Renunciation

Renunciation

ACTS OF ABANDONMENT BY WRITERS,

PHILOSOPHERS, AND ARTISTS

Ross Posnock

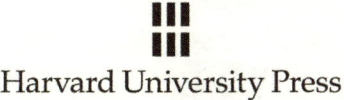

Harvard University Press

Cambridge, Massachusetts
London, England
2016

Second printing

Library of Congress Cataloging-in-Publication Data
Posnock, Ross.
Renunciation : acts of abandonment by writers,
philosophers, and artists / Ross Posnock.
    pages cm
Includes bibliographical references and index.
ISBN 978-0-674-96783-0
1. Life. 2. Renunciation (Philosophy) I. Title.
BD435.P68 2015
128—dc23

                                        2015011336

To
GDC
and
to
JLB

Contents

Overview 1

PART 1
William James, Arthur Rimbaud,
Stéphane Mallarmé, Hugo von Hofmannsthal,
Jackson Pollock, Bob Dylan, Susan Sontag 67

PART 2
J. D. Salinger, Thomas Merton,
Ad Reinhardt 135

PART 3
Søren Kierkegaard, Regine Olsen,
Franz Kafka, Felice Bauer, Philip Rieff,
Susan Sontag 208

PART 4
Glenn Gould, Thomas Bernhard 238

PART 5
Ludwig Wittgenstein 264

PART 6
Ralph Waldo Emerson, Friedrich Nietzsche,
Ludwig Wittgenstein 282

PART 7
George Oppen, Paul Celan 330

PART 8
Agnes Martin 364

ACKNOWLEDGMENTS 379
WORKS CITED AND CONSULTED 381
INDEX 407

Renunciation

Overview

RENUNCIATION IS NOT a familiar subject of study. I came to it circuitously via a repeated experience that for a long time eluded my conscious understanding. I will begin by relating that experience—not to
indulge in autobiography, but to make vivid, I hope, the way I eventually reached the topic and developed my approach to it. "Reached,"
however, is imprecise: both parts—the subject and my approach—
proved all of a piece with how renunciation found me.

Perhaps, like me, you have a propensity to collect books without
quite knowing why. Over the years I have piled up books by and about,
say, Ludwig Wittgenstein, Hannah Arendt, George Santayana, Philip
Roth, Ad Reinhardt, Philip Guston, Franz Rosenzweig, Penelope
Fitzgerald, Paul Valéry, Thomas Bernhard—and not only not read them
but have no desire to do so. I am busy working on other things. For a
decade or two at a time, these texts simply gather dust on my shelves.
But then, inevitably, I am drawn to these nearly forgotten volumes and,
strangely, they prove pivotal to a new project. I recall, for instance, that
Santayana ascended, literally, from the obscurity of a low shelf to earn
a chapter in my book on William and Henry James. Wittgenstein made
an analogous, if more circuitous, journey from the shadows, waiting
untouched, until seven years ago when I kept a long-held inner vow to
read another languishing tome, one that had stared me down so often
it had acquired an aura of intimidation—Stanley Cavell's *The Claim of
Reason: Wittgenstein, Skepticism, Morality and Tragedy*.

The peculiarities of this manner of book buying—the absence of
full consciousness and the long gap between acquisition and reading—
call to mind Walter Benjamin's 1931 essay "Unpacking My Library."
He starts with the premise that "every passion borders on the chaotic"
and finds that the passion of the book collector unleashes a "chaos
of memories"—where in each purchase "chance" and "fate" seemed
to jostle against each other. Benjamin speaks of his library as the

"accustomed confusion of these books. For what else is this collection but a disorder to which habit has accommodated itself to such an extent that it can appear as order?" (486–487). For decades the "chaos" of my own book collecting was a form of "disorder" that blurred agency and intuition, chance and fate. Though this "disorder" helped shape my intellectual life, it had been masked by habit and so escaped my reflective notice. That is, until a recent encounter with a passage from Nietzsche helped shed light. Before that, though, something else intervened to nudge me to interrogate my habit.

not unlike Mary Beard

Around 2002, when I decided to write a book on Philip Roth, I had at hand most of his novels, having dutifully acquired them over the years and, true to form, remained largely indifferent to reading them. As I burrowed into Roth's oeuvre, however, I grew aware of his close friendship with the painter Philip Guston, a relationship that became basic to my understanding of what I began calling Roth's aesthetics of immaturity. That understanding was built on what was also at hand: my pile of monographs and articles on Guston. No longer inert objects but palpable presences, this patient stack of Roth and Guston material had undergone a transformation that now struck me as more than a serendipitous accident.

For the first time I wondered what was going on: how did I explain my thoughtless buying and deferred reading; what game was my unconscious playing? It seemed to be busily working subliminally (as if behind my conscious mind's back?), replacing deliberate effort with intuition or instinct in order to quicken receptivity, keeping me in a period of prolonged incubation, as I filled my shelves in advance of my willful turn to works that would prove crucial. Was it a professorial enactment of what Emerson called "abandonment": the "one thing which we seek with insatiable desire" is to "forget ourselves . . . to do something without knowing how or why; in short, to draw a new circle" (*Essays* 414). This passage—from the final paragraph of the exhilarating essay "Circles"—had always been a personal favorite and a pedagogical touchstone of my lectures. But who knew I was *living* it?

The possibility that I was indeed living my own version of "abandonment," that I had unwittingly—hence appropriately—been drawing Emersonian circles, apparently for decades, received sharp confirmation last year. Teaching a seminar on Emerson and his avid admirer

Nietzsche, I encountered a passage from the latter's autobiography, *Ecce Homo: How One Becomes What One Is:* section nine of "Why I Am So Clever." This, at last, crystallized matters. With brazen perversity Nietzsche replaces the venerable motto "know thyself" (now a "recipe for ruin") with "self-*misunderstanding*" and describes his own self-becoming as a miracle of self-forgetting.

He begins by declaring, "At this point the real answer to the question, *how one becomes what one is*, can no longer be avoided." The question presupposes that "one must not have the faintest notion *what* one is." From this perspective "even the *blunders* of life"—the side paths and wrong turnings—"have their own meaning and value," as Nietzsche acknowledges that one's self-estrangement awakens one from the tunnel vision that plagues the certain knower. Knowledge is warded off, permitting the "surface of consciousness" to be kept clear of any of the "great" imperatives—desires, words, attitudes. All that would burden one with responsibility and goals and make one a man of knowledge. "'Willing' something, 'striving' for something, envisaging a 'purpose,' a 'wish'—I know none of this from experience" (253–255). The grand words represent "so many dangers that the instinct comes too soon to 'understand' itself" and will be clogged with meaning. Keeping consciousness clear thus allows the eventual organizing powers to grow in the dark, as it were, "deep down" in the depths. A self with the capacity to reevaluate values requires an especially intricate psychic development—"contrary capacities" must be cultivated—and must be carefully protected from awareness of the "secret labor" of the instincts (254).

His self-portrait makes manifest the self-overcoming that Nietzsche prizes—when we experience the impersonality of ourselves rather than affirming our familiar sense of identity. This impersonality—we are "strangers to ourselves, we do not comprehend ourselves," as he says at the start of the preface to *The Genealogy of Morals*—is a salutary rebuke to the fantasy dear to the Western male psyche—of the sovereign individual as self-knowing master of experience. Renouncing the deliberative self who formulates a plan of life (J. S. Mill's notion) and renouncing "know thyself" (and its correlative "to thine own self be true," as foolish Polonius put it), Nietzsche challenges us to bear *not* knowing, to live without *why*. The German mystic Angelus Silesius issued a similar challenge with his often-cited couplet which

"Because it is he,"
and because it is I."
Montaigne
on friendship

begins "the rose is without why / it blooms because it blooms" (qtd.
Heidegger, *Principle* 36).

Author and
N. comes
close to
describing
providence

The passage from "Why I Am So Clever" hit home, for it made
sense of my own self-opacity. The passage also made me feel rather
heady, as if I were now licensed to consecrate my blind book buying
on the altar of the Nietzschean *Übermensch*, Amazon unbound. My
temptation to self-transport seemed not wholly inappropriate when
I reflected that, as the Emerson-Nietzsche seminar revealed on more
than one occasion, Emerson's praise of whim, intuition, and insouciance seems at times to intoxicate Nietzsche and inspire him to new
heights of rhetorical audacity.

rhetoric
(vs truth?)

The deflationary, suspicious era of the postmodern, as is well
known, champions the constructed, the situated, and the textual nature of "the real." For decades these words and those scare quotation
marks—"the real"—have been the lingua franca of the humanities, a
vocabulary now updated to include the saturation of "reality" by the
endless flow of new media imagery. In consequence, talk of what escapes rational reflection and the rule of the concept—intuition and
whim and the pre-conceptual—smacks of the naïve or the nostalgic
(this last word a ubiquitous term of dismissal since the seventies era
of deconstruction). With notions of the immediate, of presence, of
the natural long taboo, linguistic determinism reigns as an article of
faith. The "most-in-the-know-critics"—for instance, visual theorists
expert in deconstructive, self-referential analysis—"don't want to see,
but only to read." Having "read everything but seen nothing," they
suspect "all presence of only ever being an illusionist effect of representation," remarks the art historian Thierry de Duve of those who approach visual art armed with a "radical lack of faith in images" (as he
notes in an essay accompanying *Voici*, the aptly named 2000 exhibit
that he curated (*Look* 47, 46). The command to *look* will echo in these
pages, an imperative to renounce the reflex defensiveness of naming
and clarifying everything at once.

That defensive rush to curtail looking reflects, as de Duve implies, postmodernism's master metaphor—that the world is a text or
representation. Rather than a symptom of irrationalism (the popular
charge against postmodernism's alleged indifference regarding reason and truth) textuality is a species of intellectualism, a venerable

Enlightenment creed founded on belief that the mind and its acts of knowing precede and define experience. Once it is decided that the world is a text, the sole job of humanists is to interpret—to hunt down meaning. Mastery is the goal. What flows under the radar of deliberative rationality tends to trigger a reflex "suspicion over claims of naïveté," to borrow the words of art historian Richard Shiff, who articulates frustrations about the postmodern in *Doubt* (2008). He adds: "Claims for the ubiquitous efficacy of cultural forces may be creating a more pernicious mythology than speculation on the putatively absolute value of aesthetic immediacy and naturalness. . . . Our doubt merely indicates how deeply dissatisfying it is to believe that there can be no natural self and no physical existence at all—no source of sensation that might escape the generalizing sameness of our various cultural identities" (127).

Shiff's frustration with contemporary orthodoxy spoke to me; after all, my own discipline, literary studies, had suffered a long period of programmatic suspicion of the aesthetic, which by definition is the locus of feeling—what Baumgarten, the founder of modern aesthetic theory, called "sensual cognition." This produces the "obscure" and "confused" knowledge gained from the senses. One reason the aesthetic *remains* embattled is that prestigious figures of postmodern thought continue to insist that knowledge, to be true, must explain or justify itself discursively, as in a proposition. For instance, Richard Rorty, the foremost pragmatist philosopher after John Dewey saddles his account of pragmatism with the "linguistic turn" he made in the sixties prior to announcing his allegiance to pragmatism (human beings are the vocabularies they possess and experiences are equivalent to the sentences they provoke). The result is impoverished: Rorty's version requires forsaking Dewey's aesthetics *(Art as Experience)* and nearly all of William James, who, as did Dewey, rejected mind-body dualism to make the rootedness of mind in feeling foundational to his work. There is a coda, puzzling and poignant, to Rorty's neglect of the aesthetic dimension of pragmatism. Late in life, he left academic philosophy to teach in a comparative literature department, where he wrote eloquent tributes to the power of literature, including an essay on Nabokov's work in which deficiencies of empathy and curiosity constitute moral failure.

Tired of "feeling pressured by the critical indoctrination" which trains us to "all too readily expose the superficiality, the constructed spectacle, the mirage of sensation," to "distrust our feelings more than to trust them," Shiff asks: "To what degree are we . . . willing to trust and act on feeling, especially when no theory supports it?" ("On 'Between Sense'"; *Doubt* 25). Though postmodern theory encouraged him to be "extraordinarily wary of many of the claims of the modern artists," Shiff now tries to resist his own distrust. When asked in an interview "what is worth caring about," Shiff says that we need to acknowledge our "hunger for experience that escapes conceptualization" ("Interview"). This hunger is deep in the American romantic grain.

■

Impatience with the primacy of concepts and of discursive knowing pushes back against what Charles Taylor recently called "a big mistake operating in our culture, a kind of operative (mis) understanding of what it is to know, which has had dire effects on both theory and practice in a host of domains" (61). Alert to earlier versions of this "mistake" and convinced that we are not exclusively reflective rational beings, Emerson, Nietzsche, James, and Wittgenstein revaluated "what it is to know." They assault the philosophical prestige of modern epistemology, a tradition Descartes begins, that promotes a flattering fiction of the self's Olympian disengagement, a serene spectator who knows by surveying experience. William James refused this picture's static dualism, for it preserved "refined objects of contemplation" while ignoring the world's "wildness" (*Writings* 2:496). This pacified, inert scenario testifies to a vision of the world perceived through the lens of "vicious intellectualism."

With this pungent phrase William James named his philosophic enemy. Although I had long known this, it was a barren fact that did not grow pregnant until I grappled with my bookish brush with the non-cognitive. Only after I became attuned to the power of the intuitive was I ready to realize that James's exasperation with rationalism and attempt to "think in non-conceptualized terms" occurred in the context of his quixotic effort, two years before his death in 1910, to renounce language: "I must deafen you to talk and let life teach the lesson," he told his audience, sounding literal but marooned in the figural, as he continued lecturing. James's thirst for experience that slips the grasp of fully rational control is embedded in his desire to renounce—language, books, academic philosophy, Harvard: "Exit the whole Shebang," to borrow the words of Wallace Stevens, a Harvard undergraduate admirer. Only when 1 started writing this book and turned to James did I read his 1908 words anew, discovering that they pointed back in time: his impulse to quit was revisiting a much earlier, painful renunciation—his coerced relinquishment of plans to become a painter. Something similar happened to my sense of "abandonment"— I had sung its praises without consciously grasping that its force of reference included Emerson's abandonment of his ministerial career.

My belated revelations crystallized into a suggestive pattern. This happens when one works on William James. He opens networks of connection, for he is one of those rare "through lines" in intellectual history—anywhere you look he is on his way back, as was said of Plato. All I had to do, then, was to follow his coordinates—first his own inspiration—Emerson (who blessed the infant James in his cradle according to family lore) and from there it was a short step to Nietzsche. Now another cold fact warmed to life: both Emerson and Nietzsche had severed institutional ties, which James had also yearned to do. Instead he stayed at Harvard to fight what all three regarded as one of modernity's deadening imperatives, the "vicious intellectualism" which emanated from departments of philosophy. This belief—that "reality consists of essences, not appearances," and we know these essences when we "know their definitions"—circulated as scientism or positivism in the culture at large (728). Another figure came to mind—Wittgenstein, chronic renunciator (of an academic career for a time, of his family fortune, of capital P Philosophy) and an admirer of James (especially *The Varieties of Religious Experience* and its extolling of "the old monkish poverty-worship"), and whose late work—*On Certainty*—treats man as a "creature in a primitive state," guided more by animal instinct than by conscious reason (sec. 475). In affirming the elective affinity of renunciation and receptivity to the tacit, the realm of the pre-cognitive, William James et al. readied the ground, as I had been readied, for a study of renunciation across a range of forms and figures.

Trust in attunement inspires the present book's form. It is written as
an essay—the mode of writing that "incorporates the antisystematic
impulse into its own way of proceeding" (Adorno, *Prisms* 12). By etymology an attempt that stays precisely that, "the essay as form" is the
subject of a very Emersonian essay of that title by Theodor Adorno.
The essay, he says, comes into being as a dissent from the scientific
ideal (instanced in Descartes's *Discourse on Method* with its mission
to reduce what is difficult and complex to the simple and logical by
insisting on strict definition, exhaustive enumeration, definitive conclusion). "Composing as he experiments," (*Notes to Literature* 1:17)
the essayist offers a counter-ideal that is cautious about concepts and
theories even as it absorbs them, prefers discontinuity because it does
not disguise that its "subject matter is always a conflict brought to a
standstill," and "shrinks from any overarching concept" that would
subordinate all its findings to one meaning (16, 18). Although an essay cannot avoid the work of explanation, it can try to minimize the
expository mode. The essay connects, says Adorno, "thought's utopian
vision of hitting the bullseye" to "consciousness of its own fallibility
and provisional character," a tension that "takes place not systemati-
cally but rather as a characteristic of an intention groping its way" (16).
Deferring the command of understanding—which deliberately brings
things under concepts—groping relies on the tacit and intuitive in order to quicken receptivity. "It coordinates elements instead of subor-
dinating them" (22).

This essay "coordinates" in the sense that it displays specific examples, moments, intersections rather than embedding them in a linear, progressive, historical narrative. Without ignoring them, I resist
the rules of context and of boundaries, temporal and disciplinary, the
better to let the material, the specificity of the object, take the lead
and impart something of the resonant, if ineffable, presence that often surrounds acts of renunciation. Pure presentation was the goal of
Adorno's friend Benjamin, who said: "I need say nothing. Only exhibit." This ambition put him, warned Adorno, at the "crossroads where
positivism and magic meet" ("Letter to Benjamin" 129). However, to
coordinate here does not mean to forego analysis and "only exhibit."

One form of analysis will be the constellations of relations among writers, painters, philosophers, and critics: the result will be juxtapositions, groupings, linkages, both overarching and local. This embodied mode of analysis intends to help mitigate, if not dissolve, the anomaly that as a critic I am in the business of explaining, an enterprise my figures tend to renounce.

In other words, I fashion a critical approach in the spirit of my subject, an approach more intimate but one that resists indulging in imitative form. Yet even while trying to minimize mimetic reciprocity, I seek to tap some of the renunciatory freedom of aesthetic experience without succumbing to aesthetic intoxication. I also seek to do so without succumbing to another risk: a blurring of differences, a standing temptation given that constellations work by analogies. Showing unexpected resemblances is a venture worth making because it can allow one to challenge canonical differences that veil lively affinities, present, if unstressed. Nevertheless, my constellations will note irreducible distinctions while trying to make them less dominant.

To facilitate the flowing, associative ambit of the discussion I renounce certain scholarly expectations: I refrain from notes and chapter breaks, though parts will be indicated. I do not intervene into the secondary literature on my subject, admittedly not much of a renunciation because critical commentary on renunciation as construed here is minimal. While remaining a basic topic in the study of Christian and Eastern religion, renunciation as a creative act examined across several disciplines is new. My focus will be on modernism, with the caveat that this period label, like any, is porous: modernists are inspired by far-flung predecessors and precedents. This fact and another—that renunciation respects neither national boundaries nor historical epochs—partly accounts for my zigzagging form: what follows weaves in and out of American and European periods, contexts, genres, and disciplines. Eastern spirituality will have some presence, especially as Western figures encounter it. The pace and extension of my treatment of various people accordions, expanding for some but contracting for others, depending on their pertinence to my nexus of the aesthetic and renunciatory. I have made no effort to be exhaustive and readers will be able to add examples of their own. Because my method is accretive, adding details incrementally, some repetition with a difference is built in and the hope is that the reader will grow attuned to this rhythm. Pauses will be inserted throughout, sometimes as a point of rest, other times to indicate a temporal leap or shift in direction. As I have said, though, the entirety is an extended essay.

The point of these arrangements is simple: to produce for writer and reader "an open intellectual experience" (*Prisms* 13). Mobility is also a strategy here, a way to encourage fresh juxtapositions. Two examples within American culture: Bob Dylan and William Faulkner join hands in the early sixties in shared strategic coyness; and in 1903 Henry James and W. E. B. Du Bois both present an aesthete hero— Lambert Strether, John Jones—in the throes of renunciation.

As J. D. Salinger showed in his final novel, digressiveness is intimately aligned with receptivity. Both stances are embodied in the flâneur, an emblematic figure of modernity wandering the city, untroubled by destination. The above-mentioned Angelus Silesius—the Silesian Angel—the sobriquet of one Johannes Scheffler (1624–1677), a doctor turned priest, mystic and poet—was one such walker, though tramping more rural byways, as Michel de Certeau reminds us in discussing the sixteenth- and seventeenth-century mystic fable (299). Emergent at the "threshold of modernity," the fable, often an oral tale, was soon to be discarded by the Enlightenment, which made the written, not the spoken word a priority. The fable was relegated to "fiction," hence "presumed to mask or to have mislaid the meaning it contains" (12). Out of step, "pushed aside by progress," the mystic tramps a perpetual journey whose very motion often becomes the fable's framing metaphor: "down the paths or ways of which so many mystics speak goes the itinerant walker, *Wandersmann*," often "impoverished rural nobility," let loose from a disintegrating social order (22, 13–14, 23). *Wandersmann* was part of the title of Angelus Silesius's book of spiritual aphorisms, *The Cherubic Wanderer* (1675), which included "The rose is without why." One finds an echo of this line in another solitary walker and reader of Angelus Silesius, Wittgenstein, who would have encountered him in *The Varieties* where James quotes him twice. He remarks in *On Certainty:* "Why do I not satisfy myself that I have two feet when I want to get up from the chair? There is no why. I simply don't. This is how I act" (sec.148). Wittgenstein's "There is no why" chimes with the account of our inevitable self-misunderstanding sketched above by that inveterate wanderer Nietzsche and echoes too Emersonian abandonment as doing "without knowing how or why." In "Self-Reliance," Angelus Silesius's flower seems on his mind when he praises the roses under his window: "There is simply the rose; it is perfect in every moment of its existence" (*Essays* 270).

Worth noting is that three centuries before Angelus Silesius, Meister Eckhart (1260–1327), the Christian mystic and philosopher (the two were not far apart in the medieval world), had made the phrase "without why" *(ohne Warum)* central to his "negative" theology. So in synch was Angelus Silesius with his predecessor that he has been called "so to speak, Eckhart's versifier" (Schürmann, *Wandering* 236). Living without why meant for Eckhart, among other things, forsaking the traditional metaphysical "quest for unshakable foundations" since this pursuit of godly grounding is "attached to the 'why,' to the *raison d'être* of things." Upon hearing of his indifference to security, the Rhineland nuns who were his auditors were likely "seized with dizziness" (110). To let God be, to look for nothing, launches one on a "wandering" path of "detachment" and relaxed openness that Eckhart calls *Gelassenheit*—"releasement" (110). The word, its cognates, and Angelus Silesius's poetic rendering, reverberate in the history of philosophy—extending to an Eastern version in the "empty" mind of Zen which, having banished dependency on any calculating project, any grasping after a why, is full of no-thing but latent receptivity, dynamic passivity (Suzuki 200). This state of detachment implicitly informs many of the renunciations discussed, explicitly so with the abstract painter Agnes Martin. She says her work is "about the sudden emotions that we feel without cause in the world" and speaks repeatedly of "wandering" as an alternative to ego-driven "conquest" (*Writings* 71).

The wandering Angelus Silesius is a tutelary spirit here, for he brings together embodied presence, pre-reflective doing, and openness to the unexpected, all aspects of the crossing of the aesthetic and the spiritual to which renunciation often bears witness.

■

A *dramatis personae* of the major figures to be discussed after this wide-ranging, non-linear overview: William James and his distrust of language sets the stage, in Part 1, for Rimbaud, Mallarmé, and Hofmannsthal, figures basic to any consideration of modernist literary renunciation. They are sketched in some detail but remain secondary. James also functions as a gateway to discussing a variety of artists whose reticence about "meaning" testifies to trust in the noncognitive as they renounce representation and seek to attain ineffable "presence." Jackson Pollock's drip paintings and the drama of renunciation that produces them are revisited as an iconic, almost mythic, episode. Pursuit of an ideal of resonant muteness includes the propensity of a range of figures, including Bob Dylan, to abjure public requests to explain their work. Susan Sontag emerges by the late sixties as an influential proponent of a "new sensibility" and "aesthetics of silence" of spiritual intensity. Part 2 commences with a sustained look at the most famous American renunciator, Salinger. He is overdue for revaluation and I suggest the depth of his achievement, which deserves to be far better appreciated. Another fifties and early sixties figure Ad Reinhardt, is an artist with a sustaining relation, as writer and painter, to renunciation. Together with his friend the Trappist monk Thomas Merton he in effect works through the challenge uttered by Salinger's Franny Glass—"the courage to be an absolute nobody"—an imperative that seems to haunt a number of their generation. Part 3, which examines three couples whose relations were defined by renunciation, devotes several pages to Kafka's renunciatory sensibility as he represents it in his unnerving letters to Felice Bauer. The main concern is the understudied cultural sociologist Philip Rieff: both his thought and the arc of his career, shaped by his early marriage to Sontag, play intricate variations upon renunciation.

Part 4 discusses Glenn Gould while weaving in Bernhard's *The Loser* (1983), a fictive portrait of the pianist that also superimposes the figure of Wittgenstein, who is the subject of Part 5. Wittgenstein's reading of Emerson and Nietzsche is a point of departure for Part 6 and a way to consider the intersections of all three. Part 7 is devoted to George Oppen, who will appear alongside the postwar German poet Paul Celan. The former's minimalist poetry emerges out of war and elected silence, an ascetic poetry of "clarity" made possible by renouncing modernist and symbolist hermeticism, the self-referential literariness he called "the terrible thin scratching of the art world" (*Selected Prose* 31). I will compare Celan's analogous renunciation of lyric beauty and what he called the artificiality of art, which reduces poetry to "perfumed bouquets" of metaphors and "lyrical potpourri" (*The Meridian* 149, 138). The book's final section, Part 8, takes up Agnes Martin. More rigorously than even Merton the monk, Martin—mentored by Reinhardt—took up Franny Glass's challenge. Suddenly leaving New York as her career was taking off, she renounced painting for seven years and then resumed, having become a hermit in New Mexico.

This cast and their modes of renunciation serve to generate ideas and themes which are elaborated concurrently in relation to a host of satellite figures, many of whom were themselves in dialogue with the primary group, among them Clement Greenberg, John Cage, Robert Irwin, Allan Kaprow, and Eva Hesse, each offering provocative turns and contrasting perspectives. Three key background presences should be mentioned. Paul Valéry, whose theories of poetic autonomy are foundational to modernist aesthetic renunciation. Second, Meister Eckhart, rediscovered in the postwar US (a new English translation appeared in 1941), delivered heretical sermons on the renunciatory path to "releasement," "detachment," and "wakefulness." He sounded very Zen to many and influenced Merton, Reinhardt, Cage, and Salinger. Rather than emphasizing sin, evil, and redemption, Eckhart urges the "eradication of possessing and having," including language and images, inviting listeners to become "free and empty" (*Selected* 244, 159). The third presence, Kierkegaard, is a notable connective thread, a model of how philosophy can—must—be lived and not simply known. Embodying renunciation as an existential imperative and ultimately as a source of joy, Kierkegaard exerted a profound effect on people from Wittgenstein and Kafka to Salinger and Rieff.

■

Focusing on renunciation allows us to grasp the connection between two cultural historical moments not usually regarded as complementary—the turn into the twentieth century and the American postwar era. The late nineteenth century witnesses the birth pangs of modernism, specifically the emergence of aesthetic autonomy and the avant-garde, where poetry and painting renounce the obligation to represent the

exterior world. To sketch the consequences in broad strokes: renunciation of reference initiates a "crisis of poetry" (Mallarmé) and recognition of the "sickness" of language when it imagines it corresponds to
an external reality (Nietzsche). With re-presentation renounced, presentation or presence is set free; creators are invited to evoke "the living act of perception," for which, James notes, "reflection comes too
late" (*Writings* 2:409), or "the moment when we start to live our thinking" (Valéry 8:148). These moments, says Valéry, escape "conventional
language" with its inevitable tendency to "carry us back" to "states
already experienced" (149). Instead, when we "live our thinking" we
sense thought's "transitional nature" and pre-reflective immediacy in
motion before the intellect (via language) categorizes and normalizes.
We inhabit what Maurice Merleau-Ponty calls "lived perspective" that
generates "the expression of what is before expression and *sustains it
from behind*" ("Cézanne's" 64; *Visible* 167).

I will approach these European concerns through William James's
contemporary and analogous experiment to renounce language, or at
least to attempt to "think in non-conceptualized terms." Like Valéry,
James is wary of the seductive stasis of concepts; he favors words that
suggest transition rather than fixity, such as "overflow," "margin,"
and "fringe," for they point to a "wider self"—"what quivers along
various radii like the wind-rose on a compass." These radiating possibilities are what "we can only feel without conceiving, and can hardly
begin to analyze." They convey the "manyness-in-oneness" so long
denied by "intellectualism" (*Writings* 2:760–763).

The second historical moment of renunciation, I argue, is the postwar American era, which in effect harvests the turn of the century yearning for living aesthetic experience—its pleasures and bewilderments and
trespasses. To their different generations, Greenberg and Sontag are the
two key relays from the symbolist heritage to postwar modernism. In
the postwar period I show that democratizing proponents of aesthetic
education proliferate: unwittingly working in concert, the ensemble
includes among others Greenberg, Salinger, Vladimir Nabokov, Jack
Kerouac, John Crowe Ransom, Dylan, Sontag, Reinhardt (his manifesto
of 1962 proclaimed "Art-as-art is nothing but art"), and from his piano
in Toronto, Gould, who invited listeners to cultivate what in 1962 he
called "aesthetic narcissism . . . in its best sense."

Together the turn of the century and the mid-century epochs form a narrative of the birth and promulgating of aesthetic autonomy, with its ideal of "approaching the brink of meaning and yet never falling over it," as Greenberg said of the French symbolist poets. It is an "impossible ideal," but a worthy one (1:33–34). Analogously, he said that some of the best works of abstract art "were got by flirting with representation" (4:124). Aesthetic autonomy—less as art for art's sake than as a distinctive mode of making sense—constitutes the family resemblance that threads these two historical moments together. And various kinds of renunciation form a subset that can be placed on a continuum. It ranges from emphatic prohibitions—Sontag's injunction against interpretation for an embrace of "an erotics of art" (what a few years before Nabokov called "aesthetic bliss")—to micro self-curtailments—say Greenberg's propensity to grunt instead of speak in his immediate response to encountering a new canvas, or Dylan's mocking vagueness at press conferences when asked to explain. It also includes macro acts of abandonment—the deliberate withdrawal from public life performed by a Salinger or a Gould.

Postwar aesthetic education challenges the assumption that the task of interpretation is mastery—the pursuit and seizure of meaning, which makes of the artifact a puzzle to solve and the reader or spectator a detective tracking clues. Undertaking a more spiritual, less cognitive and linguistic approach to art, these aesthetic educators tend to stay on the surface—where the presence of mystery is—and ask what art is trying to do or be rather than mean. The watchword here might be what Gertrude Stein said of herself and Picasso: they see things as they are by getting out of the habit "of knowing what one is looking at" (qtd. Meyer 162).

■

When in 2005 comedian Dave Chappelle left a $50-million contract and a hit show, he didn't specify his motives. Spending the next eight years largely outside mainstream media attention made it apparent he wanted time to meditate about life, to visit Africa, or, as he put it to *Time*—"to make sure I am dancing and not shuffling." In the process Chappelle "became a far more singular cultural figure: A renegade to some, a lunatic to others, but, most of all, an enigma," reported *The New York Times* in 2013 (Zinoman, "Comic"). This transformation from the familiar to the enigmatic neatly sums up the effect and mystique that acts of renunciation tend to engender. "Enigma" suggests as well what is often entangled in acts of renunciation—the estrangement from the immediately intelligible that marks aesthetic experience and indeed the act of thinking itself. Thinking "demands a '*stop*-and-think,'" Hannah Arendt declares: "it interrupts any doing, any ordinary activities" (*Life of the Mind* 78). Unlike knowledge, which uses thinking as a means to an end, thinking is done for its own sake (64).

Thinking's withdrawal from the world—absent-mindedness is the "only outward manifestation of the mind"—is not the sole source of the epithet "enigma" (72). More obviously "enigma" refers to the seemingly inexplicable insouciance of Chappelle foregoing his fabulously lucrative contract. He implicitly asks us to consider whether less might not be more. But in a culture and economy whose byword is "more," one imprinted upon not only our economic but also psychic and cultural life, renunciation seems bewilderingly perverse. So dependent is capital flow on "more" that even "less is more" (to adapt Mies van der Rohe's dictum about his architecture). Under capitalism, minimalism has a hard time remaining minimal. Recall the concept's postwar career: it began in the early sixties as minimal art, and after a post-Minimalism reaction, migrated over several decades from an aesthetic into a taste, marketed as a lifestyle and design option including an expensive diet regimen. The aestheticizing of the ascetic: *Vogue* models don monks' robes for a photo shoot. Renunciation says "no more"—in fact, it says no to more alongside saying no to the maximalist minimalism of "less is more." This dismissal of "more," the motor of the logic of accumulation, may be heard as implicit rebuke by those—most of us—caught up in the logic.

So a certain disappointment sets in (Chappelle was a "lunatic" to some). Especially when expectations have been raised, then willfully dashed. In 1961 *Time* predicted that Salinger would become the American Proust. Fewer than five years later he wrapped himself in silence after bidding farewell with a final work, a long and garrulous short story that antagonized many by flagrantly defying the genre's reigning template—which carefully brings the reader along a narrative journey to an epiphanic punch line. In effect he had injected "more" into the genre of "less." Soon Salinger was as famous for renouncing his career as for his fiction. In some readers and critics, disappointment grew into a sense that a lurking purism and self-righteousness might be at work in Salinger's closing of the door. Inevitably his hermit behavior aroused bitterness, on display in his daughter's memoir of a distant father. A less heated version of disappointment continues to attend Wittgenstein's practice of a philosophical "quietism"—his perverse method of not advancing philosophical theses but only reminders of what theses have obfuscated. A 2013 book concludes with this defensive admission about the thinker's minimalist achievement: "no depths have been plumbed . . . nothing has been explained or discovered or reconceived. How tame and uninspiring one might think. But perhaps, as Wittgenstein suggests, the virtues of clarity, demystification and truth should be found satisfying enough" (Horwich 211; McDowell, "Quietism"; Stone, "Wittgenstein" 111–112).

In philosophy, said Wittgenstein, "the winner of the race is the one who can run most slowly" (*Culture and Value* 34). This revaluation of slowness reminds us that part of the disappointment that some works of renunciation induce derives from the time they demand. They slow things down. Stop and look. "Everything else is on the move. Art should be still," Reinhardt said of his (almost) pure black paintings of the early 1960s (*Art-as-Art* 206). As we stand in front of one, eventually becoming absorbed in its depths where its hidden shapes and colors reside, time is suspended. Temporal arrest is basic to any aesthetic experience but here is more pointed, a quiet rebuke to the sanctity of "more" in the culture. Reinhardt had just this in mind: "the busier the work of art, the worse it is. 'More is less'" (204).

Recall another rebuke: Walt Whitman's disturbance of ideals of Puritan industry when, heedless of time, he merely "leans and loafes at his ease" at the start of "Song of Myself" (1855). He observes a "spear of summer grass" with a calmness that seems more appropriate to a Zen poem, for instance: "Sitting quietly, doing nothing, / Spring comes and the grass grows by itself." This little poem, says Roland Barthes, "really means putting oneself completely outside the universe of sin" and of "profit": "perhaps impossible for a Westerner: to do nothing without being wrong, without being in debt" (*The Neutral* 185). Flouting good economic sense—"time is money"—renunciations on one level risk arousing our inherited anxiety to make haste even as, on another, they may be impeccably Puritan in their austerity and abstention. Or in Salinger's case impeccably Eastern, given his devotion to a range of self-abnegating philosophies. Around the "enigma" of Dave Chappelle's act of abandonment—which by 2014 he had reversed—tense cultural implications are at play, which is to say, at work.

To add to the complexity, renunciation is not unconditionally antipathetic to the "more." There is not only the banal fact that renunciators depend on capital (Emerson had his late wife's estate to cushion him after he resigned his ministry; the sales of *The Catcher in the Rye* funded Salinger's decision to stop publishing) and renunciations can be profitable (Gould's turn to recording proved lucrative). Maurice Blanchot suggests a less obvious link to the "more" when he writes of Rimbaud:

> To renounce writing, when one has proven to be a great writer, certainly does not occur without mystery. The mystery increases when one discovers what Rimbaud asks of poetry: not to produce beautiful works, or to answer to an aesthetic ideal, but to help man go somewhere, to be more than himself, to see more than he can see. (*Work* 154–155)

To be more and see more comprises the "mystery" of renunciation. While Blanchot's "more" refers directly to Rimbaud's visionary ambitions, it also points beyond—to renunciation's less familiar aspect as an act of severance capable of releasing energies thwarted by webs of conventional expectations, including those encouraged by capital's fetish of the "more" and suspicion of the "less."

Not the least mysterious quality of renunciation is how it unsettles the two terms (and variations like "excess" and "austerity") by putting them into creative interplay that breaks the habit of dualistic thinking. This yoking together of opposites echoes in Zen—"zero equals infinity"—and in the so-called negative traditions (*via negativa*) of Christian mysticism, for instance, in the self-canceling words of Marguerite Porete. A Christian female heretic of the early fourteenth century, she speaks in her book, *The Mirror of Simple Souls*, of "this

Soul," who has "become nothing, thus possesses everything, and so possesses nothing" (85). She employs here an ancient rhetorical technique of unsaying called apophasis—Greek for negation, etymologically a speaking away from speech, premised on God's transcendence of any of the predicates we can use to describe Him. This mode of discourse, by naming the ineffable, makes meaning reside in a tension between saying and unsaying. With apophasis renunciation becomes in effect a linguistic strategy (Franke, Preface to vol. 1).

Because such statements refuse to be stabilized under a concept, they compel us to push beyond logical limits and ponder unsuspected ways in which less becomes more. Porete warns at the start, "Theologians and other clerks" must "proceed humbly" for her book is not to be understood by "intellect": "Humble, then, your wisdom / Which is based on Reason" and "may Love and Faith, together, / Cause you to rise above Reason" (Porete 79). While the modern renunciants to be discussed in the pages to follow tend not to use the exalted language of transcendent Love and Faith, they implicitly heed Porete's heretical reversal, her skepticism of the primacy of Reason and her teaching of thinking in and through paradox. When paradox is ignored a "less" versus "more" dichotomy can emerge, evident, for instance, at a 1993 global conference on asceticism. Participants failed to reach consensus on a definition of the term: some insisted on asceticism as deprivation and "shrinkage" of the self while others stressed "liberation" and "fulfillment of one's true nature" (E. Clark, "Ascetic" 505, *Reading* 14–15).

Often, acts of negation and withdrawal leave a silence in their wake, a silence they nonetheless attempt to articulate. Consider two examples (sketched here and elaborated upon later) of "less" and "more" changing places, from each of the two "disappointing" figures invoked above. "What is the sound of one hand clapping?" is part of the Zen koan (a terse riddle-like utterance meant to defeat logic and spark new ways of thinking) made famous as the epigraph to Salinger's *Nine Stories*, the first and last of which each concern a young man's abrupt death. Hence the book in effect is framed by the sound of silence: the single clapping hand prevails, a paradox that houses another: death in these stories is more (and less) than death, for both characters—Seymour Glass and Teddy—are transmigrating souls, each to be reborn in a new incarnation.

Wittgenstein performs another upending of "more" and "less": "There is indeed the inexpressible. This *shows* itself; it is the mystical" is a proposition he states near the end of his first book of philosophy. So precious is the silence of *showing*—the domain of values making themselves manifest in deeds—that it eclipses all the facts that can be *said*. "The right method of philosophy," he informs us in the next koan-like proposition, "would be this. To say nothing except what can be said, *i.e.* the propositions of natural science, *i.e.* something that has nothing to do with philosophy" (*Tractatus*, 6.522, 6.53). Evidently, to pursue "the right method of philosophy" is to empty it from inside—to pursue "something that has nothing to do with philosophy." Has any thinker ever done more with less?

Often logically and socially disruptive, renunciations beckon the mystical—what refuses speech but is made manifest in action. Wittgenstein's sense of the word is faithful to the Greek etymology of "mystic"—from *myein*, a closing of one's eyes or mouth (Emerson, *Essays* 663). This shutting recalls Eckhart's "releasement" from all attachment. Those who want to understand "my teaching of releasement," he tells us, must themselves "be perfectly released." They must be "equal" to the truth he preaches. Glossing this, Reiner Schürmann, a philosopher who wrote an important book on Eckhart, notes that "an attitude is required for thinking to succeed. We propose to define mysticism as this reciprocity between existence and thought: to think of *being as releasement* one must first of all have a released existence" (xx–xxi). Many of the renunciations I discuss insist in various ways on this reciprocity, on *living* one's convictions rather than confining them to the page, the canvas, the pulpit, the classroom, the concert stage. They often pivot around versions, more or less secular, of "released existence"—what I will call aesthetic living. Renunciation here enacts the "letting go" which initiates "every form of spirituality . . . a renunciation of the limited and limiting self," in Pierre Hadot's quote from a history of Chinese thought (*The Present Alone* 86). This letting go is at the heart of the "less" that renunciants live as the "more."

■

Before Chappelle, Garbo did it, becoming its veritable icon; or perhaps to Emily Dickinson belongs that laurel; after all, she barely published her whole reclusive life, outminimizing Kafka, who prided himself with good reason on what he called his "fabulous innate capacity for asceticism" (qtd. Stach, *Decisive* 421). He loathed yet nurtured his busy bachelorhood, until he refined it to a vanishing point with his deathbed request that nearly all traces of his (writing) life be burned. In the US Salinger is usually regarded as its patron saint. Depressed war veteran, mystic, Buddhist, Vedantist, Salinger fell under the influence of a past master at it, Kierkegaard, that unlikely spiritual mentor to sensitive young American postwar intellectuals. After a cosmopolitan bohemian life, Laura Riding gave up poetry, spending her last fifty years in central Florida in the citrus growing business, making good on the title of one of her last collections: *Poet: A Lying Word* (Ashbery *Other* 100). Jean Toomer, author of the Harlem Renaissance classic *Cane* (1923), issued only one other significant work, in 1936, and died thirty-one years later, leaving voluminous unpublished self-reflections, enacting, via public silence, his disavowal of fixed racial identity for a universalism inflected with mystic yearning for what he called a "united human race."

After their first novels, *Call It Sleep* and *Invisible Man*, both Henry Roth and Ralph Ellison refrained from publishing another for more than half a century. Whether these silences testified to renunciation or to writer's block was a question clarified only at the end of their parallel careers, but clarified in the most startling way. Roth in his mid-eighties issued the first two volumes of *Mercy of a Rude Stream*, the collective title of what eventually became a published four-volume sequence (with another 2,000 pages—two novels—remaining in his archives). Five years after his death Ellison's novel-length fragment, *Juneteenth*, appeared in 1999, followed by the source of that piece eleven years later—*Three Days before the Shooting*, over 1,100 pages long. It is less a novel than an archive of an unfinished one. (Salinger may also have a posthumous life, with rumors of several novels waiting in the wings.)

Arthur Rimbaud renounced with spectacular decisive abruptness, as did Glenn Gould, who turned not to gun running in Abyssinia but to the holy hush of the recording studio and to making radio meditations about the solitude of Canada's northern reaches. He was never to perform a concert again once he announced his public retirement at the age of thirty-one in 1964. He was among the first to flourish in the hermetic world of virtual life decades before technology made the possibility available to anyone. Djuna Barnes did it, decade after solitary decade, an immobile Thoreau in her tiny Patchin Place apartment off Washington Square. George Santayana resigned at forty-eight from a tenured post in philosophy at Harvard: "a rather difficult renunciation," he called it, but imperative since in his department "philosophy was most modern, most deeply Protestant, most hopefully new: the very things" in which he could place no faith. For the next forty years he lived out of four suitcases, preserving his "essential character of stranger and traveler," ending his very productive career in a monastery near the Vatican (*Persons* 426, 467). Nietzsche renounced university life in no uncertain terms: to hold an academic chair—"being obligated to think in public about predetermined subjects at predetermined hours"—makes philosophical thinking "emasculated from the first" (*Untimely* 186). Rieff, in contrast, made the classroom his sanctuary and expressed his lofty disapproval of the surrounding culture by ceasing to publish. Like Andrei Rublev by the end of Andrei Tarkovsky's mammoth glorious film, the poet Valéry did it and then undid it. As did George Oppen, returning to poetry after a quarter-century political odyssey as a Communist that began in mid-1930s Depression America and continued through the McCarthyism of the fifties that forced him and his family to flee to Mexico for eight years. In between both disasters he enlisted for another, serving in an infantry unit and, in 1945, being wounded in Germany. "Twenty-five years to write the next poem" was how Hugh Kenner summarized it, a comment to which Oppen assented. The remark leaves out what Oppen would clarify many times in interviews and letters: that he stopped writing and publishing out of a conviction that "there are situations which cannot honorably be met by art" (*Speaking* 20, 217; *Selected Prose* 36).

Abandonment of career, elected renunciation, comes in all shapes and sizes, and with a range of affects, effects, and consequences. Sometimes a writer renounces a portion of an oeuvre: Barthes speaks of the capacity to "shift ground" or "to abjure" in reference to the Italian writer and film maker Pasolini, who disavowed his *Trilogy of Life* films: "to abjure what you have written (but not necessarily what you have thought) when gregarious power [in Pasolini's case the Catholic Church] uses and subjugates it. Pasolini was thus led to 'abjure' (as he said) his *Trilogy of Life* films (based on Boccaccio, Chaucer and the *Arabian Nights*) because he realized power was making use of them—yet without regretting the fact that he wrote them in the first place" (Barthes, "Lecture" 9). Another shape of renunciation occurs when an author renounces one genre for another: Hugo von Hofmannsthal left lyric poetry for essays, opera librettos, and folk art. In itself this shift is minor but attained significance when Hofmannsthal generalized his leaving of poetry into a fable of renouncing language in his remarkable "Letter to Lord Chandos" (1902).

Marcel Duchamp wove renunciation and creativity into a tight knot that changed the course of modern art. "Marcel, no more painting, get a job," he noted to himself in 1912, feeling his work was no match for a Matisse or Picasso. Instead of ending his relation to art, he eventually memorialized it with the notorious found objects he called "readymades"—a bicycle wheel, a coat rack, and, his most famous, a urinal named "Fountain" (1917). "The readymades (and to some extent the 'Large Glass') are the other side of Duchamp's abandonment of painting," says de Duve. "If he had relinquished every artistic ambition when he renounced painting, no one would speak of him today. Obviously, the readymades are, among other things, Duchamp's way of registering his abandonment of painting, of getting it on the record." Duchamp "succeeded in recording *the impossibility of the making* by making something nonetheless." De Duve calls this "the genius of impotence" (*Kant After* 150, 167). The readymades had an anarchic effect; they scrambled and besmirched the lofty category of art, abolishing the classical aesthetic judgment—"this is beautiful"—and replacing it with a new modern one—"this is art." "Whether or not, 'this is art' still means 'this is beautiful' or something similar is irrelevant," notes de Duve (303). A decade or so later, Duchamp renounced art, retiring to play chess, a move itself regarded as an artwork.

Kafka never needed formally to renounce because he lived it daily, honing it to a sharp point against the flint of his long-term engagement to Felice Bauer. "Everything is obscured by the apprehensions I feel at the idea of not renouncing," he admits. To her he dangles the prospect of marriage only endlessly to defer it. Kafka stages this slow-motion renunciation so to dramatize his deepest identity: "I am nothing but literature; I can and want to be nothing else," he declared (*Letters to Felice* 304). "I am not a human being," he told her again and again. He was wedded to "I don't."

Kafka recognized his predecessor in the marriage of renunciation and writing. In a 1913 diary entry, Kafka records reading Kierkegaard's journals and acknowledges the Dane's commitment to renunciation as kindred to his own. Philip Rieff enacted an elaborate *imitatio* of Kierkegaard, in his version scripting a part for ex-wife Susan Sontag, who came to embody for Rieff the hedonism of the sixties from which he fled. He did not publish a book for over thirty years after writing two major works by the early sixties. (A few months before dying he issued a volume, followed posthumously by three more.)

Emerson published steadily but his act of abandoning the Unitarian pulpit to become a man of letters set his words and body in motion as peripatetic Lyceum lecturer, anti-slavery speaker, journal keeper, and essayist, a range of movement shaping the very rhythm of his thought and the pulse of his writing. Melville did it, and it stayed done, his refusal admitting no wavering about publishing more fiction, but did admit *Billy Budd* into the world, if only the darkness of a desk drawer. It languished there for decades until posthumous discovery. After five novels, the last and greatest published when he was forty-five, E. M. Forster stopped publishing fiction, enacting his belief that "all literature tends towards a condition of anonymity. . . . To forget its Creator is one of the functions of a Creation" (82). Forster lived to ninety-one, keeping closeted his gay novel, *Maurice,* for over half a century (until it appeared a year after his death in 1971). Merton renounced, drastically, and wrote a bestseller about it in 1947, and for two decades book after book kept flowing from the silence he had embraced after joining a Kentucky monastery. He lived a paradox not unlike one that guided his Columbia college friend Reinhardt, whose series of (almost) pure black paintings attempt the bizarre task of making a "painting that can't be seen." His canvases are vibrant arenas of renunciation.

So it can generate a lot of creative energy, this act of negation. About the power of "negation," said Glenn Gould, "you must constantly examine" it and "must never forget to pay homage as the source from which all creative ideas come" (*Reader* 7). Hegel made negation the engine of thinking, explicitly inspired by Meister Eckhart's ideas sermonized 500 years earlier. Linking "negation" to solitude and contemplation, Gould was drawn to releasement (if not in a specifically Eckhartian way) both emotionally and in its geographical embodiment in the desolate Arctic reaches of Canada, a world he dubbed "the idea of North."

Modern literature could be said to inhabit its own version of Northern extremity. Edmund Wilson in his pioneering work *Axel's Castle* (1931) argues that negation takes the shape of a dedicated inwardness indifferent to the external world, absorbed in elaborating artistic designs. Modernism is, for better and worse, argues Wilson, a post-romantic continuation of the hermeticism of French symbolism as it fuses with or conflicts with naturalism. The book gets its title from the 1890 French symbolist prose poem *Axel* by Villiers de l'Isle-Adam. Wealthy, melancholy young Count Axel occupies an "ancient and isolated castle in the depths of the Black forest" where he studies alchemy and is being prepared by Rosicrucians into revelation of the ultimate mysteries. When his lover urges him to leave his castle to "come and live," to realize their dreams, he replies: "Live? No. Our existence is full—and its cup is running over! . . . To consent, after this, to live would be but sacrilege against ourselves. Live? Our servants will do that for us" (qtd. 209). After such insouciance what forgiveness? *Axel* concludes with hero and beloved drinking poison together: "Oh, the external world! Let us not be made dupes by the old slave."

For Wilson, Axel's renunciation is not aberrant but suggests the quintessential modernist type. He notes that the "supine and helpless" "heroes of the contemporary writers with whom I have been dealing in this book are in general as uncompromising as Axel—sometimes, indeed, the authors themselves" seem "almost to have patterned their lives" on symbolist aesthetes (211). Rimbaud, Yeats, Joyce, Valéry, Proust, Gertrude Stein, and T. S. Eliot all flaunt various modes of withdrawal, with Stein spinning "herself a more impenetrable cocoon" than any of them (212). Although Wilson exaggerates their isolation, he respects the rigor and difficulty of these authors. It is hard not to hear relief in his declaration near the end that "though we shall continue to admire them as masters," they "will no longer serve us as guides. Axel's world of the private imagination in isolation . . . seems to have been as exploited and explored as far as for the present is possible" (231).

As Wilson depicts it, renunciation is an act of luxurious and perverse choice, one sewn into the fabric of literary modernism. Another choice, naturally aligned to the renunciatory, is asceticism, exemplified in a figure who hovers on the edge of *Axel's Castle* and is a favorite of Wilson's. Flaubert, high priest of the religion of art, who confided that he loved his work "with a love that is frenzied and perverted, as an ascetic loves the hair shirt that scratches his belly," inspired Mallarmé, Joyce, and Henry James, and yearned to write "a book about nothing, a book dependent on nothing external, which would be held together by the internal strength of its style" and whose "subject would be almost invisible" (*Letters* 154, 158).

Isolation and withdrawal, enforced rather than chosen, are equally central to modernity in another pioneering critical work, Tillie Olsen's *Silences* (1978). The stunted careers of Olsen's figures testify to "the unnatural thwarting of what struggles to come into being but cannot." Her book, originally a talk at Radcliffe in 1962, would become a foundational text of feminist literary history. It begins with elected renunciation: not only Rimbaud and Melville but Gerard Manley Hopkins, the Jesuit priest whose writing of poetry depended on permission from his superiors until he surrendered to silence, with intermittent lapses. Thomas Hardy, frustrated by Victorian prudery, eventually abandoned novels for poetry. Above all though, Olsen is concerned with coerced abandonment or arrest of writing careers—"work aborted, deferred, denied." These are the "hidden silences" inflicted by poverty and racism and, above all, gender inequality, borne by those "consumed in the hard, everyday essential work of maintaining human life." Another burden is censorship by government and by publishers. Olsen also speaks of "foreground" silences, those occurring prior to major achievement—as with Kate Chopin, George Eliot, Conrad, Sherwood Anderson, Laura Ingalls Wilder (8, 10). Olsen found personal inspiration in Kafka's diary entries narrating his relentless effort to snatch moments to write amid the demands of office work and family. Her refusal of self-pity and resolve to show the fatality entwined in material circumstance and socially dictated incapacity only sharpens the pain of the silences she sets before us. We are a long way from the elected decadence of Axel in his castle.

Social position blights opportunity but can also create it. For the sixteenth- and seventeenth-century *gentilhomme*, for instance, a Montaigne, a Descartes, retreat from the city to the country was practically de rigueur (Gaukroger 188). It was a strategic cultural and social ritual: one seeks distance from court if one is to influence the wider society. Less class-bound or strategic and far more hedonistic in their teaching were anarchic 1960s gurus who preached "turn on, tune in, drop out." This mantra of Timothy Leary was taken up by his friend Ken Kesey and the Merry Pranksters, all seizing the baton of Jack Kerouac (whose buddy Neal Cassady, the model of *On the Road*'s Dean Moriarty, drove the Prankster bus). Even in the fifties Kerouac's own road trip was already a venerable trope of American pastoral as first practiced by Walt Whitman on the open road, himself inspired by Emerson's praise of abandonment. As a counterforce to the imperative of movement, Kerouac, like many fifties artists, took up Zen, abandoning Western reason and conscious thinking to pause and bask in silence, patience, serenity, though he mixed his bouts of asceticism with occasional "Zen Free Love Lunacy orgies" (Kerouac, *Dharma* 30). To this heady brew, Kerouac and Allen Ginsberg added a dash of Rimbaud, whom they revered as a mystic poet-outlaw and *enfant terrible.* They shared the enthusiasm of that hipster *avant la lettre,* Henry Miller, who shamelessly took Rimbaud as a mirror on which to dwell: "He did not 'belong'—not anywhere. I have always had the same feeling about myself" (Miller 6).

Our homegrown renunciators are familiar to even casual readers: not only Emerson from his ministry and Melville eventually from fiction writing, but also the recluses Thoreau and Dickinson and Hawthorne. Each embodies a "No! in thunder," the pithy signature of native negativity that Melville called "the grand truth about Nathaniel Hawthorne." The latter absented himself (for twelve years) from (social) life itself. His gallery of renunciators is indelible, above all his character Reverend Hooper, who one day preaches his Sunday sermon with his face hidden behind a black veil. For the rest of his long life he never removes it in public or private, even on his deathbed. As a reproach to the hypocrisy of his parishioners, Hooper has turned himself into a solitary living symbol of sin and a notorious village eccentric. His monomaniacal self-erasure simultaneously magnifies the ego, an irony that seems almost built in to renunciation.

Authorial anxiety runs deep in an American culture founded on Calvinist suspicion of art, indeed of subjectivity itself. This is a venerable theme that has been discussed often and well; from it I will distill a figure to return to—Melville's laconic scrivener, Bartleby. He stands with another opaque presence, Babo, that "hive of subtlety" whose death head on a pike calmly gazes at us at the end of Melville's *Benito Cereno*. Babo and Bartleby affront our urge to unravel mystery into meaning and, in their brooding silence, forecast Melville's own renunciation of prose fiction. Bartleby, lately beloved of European theorists, has also lent his name to a "syndrome" denoting literary abandonment: "Those in the No" is the subject of Enrique Vila-Matas's engaging and erudite *Bartleby & Co.* (153).

Renunciation is as American as apple pie, and as old as the Greek cynics. The first self-conscious dropout, the vagrant Diogenes, a fourth-century BCE Athenian troublemaker, was notorious for scorning all decorum. With all his worldly possessions kept in a knapsack, Diogenes's renunciation combined animal excess with an ascetic refusal of comfort and routine. William James's airbrushed late Victorian version of Diogenes saluted him for possessing the pragmatist spirit of anarchic vitality and the Cynic was a touchstone for freethinkers throughout the eighteenth and nineteenth centuries. "The highest thing that can be attained on earth," said Nietzsche of cynicism (*Ecce* 264). Thoreau was called a "Yankee Diogenes" and Whitman revered him as a predecessor. Giving bite to the etymology of Cynic as the dog *(kuon)*, a creature immune to shame, Diogenes has a programmatic commitment to outrageous acts that mock the Greek esteem for rational thought. He turns private behavior public by masturbating, defecating, and urinating in the town square. Diogenes's aggressive naturalism regarded "canons of decency" as "artificial and thus irrational," so he scorned material comfort and sought to perfect through rigorous discipline a wholly natural self-sufficiency (Geuss 26). He spoke rather than wrote his philosophy, making it a perishable thing of this world rather than print on a page. Whereas the reclusive Gould effaces his public presence, Diogenes is nothing but; yet both their acts of renunciation invite us (explicitly in Gould) to make our life and music one, our life and philosophy one, even while relocating them in opposite realms.

Renunciation preoccupies several distinguished novels. A narrated interior monologue, Hermann Broch's *The Death of Virgil* (1945), interrogates, via the Roman poet's effort on the last day of his life to burn his *Aeneid*, the status of art's possibility in the wake of genocidal catastrophe. Thomas Bernhard devotes novels to exploring forms of creative self-erasure in Gould *(The Loser)* and in Wittgenstein *(Correction)*, including the propensity of their genius to unleash around them a mimetic contagion of self-doubt. Richard Powers's novel *The Goldbug Variations* (1991) presents a meditation, with Gould invoked humming in the background, on American success and failure by charting the withdrawal of a gifted postwar molecular biologist. He speaks of "that saving grace of *Homo sapiens:* the ability to step out of the food chain and, however momentarily, refuse to compete" (165).

As I suggested regarding Ad Reinhardt's "black" paintings, I do not restrict renunciation to biography, to the abrupt forsaking of a career or of novels about it. Less dramatic acts of abandonment occur *in the making* of art; that is, refusals help constitute certain artistic forms— the refusal, say, of explanation, of reference and likeness, of definitions, indeed of determinate concepts, in short, the basic tools in the intellectual arsenal that enable clear communication with an audience. For instance, the riddle of a Zen koan eluding logic is a miniature embodiment of strategic refusal. In the West, by the late nineteenth century, "the symbolist movement in literature" (as Arthur Symons titled his influential 1899 book) had been rebuilding poetry upon opacity and mystery; "this revolt against exteriority, against rhetoric" addressed the "soul" and "in speaking to us so intimately . . . becomes itself a kind of religion" (Symons 5). French symbolist poetry was to leave a rich inheritance among high modernists (T. S. Eliot, crucially). Eliot mocks meaning as what the poet provides the reader while going about his work, the way the burglar offers the guard dog a bit of meat to distract him. The symbolist inheritance in literary modernism, combined with Dadaist and Surrealist contempt for the rational and the received in the wake of the First World War, prepared the way for fascination with Zen in the US postwar era. These movements invested in artistic and spiritual expression that abandoned both conventional intelligibility and the priority of Meaning.

Here the *locus classicus* is John Cage's Dada/Zen-inspired silent piece for prepared piano *4'33"* (1952). Emptied of ego and assertion, moving "from making to accepting," it wittily deflates the "vogue of profund-ity" and "genius" that assumes "Art comes from within" (Symons). This assumption "elevates the man who made it a-bove those who ob-served it or heard it." Among the elevations of self that Cage hoped to topple were the heroic existential performances of the macho Jackson Pollock, whose drip paintings made him the best-known exemplar of abstract expressionism, the reigning artistic movement of the time (Cage, 129–130; Jones, "Finishing").

Valéry, the poet and critic who renounced poetry for twenty years, noted that "painstaking work, in literature, is manifested and operates in terms of *refusals*. One might say that it is measured by the number of refusals" (8:250). He has in mind his mentor, the mystifying Mallarmé, who once remarked: "To *name* an object is to lose three-quarters of the pleasure of the poem." To impede direct communication or at least make it difficult has historically been the *raison d'être* of avant-garde painting and poetry (roughly the experimentalism that starts in France in the 1860s). When later artists balk at requests to explain their work they are invoking, wittingly or not, a symbolist inheritance that spurns obligations of representation. Recall the public shrugs of Bob Dylan (whose *Tarantula* is a collection of his symbolist prose poems) or William Faulkner, both youthful enthusiasts of Rimbaud and Mallarmé, respectively.

This defiance of the plea for understanding extends to renunciation's motives. Even when reasons can be deduced—Melville quit fiction because he was tired of not earning a living by it; Glenn Gould, at thirty-one, ceased live performance the better to purify the sound of his piano—even with reasons their elected silence abides in mystery, overshadowing the facts. A "without why" remains. As Richard Howard (adapting Walter Benjamin) writes of Frank O'Hara's early death: "A man who dies at forty is at every moment of his life, we say, a-man-who-has-died-at-forty. . . . On the level of life, real life, the formula has no meaning; in the order of memory there can be no escaping it" (466–467). Like those ambushed by premature death, artists who abandon their art will be, in memory, forever defined by that act. Yet this idealizing impulse must also confront its opposite—the unglamorous possibility that renunciation expresses an end of creativity, the act of a burned-out case with nothing left to say. This has been suggested about Rimbaud and Salinger, one an adolescent poet, the other preoccupied with adolescents, who both grew up and quit.

Motives can be speculated upon. Or ignored. Barthes prefers the latter; "the very idea of a motive would be useless, insufficient here: that's how it is, period, that's it," which is how he describes "the absolute impenetrability" of Rimbaud's decision to quit (*Preparation* 151). It is tempting to generalize these remarks if only to suggest that the act or the art of silence admits of no sweeping generalizations or master plot, a conclusion Gore Vidal reached about homosexuality: how can one regard it as a category of identity (as opposed to behavior) when it includes both Eleanor Roosevelt and Roy Cohn? Nor does renunciation have a particular political identity; it ranges across the spectrum of responses to modernity—bookended by Rimbaud's now lost "communist constitution" for the Paris Commune of 1871 and George Oppen's Communist commitments on one end and on the other by Philip Rieff's screeds against the sixties counter-culture. The "why" of renunciation, its motives, will be set aside in some cases (Rimbaud's) but will be taken into account when they impinge upon what most counts in a renunciation—its *form*. In some important cases (Gould's) the particularity of the form it takes emerges from renunciation's interplay with why.

The figure who functions in this book as a kind of nexus threading together various authors and movements is the profoundly cosmopolitan William James. After Thomas Jefferson and Benjamin Franklin, he is

the uncannily ubiquitous American intellectual—influencing philosophers, writers, and scientists in Russia, Japan, Germany, France, and
Italy, to suggest his breadth of impact. But not only global intellectual
range makes James exemplary here. So does the urgency of his desire to
renounce the rule of concepts. James's reach—nodding to the ancients,
ranging from West to East—encompasses the scope of renunciation in
these pages.

He allied himself with the primal renunciator, Diogenes; he host-
ed at Harvard in 1896 the visiting Swami Vivekananda, who export-
ed Yoga and Vedanta to the US; James was so impressed he wanted
to arrange a Harvard professorship for him. James influenced D. T.
Suzuki, who would become the key relay of Zen to the West, thanks
to books and a seminar he conducted at Columbia in the early fifties (Leonard 151). James looks back to Emerson and ahead to his admirer Wittgenstein, and even indirectly to Salinger, who, after leaving
Zen for Vedanta, depended for spiritual guidance on the Vivekananda
House in Manhattan. In sum, James's intellectual legacy embodies the
"wider self" of "manyness-in-oneness" he posited in his efforts to defeat the reign of intellectualism.

Suzuki is a key transmission point in bringing James to the East.
By the 1890s Suzuki was already active in the US, reading and writing
on Emerson (the subject of his first published essay) and James—and
his wife was a former student of James's. When Suzuki declares, "Zen
is not to be conceptualized . . . if it is to be experientially grasped;
but inasmuch we are all human . . . we cannot remain dumb," he
could also be describing the conundrum we will witness James grappling with in 1908 (Suzuki 260). Suzuki was so excited about James's
thinking that in 1904 he sent James's just published essay "A World of
Pure Experience" to a friend in Japan, Kitaro Nishida, who had briefly
practiced Zen meditation and who would become the most important
Japanese philosopher of the century (Yusa 358n.54). In his first book,
published in 1911, Nishida explicitly makes central James's phrase
and idea "pure experience"; it functions for both thinkers as a provisional designation for pre-reflective Being, "without the admixture of
any thinking or discrimination" (qtd. Sharf 21, 22). A year before, in
1910, Nishida had commended James's *Essays in Radical Empiricism*,
noting "they seem to bear clear resemblance to Zen" (qtd. Friedl,

"Global" 199). Pure experience chimes with the Zen Buddhist idea of *sunyata*, a plenitude of no-thingness or emptiness. Suzuki, in turn, made Nishida's notion of unmediated experience the cornerstone of his own version of Zen.

Japanese appropriation of Jamesian themes at the turn of the century complements earlier American fascination—Emerson and Thoreau, for instance—with East Indian and Buddhist thought. This cross-pollination would nurture Cage, Suzuki's best-known American student. He expressed this fusion in 1975 when he noted that Thoreau was the source of "just about every idea I've ever had worth its salt" (qtd. Leonard 151). Rather than nationalist, this remark, once unpacked, makes perfect global sense given that Suzuki shared Cage's enthusiasm for the Transcendentalists and that Thoreau revered the sacred Hindu text the *Bhagavad Gita*, with its praise for "the supreme perfection of actionlessness . . . through renunciation."

■

In the West renunciation starts as a religious imperative: Leave father and mother, house and land, and follow me, Jesus said. Obedience by the exemplary few to the call to continence was a cornerstone of early Christian spiritual purity. By A.D. 70 exponents of the ascetic ideal in Palestine, claiming to be Jesus's true followers, submitted to "drastic dislocation of the normal course" of their lives and beckoned householders to abandon their own settled existences and ancestral ties. By the late second century, *apotaktikoi*, the withdrawers, "bands of rootless persons," sworn to chastity, fasting, and begging, filled "the nooks and crannies" of the Nile Valley (Brown 42, 244).

Joining a flock of wanderers is one form of self-effacement. An individual act of renunciation is another, one that suspends business as usual to become, intended or not, an act whose spiritual rigor might reverberate out into the world. This centrifugal move from within to without had literal counterparts. The worldliness of even the solitary hermit is evident in the so-called pillar saints, the stylites of the fifth century, "who spent their renunciatory careers atop narrow pillars and who from their lofty perches became the focus of intense admiration" (E. Clark, *Reading* 35). The great stylite, Simeon, stood high above for twenty-eight years. But rather than isolated he acted as a wise man in the community, attended to by a flock of acolytes as he moderated disputes, performed cures, exhorted mobs, and foretold natural disasters. Renunciation was even for some a career move. "Somewhat ironically," it became for female ascetics, excluded from the priesthood, "an avenue for patronage and for monastic leadership" (37).

Just as renunciation entangles the solitary and communal, the act's ascetic moment is often in disconcerting interplay with excess—a version of the dialectic of "less" and "more" that Diogenes the Cynic incarnates. The most glamorous renunciations have about them an extravagant asceticism, a flagrant austerity. Rimbaud, Wittgenstein, and Gould embody near mythic rebukes to dependency of any kind: they seem in their hermetic rigor indifferent to applause or recognition and force the powers that be to play by a new set of rules. These three have captured modern imaginations by tapping into fantasies of omnipotent individualism, though their *ideas* explode the notion of a sovereign subject in control. Of Wittgenstein's style of philosophic debate it was said he takes "all the sides himself; he answers before you've said it—you can't get in." This was less "arrogance," noted F. R. Leavis, who reported about his Cambridge colleague's manner in discussion, than "an intensity of concentration that impressed itself on one as disinterestedness" (130).

Visible in the philosopher's devouring disinterestedness is something of the "divine fury" that has been the nimbus of genius since the ancients. The poet and the pianist sought nothing less than to rearrange temporal order, hoping to banish all tenses save futurity. In their solitude, impatience, and perversity these forbidding figures possess an air of "compulsive fury" (borrowing the words of a close friend of Gould's characterizing the pianist), which they "applied to everything" they "ever touched" (Ostwalt 303). The "little savage" Rimbaud was notoriously sadistic and menacing, and of Wittgenstein his literary executor remarked: "I believe that most of those who loved him and had his friendship also feared him" (qtd. F. Sontag 63). Indeed, Wittgenstein and Gould were both explicitly regarded as threats not simply to their professions but to the very existence of philosophy and music making. "Art should be given a chance to phase itself out," said Gould, an attitude comparable to how Wittgenstein felt about philosophy and Rimbaud about poetry (324). To varying degrees, all three inhabit an "inhuman state," as Thomas Bernhard says of his "Glenn Gould," a state in part composed of "hatred" and "ruthlessness" and "simplicity," qualities marking a life "so possessed by . . . art" (*The Loser* 6, 4, 75–76).

Renunciation's lability, its hospitality to contrary motives and needs, makes it elusive conceptually. Its connotations are diffuse, suggesting deliberative finality, dignity, even grandeur, though not as solemn as abdication. From another angle it involves creative resistance to conventional expectations. Yet from still another it sounds Puritan, evoking guilty, self-abnegating surrender. One is tempted to desert renunciation for nearby cognates—relinquishment, abandonment, leave taking, dropping out, or even its cousins, failure and silence. An anti-subjectivist cognate, "letting be" *(Seinlassen)*, suggests an act of abandonment that allows things, the world, others, to show as they are. Rather than worrying semantics, I accept the imprecision of the word. Most frequently, I link abandonment and renunciation, while aware that they are not strictly synonymous. A bad husband abandons his wife and children; he doesn't renounce them. But if he left for the sake of a higher calling—for God or Country, say—we might say he renounced his family.

With conceptual and linguistic instability a given, one way to harness this flux is via Immanuel Kant's anti-concept concept he calls an "aesthetic idea." This is the basis of aesthetic autonomy, that flirtation with meaning Greenberg praised above. Because it refuses fixed limits, disrupts common-sense logic, and induces unsettlement, the "aesthetic idea" in its indeterminacy is analogous to Kant's more celebrated notion of the sublime, which produces "soul-stirring delight" in nature's terrifying power, "provided our own position is secure" (91–92). Unlike the "workaday world of conceptual determinacy" with its operative fiction that our words mean what they say, an "aesthetic idea" is modeled not on transparency or cognition but closer to its opposite—on the bewilderment art provokes in us (Pillow 92). In *Critique of Judgement* (1790), where Kant builds a place for aesthetic judgment in his larger system, he calls the "aesthetic idea" "that representation of the imagination which evokes much thought, yet without the possibility of any definite thought whatever, i.e. *concept*, being adequate to it, and which language, consequently, can never quite fully capture or render completely intelligible" (Kant 142). This sounds close to the teasing, evocative suggestiveness of our experience of artworks. They induce "mutism" in us, the sense of "not knowing how or where to begin speaking in the face of the artwork," which is the "most common initial response to works of art," to quote a recent observer (de Bolla 4).

Renunciation, as conceived here, is not itself a Kantian aesthetic idea but rather works like one. It finds a seed of its silence in the "mutism" experienced in our first apprehension of an artwork when one points to a "mere *that*" which is not yet a "what"—the pre-cognitive moment that William James and Zen ask us to ponder. Which is to say that certain acts of renunciation remain a mystery in a way that recalls what Friedrich Schiller, writing three years after Kant, says of the beautiful: "A form is beautiful, one might say, if it demands no explanation, or if it explains itself without a concept"; "a triangle explains itself but only through the mediation of a concept. A curving line explains itself without" (Schiller, "Kallias" 155). Exceeding our conceptual grasp and language's purely practical use—to understand and be understood—"aesthetic ideas" are nothing if not thought provoking. Indeed Kant calls them the mind's "animating principle," its "spirit," for they spark reflection. In aesthetic reflection, judgment is not immediately subject to the control of the understanding, the faculty that produces concepts. As an anti-concept, the "aesthetic idea" is, by definition, skeptical of definition or explanation. Says Kant: "Now since the reduction of a representation of the imagination to concepts is equivalent to *expounding* it, the aesthetic idea may be called an *inexponible* representation of the imagination (in its free play)" (171).

Commentators have stressed "just how unique Kant's embrace of aesthetic indeterminacy is": by contrast, both Hegel and British and Scottish empiricist aestheticians "subordinate the imaginative 'wit' of aesthetic play to the sound judgment of rational rules and determinate conceptual unity" (Pillow 9). Refusing this subordination, the German romantics exploit the radical potential in Kant to construe the aesthetic as a new mode of making sense, non-discursively. Hölderlin in 1796 declares "the philosopher must possess as much aesthetic power as the poet" ("those people without an aesthetic sense are our philosophers of literalness") and that "the highest act of reason . . . is an aesthetic act" ("Oldest Programme" 186).

The "aesthetic idea"—the volatile product of artistic genius, says Kant, hence dismissive of preordained rules—pushes against the boundaries of the intelligible. Hence it is available to being appropriated to sponsor experiments, including the expressive use of renunciation. Consider this compelling act of self-silencing from a philosopher who described his first book as "strictly philosophical and, at the same time, literary." Wittgenstein went on to say "the book's point is an ethical one," describing the aesthetic arrangement of his work, the *Tractatus* (1922), whose equation of the "inexpressible" and "mystical" we noted earlier. "My work consists of two parts: of the one which is here, and of everything which I have *not* written. And precisely this second part is the important one. . . . In brief, all of that which *many* are *babbling* today, I have defined in my book by remaining silent about" (qtd. Monk 178).

Articulate silence brings the ethical before us as anti-"babbling," as the "*not* written" pregnant with mystery. The book must be closed— disposed of like a ladder after use, Wittgenstein will implore—as if evaporating in one's hands. What counts is not language and not the page but life—the silent statement made manifest in the right deed. Here, poised in suspension, are the aesthetic (the "literary"), the ethical (for Wittgenstein they are united with the religious in being beyond propositional language), and the silence of an unsettling opacity akin to revelation. Part of a distinguished Viennese family steeped in the worship of art of the late nineteenth century, especially music, Wittgenstein has in effect put in practice the "refusals" Valéry regards as a rigorous literary work's very mode of being.

■

For Valéry, a poem is a reverberant sound of words pitched in the key of evocative suggestion rather than the sterility of precision, evoking not Meaning but a poetic state of mind attuned to beauty, "what is indefinable in things." Here Edgar Allan Poe is a decisive influence, for he reduces meaning to a suggestive undercurrent stimulated by beauty. Beauty, says Valéry, requires "the servile imitation of what is indefinable in objects." The indefinable is the inimitable (how Adorno glosses Valéry's phrase) and attending to particularity is what the beautiful demands of us. "Pay attention," Valéry tells us, "to this subtle continuous sound; it is silence. Listen to what one hears when one no longer perceives anything" (qtd. Adorno, *Notes* 1:172). Of the above passages, Adorno comments that here "nuance comes into its own" and we reach, he says, "the utopian promise" of the aesthetic: "the yearning for a form of thought freed of its own coerciveness" (172). Nuance's career in the hands of Salinger, who finds it a key to freedom from coercive literary form, will be charted later. As will the contradiction latent in the effort to represent the inimitable. "This pure oxymoron" (imitation of the inimitable) liberates but also "marks the impossibility of poetry," an impasse where the self-dismantling poetry of the post-Holocaust writer Paul Celan "locates the tragic" (Lacoue-Labarthe 69).

Building his notion of aesthetic autonomy upon a logic of refusal, Valéry in effect will give Kant's "aesthetic idea" a corporeal turn. We turn to a sketch of Valéry because his ideas comprise the tacit set of background assumptions that nurture many of the acts of renunciation, especially by literary figures, to be examined. Valéry's refusal to locate meaning in an author's intention, for instance, is basic to New Criticism; indeed he "virtually invented the position that dominated literary theory from this point forward" (Cronan 247).

Crucial to Valéry's poetics is skepticism about both "meaning" and "understanding": not *per se*, not as the means of enabling human conviction, but when construed as imposition rather than discovery, an imposition that moves too quickly from medium—paint and words—to message, to tidy concepts of explanation. Valéry would concur with a remark of Paul Celan's, that "poetry no longer imposes, it exposes itself." What it exposes, against the reduction of determinate judgment, is "meaningfulness without meaning." This last phrase is a contemporary formulation of the non-reductive character of Kant's aesthetic judgment (Bernstein, *Against* 58–59). "Something 'understood' is something falsified," declares Valéry, who would applaud (and heralds) Sontag's sponsorship of "pure, untranslatable, sensuous immediacy" (Valéry 14:376; Sontag, *Essays* 16). Instead of regarding an author's intentions as the path to understanding, Valéry submits that it is fine for an author to tell us his intentions, but they are beside the point: rather, "it is a question of what subsists, what he has made independent of himself" (7:158). What subsists apart from the author is "silent"—a resonant, manifest presence "independent of any meaning." At other times, he says this impenetrable silence provokes the reader to become a co-creator. In sum, Valéry's emphasis on the "is"-ness of the object's pure presence is in unresolved tension with his other stress—the "I"-ness of that rare fit reader who participates "as partner of the writer" (8:221). (New Criticism inherits this conflict, for it shares Valéry's anti-intentionalism—denying the author as source of meaning—but, unlike him, also invokes the "affective fallacy," which bans the equating of meaning with the reader's experience.)

Animating Valéry's aesthetics is his often-repeated conviction that "poetry" (by which he means all artistic uses of language) "implies a decision to change the function of language." Prose has a utilitarian mandate—to express aims, wishes, and commands—that annuls itself upon achieving its goal; he always analogizes prose to walking: the end absorbs the means, "only the result remains." "I shall know I am *understood* by the remarkable fact that my discourse no longer exists. It is entirely and definitively replaced by its *meaning*" (7:208). Such is the "fate of prose": "it perishes once it is understood, and because it is understood" (156). If someone has not understood, "he preserves and *repeats the words*" (208). "Repetition answers incomprehension. *It signifies that the act of language has not been able to complete itself*" (156). Here in embryo, in this moment when stalled or inconclusive speech becomes fertile incompletion, is the move from the transitive to the intransitive, from a practical, prosy use of language to a poetic one, from walking to dancing, from language that dies with understanding to what outlives it, reproducing "itself in its own form," as it "stimulates our minds to reconstruct it as it is" (209). Whereas "content alone is to be extracted from prose," in poetry form alone "commands and survives." Form's material elements—sound, cadence, "the physical proximity of words, their effects of induction or their mutual influences"—work on us physiologically, stimulating "the muscular organization by its rhythms" (211). "The greatest possible poet is—the nervous system" (14:541). All of this intense bodily feeling dominates "at the expense" of the "capacity for being consummated in a defined and particular meaning" (7:156–157). Poetry is "altogether pagan," Valéry discovered; "the muse imperiously demands no soul without a body" (8:288).

Around 1892, after a romantic and emotional crisis, he decided to stop writing, a vow which lasted for two decades. Valéry sought relief in the pursuit of another kind of formal purity—higher mathematics. His leaving of poetry was partly inspired by the rigor of intellection that one of his heroes—Descartes—practiced by "renunciation." It allowed Descartes "free play to his boldness in the realm of abstract thought." Yet even Descartes could not screen out all distractions. "Exacting" intellectual work, wrote Valéry, is "necessarily obstructed" by the fact that man is "not simply a disembodied mind" (9:52–53). Yves Bonnefoy has said of Valéry: "He was a very physical, sensual man, and he felt that thought deprived him of the best part of existence." Bonnefoy reads the end of "Le cimetière marin" ("The Graveyard by the Sea") as (retrospectively) narrating this turn to silence: "The wind is rising! . . . We must try to live! The huge air opens and shuts my book . . . pages whirl away in dazzling riot" (Bonnefoy, "Art of Poetry"). The unraveling book chimes with Valéry's remark that "seeing is forgetting the name of the thing one sees." (The phrase became well known as the title of a biography of the artist Robert Irwin, discussed later.)

Poetry is a doing, an act rather than a representation, and its aim—if autotelic activity can be said to have an aim—is to make one alert to what "the name" hides—the indefinable both in oneself and in the world. That is, the poem, for Valéry, causes a "vibration" and stirs "spontaneous movements of thought" (whereas in prose "one can draw up a plan and *follow* it!") (7:176). A circuit of refusals—of meaning fixed in a name and clarified understanding anchored in authorial intention—brings forward poetry in its manifest presence. "My intention was merely *my* intention and the work is—what it is" (14:109). Intruding on this transparent opacity is the "Philosopher: a Child wanting to know the Why and How." A "man interrogating needlessly is a child; he lacks the majesty of the tiger resigned to be magnificently what he is, just as he is, whatever he is" (14:373).

That blissful tautology of pure presence will also attract a number of my figures in the shape not of the majestic tiger but of the "rose without why," that emblem of mystery that surrounds some acts of renunciation with a margin of silence. I will call this the terminal moment of renunciation, and it depends on formal discontinuity between life and art. Most dramatic is when this autonomy is pushed to a definitive abruptness as in the self-erasures (each distinctly different) of a Sylvia Plath or a Rimbaud. (I have in mind Plath's late poem "Edge"—"the woman is perfected"—invoked below, and not her more famous confessional blurring of life and art, whose motto is from "Lady Lazarus": "Dying / is an art. . . . I do it exceptionally well") (7). Terminal autonomy is one form of renunciation, whose other mode is the existential or generative—when abandonment *of* one thing and *to* another—performed by an Emerson, a Nietzsche, a Pollock, a Gould—renews creative energy, undoing boundaries between art and life. Rimbaud is a rare instance of both forms of renunciation: while his sudden abandonment of poetry is terminal—hence its "mystery"— his overthrow of canons of restraint, including the boundaries embodied in propriety (self-control) and the proprietary (self-possession), is a renunciation generative for his visionary art. I will return to these distinctions between terminal and generative forms of renunciation.

In what follows "renunciation" is emancipated from its familiar grim role as featured performer in the long-running Germanic tragedy entitled "civilization and its discontents." Freud speaks of "the "organic repression" that replaces the nose with the eye as our primary sense organ upon man's assumption of verticality and optical mastery. The repression that is civilization is emblematic of a larger regime of renunciations of immediate, libidinal gratifications that ensure man's mastery at the price of discontent. "Renunciation is the principle of bourgeois disillusionment," remark Horkheimer and Adorno in *Dialectic of Enlightenment* (1944), fourteen years after Freud. With the Nazi genocide raging in Enlightenment Europe, they retell Freud's sobering drama with a dash of Homeric color but leached of heroism. Set before us is Homer's bound and gagged Odysseus on the mast (after ordering his crew to perform the binding and then fill their own ears with wax to resist the Sirens' allure as they row fiercely past).

Horkheimer and Adorno appropriate this episode as the primal image of modern man surviving "at the price of the abasement and mortification of the instinct for complete, universal, and undivided happiness" (57). The self is a sacrifice to itself; "the history of civilization is the history of the introversion of sacrifice. In other words: the history of renunciation. Everyone who practices renunciation gives away more of his life than is given back to him: and more than the life he vindicates" (55). He gives away impulse and spontaneity; "he has always to wait, to be patient, to do without" (57).

After the war Adorno thought the West deserved to do without art. "To write poetry after Auschwitz is barbaric," he wrote wrote in 1949; and "traditional culture," "neutralized and ready-made," has "become worthless" (*Prisms* 34). To create work of lyric beauty in the aftermath of the death camps not only exposes art's impotent irrelevance but also subjects the genocide to "the aesthetic principle of stylization" that inevitably transfigures horror by endowing it with "some meaning" ("Commitment" 189). Only art that somehow internalizes the barbarism deserves to be spared.

Holocaust survivor Celan, who was a prisoner in a forced labor camp and whose mother the Nazis murdered, is the writer (along with Samuel Beckett) that Adorno would later suggest as exempt from the Auschwitz interdiction. Celan spoke of his first published (1947) and most famous poem "Todesfuge" ("Death Fugue," with its refrain "Black milk of daybreak we drink you at night") as "an epitaph and a grave" for his mother and responded to a critique of the poem as "desecrating the graves. My mother too has only *this* grave" (*Correspondence* 195). In regarding "Todesfuge" as a "grave," Celan in effect undoes representation, replacing the "aboutness" of mimesis with embodied, if deathly, presence.

Battle of the Bulge veteran George Oppen will in effect suffer the force of Adorno's severity about poetry after Auschwitz, even while finding his way back to writing after a quarter century. Wounded in combat yet guilty about surviving enemy fire, he makes the page into a battlefield, basing his return to poetry on the belief that it is "Possible / To use / words provided one treat them / As enemies. / Not enemies—Ghosts" (*New Collected* 116). Poems as graves; words as ghostly enemies: both Celan and Oppen renounce the conventionally poetical and the beautiful, electing a "greyer" language (Celan's word) to bear witness to contemporary history. Refusing to renounce after Auschwitz, Celan and Oppen instead make renunciation the basis of historically answerable poetry. Renunciation becomes for them a generative poetic practice.

Another Battle of the Bulge survivor, J. D. Salinger, starts withdrawing in 1953, a dozen years before ceasing to publish, a period in which he organizes his fictional universe around an absent center, a saintly sudden suicide, one who is both a Zen poet and a Zen riddle ("Did you see more glass?" asks Sybil, the little girl on the beach, to Seymour Glass, a returned combat veteran, shortly before he shoots himself at the end of "A Perfect Day for Bananafish"). This pun bewilders in a way analogous to that already mentioned Zen koan: "What is the sound of one hand clapping?" Renouncing conventional sense making for silence, Salinger anticipates his own elected silence but also his later prose experiments. One reason his last novel, *Seymour: An Introduction*, renounces tight plotting—indeed any narrative momentum—is because its narrator describes himself as "ecstatically happy," in tune with the Zen edict that abolishes closure and hierarchy for receptivity to the ubiquity of the divine in the things of this world. Salinger turns this openness into the writer-narrator's confessed compositional principle of digression and deferral, qualities that also characterize his own ambivalence about finishing a portrait of Seymour. Writing inside this Zen indifference to all goals save the abolition of desire, Salinger beckons his reader toward a higher spiritual state beyond the conditional world—the "pure consciousness" of satori.

I redescribe renunciation by tracking its other life: instead of its familiar identity as the condition of the immiserated self in modernity, indeed as the definition of civilization itself as a barren loop of perpetual frustration, here renunciation is an act of freedom. This equation revives ancient associations. If renunciation in any of its manifestations has a common thread to grasp it might be found in a phrase of Peter Brown's in *The Body and Society*, his magisterial study of sexual renunciation in early Christianity. In describing why "a virgin of either sex" in the third century A.D. refuses to marry, Brown notes that it has nothing to do with redeeming the ravages of lust, a later, Augustinian

view. The "intact flesh"—a "waxen seal" of the "untarnished soul"—
is a "fragile oasis of human freedom" and "mirrored the right of the
human being, the possessor of a preexistent, utterly free soul, not to
surrender its liberty to the pressures placed upon the person by society" (170). This margin of freedom, which anticipates the function
of the aesthetic in these pages, is what renunciation keeps faith with
while shaped by a multitude of permutations and motives.

Renunciation as freedom does not, of course, take place in a vacuum; indeed renunciants are often protesting the disturbing degree of
unfreedom in modernity, where "life does not live" (to quote Adorno's
epigraph to *Minima Moralia*) despite (or because of) the achievement of
scientific and industrial mastery beyond the dreams of Enlightenment
philosophers. That the accomplishments simultaneously degrade living life, not least because of the psychic desiccation imposed by positivist science and technologism, is a virtual given for, say, William
James and Nietzsche and for another war veteran, Wittgenstein. "I am
not aiming at the same target as the scientists and my way of thinking
is different from theirs," remarked Wittgenstein. For them, "Progress"
is the supreme end and even "clarity" becomes a means to an end.
This fixation is one reason that "science is a way of sending" us "to
sleep." However, "man has to waken to wonder—and so perhaps do
peoples" (*Culture and Value* 7, 5).

In the nation of unfettered Enlightenment reason and personal liberty the rule of instrumental thinking has produced a paradox—the
stunted state of human flourishing amid unprecedented prosperity.
American literature, from *Walden* to *The Human Stain*, has pondered
this tension. The ascetic Thoreau, at the end of *Walden*, remarks
"there is not one of my readers who has yet lived a whole human life"
(222). Roth's version: "There is the drive to master things, and the
thing that is mastered is oneself" (273). Colliding against the drive of
mastery, upending its harsh, self-ambushing demands, acts of renunciation challenge the rationalist imperative of Enlightenment.

Renunciation's other life of creative abandonment is often a protest
or refusal that is made on behalf of the ideal of "a whole human life"—
but without turning ideal into a metaphysical essence, whose pursuit
inevitably becomes fixated on the pre-lapsarian. Avoiding the lost paradise of "undivided happiness" (Horkheimer and Adorno's holy grail),

the key acts of renunciation examined below avoid as well the fetish of origins and of primitivism. Instead of pining for Adamic freshness, the act survives for us thanks to the narrative of its own existence, its material trace, be it on a page, a canvas, a recording. So these acts of what I am calling generative renunciation can be said to proceed immanently—they are always reliant on the instruments—language, concepts, culture, an audience—that they seek to assault or abandon.

Indifferent to going beyond or behind or under, this immanence encourages receptivity to the solicitations of surface rather than depth. Lightness replaces the heaviness of metaphysical questing. This shift is already apparent in Montaigne, one of the great renunciators, and a modernist *avant la lettre*. Initially he was spurred in part to withdraw from the world out of dismay over the treachery of surface, of masks and appearances, including their accomplices in deceit, words and language—"a commodity so vulgar and so vile." But silence eventually makes Montaigne restless so he begins, contrary to expectations, to essay a dialogue with himself and discovers he has to revise his relation to language. He learns, Jean Starobinski tells us, that "our language is powerless if what we expect from it is revelation of a truer world, but it offers us fullness if we agree to live in it, in this primary world of trouble, pleasure and suffering" (244–245). Because William James pursues revelation, a "truer world" of "raw unverbalized life," he cannot, we will see, quite manage the Frenchman's equanimity. We are however urged to do so by two of Montaigne's admirers, who applauded his "gaiety"—his fellow renunciators Emerson and Nietzsche. "We live amid surfaces, and the true art of life is to skate well upon them," says Emerson in "Experience," a subject Montaigne first made his own (*Essays* 478). Nietzsche's praise of the Greeks can stand as a watchword for the other life of renunciation traced in these pages: "to worship appearance, to believe in shapes, tones, words—in the whole Olympus of appearance. Those Greeks were superficial—*out of profundity!*" (*Gay*, "Preface" 4).

■

To plumb the depths of surface (and "nothing is deeper in man than his skin," says Valéry) is a dream that accords with literary and visual

modernism's formalist emphases (5:33). "The history of modernism is
the history of purgation," to cite Arthur Danto's capsule definition that
refers first of all to Greenberg's stress on the avant-garde distaste for
"subject matter or content" as "something to be avoided like a plague,"
a purism that turns content into form, making the work irreducible to
"anything not itself" (Danto, *After* 70; Greenberg 1:8). Liberation from
content or Meaning doesn't end in Axel's castle though; something of
this dream survives even in mid-twentieth-century writers committed to sumptuous verisimilitude. So we hear Saul Bellow, an art novelist but hardly avant-garde, in a letter and then in an essay against
"deep readers," disown not reference but novels, including his own,
that "pant so after meaning. They are earnestly moral and didactic,"
in flight from feeling (*Letters* 138; *There Is* 94).

To make feeling the preserve of aesthetic power and to pit it against
the machinery of the Intellect is a move basic to modernism and to the
critique of modernity many modernists carry over from the romantics,
and is performed alike by symbolist poets and realist novelists. The
cost for Bellow in turning a "cognitive profit on imaginative activities" by trumpeting capital M "Meaning" is "loss of the power to experience life," a concern not unrelated to his well-known belief that "art
has something to do with the achievement of stillness in the midst of
chaos" (*Conversations* 203, 229, 70). Think of his Herzog: after torrential efforts to justify himself, "to have it out," he concludes that "if
the unexplained life is not worth living, the explained life is unbearable, too"; he ends with "not a single word" for anyone (*Herzog* 322,
341). Within garrulity is the yearning to honor stillness and redeem
experience from explanation's "unbearable" weight. So the lightness
achieved in renunciation beckons authors for whom it is not a live
career option.

It even haunted the indefatigably industrious poet, dramatist, and
novelist Charles Reznikoff (1894–1976), who was so adamant about
getting his writing into print that he relied on a personal printing press
he kept in his parents' basement. He refused to be silenced by indifferent publishers. Yet even Reznikoff entertained a fantasy of renunciation that he dramatized in one of the few pieces of writing that he
wrote but did not publish. Found at his death in a meticulous type-
script (awaiting publication) and then posthumously issued by Black

Sparrow, *The Manner Music* is a novel that culminates in the gifted, ignored, now mad musician Jude Dalsimer reducing his life's work to a "heap of ashes." Of his friend Reznikoff, George Oppen once said that in enduring "much more than twenty years of neglect, very near-ly total neglect," he learned "the tactic of total humbleness" (*Letters* 194). In *The Manner Music* he dispenses with the tactic that controlled his public face of fortitude by which he contained the pain of non-recognition, and exposes the other side of his determined humility: Reznikoff's fictive conflagration—deliberately kept private but ready for publication—enacts renunciation not as redemption but as rage.

Bellow's yearning for the stillness that ensues when one stops pant-ing after Meaning is a wish not unrelated to avant-garde modernism's assault on understanding. As Adorno said of Beckett's *Endgame*, "un-derstanding it can only mean understanding its incomprehensibility" (*Notes* 1:243). The challenge of modernist artifacts includes the de-mand we recognize that understanding qua understanding is itself "in want of understanding." We will pursue this line of inquiry later but note here that modernism tends to renounce the usual form of un-derstanding that comes to a "halt" with the "self-securing of cogni-tive reason" and the "production of meaning." Instead modernist ex-periments transfigure understanding into something requiring its own undoing by "turning toward what is unsaid, toward silence, speech-lessness, and muteness," that is, toward what preserves singularity by escaping assimilation into general concepts and types (Hamacher 1, 5, 10, 21, 83). But authors are hostage to words, to what Nietzsche calls the "seduction of language." (*Geneaology* 1: 13). The trick is to find a way to write whereby one is, to borrow from Emerson, "not . . . sub-dued by" one's "instruments," that is, by words and books (Emerson, *Essays* 58).

In their suspicions about language, if not in each of their unique responses to the dilemma, Nietzsche and Emerson are waging a vener-able romantic fight, descendants of Schiller ("the art of the poet wants *intuition*, language provides only *concepts*" and thus "robs the object of its sensory nature, of its individuality") and of Wordsworth (Schiller,

"Kallias" 182). The poet begins *Lyrical Ballads* (1800) by urging his readers in "The Tables Turned" to "quit your books" and enough of "meddling intellect": "Let Nature be your teacher" (59–60). A direct line of descent has been traced from this injunction to the moment, 152 years later, "with John Cage and David Tudor sitting silently before an untouched piano, listening to the rain strike the leaves outside the Woodstock concert hall" (Leonard 78). These bids to renounce art or at least erase its difference from life are of course only figurative pleas. Wordsworth doesn't heed his own directive; Cage's silence, an ideal rather than reality, is sculpted and timed, inextricable from the concert hall trappings in which it occurs. (The setting cues our expectation of musical sounds but the ensuing silence is meant to convert that expectation into openness to the vagaries of ambient noise. In short, *4'33"* is a crash course in achieving the Zen state of empty mind.) The pleas are from two who, unlike a Nietzsche or an Emerson, never actually undergo the experience of abandoning a career. The philosophers are caught in the same contradiction as the poet—their linguistic skepticism is expressed in language—but with this difference: leaving sclerotic bastions of authority, Emerson and Nietzsche channel that energy of abandonment into their writing, as they *inscribe* movement and instability into their sentences. Which is to say they let the hermit speak. Which is one way to describe the immanent thrust of generative renunciation.

Letting the hermit speak invokes a favorite self-description of Nietzsche's, suggesting a misfit's rudeness toward received wisdom, one who conducts a "schooling in suspicion" that he formally enacts in writing bristling with "snares and nets for unwary birds" (*Human*, 1: "Preface" 1). Late in *Beyond Good and Evil* Nietzsche tells us that "the hermit does not believe that any philosopher . . . ever expressed his real and ultimate opinion in books: does not one write books to conceal what one harbors? . . . Every philosophy also *conceals* a philosophy; every opinion is also a hideout, every word also a mask" (sec. 289). This confession of masking all the way down is itself another mask. With a vengeance, Nietzsche's hermit renounces trust in linguistic stability, in transparency grounded in the correspondence of word and thing: that is, he makes the thwarting of communication—the concealing of a mask—constitute the very condition of communication. To produce concepts requires overlooking the individual, Nietzsche says, "whereas nature knows no forms or concepts . . . but only an X that is for us inaccessible and indefinable" ("On Truth and Lies" 117). "Only the inaccessible—as something different from whatever is grasped—is individual, whereas the object caught by the concept of individuality must bow to the reservation that it could be fictional" (Hamacher 177). Nietzsche prefers to face up to the abyss hidden beneath every grounding—"another deeper cave"—and treat language as a mask rather than to accept as truth the errors handed down by metaphysics (*Beyond* 289). In this case the error is "belief in language" as "expressing supreme knowledge of things." Rather than give us knowledge of the world, though, the reign of concepts subsumes the incomparable, incommensurable individual under the general type to produce a fiction of particularity (*Human* vol. 1, 1: 11). A mask, disabling the illusion of transparency, is precisely what reveals the individual in its freedom.

In other words, both Nietzsche and Emerson turn on its head Plato's conviction, backbone of the classical philosophic tradition, that the fixed essences to which language is said to give us access constitute the definitions that are the precondition for knowledge. Like the romantic poet, both thinkers take their cue from nature but turn it into a tutelary skeptic: it offers only an inaccessible X says Nietzsche, and Emerson remarks: "You are one thing, but nature is *one thing and the other thing*, in the same moment" (*Essays* 581). Nature's ferment models Emerson's sense of language's volatility; "no sentence will hold the whole truth" so must contain its contrary. He launches this remark from his own hermit perspective, that is, he makes it after talking with a "pair of philosophers" for whom "out of my poverty of life and thought, [I] had no word or welcome . . . when they came to see me" (585, 587). His "poverty" registers discrepancy—that "however sincere and confidential we can be, saying all that lies in the mind," still we "go away feeling that all is yet unsaid," although we "use the same words!" (587). His pun on "lies" is already eroding his sincerity and mocking his claim that we "use the same words," an unraveling that enacts his sense of the tension between language and truth. In their own crafty work with words these two generative renunciants practice the hermit's radical interrogation of language.

In the next century another hermit would revolt against the Platonic mandate that pure essences ground knowledge and language. "Solitary exile seems to be suiting him," remarked a friend of Wittgenstein's, recalling the philosopher's plan to "live entirely alone and by himself— a hermit's life—and do nothing but work in logic" (qtd. Klagge *Exile* 54). Solitary, dubious of essences, Wittgenstein was drawn to a classical (rather than Cartesian) skepticism that also informs Nietzsche and Emerson's hermit perspective. The skeptic, says Sextus Empiricus, uses language and definitions "in a loose and inexact sense" for practical purposes of living; "our aim is to indicate what appears to us" rather than to represent "realities" (111, 113).

Wittgenstein is not a Master of Suspicion—the role Nietzsche is often asked to play in postmodern thought—he does not demand anything as sweeping and grand as a "radical interrogation" of language or resistance to the conceptual. Instead, his hermit vantage, his adamant independence, in effect counseled insouciance. Wittgenstein says that we resist essentialism when we develop the ability to lower our expectations (nurtured by Plato) that legitimate concepts need to be anchored in essences. That this expectation is misplaced is confirmed quite easily—by reflecting on our everyday life with language, where only some kinds of language—mainly scientific ones—use concepts to make knowledge-claims that depend on fixing meaning in an essence. The majority of other concepts—employed, say, to command, question, joke, chat, recount—require only a loose, flexible unity based on similarity ("family resemblance" Wittgenstein calls it) that varies with occasion and use.

Alertness to these actual practices will assuage our anxieties about needless foundational questions; this calm is what philosophy can instill in us. Which is to say: "it leaves everything as it is" (Wittgenstein, *Investigations* sec. 124). The "originating cause of skepticism," for Sextus Empiricus, "is, we say, the hope of attaining quietude" (*Outlines* 9). The matter-of-factness that typifies Wittgenstein's later thinking—"We want to *understand* something that is already in plain view"—enacts nothing less than a revolutionary attitude (and brings him closer to Nietzsche): that philosophy needs to renounce its traditional grand ambitions to get to the bottom of things, to offer grounds, justifications, and explanations (*Investigations* sec. 89). To offer them is to be held captive yet again by the Platonic demand for essences, which only brings us to the abyss of an infinite regress familiar to Cartesian skepticism (but how do you *know* it was your brother and not a robot version of him?). Instead, philosophy should provide reminders and truisms. To house his deliberately deflated philosophy Wittgenstein fashioned what he called provisional "sketches" made in transit, as if "this work, in its poverty" records the thinking of a hermit in his preoccupied perambulations (*Investigations* v–vi). This deflation would help cure "our disease" which "is one of wanting to explain" (qtd. Klagge *Exile* 208).

■

These figures of hermit vision share an orientation that might be suggested by a pair of complementary quotations. First is Arendt's "stop and think" (to recall her imperative, the urgency of which she discovered studying Adolph Eichmann's "thoughtlessness"). Yet by stopping we have already converted intuitive groping to conceptual order. So to "stop and think" these thinkers in effect add a self-reflexive challenge—summarized in Wittgenstein's "Don't think, but look!" Strange coming from a philosopher, this remark (which will be appropriated, we will see, by an artist and a mystic theologian) decouples thinking from looking to remind us that the order imposed by thinking's work of retrospective analysis and explanation is inevitably biased toward looking *through* the surface—what is front of our eyes—in search of a simplifying crystalline essence. This looking *through* occurs whenever we "sublime" looking into god-like detachment (*Investigations* sec. 66).

Refusal of such (illusory) disengagement is a root conviction—anti-Cartesian and anti-dualist—that animates the figures of renunciation here. They share an implicit critique of philosophy's traditional elevation of rationality and concomitant neglect of the ordinary. These emphases "mistake the nature of reason and the role it plays in most of our behavior" and ignore the "nonrational features which are inborn or are acquired" through custom, habit, or our bodily involvement in the world (Braver 215). This reinstatement of the nonrational (as distinct from the irrational) is not a romantic corrective that merely reverses dualisms and enthrones impulse, but rather insists we are embodied subjects, that is, our rationality is joined to our participation in nature. We act with a spontaneous adaptiveness that is goal-oriented but "often not chosen for reasons" (Siewert 220–221). The fact that non-renunciants—for instance, David Hume, Walt Whitman, John Dewey, Heidegger, Faulkner, and Arendt—more or less uphold this perspective should caution against imputing any causal or necessary relation between it and renunciation. While anti-Cartesianism is not exclusive to those who renounce, many of the figures I concentrate on do have a distinctively visceral relation to it; they make the critique a shaping pressure in their work *and* lives, as if enacting Hume's baseline warning: "Be a philosopher; but, amidst all your philosophy, be still a man" (qtd. Braver 220). "Let us be human" is Wittgenstein's version and this dauntingly simple imperative drives in multifarious, contradictory ways the renunciations to be examined (*Culture and Value* 30).

Respect for the human limits of reason and for the world as phenomenal appearance rather than knowable essence: this hardly sounds incendiary. Yet any philosophy that validates the pre-cognitive is vulnerable in certain historical moments to hijacking by demagogues promulgating a cult of unreason. Consider the fate of *Lebensphilosophie* (life philosophy), the turn-of-the-century rubric under which thinkers such as James, Bergson, and Nietzsche have at times been placed, A main mediator of this anti-dualist mode of thought, Wilhelm Dilthey, rejects intellectualism since life is not reducible to logical formulae, for we often act on feelings and intuition, on what is beyond or over or prior to reason. For Dilthey, positivist science ignores the "whole man" and the fact of "real blood flowing in the veins of human beings" (qtd. D. E. Cooper 95). In the 1930s German ideologues of vitalist irrationalism appropriated *Lebensphilosophie* to provide support for reducing culture to biology and nationalism to blood and soil, upholding the racial supremacy of the Teutonic. The Nazi Alfred Rosenberg hailed Eckhart as the "apostle of the Nordic West" (Moran). Hitler bestowed upon Mussolini a specially bound complete edition of Nietzsche's work for his sixtieth birthday. The uses made of Nietzsche and Eckhart were distortions, their ideas and words ripped from their contexts and cobbled together to rationalize murderous ideology. Analogously, the benign "without why" was twisted into a byword of terrorist fanaticism in the thirties. Fiction of the period gave ample indication of such pure resoluteness. "The question 'why' was eliminated in our endless struggle," declared a character in a 1930 German novel about a terrorist, a book that influenced André Malraux's fiction. Terrorists "asked no questions," he writes in *Man's Fate* of an ecstatic suicide who seeks to maximize his sense that the purest acts are pointless (qtd. Collins, 915). No idea is exempt from ideological enlistment.

The brutal simplifications of such political enlistment would have no patience for renunciation's quality of reverberant aura, its tendency to elude full intelligibility and become a "center of vibratory suspense" (how Mallarmé describes what words do in his poems) (235). Wallace Stevens ends "Notes toward a Supreme Fiction": "You will have stopped revolving except in crystal." Both poets capture something of this pulsating aftermath, at once moving and still, of this terminal moment of renunciation. Rimbaud's quitting—never explained, never rescinded—has this aura or "mystery," as Blanchot puts it. What we hear in the aftermath are "the echoes!" as Sylvia Plath writes in "Words," fittingly a posthumously published poem (in *Ariel*). It begins: "Axes / After whose stroke the wood rings, / And the echoes! / Echoes travelling / Off from the centre like horses" (85). The fact of Plath's suicide cannot help but make us feel these echoes more acutely. Even against one's better (detached) judgment, when death occasions the silence, renunciation tends to gain authenticity and dramatic intensity.

In "Edge," one of her very last poems, also from *Ariel*, Plath makes terminal renunciation an aesthetic event, as she memorializes suicide as an artwork, narrating, as if from the grave, her own imminent leave-taking: "The woman is perfected / Her dead // Body wears the smile of accomplishment / The illusion of a Greek necessity // Flows in the scrolls of her toga." Although "feet seem to be saying: / We have come so far, it is over," this sense of ending turns out to be merely a pause before we make the discovery of what "we" includes and what "over" and "perfected" "accomplishment" actually entail. The next line discloses the corpses of two children: "Each dead child coiled, a white serpent / One at each little // Pitcher of milk, now empty. // She has folded // Them back into her body" (84). Embodying a marmoreal coldness of deadly self-sufficiency, the woman's defiant serenity of aesthetic autonomy (a serenity admittedly pressured by the macabre "dead . . . smile" and the fragile "illusion" of "necessity") silently refuses a reader's urge for explanation, an intransigence that pervades the final poems of *Ariel*. "We stand before the *Ariel* poems," Janet Malcolm has said, as Plath's baffled sister-in-law stood before the "stone-faced Sylvia" wondering "Why doesn't she *say* something?" "Like the life, the work is full of threatening silences . . . with surrealism's menace and refusal to explain itself" (109).

Though a stunning assault on explanation, Plath's suicide seems to me terminal—renunciation that has the last word—rather than generative—abandonment of one thing for another. Her poetry's preference for casting the speaker as a spectacle performing for a spectator (reader) sets up an isolating distance forbidding, or at least discouraging, exchange or intimacy. Especially in these late poems where she narrates her imminent renouncing of life, writing, and motherhood, Plath frames—and freezes—her impending death in a formalist perfection of the irretrievable ("We have come so far, it is over") that makes it impossible to pose the existential question how might one live, which is the implicit interrogative force of generative renunciations.

In other words, terminal renunciation is synonymous not with suicide in itself but rather with the election of an engulfing implacable silence—a folding back into one's self that marks a turn away from the reader, and from life. Paul Celan, for example, also a suicide, renounces poetry as an art form of lyrical beauty and eloquence and re-invents it "for the sake of an encounter," "the mystery of an encounter," with an Other; in short, he makes renunciation a formal and moral pressure that shapes his poetics from the start (*Collected Prose* 49). That is, Celan's hermit perspective (to recall Nietzsche's term) allowed him to internalize renunciation and make it generative of poetry that wends its way between silence and eloquence—saying too little and saying too much. In contrast, terminal renunciation is Plath's trajectory, a horizon to which she is headed, as the kinetic end of "Ariel" suggests: "And I / Am the arrow, // The dew that flies suicidal . . . / Into the red // Eye, the cauldron of morning" (27).

I will set aside the notorious disappearing acts of American literature—Ambrose Bierce, B. Traven, Weldon Kees, and, most poignantly, Nella Larsen. For decades she hid in plain sight as a working nurse,

having left behind her literary life in Harlem in the wake of a plagiarism scandal. Instead of the terminal I will emphasize the generative or germinal; by that I mean the existential *uses* in life and art
of renunciation, how it or its threat orients a life and functions as a
compositional resource in writing and in art making. Renunciation is
generative when, without dying or disappearing, one instead writes,
plays, or paints it.

■

A signal instance of generative renunciation is the founding work of
philosophical Taoism, Lao-tzu's *Tao Te Ching*, said to be the most
translated book in the world after the Bible and the *Bhagavad Gita*.
Like Eckhart's sermons, the *Tao* became a basic text for postwar
American renunciants. Compiled orally in China over the course of
three centuries, circa 650–350 BCE (*Lao* 120), the *Tao*, while not a religious work, counsels ethical and spiritual cultivation. Its central concept of *Wu-wei*—not-having and non-action (or, more precisely, nondeliberative, non-calculative acting) is the basis of individual, social,
and political ideals opposed to the self-interested pursuit of desire,
which is endless and inevitably creates disorder. The name Lao-tzu
is a generic rubric meaning "old master"; the actual author of the *Tao
Te Ching* is unknown, appropriately enough given the priority of self-
effacement. He and his book are worth pausing over here and rendering even in broad strokes because his philosophy of self-effacement so
vividly shapes his life and writing. He consigns wisdom to silence as
the very condition of knowing and communicating. "One who knows
does not speak; / One who speaks does not know," the *Tao* remarks
(25). Devising a variation on this, Wittgenstein in the famous final
entry of the *Tractatus* writes: "Whereof one cannot speak, thereof one
must be silent." In effect they wrap their inwardness with the *tao* in a
silence whose meaning is accessible to others similarly endowed with
intuitive understanding. Given this logic how did the *Tao Te Ching*
ever come to be?

According to legend, Lao-tzu wrote it at the behest of a Gate Keeper
who asked the aged thinker, who was about to depart his declining
homeland, to record his thoughts in a book so that the official might

gain enlightenment. After a few days of work, the old man submitted eighty-one highly compressed aphoristic maxims presenting the *tao*. Lao-tzu "solved" the Gate Keeper's command to renounce silence and codify ineffable thinking by making mystery—including the "mysterious integrity" gained from surrendering possession and control of what one gives birth to—into the stylistic and thematic premise of his work (69). Hence paradox presides: "Act through nonaction, / Handle affairs through noninterference, / Taste what has no taste, / Regard the small as great, the few as many, / Repay resentment with integrity" (33). In sum, Lao-tzu practices his own version of "letting the hermit speak": he foregoes the transmission of knowledge via definitions, essences, and explanations, instead letting language's slipperiness impart the *tao*'s inaccessibility.

From the start, Lao-tzu sets words on the page that at once refuse and confirm the illusion that *tao* can be distilled into words on a page: "The ways that can be walked are not the eternal Way / The names that can be named are not the eternal name" (59). As a passage or channel *tao* is enabling but its meaning cannot be possessed—only intuited—and its name only approximated—usually as "the way." "Not knowing its name, I style it the 'Way.' / If forced to give it a name, / I would call it 'great.' / Being great implies flowing ever onward, Flowing ever onward implies far-reaching, / Far-reaching implies reversal" (90). Even nature's flowing is not smoothly predictable but instead offers "reversal," surprise, echoing his qualified, provisional acts of naming. To name is, inevitably, to "divide things up" (as William James will also say) and create dualisms, hence to obstruct the "Way" of "flowing," which is without desire or possessiveness: "Rippling is the Way, flowing left and right / Its tasks completed, its affairs finished, / Still it does not claim them for its own" (99, 101). At one with the rippling flow, Lao-tzu vanished after complying with the Gate Keeper's request; he was true to his elusive word. His self-effacement aptly mirrors his act of making a self-renouncing book, words of wisdom that at once say and unsay. "To withdraw when your work is finished, / that is the Way of heaven" (69).

It is hard to resist turning the origin myth of the *Tao Te Ching*—the Gate Keeper's command that Lao-tzu write out his teachings and renounce the purely inward and intuitive—into an allegory of humans' frustrating lot with language. The origin myth shows how a creator works within the compromises—the betrayals—that language inflicts as a condition of its expression. Not only is language unreliable, so the human act of seeing distorts. "We suspect our instruments," says Emerson, for "we do not see directly but mediately" because propelled by desire and the urge to possess (*Essays* 487). Art's emergence from the reifying matrix of language and vision is immanent when it bears the scars of its struggle, when the work incorporates what menaces it. Hence Lao-tzu obeys the Gate Keeper's freezing command without wholly betraying the ineffable *tao*, by making the mystery and vacillations of paradox his muse.

For twentieth-century readers, the myth of the *Tao Te Ching*'s origin announces humans' accession to the gate-keeping interdictions of the law of the father, of language and culture, of the socializing agencies of the superego. (The *Tao* has served as a handbook for the would-be political leader.) Modern art's notorious hostility to these authorities encourages in some makers a fantasy of banishing the dead weight of the preordained, the already written. Thus the yearning to render experience fluent and flowing, as if liberated from words. However, to erase the "as if" and treat the clean-slate fantasy as actual produces only frustration, for one is still relying on language to defeat language's deformations: witness, as we soon will, William James's futile pursuit of "experience in its immediacy" which he finds "self-luminous and suggests no paradoxes" ("The Thing" 45).

The modernist fantasy to overturn mediation for transparency or luminous immediacy would be regarded as Promethean arrogance in a God-centered universe where submission is the cornerstone of faith. In a medieval world where the absolute or God is by definition unknowable, save by the presence of his absence (the premise of "negative theology") how does a painter paint Him? An answer is generative renunciation—turning prohibition into artistic stimulus.

Witness the immanent power that accrues within a sublime expression of humility: Fra Angelico's *Annunciation*, a fresco in the convent of San Marco in Florence, completed in 1445. If Lao-tzu finds a way to represent in language the ineffable *tao*, the painter, a Dominican friar, finds a way to render the unrenderable. In his "minimal" or ascetic depiction of a familiar biblical and artistic trope—the Angel Gabriel visiting Mary to tell her she will become the mother of Jesus—Fra Angelico has renounced the usual symbols, allusions, and props. The meeting occurs, in Fra Angelico's version, amid the monastery's low white walls and columns, which separate the two figures and dominate the fresco. The space, stripped of ornament and iconic detail, is rendered as cramped—emphasized by the hunched posture of both— yet also possessed of depth, one can see into the room behind Mary. This has the effect of making palpable the mystery of the event, its resistance to being captured by "mere visual appearance," as Norman Bryson writes. Fra Angelico "refuses to map the world in terms of perception or optics" or to impose a "coherent narrative." Moreover, "theologically, the picture insists on nescience: its God is truly Other, unknowable, unrepresentable, and in the face of that unknowability, the picture voids itself as representation, sacrifices itself, hollows itself out. The insistence on making a representation that abjures its own powers of narrative and optical resolution corresponds to a whole doctrine of sacred ignorance: God's presence is felt and known in the failure of representation, not its success. The mystery of the faith is found where the project of visually capturing the world comes to an end . . . in the white walls of the monastery cell" (336).

Failure as success in affirming the mystery of faith: Fra Angelico makes the ineffable present by, like Lao-tzu, abstaining from clarity and mastery. The medieval friar, working within the artistic and theological strictures of "sacred ignorance," and the ancient man of wisdom, working within a mystic philosophy of the unsayable, both turn renunciation into a generative resource for making work that eludes the legibility of intellectual knowledge.

■

Abruptly drafted into authorship, Lao-tzu teaches that reversal is the only rule. Montaigne will affirm this paradox even though the circumstances of his generative renunciation could not be more different—he initiates it deliberately, even ceremonially. Montaigne, we will recall, freely removes himself from the world to his tower library and reflects on the power that withdrawal will accrue; yet eventually he becomes impatient with its limits. The formal inscription he had painted on his library walls to mark the occasion reads: "In the year of Christ 1571, at the age of thirty-eight years . . . the anniversary of his birth, Michel de Montaigne, long since disgusted with the slavery of the court of parliament and still feeling fit, came away to repose on the bosom of the learned virgins in calm and security; there he will pass the days he has left to live. Hoping that destiny will allow him to perfect this residence, this sweet paternal retirement, he has consecrated them to his freedom" (qtd. Starobinski 311). Montaigne's care with dates, notes Jean Starobinski, "marks a caesura in time" and "reinforces the idea of a voluntary *birth*. Time takes on a new origin" and "acquires a new meaning. . . . The new order is no longer that of *servitium* but that of *libertas*. Liberation goes hand in hand with constriction" (7). He "felt under no obligation to reside there permanently" though; at times Montaigne left his tower to immerse himself in civic affairs and to discharge his political obligations. What mattered for him "was to have secured the *possibility* of occupying his own private territory, the possibility of withdrawing at any moment into absolute solitude, of quitting the game" of flattery and deception and hypocrisy rife at court (7). Denying neither the life of the flesh nor the world, Montaigne seeks to "maintain as much *presence* in the world as is compatible with his refusal of servitude" (13).

Less than a decade after his withdrawal the first edition of his *Essais* appeared. What had been intended as a new birth into repose migrated into creative ferment; not expecting that his freedom from worldly falsity would induce a melancholy solitude, he found relief in writing, and in so doing came to terms with artifice, affirming what would be a guiding theme of the *Essais*—that change is the only constant. This reversal sets "Montaigne in motion," to cite the title and subject of Starobinski's exhilarating study. He observes that the modern reader may detect a pattern of regression in Montaigne's wall inscription, given its images of withdrawal to a hidden place where he is to be nourished at the bosom of the female Muse. Although the inscription, says Starobinski, is not "primarily a psychological document" since it is a standard humanist formula, it is one into which Montaigne poured his deepest emotions, making, in sum, "full 'instinctual' use of a coded language" (8).

In his memoirs the philosopher Santayana also makes "full 'instinctual' use of a coded language" as he too speaks of renunciation as a power sharpened by constraint. In his case constraint springs from his need to conceal his homosexuality in the genteel Boston of the early twentieth century. He says: "If you renounce everything, you are master of everything in an ideal sense, since nothing can disturb you." His model is the "*perfect* lover"—one who "must renounce pursuit and the hope of possession" for the "passion of love, sublimated. . . . The psyche is not thereby atrophied; on the contrary, the range of its reactions has been enlarged. It has learned to vibrate harmoniously to many things at once" (*Persons* 257, 429). Igniting this psychic enlargement is "the spiritual flame of a carnal fire." Santayana's idealized vision construes renunciation as self-cultivation grounded in the power of self-denial.

Yes, renunciation generates vitality, Nietzsche agrees, but it does not do so via the ascetic economy of sublimation that Santayana posits. Nor does the "pessimism of the renunciators, the failed and defeated," attract him (*Human* vol. 2: "Preface" 7). He calls this "romantic pessimism" and contrasts it to the "*superabundance of life*," a "Dionysian" pessimism, that includes "absolute skepticism towards all received concepts" that free thinking requires (*Gay* sec. 370; *Late Notebooks* 13). Nietzsche has special pertinence here because of how emphatically he links this skepticism to abandonment of a professional career. He poses the question: "What does it mean to us today to *live* philosophically, to be wise? Is it not almost a way of *extricating* oneself cleverly from an ugly game? A kind of flight?" He answers that "the wise man" is not the scholar chained to his desk and his classes but rather someone who lives in a "remote and simple way," who has "tried out life personally in a hundred ways." He "must have lived absolutely 'unphilosophically' according to the received ideas, above all not to have lived in timid virtuousness" (*Late Notebooks* 20). Here he prophesizes Wittgenstein.

So it turns out that to *live* philosophically is to live "absolutely 'unphilosophically'"—recall Diogenes the Cynic, whom Nietzsche regarded as a model. Nietzsche's inverted logic drives the iconoclastic energy of modern renunciation: a Pollock or a Reinhardt paints by abolishing the received practice of painting, a Gould plays by abolishing the practice of a musical career, a Wittgenstein philosophizes by abolishing the practice of capital *P* Philosophy. In his riddling claim about what and who counts as living philosophically, Nietzsche demands we work through the logic of his transvaluation of values. He challenges us to abandon our reflex, unthinking assumption of consistency and self-identity, substance and being, all of which Nietzsche calls the "regulative fictions" by which "a kind of constancy and thus 'knowability' is inserted into, *invented into*, a world of becoming" (21).

The "flight" from the "ugly game" of academic careerism is not only a salutary escape from the torpor of routinized labor but also from the metaphysical illusions that feed the intellectual torpor of professional philosophy. "I teach the renunciation" of belief "in grammar, in the linguistic subject, object, in verbs." These all are "indispensable" "condition[s] of life," but nevertheless "invented," including the "conscious 'I'" which is only a "tool" of one's "whole organism" (21, 2). To grasp as contingent, historical, and invented that which we assume is man's natural birthright as the higher animal is to humble the vanity of self-congratulatory humanism and to practice "the taste and privilege" of "refined contempt." It is permitted only when one is distant from repositories of received wisdom such as state institutions (*Gay* sec. 379–380). That distance takes one "beyond one's time; to create for oneself eyes to survey millennia." It encourages escape from sensual atrophy, for by the late nineteenth century "our ears have grown more and more intellectual"; "pleasure is transferred to the brain, the sense organs themselves grow blunt and feeble" (*Human* vol. 1, 4: 217). To be unaffiliated makes one, says Nietzsche, "the most modern of moderns" (*Gay* sec. 379). In other words, generative renunciation is the gateway to overcoming one's own time in oneself and becoming the "human being of such a beyond" (*Gay* sec. 380). Renunciation in this heroic (perhaps megalomaniacal) Nietzschean mode is for many of our figures in effect the basic template upon which are played softer variations. These latter versions refuse the pugnacious and defiant by deflating the self into a channel for what Agnes Martin evokes as the ideal of the "untroubled mind" and George Oppen as "faith" in "the life of the mind" as intuitive "awareness of the world, a lyric reaction to the world" (*Speaking With* 11–12).

This relaxed mood orients as well Lao-tzu's *Wu-wei* and Eckhart's "released existence" and recalls a canonical account of aesthetic experience, one imbued with Eastern and Christian mysticism. When contemplating the beautiful in art and nature, says Schopenhauer, we experience "absorption in perception, being lost in the object, forgetting all individuality, abolishing the kind of knowledge which follows the principle of sufficient reason." It is "the painless state of the gods; for at that moment we are delivered from the miserable pressure of the will" and temporarily attain absolute objectivity (we become "that *one* eye of the world") (*World* 1:196–198). Here Arendt's equation of stopping and thinking achieves a kind of aesthetic apotheosis. Schopenhauer's evocation of the self-forgetting bliss of "pure contemplation" (he regards music as the highest art form) suggests spiritual liberation bordering on self-dissolution. Since he understands existence as comprised largely by pain and suffering due to the tyranny of the will, human beings can heroically withdraw by ceasing to will and to embrace death. "Art plays a role in this ascetic resignation," says one commentator, "that of a 'tranquilizer' that frees us—at least temporarily—from the tyranny of the desires and drives; through it . . . we glimpse the peace of a definitive annihilation, Nirvana" (Schaeffer 203). Schopenhauer's tranquilizing, compensatory view of Art dominated European thought in the second half of the nineteenth century. The young Nietzsche and the young Wittgenstein devoured *World as Will and Representation* and admired Schopenhauer's own dyspeptic maverick ways. Wittgenstein imbibed something of the philosopher's enthusiasm for the Buddhist ideal of quietism and self-extinction. Nietzsche was later to look back and mock Schopenhauer's animus against sensuality.

Schopenhauer's love of the *Upanishads* (he remarks in his first preface that acquaintance with "the divine inspiration of ancient Indian wisdom" will best prepare us to read him) (xv) produces one of the first crossings of Western aesthetics and Eastern thought. The ground of that crossing is renunciation. "In spite of fundamentally different dogmas, customs and circumstances," the philosopher tells us, "the endeavour and the inner life" of a Christian penitent or saint and that of an Indian "are absolutely the same" (389). Ascetic denial of the will is central in Hindu literature and ethics and, adds Schopenhauer, the ethics of Christianity lead "not only to the highest degrees of charity and human kindness, but also to renunciation." This tendency, developed in monasticism, penitents, and anchorites, is brought to full flower in "the writings of Christian saints and mystics" (386–388).

If the spiritual serenity of near self-annihilation is at one end of the experiential continuum of aesthetic disinterestedness and death, the ultimate renunciation, lurks at the other end, then receptivity as relaxed openness is in the rich middle zone. Such openness "calls for something other than intellectual endeavor, questioning, and skepticism," or reaching conclusions, to borrow Thierry de Duve's words about the need to give in to appearances when we "really look" at a painting (*Look* 16, 15). Suspending the pursuit of objective knowledge—be it about art or the ordinary—the surrender involved in intense looking leaves one absorbed in and by the arresting presence of the things of this world. This attunement as surrender to the object— to the horizontal revelation of presence—comprises the life of art or what will be called aesthetic living. The aesthetic, as its etymology tells us, is grounded in the senses, and aesthetic living at once effaces the ego while recovering "that other knowledge," neither objective nor detached, which we have of the body "in virtue of its always being with us and of the fact that we are our body" (Merleau-Ponty, *Phenomenology* 206).

As practiced by renunciants, the life of art seeks to bid adieu to the priority of books so as to let life "teach the lesson," to borrow a phrase of William James. That "lesson" poses the question how *might* one live, which for Nietzsche, after God's death, can now be asked for the first time. It replaces how one *should* live or act, which depended on the guidance of transcendental standards that no longer exist. To move from the anxious obligations of *should* to the life affirmation of *might* is to admit new possibilities. "In Nietzsche's hands, this new question becomes a challenge, a gauntlet thrown at the feet of those whose lives are too narrow" (May 7). Aesthetic living is one answer to how might one live and invites the practice of Nietzsche's skeptical hermit thinking.

The receptivity of an aesthetic life is often a spiritual venture but need not as a matter of logical necessity involve assent (and ascent) to metaphysical idealism, to belief in the noumenal, a "truer world" underwritten by a transcendent "theological ontology." Emerson pithily sums this up in 1862: "Other world? There is no other world. God is one and omnipresent: here or nowhere is the whole fact" (*Later Lectures* 269). In the decades following Emerson, hunger for experience that escapes rigid conceptualization tends, in the work of renunciants discussed here, to precipitate horizontal rather than vertical movement. "I am thrown back to the earth . . . and rough reality to embrace!" declares Rimbaud near the end of *Une saison en enfer*, in a rare moment where he sets aside the imperative of visionary derangement (*Complete* 209). "Human being and human earth are still unexhausted and undiscovered," Zarathustra proclaims (58). "The earth of things, long thrown into shadows by the glories of the upper ether, must resume its rights," says William James in announcing that he is rotating the axis of philosophy downward, de-centering the divine authority of the vertical and its reign of metaphysical abstraction (*Writings* 2:540). The antivisionary George Oppen (who dismissed Rimbaud's sensory "derangement" as "mere prose poem artiness") would return to poetry lured by the force of what he called "the fact of actualness" as "*the* miracle, the source of emotion"; and one of his best-known poems begins: "In the small beauty of the forest / The wild deer bedding down— / That they are there!" He calls the poem "Psalm" (*Letters* 56; *Speaking* 55; *New Collected* 99). These are exemplary modernist moves to the descendental. Wittgenstein marks out a similar path at the start of *Philosophical Investigations:* Abandon the sublime verticality of metaphysics and theory and go "back to the rough ground!" where we can minutely observe our everyday life with language. This claims the horizontal as the human realm (Wittgenstein, *Investigations* sec. 107).

These figures recovering the ground are opposed, tacitly or explicitly, to the foundational (vertical) thinking of metaphysics. At the same time another trajectory is at work fortifying grounds in order to rebuild foundations. In modernity, as Hans Blumenberg notes, "the gaze now sinks toward the earth; it is also directed purposefully and in a concentrated way to the question of foundations instead of toward vaults and tracery, tower and peaks" of medieval cathedrals. Descartes, he reminds us, imagined that the "science made possible by his *Discourse on Method* follows the model of rational urban planning," which requires the literal leveling to the ground of what had been previously built so that work can commence according to rules

(Blumenberg, *Care* 71–72). The founder of the Vienna Circle of logical positivism (Schlick) returns to the ground as the basis of erecting "The Foundation of Knowledge," to borrow the title of his 1934 treatise. His text extols those who "search for the rock that is there before all building takes place and that doesn't sway" (qtd. 73). Modernity, we shall see, is nothing if not antinomical.

■

Aesthetic living's openness involves acceptance, tacit or explicit, of art's sacral quality. Here the sacral refers neither to Fra Angelico's faith in his art's power to evoke unrepresentable mystery nor to an Arnoldian view of art as a secular culture's surrogate expression of religious belief. Rather, says de Duve, the sacral makes "the mere willingness to let oneself be visually touched"—whether by a challenging painting or an unexpected encounter in nature—"tantamount to an act of faith." It only appears that with the triumph of abstract art "anti-humanism has won the day." This however is not the case, for "the best modern art has endeavored to redefine the essentially *religious* terms of humanism on *belief-less* bases" (*Look* 15, 14). That redefinition discriminates between belief (often superstition) and the act of faith, which "by necessity is to have faith *in* someone else . . . an ethical act of the surrender to the freedom of others." This adumbrates an ideal community, where one lets others judge without surrendering one's own judgment. Kant is the first, says de Duve, to see that this mutual granting of the faculty of judgment and of the capacity for agreeing becomes the seed of an idea of a (potentially) universal community (qtd. Elkins and Morgan, *Re-Enchantment* 131, 134).

Faith is what "aesthetic judgment invariably calls for"—"a readiness to be touched" (de Duve, *Look* 38). By definition such readiness is a demand for tactility and feeling. "Seeing is touching, eyes feel light waves," Ad Reinhardt reminds us (*Art-as-Art* 111). Tactile encounter makes of art a showing and presenting rather than representing, a spiritual immediacy that suffused the medieval cult of sacred icons or saints' relics that the illiterate were said to regard as miraculous. The icon's living presence is still available—the Shroud of Turin is not a representation of Christ but his materially embodied divinity.

■

Glenn Gould was well known for his faith in art as the lifelong cultivation of what he called "a state of wonder and serenity." He achieved such receptivity and calm by the vigilant confinement he imposed upon his existence: this may be the governing irony in a life full of them. Another is that the hermit Gould, largely self-exiled from the outer world, performs a generative renunciation that attains serenity by his commitment to moving from art to life and challenging their boundaries. He in effect provides an aesthetic hermitage to his listeners, offering to make each one of us a version of Gould living saturated in sound: "the audience would be the artist and their life would be art" (*Glenn Gould Reader* 353).

If Gould sought to enlarge our aesthetic capacities with technology, Rimbaud wants to expand human consciousness using his own body as a model and drugs as his catalyst. Akin to Nietzsche going "beyond" his time and becoming "the most modern of moderns," Rimbaud envisions the poet as a Promethean advance guard in the struggle for modernity. As he wrote, the poet is "truly the thief of fire. He is responsible for humanity, even for the *animals*" (Rimbaud, *Complete* 309). His imperative is to renounce inhibition, to "open the senses" to "the *new* ideas and forms" (309, 307). The poet, to recall Blanchot's words, conceives of literature not as an "answer to an aesthetic ideal" but as "an experience that concerns the whole of life" (*Work* 154–155). Rimbaud's version of aesthetic living makes the avant-garde the art of life. Yet in his very commitment to perpetual movement he will submit to the self-annihilating logic of this project.

Combining Valéry's depiction of the poetic state of mind as intense attunement to silence with Blanchot's account of Rimbaud bringing life and literature together, Yves Bonnefoy, the contemporary French poet, literary and art critic, and Rimbaud scholar, builds renunciation into his basic understanding of writing. "In the very heart of writing there is a questioning of writing" ("Image" 444). The "kind of reading that tends toward poetry," he writes, asks us to "lift our eyes from the page and to contemplate the world, that is always so unknown" ("Lifting" 806). Poetry urges us to "turn away from poems" for "the text is not poetry's true place" since poetry aims at what escapes

representation—"lived experience," the "presence of the world," domains that "no word of a language" can designate without estranging
them ("Lifting" 798–799). Poetry's "spirit of responsibility," its quality
of "hopefulness" is entwined with the "dissatisfaction" it provokes
in us—frustration before the "fact of textuality" (798). Rather than
inviting us to regain some preverbal plenitude, an impossible goal,
"dissatisfaction" helps us "remember that we miss it and to prove to
ourselves the value of those moments when we are able to encounter
other people, or trees, or anything, beyond words, in silence" ("Art of
Poetry"). The reader rediscovers hope in poetry when "he closes his
book anxious to live out the promise" the poem can never fulfill: a
"more direct intuition of presence" ("Image" 440; "Lifting" 803). We
pause, to begin again.

Part 1

IN 1908 TWO years before his death William James is closing the book,
renouncing "words, words, words," as Hamlet wearily, wittily says
when asked what he is reading. As a young man he was haunted by
Shakespeare's Prince, with whom he shared a guilty sense of indeci-
siveness, in the philosopher's case exacerbated by sitting out the Civil
War at his father's insistence (Cotkin 33). Though he balks at literally closing the book on and of words, James's need to "return to life"
shapes his antagonistic relation to language and philosophy. In his
Hibbert Lectures at Oxford (published as *A Pluralistic Universe*) he
is pushed to the edge of renunciation by frustration at how the rule of
concepts "arrest[s]" life, "cutting it up into bits as if with scissors,"
so inveterately are they "retrospective and post mortem" (*Writings*
2:739). Concepts function to generalize, to classify, and hence devour
particularity: "A concept means a *that-and-no-other*" (746). It leaves
no remainder, no "fringe," no "muchness," the excess James esteems
as precious freedom. As if recalling Emerson's praise of silence—"if I
speak, I define, I confine, and am less"—he offers his own silent conduct as an "example" to imitate: "No words of mine will probably
convert you, for words can be the name only of concepts"; "the return
to life can't come about by talking. It is an *act*" (Emerson, *Essays* 426;
James, *Writings* 2:762–763). Anticipating Wittgenstein's wish fourteen

years later that we treat his statements as a ladder to be tossed once grasped, James urges his listeners to ignore his words and plunge into the preverbal flux. But his urging is in vain; he must face the frustrating fact that his vow of silent action is merely figurative. Unlike Wittgenstein who offers his exit strategy as the *Tractatus* concludes, James announces his in the middle of a long lecture, shackled to words as he tries to escape them.

Stalled in merely figurative gestures of farewell, James is enthralled by his new ally Henri Bergson, whose style, he admits, "seduces you . . . he's a real magician" (*Writings* 2:732). Many regarded the Frenchman in these rapt terms; in the second decade of the century he would lecture to crowds within and outside the academy. Although he regretted that Bergson had erected a "great system" with the *élan vital* as its metaphysical foundation, James welcomes his life philosophy as a deathblow to "intellectualism," which promotes the tyranny of concepts by positing that experience is above all a mode of knowing (James, *Letters* 2:292). So eager is James to reach "the inner life of the flux" that he gainsays (while granting) the cost of abandoning himself to the non-conceptual: "Both theoretically and practically this power of framing abstract concepts is one of the sublimest of our human prerogatives" (*Writings* 2:728). Hence he admits that to renounce concepts is to "regress" and shed our "proud maturity." But "difficult as such a revolution is, there is no other way" (755). And with equal resolution he vows to "close" his "ears" to the "intellectualist."

James has imprisoned himself in a stifling dichotomy: either submit to the "conceptual decomposition of life" or dive into the flux of "immediate experience" (747, 749). About this impasse, a philosopher friend wrote him: "Is choice limited to these alternatives? Here I think is the crux of the whole problem." The friend mentions that "concepts are of various sorts," noting Hegel's "concrete universal" and adds that Kant speaks of a kind of concept that has "no fixed limits"— apparently an allusion to the "aesthetic idea" (James, *Correspondence* 10:322–323). But James seems willfully to insist on his either/or. He certainly wants no help from Kant: "Think of the german literature of aesthetics, with the preposterousness of such an unaesthetic personage as Immanuel Kant enthroned in its centre!" he fumes in another lecture (*Writings* 2:638). After all, Kant's "aesthetic idea" was the exception in his system whose rule was a narrow notion of cognition as the subsuming of particulars under concepts.

Not only has a false dichotomy brought James to this strange impasse; even stranger, few knew of its falsity more profoundly than did he. In *Some Problems in Philosophy* (1911), his final, posthumously published work, he stressed how we rely on both percepts and concepts, "as we need both our legs to walk with," and urged that we treat concepts functionally, as leading us back to reality's thickness (*Writings* 2:1008, 1010).In *Pragmatism* (1907) he noted that we do not need to abandon ourselves to the precognitive because we already have done so; "we are like fishes swimming in the sea of sense." He elaborates his simile: the sea is the "world of sensible facts" and the air above is the "world of abstract ideas"; both are real and they interact. Though we are "unable to breathe" the air of abstract ideas "pure," we "get our oxygen from it" while the "*locus*" of "everything that happens to us" is the water of experience (*Writings* 2:541). Here James offers what he will jettison in his Hibbert Lectures—the reciprocal interaction of a homeostatic system in which neither abstract reasoning nor "unverbalized life" rule (755). But his deliberate simplification doesn't make any less significant—indeed makes more intriguing—his need to stage a renunciation of words and become a child again as a way to honor the non-conceptual. His willingness to "regress" is a kind of martyrdom to his belief in "the fact that life is logically irrational" (724).

Though he ultimately became a revered professor, James was uneasy in that role. This self-described anarchist was impatient with the confines of the classroom and with Harvard's aloofness from "the tangled and muddy" hard facts of life. In *The Varieties of Religious Experience*, he decried how "wealth-getting enters as an ideal into the very bone and marrow of our generation" and hence "we have grown literally afraid to be poor." He envies monks' poverty as an enactment of the "strenuous life" absent from the modern world, and praises "the right to fling away our life at any moment irresponsibly" (*Writings* 2:333). The Hibbert Lectures uphold that right: they are a barely sublimated act of flinging away. Seeking to divest himself of words and flirting with a vow of silence, James declares his own attraction to a monastic regime via his late Victorian experiment in regression as emancipation. He extols "poverty" as redemptive in ways that recall

Meister Eckhart and his praise of the riches of spiritual poverty in his famous sermon "Blessed Are the Poor in Spirit." Josiah Royce had already drawn his colleague James's attention to Eckhart in a chapter devoted to him in *Studies in Good and Evil* (1898).

James found philosophy less a consolation than a "maze . . . and what he was looking for was the way out," as his colleague Santayana noted, quipping that James remained "a sort of Irishman among the Brahmins" (*Character and Opinion* 62–63). But unlike Emerson or Nietzsche James never found the exit. Instead, he devised a philosophy that embodied his restless urge to renounce institutions: his pragmatism, though a method based on scientific experiment and respect for "the triumph of the Darwinian theory," was, finally, an antiphilosophy that mocked what his colleagues revered: the rationalist mind's love of system. In all this James shows kinship with Nietzsche. Of philosophers Nietzsche remarks: "Their trust in concepts has been as unconditional as their mistrust of the senses" (12). James's word for this mistrust of the senses is "refinement," both as a defensive refuge in abstraction and as an insulating patrician value.

James's attraction to irrationalism in 1908, his need to shed maturity, point back to possible roots in an earlier renunciation—of his love, at seventeen, of painting and drawing. By 1860 James had plans to make art a career until his pseudo-benign, meddling father soon squelched them. An astute biographer narrates this collision in terms of "the murdered self," referring to the violent imagery of James's own drawings at the time of his decision to quit painting; in one, an ogre devours a man whole (Feinstein 144). James's late urge to renounce words for life emerges as a subliminal effort to be reborn, or at least redeem his forced desertion of the wordless medium of art by now championing the very heart of the aesthetic—the non-conceptual. "It ought to be called a 'Defense of Poesy,'" noted James's friend John Jay Chapman (after hearing the Hibbert Lecture on Bergson), a shrewd remark that grasped the relation between the aesthetic and James's impatience with concepts (Chapman 231).

It is a defense of painting, as well. Listen to James's lyrical evocations and pleas to "place yourself . . . inside of the living, moving, active thickness of the real, and all the abstractions and distinctions are given into your hand. . . . Install yourself in phenomenal movement . . .

put yourself *in the making* by a stroke of intuitive sympathy with the thing." His diction suggests a moving hand in the act of making brush and pencil strokes, achieving an "active thickness" as the touch of the brush smears viscous paint onto canvas (*Writings* 2:750–751). Who more than the working artist or artisan feels from literally hands-on experience that "what really exists is not things made but things in the making"? I am seeking "the instantaneous," said James's contemporary, the Impressionist painter Claude Monet, "to see the world through the eyes of a man born blind who has suddenly regained his sight: as a pattern of nameless color patches" (qtd. McEvilley, *Exile's* 18).

While James's fantasy of art making remains latent within his yearning for silence, in *The Principles of Psychology* (1890) he had made more practical efforts to loosen the hold of concepts. He urged replacing their stolidity with the "transitive" rhythms of language—"alternation of flights and perchings"—that evoke experience "fringed forever by a *more* that continuously develops" (*Writings* 1:159; 2:1173). He seeks to explode "the ridiculous theory of Hume and Berkeley that we can have no images but of perfectly definite things." In this same passage he sums up what he is "so anxious to press" on our "attention": "the reinstatement of the vague and inarticulate to its proper place in our mental life" (*Writings* 1:164). These commitments to "possibles not yet in our present sight" would capture the imaginations of Gertrude Stein, Robert Frost, and Wallace Stevens, all Harvard students influenced by James's teaching.

His impassioned futile protest in 1908 against abstraction on behalf of life and the life of art and his praise of poverty anticipate some of the most radical modernist innovators in their war against culture. James's reanimation of the act of painting also looks back—to a pre-Enlightenment era when image, not word, had affective power. The medieval icon—the image as "immediate evidence of God's presence"—challenged the traditional privilege accorded God's word in Scripture. The Reformation, by reinstituting the priority of language—"only the abstract word . . . is the bridge to God," John Calvin insisted—enthroned hearing and reading while devaluing seeing and the senses and the surface appearance of the visible world (Belting 15, 550).

Residues of the premodern cling to James's modernism, a pattern pervasive in twentieth-century art and thought. Linguistic and spiritual forms of poverty, including the apophatic discourse of the *un*sayable, which began with Plotinus, fascinate modernists in their revolt against representation. In the 1930s Antonin Artaud reinvents theatre that escapes the Enlightenment priority on words to express emotions and ideas. He is inspired by fourteenth-century Japanese Noh drama. Seeking to undermine the authority of the written word (without jettisoning it), Artaud creates "a language designed for the senses" and "independent of speech," where sonority rather than grammatical meaning has priority, a "concrete language" of sounds, gestures, pantomime expressed in the bodies of the actors (231–233). To help himself reach a preverbal consciousness Artaud experimented with peyote. James himself tried nitrous oxide to "stimulate the mystical consciousness," his experience of trance verifying his belief that our "normal waking consciousness, rational consciousness as we call it, is but one special type . . . whilst all about it, parted from it by the flimsiest of screens there lie potential forms of consciousness entirely different" (*Writings* 2:349). His last published essay celebrated the thought of the "pluralistic mystic" Benjamin Paul Blood (reason, Blood wrote, "is but an item in the duplex potency of the mystery") and James concluded with the imperative that "Philosophy must pass from words . . . to life itself" (1313).

In Japan, in 1911, Kitaro Nishida made the same move from abstraction to life, employing not drugs but the mind-altering Zen practice of *koan*. This meditation allowed him to reach a state of non-attachment regarding "his arid intellectual desire for secular fame and success," in the words of his biographer (Yusa xviii). Renouncing worldly desire, Nishida next renounced the priority of the concept. Inspired by reading James in 1904, he immersed himself in Being as "pure experience"— what is prior to conceptual appropriation and the split into subject and object. "At the instant of seeing color or hearing sound . . . before even the judgment of what this color or sound is, has been added"— this is what Nishida calls "experience in itself" (qtd. Sharf 21) and James calls "the instant field of the present" when knowledge is still "in transit," "on its way" to being verified (*Writings* 2:1175). "Nishida could follow James," says Herwig Friedl, "because his Zen training had conditioned him" to cope with the permanently "*indeterminate term* of Being as nothingness," a no-thing, a mere "that," perpetually beyond the reach of conceptual modes of awareness. It has to be kept undefined lest it become a separate entity and summon the specter of an epistemology grounded on "aboriginal dualism" (Friedl, "Global" 204). Retrospectively, upon reflection, we rationally reconstruct what we see and hear. But, James, as does Nishida and, later, Merleau-Ponty and Heidegger, dwells in what rationalism ignores or discredits—the pre-cognitive transitional realm of perception—"a simple *that*, as yet undifferentiated into thing and thought" (*Writings* 2:1175). At least in 1905, however, James restricts pure access to immediacy to "only new-born babes or men in semi-coma from sleep, drugs, illnesses, or blows" ("The Thing" 46).

James's late thinking affirms that life (experience) defeats intelligibility (meaning), a tension that Barthes, a student of Zen, finds fundamental in modernity, especially literature. Literary realism's "reality effect" turns out to depend on "futile" and "useless" details—a "luxury" of insignificance. Such "superfluous" excess produces potential "vertigo" if not brought to a halt by the imposing of meaning ("The Reality Effect" 141, 145–146). Analogously, if sensory experience "seems to have a meaning, we are at once suspicious of its authenticity," as Fredric Jameson has recently glossed Barthes. "If it means something it can't be real; if it is real, it can't be absorbed by purely mental or conceptual categories" (Jameson 34, 37).

If even as conservative a genre as realism—invested in the solidity of bourgeois reality—possesses an animus to the intelligible, then visionary projects magnify animus to Meaning. The most influential is Rimbaud's campaign, commencing in 1871, of "making" himself a "*seer.*" Like James, the poet is drawn to the flux, which the seventeen-year-old prodigy calls "the *unknown!*"—a forever beckoning non-place of vertiginous immediacy that defies conventional logic and language. "And when, bewildered," the seer "ends by losing the intelligence of his visions, he has seen them. Let him die as he leaps through unheard of and unnamable things" (Rimbaud, *Complete* 307). Afoot with his vision, the poet is in no need of understanding. So relentlessly did Rimbaud ride the momentum of forward movement that before long he left literature altogether, moving past poetic to geographical experiment, abandoning Europe, pushing into places in the Horn of Africa "where no white man had ever yet penetrated" (Starkie 358).

■

Literature's modernity is the (unrealizable) effort, says Paul de Man, to slough off the past and at last to reach a "true present, a point of origin that marks a new departure." "Some of the impatience of Rimbaud or Artaud echoes in all literary texts, no matter how serene and detached they may seem" (148, 152). Artaud's battle cry is "no more master-pieces." Art becomes the "enemy of artists," Sontag explains, because it is practiced "in a world furnished with second-hand perceptions, and specifically confounded by the treachery of words" (Introduction 293). As impatient as James with the conceptualizing power of language, Rimbaud's manic urge for new departures of all kinds marks his com-mitment to being "absolutely modern." But even Rimbaud, for all his verbal and psychic tumult, remains a believer in "truth" and hopes to heal a psychical breach inflicted by modernity—the mind/body split that Cartesian rationalism inherits from Christianity: "I shall be free *to possess truth in one body and soul*," is how he concludes *Une saison en enfer* (*Complete* 209).

To be a seer, says Rimbaud, requires nothing less than a "ratio-nal derangement of *all the senses*" (*Complete* 307). The oxymoronic "rational derangement" can be regarded as the banner under which Rimbaud sails, suggesting his mix of pagan contempt for Christianity, his breaking of poetry's referential circuits, *and* his faith in reason; in-deed, he was drawn to the radical politics of the Paris Commune where one splinter group urged the "people" to seize "science": it is "your conquest, science belongs to you, come and take it" (qtd. Oxenhandler 51). Analogously, Rimbaud's unprecedented expeditions were not sim-ply acts of visionary rambling but made him a prosperous financier: by 1888 "most of the foreign trade in southern Abyssinia revolved around Rimbaud" (Robb 401).

Rimbaud's example reminds us of the slippery relation—of opposi-tion and affiliation—between Enlightenment modernity and artistic modernism, a doubleness inevitable given that both are constituted by analogous contradictions that reflect the double imperatives of capitalist modernization—investment in risk, fluidity, experiment co-exists with disciplinary and normalizing regimes of control and organization. Recall that the imperative to make a "new departure" is shared by anti-metaphysical thinkers eager to recover the ground, suspicious of the transcendent, and by logical positivists inspired by Descartes. Modernism at once seeks to repair the psychic damage modernity inflicts and displays an exhilarated mimicry of modernity's ease with change and innovation. So T. S. Eliot writes poetry of fragments "shored against" the world's "ruins" while crafting an aesthetic that joins what has been torn asunder—thought and feeling, the intellectual and emotional.

Contrary impulses also shape modern art: a quest for the pure beginning—Pollock's dream to paint the first painting or Artaud's ambition to create theatre before "the split between language and flesh" has a flip side in the quest for ending (Sontag, Introduction xxxv). Each pursuit has provided fertile strategies of renunciation. Regarding the effort at ending, Yves-Alain Bois argues that the "whole enterprise of modernism, especially of abstract painting" in the postwar era, "could not have functioned without an apocalyptic myth." The earlier generation's "liberation from tradition" could "not but function as an omen of the end." "Freed from all extrinsic conventions, abstract painting was meant to bring forth the pure *parousia* [presence] of its own essence, to tell the final truth and thereby terminate its course." Ad Reinhardt's "last paintings" in the sixties echoed earlier apocalyptic claims by Malevich, Rodchenko, Duchamp, and Mondrian among others (Bois, *Painting as Model* 230–231).

Modernity inspires and repels; Baudelaire was the first to insist on its double character as at once ephemeral and changing but also eternal and immutable. So the familiar critical term "anti-modernist," a tempting label to apply to many who renounce, usually simplifies: excepting such celebratory urban ventures as, for instance, French Impressionism, Italian Futurism, and American Pop Art, the modernist's relation to modernity tends to be messy and ambivalent rather than defined by unconditional embrace or opposition. Even deliberate flights into monastic sanctuary—Thomas Merton's, for instance—are hardly immune to worldly temptation. John Cage, also in pursuit of mystic egolessness, at times incorporated technology into his musical performances. Inspired by Eastern mysticism, he was open in whatever circumstances to the "experimental"—"an act the outcome of which is unknown"—and to renouncing Western understandings of

intentionality (*Silence* 12; Goehr, 63). By the mid-sixties the blending
of East and West, an instance of what has been dubbed "*technê*-Zen,"
had become widespread, made canonical in Pirsig's *Zen and the Art of
Motorcycle Maintenance* (1974), which argues: "hatred of technology
is self-defeating" (qtd. R. John Williams 33). By the seventies "*technê*-
Zen" set the stage for "corporate Zen," and it remains the ethos of
management gurus spreading global capitalism. Cage had anticipated
this: "The world is one world now," he said in the late fifties, meaning there is no longer any oppositional "outside" to capitalism. Here
he was borrowing an insight of his friend Buckminster Fuller (*Silence*
75; Joseph 19–20). Capitalism's passion for what Joseph Schumpeter
long ago named "creative destruction" is hospitable to its seeming opposite, the mystical and contemplative: each esteems flexibility, flow,
and chaos as sources of creativity. Cage himself noted that Zen is not
a "fixed tangible" but changes according to time and place, yet always
invigorating action (xxxi).

By 1966, Cage had married his Zen openness to the aleatory—
which lets sound be itself—and to the expansive reach of technology. He collaborated with Bell Telephone Labs on *Variations VII*
as part of an evening of "theatre and engineering." Instead of using
recorded sound, Cage sought it from live feeds emanating from an
array of devices, coordinated from a control room, to insure simultaneity and to eliminate pre-established hierarchy. This production
of randomness involved, among other devices, ten telephone lines
to pick up ambient noises in various New York locations, six micro-
phones to amplify the transistor radios, electric juicers, and mixers
on hand, and even two Geiger counters (their signals converted into
noise) that the performers turned on as they themselves triggered
new sounds when passing thirty electric photocells (electric eyes)
located at ankle level (Bonin). As always, Cage in 1966 regards art as
life and the "purposeless play" of music as "an affirmation of life"
rather than an attempt "to bring order out of chaos," a "way of waking up to the very life we're living, which is so excellent once one
gets one's mind and one's desires out of its way and lets it act of its
own accord" (12).

This adaptability of the spiritual and technological reminds us how
dubious is the assumption that one could possess a coherent single

attitude toward modernity, though we have been invited to articulate one ever since Max Weber made the problem of modernity a subject. Yet, as David Walsh has argued, "no account can finally be given of that within which we live." Therefore "neither the contradictions nor the crises of modernity constitute a problem, for they are the very horizon within which we exist. There is no stepping back to secure a vantage point of theoretical penetration" (466, 462).

This reminder of immanence, a useful corrective to idealist illusions of an Archimedean space outside culture, is logically true but experientially less than compelling. For, however deluded, intellectuals tend to step back, deriving their orienting values and self-definitions by reacting for and against modernity and modernism. Look, for instance, at how Cage engages both. His avant-gardism begins with his renouncing sounds as defined by music theory (which regards them as inseparable from exposition and thematic development) for random noises of city life. Cage will bring the noisy intrusions of Life into the formal sanctuary of modern music. In the course of his 1959 "Lecture on Nothing" Cage declares that he turned from sounds after studying modern music and learning that "intervals have meaning; they are not just sounds, but they imply in their progressions a sound not actually present to the ear. Tonality. I never liked tonality." So he "began to see that the separation of mind and ear had spoiled the sounds,—that a clean slate was necessary. This made me not only contemporary, but 'avant-garde.' I used noises They had not been in-tellectualized; the ear could hear them directly and didn't have to go through any abstraction a-bout them" (116). It would be hard to find a more compact instance of the mixture of affiliation and critique: inspired by modernity's clamorous vitality, Cage (who when young admired the Italian Futurists' incorporation of noise into musical compositions) enlarges the definition of music while also suspicious of system and of the abstract "meaning" it produces.

With impeccable Jamesian logic, Cage seeks to recover "the old sounds" that "thinking" had "worn out." "And if one stops thinking about them, suddenly they are fresh and new" (117). Listening requires purging oneself of the habit of retrospective reflection. Cage heals the wound of intellectualism inflicted by Cartesian dualism ("the separation of mind and ear") with the vow of a "clean slate." (This cleansing is itself a Cartesian project, as we have seen.) This new departure is precisely what modernity and modernism both depend on ("new and improved" is the perennial promise of free market economy). For Cage and other modernists, the "clean slate" may be illusory and unreachable, merely a "temptation of immediacy" (de Man's, if not Rimbaud's and Cage's, point); but what counts is the effort (de Man 152).

■

In shutting the book on words and seeking to make a fresh start, James, we have seen, unconsciously revives the experience of making art. He implicitly confirms what Bonnefoy will declare: that to stop reading "means becoming a painter": for painting begins by evoking "in a direct way, and through means that are non-verbal, that unity that words destroy" ("Lifting" 806). No wonder James's "Defense of Making" (a small revision of Chapman since "Poesy" derives from the Greek word *poesis*, meaning making or fashioning) sounds so familiar when we read statements of postwar artists talking about their aesthetic practice. James loves imagining himself inside moments of artistic making because that is when concepts are kept at bay and we enter a pre-cognitive, "pre-mediated perceptual field," as the minimalist artist and theorist Robert Irwin (b. 1928) has argued. Never a sustained renunciator, though he relished eight months in absolute solitude where he "almost stopped thinking in terms of language," Irwin has "become increasingly convinced that perception precedes conception," his biographer observes. And Irwin himself says: "It all comes down to how you answer a single question: Is the moment of perception—that first moment, before all the abstracting, conceptualizing processes that follow—is that moment closest to or furthest from the real?" (Weschler and Irwin 41, 182, 259).

For James and Irwin it is closest, as it is for Bridget Riley (b. 1931), the painter known for her early sixties kinetic, vertiginous, op(tical) art. "Pure perception," Riley says, is so "startling, exciting . . . a kind of primary experience" that in "normal life" one must quickly put it into "whatever conceptual envelope one can." When one paints one dwells with what one *really* see[s] for the split second before knowledge moves in" to tidy things up into "manageable entities in the world.

Then they are no longer startling—or, if you like, pure" (Riley 321). She acknowledges how difficult it is for a painter "to rely on this purity of perception" and—perhaps more difficult still—have it "remain unavailable to the logic of the intellect" (11).

The pre-cognitive is fugitive, at once sought and continually renounced, for it is always on the way to being assimilated to knowledge and communication. We live and move on a path Irwin calls (in an ungainly phrase) "compounded abstraction": from pre-cognitive perception—adrift in "undifferentiated sensations—they are not even defined yet as sounds versus colors . . . they exist as the plenum of experience"—the road leads to conceptions, then naming, then codification into formal patterns—the reified, standardized instruments of efficiency that humans and culture depend on to allow us to communicate and to know (Weschler and Irwin 183). Though "at any given moment, for any given individual" all phases are operating simultaneously, the pre-cognitive is the "foundation of everything and the hardest to reach" (183). As Hegel was one of the first to note, when we name something we lose the thing we name: "Adam's first act, which made him master of the animals, was to give them names, that is, he annihilated them in their existence (as living creatures)."

Quoting this passage, foundational in French theory, Blanchot commented in 1949: "Hegel means that from that moment on the cat ceased to be a uniquely real cat and became an idea as well." Only then did living things take on meaning for man: he "was condemned not to be able to approach anything or experience anything except through the meaning he had to create" (Work 323). A James, a Bergson, pledge themselves not to the Idea or meaning but to the "Here and Now which Hegel proudly revoked in the name of language." In effect, they concur with Hegel's fable of naming as renunciation but see it as incitement to action, to seeking a cat in its living thereness (Bonnefoy, The Act 97). For Blanchot this effort would be analogous to modern literature's insistence on presence: "Literature says, 'I no longer represent, I am; I do not signify, I present.' But this wish to be a thing, this refusal to mean anything" is "an insane effort," for to negate meaning still asserts the "very possibility of signifying" (Work 329). Literature's "irreconcilable tasks" are, for Blanchot, precisely the source of its power, what "keeps the work in suspense" by reserving a "point of instability," a "disintegrating force." Blanchot, in "Literature and the Right to Death," calls it *that life which supports death and maintains itself in it*—death, that amazing power of the negative, or freedom, through whose work existence is detached from itself and made significant" (342–343). Here entangled are renunciations germinal and terminal.

The precariousness of the pre-cognitive in a fallen world of instrumental efficiency: this is a version of the fable called the "disenchantment of the world." Weber's phrase refers to whatever in modernity preaches rationality at all costs. Intellectualism is one of disenchantment's protean tools in an arsenal that includes positivism, scientism, academic philosophy, technology, and European civilization; these are the usual suspects. Their proponents "idolize concepts," they "kill and stuff whatever they worship": "nothing real escaped their hands alive," warns Nietzsche in typically mocking exaggeration (*Twilight*, "Reason" sec. 1). After all, he, like James, was a scientist (of philology).

■

"Everywhere *language* is sick," says Nietzsche in 1876, sick because out of synch with its most basic function—to express feeling, "needs and distress." Instead it has become "a power in its own right," leading man where he does not really want to go: "With the decline of language we are the slave of words . . . no one is capable of revealing himself, of speaking naively but are entangled in the net of 'clear concepts.'" If James later would offer, tacitly, the artist as a cure for the same sickness, now Nietzsche offers Wagner's unique fusion of music and poetry. Wagner has recovered the "language of true feeling," enthuses the young Nietzsche, destined to suffer disappointment with his revered friend. As poet and composer, Wagner "speaks in visible and palpable events, not in concepts" and forces "language back to a primordial state in which it hardly yet thinks in concepts and in which it is itself still poetry, image, feeling" (*Untimely* 214, 236–237).

A gripping evocation of the dislocation between language and feeling, Hofmannsthal's *The Lord Chandos Letter* (1902) describes a fictional seventeenth-century gentleman-aesthete, suffering "mental paralysis," who renounces words, for they chronically fail him. The irony (from Nietzsche's viewpoint) is that it is a flood of "poetry, image, feeling"—"thinking with our heart," not head—that *blocks* Hofmannsthal's character from speaking and isolates him in transporting vision (125). What taps his reservoir of feeling are "trivialities," things that would leave nearly all of us indifferent: "a dog, a rat, a beetle, a stunted apple tree." When observing these mute beings, "this confluence of trivialities shoots through me from the roots of my hair to the marrow of my toes with such a presence of the infinite" (124–126). Whereas the large "abstract words which the tongue must enlist" to articulate an opinion "disintegrate" in his "mouth like rotten mushrooms": "I felt an inexplicable uneasiness in even pronouncing the words 'spirit,' 'soul,' 'body'" (121). (Hemingway, after World War One, will similarly recoil from abstract words like "glory" and "honor" meant to induce patriotism). The only relief is when he feels "vast empathy" for "shabby and crude objects of rough life." If only we "could think with our hearts," Lord Chandos opines at the advent of wordless "blissful" moments, if only he possessed a language "in which mute things speak to" him. But it is a "language of which I know not one word" (125, 128).

The Chandos Letter is a kind of self-administered homeopathic cure for the Viennese aristocrat Hofmannsthal's own aestheticism, the lyric poetry of a youthful decade comprising the 1890s (Broch, *Hugo* 117). He depicts a bored, arrogant aesthete and author filled with "heavenly feeling" but also paralyzed by it; his affective receptivity occurs in a solipsistic void, never softening his own cold detachment toward all around him. Hofmannsthal was renouncing lyric poetry for more popular genres, which would require "comprehensibility": theatre and "folk art" of local dialects celebrating the Austrian homeland (*Hugo* 125). In effect he will socialize Lord Chandos's intoxicating visual imagery and his capacity for "wordless, infinite rapture" (126), converting poetic ecstasy into a constructive project of uplifting the folk (139).

But there is an ironic counterpoint complicating Hofmannsthal's desire to turn to comprehensibility. From the lush and unsettling imagery of the Chandos Letter a disruptive motif emerges: the lord's startling immediacy of visual imagination is expressed in images that bring us not to accessible, more popular forms. Rather, words unravel into their material medium, a dissolving of resemblance not unlike that which is coming to the fore in late nineteenth-century French painting. Before and during Hofmannsthal's own lyric decade, advanced French painting, forsaking the distractions of anecdote or message, had embraced a formal autonomy indifferent to subject matter. So when Lord Chandos speaks of being sodden with feeling—"as if I myself were beginning to ferment, to foam, seethe" in a "a kind of feverish thinking, but thinking in a medium more direct, fluid, and passionate than words" (127)—one can hear a description of a "medium" that evokes the "thousand conflicting vibrations" of light, the "rich prismatic decompositions of color" that Jules La Forgue in 1883 found in Impressionism's challenge to the primacy of representation (qtd. T. Clark, *Painting* 16).

This Impressionist motif had first occurred as Lord Chandos admonished his young daughter always to tell the truth; "the ideas flowing into my mouth suddenly took on such iridescent hues and merged into each other to such a degree" that he sputters, barely able to finish his sentence (*Chandos* 121). Ideas and colors fuse, and again point to Impressionism, which "becomes more an exercise in color vibrations than representation" (Greenberg 1:29). The lord's disorder broadens "like spreading rust" making him acutely vulnerable, stripped of the "simplifying gaze of habit" as his mind forces him "to see everything that came up" in conversation "as terrifyingly close to me. Once I saw through a magnifying glass that an area of skin on my little finger looked like an open field with furrows and hollows. That's how it was for me now with people and their affairs. . . . Everything came to pieces. . . . Isolated words swam about me; they turned into eyes that stared at me and into which I had to stare back" (*Chandos* 122). Now magnified and defamiliarized, words lose their everyday function—as transparent means of communication—and acquire an uncanny life of their own, congealed into broken "pieces" with eyes that demand reciprocity. When language is no longer effaced in and by its function, then the medium again asserts itself—the enabling condition of avantgarde art contemporary with Hofmannsthal.

The disturbing erasure of distance causes Lord Chandos's vision to abandon its optical function and become haptic, undoing recognizable representation: skin transforms into a furrowed field. The shift from the optic to the haptic (a term from physiology, *haptein*—to fasten—and also from *haptikos,* to touch or grasp) is a distinction that originates with turn-of-the-century German art historian and theorist Alois Riegl. Whereas optical vision sees subject and object at a certain distance to preserve their distinction in deep space, the haptic touches, feels (and fastens upon) the surface of things (texture), no longer preserving the illusion of depth (form). The haptic emphasizes the sensuous "material presence of the image" that resists assimilation into narrative, while optical perception stresses its "representational power" (Marks 163). Thwarting his own move toward more comprehensible genres, Hofmannsthal links his rendering of Lord Chandos's renunciation of words to the new non-referential ambitions of French painting, which is staging its own crisis of representation.

Contemporaneously and analogously, French symbolist poetry (building upon the breakthroughs of Baudelaire who died in 1867) is devoted to the "possibility of an independent life of art," as Valéry recalled in 1936. The movement from 1860 to 1900 called "symbolism" was united not by aesthetic but by ethical aims. The goal of independence for these "heroes and martyrs of *resistance to the facile*"—manifested in contempt for the public at large, for the critical arbiters of taste, for public honors or large readerships—is at one with an "attitude of renunciation and negation." This attitude is what unites the movement (Valéry 8:250, 220–221). Writers "stopped at nothing that might rebuff or shock a hundred readers, if they judged it might win them a single reader of superior merit" (221). That reader would become an "active intellectual" partner in grappling with poetic experiments and in so doing become a member of an aesthetic elect founded on renunciation. All the rejection of public esteem and advantage and audience bred "the creation of *an entirely new and singular state of mind.*" Valéry dubs it *"ascesis"* (from the Greek: *asketes,* monk or hermit) and explains: "Renunciation, as we know, bears some resemblance to mortification. When we mortify ourselves, we are trying to regenerate and reconstruct ourselves by harsh and even painful methods that will raise us, we hope, to a state forejudged to be superior. The desire for such elevation, such *ascesis,* expressing itself in the domain of art" became a "condition of the true artist's life and a prerequisite for masterpieces" (224). Implicit in Valéry's remarks is the convergence of the spiritual and aesthetic, which he makes explicit after he describes "devotion to pure art" as a "sometimes miraculous union of thought, sentiment, fantasy, and logic, and also delight mysteriously conjoined with energy." Of this devotion, he comments: "The barest statement of this condition compels me to use terms only to be found in the vocabulary of religious ecstasy" (230).

No wonder Valéry as a young man took as his bible J.K. Huysmans's classic of decadence *À rebours* (*Against Nature*, 1884), for it fuses aesthetic cultivation and renunciation (the novel's protagonist is a feverish voluptuary who hides himself away from the world) with religious conversion, and concludes with the hero seeking God's compassion as illness forces him to rejoin society. This plea became the seed that blossomed eight years later when Huysmans entered a Trappist monastery.

The two great French poets of the era, Rimbaud and Mallarmé, are each (distinctly different) virtuosos of renunciation and *ascesis*—to the point of indifference, at times, to having need of even a single reader. Both poets aimed to defeat art, yet by very different means: Rimbaud quit writing by 1875 but not before reinventing selfhood and poetry by exploding their alleged coherence, setting both in motion. This unmooring (which began with his father's abandonment) is emblematized at the start of one of his great poems: "I no longer felt myself guided by haulers!" says the drunken boat of its wayward freedom after its crew has been massacred at the start of "Le bateau ivre": "When with my haulers this uproar stopped, / The Rivers let me go where I wanted. . . . I bathed in the Poem / Of the Sea" (Rimbaud, *Complete* 115, 117). Rimbaud's insistence on opening art and life to the turmoil of improvisation and risk contrasts with the asylum of the page Mallarmé fastidiously arranged. No wonder Mallarmé condescended to Rimbaud; after his death Mallarmé spoke of Rimbaud's "unique adventure in the history of art. That of a child too precociously and peremptorily touched by the wings of literature, who, barely having had time to live, used up its stormy and magisterial destiny, without recourse to any possible future" (Mallarmé 71).

Rimbaud's manifesto of visionary poetry, known as his "Lettres du voyant" (from which I quoted earlier) was the work of a sixteen-year-old high school student writing his English teacher. From his hometown, Charleville in northeastern France, the most "idiotic" of provincial places, he called it, Rimbaud soon found his way to Paris where he was to make good on his pledge to explore the "unknown." Rimbaud's addiction to risk is part of an intensely futurist project, one conducted under the auspices of modernity and in the spirit of science, which, though "it moves too slowly" and can inflate man's ego, at least is immune to Christianity's paralyzing sense of sin ("O Christ, eternal thief of energy") (205, 101). A number of poems in *Illuminations*, his final work, (collected by Paul Verlaine in 1886) emphatically seek solidarity with progressive modernity—"To Reason," for instance, speaks of the conscription of "new men" who hear the "new harmony," a fulfillment of what the earlier visionary letter urged—a *"march toward Progress!"* Rimbaud believes that "poetry will not lend its rhythm to action, it will be *in advance"* (247, 309). In short, the pioneering role of the avant-garde includes political emancipation, a radical democratic extension of freedom to the enslaved: "When the endless servitude of woman is broken . . . she too will be a poet!"—this last word proclaiming the overlap of the aesthetic and the ethical (309).

Rimbaud's political vision instances his deliberate, violent affronting of authority, whatever the context. He was equally aware of the impossibility of absolute severance. He never, for instance, broke his ties to home and mother, though he professed to loathe both. And the allusive texture of his poems reflects how devoted and erudite a student of literature was this prize-winning Latin scholar. Nevertheless, Rimbaud defined himself as seer by acts of ferocious renunciation targeting the rule of tradition, be it moral or literary. His idea of freedom, he once explained to a friend, was embodied in the orphan: "Oh! How happy the abandoned child, brought up any which way, reaching adulthood without any idea inculcated by teachers or by family" (qtd. K. Ross 64). The fatherless Rimbaud was making the best of paternal absence, linking abandonment and opportunity.

"Rimbaud in Paris was not poor so much as passionately addicted to poverty" (Bonnefoy, *Rimbaud* 46), that is, using poverty as a stimulus to be "deranged" or shocked out of routine, readying himself to remake language that would be "of the soul, for the soul, containing everything, smells, sounds, colors, thought holding on to thought and pulling" (Rimbaud, *Complete* 309). The ideal is to fuse non-cognitive sensation with thought, the latter the motor of this poetic craft (powered by thought "pulling" oars). This dream of a self-sufficient poetic language of the "universal soul" abolishes metaphor—which requires distance in order to present likeness—for incarnation. A famous instance concerns another boat: "As I was going down impassive Rivers" are the words of *le bateau ivre* itself and they begin the poem of that name. This confused Théodore de Banville, the dean of the Parnassian poets (Paris's complacent aesthetic orthodoxy in the 1870s) who complained: why had not Rimbaud clarified matters by writing "*I am like a drunken boat*" (qtd. Robb 118). The young poet's banishing of simile for startling embodiment, like his vision of a "universal" language of soul, comprised his demand for an impersonality that would retire what he dubbed "subjective poetry," lyrical, aestheticized, full of familiar tropes—flowers and florid emotion. In its stead he sought to pursue "objective" art, which consigns convention to the devouring fire of the "unknown" that is inseparable from "vision" (303).

Hence Rimbaud's willingness to open perception and poetry to stimulations and sensations hitherto censored: he savored the stench of latrines and sticking his fingers into his eyes to prompt visions, as his early autobiographical poem "Les poètes de sept ans" discloses; in another, "Le coeur volé," the speaker recounts being raped by soldiers during his visit to Paris during the chaos of the Paris Commune: "my heart covered with tobacco-spit! // Ithyphallic and soldierish, / Their jeerings have depraved it" (Rimbaud, *Complete* 77, 81). According to Rimbaud, such candor about the corporeal was lacking, not only in the Parnassians but also in Baudelaire, his mentor in artistic contempt and misanthropy. Rimbaud ranked the older writer the "first seer, king of poets and yet he lived in too artistic a world; and the form so highly praised in him is trivial. Inventions of the unknown call for new forms" (qtd. Robb 311). The enemy for Rimbaud, as it will be for his translator Paul Celan, is what the culture already admires as "artistic," which was a reason he called himself a seer of the future rather than a poet.

His bravado was encouraged by the revolutionary moment in which he lived; Rimbaud was excited by the ideals of the Paris Commune and shared their revolt against the division of labor and specialization. Such atomized arrangements make any single name, like any finished object, depend for meaning on a fixed place in a hierarchy. The Communard "attack on verticality" fueled Rimbaud's larger suspicion of stable identity; to dissolve this fiction is one point of his fabled declaration: "Je est un autre" (Ross 19, 5; Rimbaud, *Complete* 304). Rimbaud turns this statement into a (dis-) organizing anti-principle of ceaseless metamorphosis in the stunning prose poems *Illuminations*. Filled with images of urban modernity (many poems were composed while Rimbaud lived in London) these depthless, dreamy, disjointed, anti-referential verbal artifacts insinuate meaning and then, teasingly, suspend it. His other major work, *Une saison en enfer*, is conventional compared to *Illuminations*, for in its effort to explain his private hell, Rimbaud relies on (often hallucinatory) narrative.

Une saison en enfer is the only book he ever saw to publication. Being Rimbaud, he turned the act of publishing inside out, carefully launching the work into the unknown. Having ordered 500 copies in 1873 from a Brussels printer, he left unpaid the printer's bill while walking away with ten free authors' copies that he gave to friends. Three decades later the rest were discovered in the shop's attic store-room. Until then the poem was mentioned publicly only once, in 1883. "The finished book was simply not that important to him" precisely because it was finished: the already done never compelled him—it belonged to the past (Robb 235). Rimbaud was likely correct in deciding there was not yet an audience for his fifty-four page experiment, a surreal autobiographical blending of prose and poetry.

Often read as his farewell to poetry, though he published important work after it, *Une saison* recounts the failure of his ambition to "reinvent love" in his affair with Verlaine, his married lover who had invited the younger poet to Paris in September 1871. The poem admits as well his failure to turn himself into a seer ("I have tried to invent new flowers, new stars, new flesh, new tongues. . . . Well! I have to bury my imagination and my memories!" (Rimbaud, *Complete* 207). Out of the ashes of these debacles he is inspired to seek some resolution though contemptuous of the means. Although via "science and Christianity, man deludes himself," Rimbaud calls on "God" to grant "freedom in salvation" (203, 181) and looks forward to "new wisdom" and a new "Christmas on earth. . . . Slaves, let us not curse life. . . . Let us welcome all the influxes of vigor and real tenderness. And, at

dawn, armed with ardent patience, we will enter magnificent cities"
(207, 209). The Future is his domain; hence, like Nietzsche, he refuses
ressentiment's obsessive nursing of past grievance. These late grace
notes of redemption, powerful in themselves, are however set within
a work of frenzied defiance, an extended interior monologue at once
self-abasing and affirming. It moves outward in one section to imper-
sonate novelistic speech when he has a Verlaine figure step forth to
recount an affair. Rimbaud maximizes his own diabolic role, casting
his lover as the "foolish Virgin" seduced by the "Infernal Bridegroom"
(Rimbaud). Everywhere his language's energy is battening against what
the poet was born into and, finally, could not surmount—the subjugat-
ing designs of Christianity, Western rationalism, and European coloni-
zation: "I am a slave to my baptism" and to its "filthy education" in
self-abnegating religious piety (189, 205). He knew it from birth in the
person of his mother, a rigid, death-obsessed Jansenist Christian whom
he loathed and loved without reciprocity.

Rimbaud's assault on the culture's crippling equation—subjectivity as enslavement—begins with the poem's premise—that the self,
if unfettered, is somebody else, is already in excess, unbounded and
multiple: "To each being it seemed to me that several *other* lives
were due": "I have lived everywhere. I know every family in Europe"
(201, 175). Like his contemporary and fellow visionary vagabond,
Whitman (adored by the French symbolists when first translated into
French starting in 1872 and likely read by Rimbaud), for whom time,
space and distance "avails not" and instant inhabitation of others
is a given ("I am afoot with my vision"; "I am the hounded slave";
"through me forbidden voices, voices of sexes and lusts"), Rimbaud
is free to enter identities at will (Whitman 53, 65, 44). He becomes at
one with "the history of France," "but always alone, without a family. . . . I am of an inferior race from all eternity" (Rimbaud, *Complete*
177): "As a serf I would have made the journey to the Holy Land. . . .
Among a thousand profane visions—I, a leper, am seated on shards
and nettles, at the foot of a sun-devoured wall—Later, as a mercenary,
I would have bivouacked under German nights" (175). Soon he is entering "the true kingdom of the children of Ham" and is swept up in a
frantic whirl: "*No more words.* . . . Yells, drum, dance, dance, dance,
dance! I can't even see the time when the whites will land and I will

fall into the void. . . . The white men are landing. The cannon! We will have to be baptized and put on clothes and work" (181). Before Rimbaud decided on the title *Une saison*, he called it "the Pagan or Negro book" (Robb 203).

Its ambitions are prodigious: untethering language and self, letting them float, guided by an hallucinating consciousness ("I looked on the disorder of my mind as sacred"), and becoming a martyr—a "beast, a savage"—bearing witness for those "conquered" by the West ("my spirit is insistent upon taking over all the cruel developments which the spirit has undergone since the end of the East"). He mocks while reanimating his own aspirations to be the visionary liberator of literary and sexual convention ("I prided myself on inventing a poetic language accessible some day to all the senses"; "the horror of my stupidity"); and then he resolves to live on earth ("I am thrown back to the earth"). All these simultaneous avowals and disavowals required that the poet "cultivate"—which is to say deform—his "soul": it "must be made monstrous," indifferent to all forms of constraint and fixity. So in his "visionary" letters of May 1871 he announced his martyrdom to a kind of Dionysian *ascesis* (to borrow Valéry's word) (Rimbaud, *Complete* 179, 185, 203, 193, 209, 307).

Making Verlaine his instrument, Rimbaud fulfilled his outlaw vows with the help of opium, hashish, and absinthe, plunging with the older poet into abjection, delirium, and destitution. Two years later, he had helped wreck a marriage and disgusted literary Paris with his violent acts of contempt, including writing poems they could not understand. Having abandoned his book at the printer's, before long he himself followed suit and abandoned Rimbaud the poet. Both orphans were left to fend for themselves: both eventually prospered.

This severance, this gamble, are what it means to respect the "unknown." In other words, Rimbaud sought somehow to balance himself on the rushing wave of time, poised in a stance of pure possibility facing the future, with no past at his back. He limns this position in "Motion," the apt title for his most explicit ode to the future. Near the end of *Illuminations*, "Motion" places us on the boat of modernity—Bonnefoy calls it the "second Ark"—in "swaying motion," the current jumping, guided by "unimaginable lights": its "voyagers" "are the conquerors of the world / Seeking a personal chemical fortune" and undertaking "the education of races, classes, and animals, on this boat." The poem ends with a glimpse of a "youthful couple" on board yet apart from the "repose and dizziness." Here Rimbaud finds a place for the poet, who "sings and stands guard" as he "withdraws into the archway," our witness to "the most startling atmospheric happenings" (Rimbaud, *Complete* 251–253).

After *Une saison en enfer*, Rimbaud's second major publication was a report published by the Geographical Society on the Ogaden region of eastern Ethiopia, "one of the world's largest remaining unexplored regions. . . . Some of the tribes mentioned by Rimbaud had never been heard of, let alone seen" (Robb 348–349). To Africa by the mid-1880s would come word that "the late" Arthur Rimbaud's early poems were now all the rage in Paris (Starkie 380). By then the current incarnation of Arthur Rimbaud, having renounced Christian Europe for pagan Africa, was no longer a "savage" but a colonialist, a successful, respected, and ascetic trader (not in slaves, as the myths have it) but in coffee and ivory and rifles in crisis-ridden Abyssinia. To the literary news from Paris he expressed brusque dismissal.

In sum, just as he had pledged in the "Lettres du voyant," for Rimbaud life and art proved to be a single project of willed "derangement" (*dérèglement*—unruliness). Was his program, finally, "a trick, a radical failure, a trap full of magnificence, or a truly legendary attempt"? To his own questions Blanchot answers that "no one can decide. . . . This uncertainty makes the power and the enigma of Rimbaud. He pushed ambiguity . . . to the utmost" and no matter how many new facts and documents about his life turn up, nothing will reduce it (*Work* 156). "He was born a seed and he remains a seed," remarks Henry Miller (100). As for the "Seer" project, failure and estrangement were native to it. That was the very point, the price of always being "in advance" (like his poetry) and on the move (like his life). Permanently on the road, even anguish proved a prod to movement. "To roll with one's wounds, through the wearying air and the sea; with physical torment, through the silence of murderous water and air," as he wrote in "Angoisse" ("Anguish"), in *Illuminations* (113). Those who came after—the Beats and their legion progeny stretching til now—could (and would) only envy and imitate him. Even on the last day of his life, his leg amputated, still in agony on his deathbed in a Marseilles hospital,

Rimbaud was busy making plans to leave and return to Africa. Under "address" on the registry recording his death the clerk wrote "de passage." Rimbaud died in transit (Nicholl 313).

From where did the poet's compulsion to move forward, an urge that fed his creativity but also his chronic sense of impatience and futility, come? Likely from an intimate encounter, starkly literal, with the avant-garde—the phrase derives from a military formation "in advance"—in the person of his father, an outstanding soldier. To his very young son, the scholarly and adventurous French army officer Captain Frederic Rimbaud taught (by embodying) a profound lesson: mastery is comprised by the capacity for abandonment, and abandonment is the quality of being "absolutely modern," i.e. avant-garde. Captain Rimbaud had distinguished himself in the conquest of North Africa but was defeated by his provincial wife. Evidently unable to bear her emotional iciness, he left the family when his genius son was six, never to return or to contact him or his three siblings. The deserted mother henceforward called herself the "Widow Rimbaud" to ease the public stigma of abandonment. "Oh! How happy the abandoned child." Rimbaud became a version of his father, master of leave-taking. Father was now "dead" just as his son would later be "dead" in Paris in the season of his celebration. The captain too left behind texts, a massive annotated grammar book and his own voluminous papers, including a translation of the Koran and a compendium of Arabic humor, both of which Arthur was to use in Africa (Robb 12). Rather than turning his life and art into a "melancholy search for the father" (a frequent conclusion of Rimbaud biographers, according to Wyatt Mason), the poet—not without grief—entered into a remarkably rich identification with the aggressor: he nourished himself on his father's example (xxx). Writing and renunciation were impressed into Rimbaud's psyche deeply and early.

■

Less literally than Rimbaud, but just as decisively, Mallarmé depends on the power of absconding: in "The Crisis of Poetry" Mallarmé speaks of the "disappearance of the poet as speaker, yielding his initiative to words." "Everything in the world exists to end up as a book" was a guiding belief (Mallarmé 226, 208). The material page, including its virginal white spaces, becomes the arena for "Language, playing.— Words, all by themselves, light each other up on the sides that are known as the rarest or most meaningful only for the spirit, the center of vibratory suspense" (235). That vibration depends on mystery; "to *name* an object is to lose three-quarters of the pleasure of the poem . . . to *suggest* it, there is the dream" (qtd. Candida-Smith 37). With speech's usual task of exchange short-circuited, language can be made into a symbol, which works by evocation, wedding ideas to emotions and sensation. This liberation from communication permits "utterances that cannot be resolved into clear ideas" and sacrifices intelligible meaning to sonority and tempo of the voice, hence what has been called the "crisis of the word" that Mallarmé initiated before his death in 1898 (Valéry 8:279).

Mallarmé had announced his death decades earlier—as a fledgling poet in the provinces, he writes "Je suis mort" in an 1866 letter, an effort to make palpable his fascination with anonymity—the "disappearance of the poet as speaker." Soon after this announcement he tells another friend: "I am now impersonal and no longer the Stéphane you once knew, but one of the ways the spiritual Universe has of seeing itself and developing, through what used to be me" (qtd. Bersani 5, 86). For the next seven years he does no writing; "the mere physical act of writing sets off an attack of hysteria," he confided to a friend. Simultaneously, he is planning a multi-volume book of prose poems, starting with a volume devoted to Nothingness, another to the Beautiful. He imagines a minimum of ten years (soon extended to twenty) for completion. As Leo Bersani has argued, Mallarmé "considers the death he speaks of in his letters not as the end of his literary career, but as the condition of literary productivity. Mallarmé's arrival in Paris in 1871, where, on the basis of a few poems seen by a few other writers, he is already welcomed as an authoritative voice in the world of letters, would seem to herald the start—after a long crisis of threatened sterility—of an exceptionally productive poetic career" (26).

But this promising scenario was not to be; instead, Mallarmé, to recall his disciple Valéry's words, embraced *"an entirely new and singular state of mind"* founded on creativity as renunciation. In effect, Mallarmé devises a way to marry poetic creativity to his confessed "death" and impersonal rebirth at one with a "spiritual Universe." He does so via his endlessly deferred Book—it will be "anonymous—the text there to be on its own, without the voice of an author," as he put it in an 1885 letter to Verlaine summarizing his own career. Mallarmé dismisses his published "album" of selected poems and prose as merely a way of "keeping my hand in" and finds them without "immediate value." He chalks up his other published work to having "had to grab whatever offered itself as a lifeboat in hard-up moments" (Mallarmé 3–4). His actual works pale next to his unwritten "Great Work": "I have always dreamed and attempted something else, with the patience of an alchemist, ready to sacrifice all vanity and all satisfaction. . . . What would it be? It . . . is hard to say: a book, quite simply, in several volumes. . . . I would even go further and say *the* Book, convinced as I am that in the final analysis there's only one, unwittingly attempted by anyone who writes, even Geniuses. The orphic explanation of the Earth, which is the poet's only duty" (3). Its "rhythm" would be "impersonal," at one with the universal quality of the subject and thus attaining the "natural fullness" of pure Presence (184). Rendering author and reader irrelevant, the Book, as Blanchot notes, "speaks *itself* and writes *itself*. That is the condition of its authority" (*Work* 41).

Yet just as Mallarmé is beseeching Verlaine to believe in his sincere devotion to *the* Book and its orphic ambition—"I am possessed by it and will succeed, perhaps . . . in showing a fully executed fragment, making its glorious authenticity glow from the corner"—he starts unraveling that devotion. His attention starts "wandering" (which is also how he describes his love of *flânerie*—he wanders whenever his "mind gets dead tired, on the edge of the Seine" and he memorializes his love of "objectless divagation" in the title and form of his 1897 collection, *Divagations*) (Mallarmé 3, 5, 224). His wanderings include his invention, (anonymous) editorship, and publication of a woman's fashion magazine, *La dernière mode*, which ran eight issues and still compels him; "when I divest them of their dust" perusing them suffices "to plunge me into a reverie for a long time" (4). Such reverie, rather than resolution, comes easy in the era in which both he and Verlaine find themselves—an era Mallarmé calls "a kind of interregnum for the poet." This period of absent authority not only keeps the poet detached but empties him of initiative, breeding casualness about productivity:

Mallarmé says he can do nothing but "keep working, with mystery, so that later, or never, and from time to time sending the living his calling card—some stanza or sonnet—so as not to be stoned by them, if they knew he suspected they didn't exist. Loneliness necessarily accompanies that type of attitude" (4).

By the end of his letter to Verlaine, one wonders what has come of Mallarmé's devotion to *the* Book. Perhaps his casualness was an instance of his "taste for flirting with the Absolute," as Valéry once remarked of his mentor's temperament (Valéry 8:377). In fact, as Bersani says, Mallarmé, "especially after settling in Paris, was engaged in an extraordinary diversity of literary projects" that betrayed his avowals of concentration on the envisioned chef-d'oeuvre. "But the very frivolousness detectable in Mallarmé's career as a man of letters" is, for Bersani, the very point, as it indicates a "radical reassessment of writing as a *value* of culture" (46). The elaborate engagement with a fugitive text of absolute autonomy that Mallarmé wants to convince Verlaine is the measure and telos of his poetic career is, finally, a willed pretense. The flirtation disguises Mallarmé's rejection of the very notion of a literary masterpiece and preference for "wandering," for easy receptivity to doing all sorts of writing, high and low (including nursery rhymes) and to promoting literary life—his celebrated "Tuesdays"—all the product, says Bersani, of an "intense, even voracious, and yet disarmingly light sociability" (47). "We might even define Mallarmé's major enterprise . . . as an effort to do away with literature" (45). This audacious project would require the subtlest tactics in a national culture where literary tradition is so sacred that to tamper with the alexandrine couplet ignited a riot, as Hugo discovered at the 1830 premiere of his verse drama *Hernani*.

The gambit of "pure poetry" according to Valéry "is only a limit situated at some infinite distance, an ideal of the power of linguistic beauty" (8:267). Mallarmé's Book confirms his belief that, as "opposed to a denominative and representative function . . . speech, which is primarily dream and song, recovers in the Poet's hands, of necessity in an art devoted to fictions, its virtuality" (Mallarmé 211). This is his often-cited example of virtuality: "I say: a flower! And, out of the oblivion where my voice casts every contour . . . there arises, musically, the very idea in its mellowness; in other words, what is absent from every bouquet" (210). Poetry, in short, severs any connection of language to that which it might refer; nature and the world are rendered irrelevant.

Yet, paradoxically, the emptying out accomplished by poetic virtuality—speaking of things in their absence—is propitious for the emergence of the materiality of the medium. The logic of this is latent in a rhetorical question posed by an anonymous critic in 1876: "Is Monsieur Mallarmé in good faith, does he want to replace poetry that says something with a new poetry, like Manet in painting, which limits itself to giving an impression?" (qtd. C. Rosen 359). Instead of saying "something"—which implies reference to the external world— the poet and painter will give an impression limited by—*and about*— the artistic means at hand. Whereas "realistic, naturalistic art had dissembled the medium, using art to conceal art," modernism "uses art to call attention to art" (Greenberg 4:86). Mallarme's visual poetics fully flower by the late nineties, as he makes readers attend to the presence of his page by experimenting with typography, layout, and spacing. Facilitating this visual formalism is the waning of the prestige of the literary paradigm, which had served as a model for all the arts. Replacing it is the pure form of music, incapable of communicating anything but sensation. Throwing off literature's obligation of reference or mimesis, the poet will make poems about words and painters paintings about paint—materiality is primary. This account sketches Greenberg's views, the American critic who stakes his immensely influential career on the renunciatory energy of the formalist turn.

Pushing the crisis of language to its limits, Mallarmé's renunciation compares with William James's in 1908. James and the Frenchman both want to banish representation while moving in parallel but opposite directions. Whereas the poet renounces world for word, James renounces word for world. For each, ordinary language is the problem: James locates the trouble in language's too ready availability for use as a tool to "name and class" what is "as yet unnamed or classed" (*Writings* 2:727); Mallarmé sees language as deformed by its obligation to represent and correspond, to stand for things "out there," a servant to external reality. If James wants to be done with words, Mallarmé seeks to retire them from service and grant them the freedom of infinite "metaphoric becoming" *within* their "lexical grammatical universe" (Steiner 97–98). This is to "purify the words of the tribe," to recall Mallarmé's often-quoted words about Poe, whom he regarded as his master predecessor in making poetry approximate music.

■

The formalist avant-garde in French art includes Courbet ("the first real avant-garde painter" who "tried to reduce his art to immediate sense data by painting only what the eye could see as a machine unaided by the mind"), Manet (who within his canvases stages the abandonment of subject matter for form), and Mallarmé in literature (1:29). As Greenberg's capsule summary of Courbet suggests, the formalist turn from ideas and subject matter—i.e. a flight from the province of "literature, which was subject matter at its most oppressive"—included painting without the mind in control, releasing intuition and impulse. In other words, receptivity to immediacy opens the door not only to the "materialist objectivity" of Impressionism which, Greenberg tells us, went "beyond Courbet" to "emulate the detachment of science," but also to what Greenberg doesn't mention—the annulment of mastery when we "do something without knowing how or why" (Emerson, *Essays* 414). *This* force of impulse is an imperative that exceeds "the expressive resources of the medium" and opens the self to the "immediacy" of "sensations, the irreducible elements of experience" (Greenberg 1:30). These phrases summon, for instance, a Rimbaud submitting himself to the dangers of sensory "derangement."

In short, Greenberg's rhetoric, if not his intention, points beyond formalism to the *poète maudit*—the accursed poet—whose life is regarded as one with his art. The role is exemplified by Vincent van Gogh, saintly tormented ascetic who killed himself in 1890, a year before Rimbaud's death. By the 1920s both men had been consecrated as mythic culture heroes. Jackson Pollock joined their pantheon several decades later as the postwar American archetype of the "damned" genius who makes his life and art an arena of perpetual turbulence. Pollock literally abolishes formalism's defining division between art and life by abandoning the traditional space of easel painting, instead working with his canvas on the floor.

Pollock gets into the "middle of experience, in the very thick of its sand and gravel," to borrow words from one of William James's 1908 arias to the horizontal. Bergsonism, James tells us, sets him into the dirt, whereas all other philosophy "is essentially the vision of things from above" (*Writings* 2:756). James's posture prefigures a (deliberately low) trajectory of postwar art; the former painter and draughtsman, forced to renounce his brush, anticipates Pollock. In his drip paintings Pollock too will set brush aside—for turkey baster and sticks— and make paintings by taking the canvas horizontal, circling around it seized by a "sort of ecstatic blindness." So remarked Allan Kaprow in 1958, mourning Pollock two years after his sudden violent death in a car crash (1). Inspired by Pollock's legacy and by John Cage's *4'33"*, Kaprow devised a new anti-art form called "Happenings" that turned art from a made thing into an experience. He found Pollock's open form liberating for it ignored the "confines of the rectangular field in favor of a continuum going in all directions simultaneously, *beyond* the literal dimensions of any work." Giving the "impression of going on forever," Pollock's scale "allows us equal pleasure in participating in a delirium, a deadening of the reasoning faculties, a loss of 'self' in the Western sense of the term." Kaprow detects a "Zen quality" in Pollock's blind "kind of knowing" (5, 7). James would have applauded Kaprow's breaking of boundaries, experiments for which Kaprow found crucial inspiration in Dewey's work of pragmatist aesthetics, *Art as Experience*.

The devaluation of "reasoning faculties" was contagious in the postwar New York art world. Consider Willem de Kooning. An occasional reader of Wittgenstein, the painter was fond of his remark, "Don't think, but look!" (*Investigations* sec. 66). Indeed, de Kooning devised his own variation: "Don't look, paint." When Harold Rosenberg reminded him of his phrase, de Kooning answered: "That's right! There is this strange desire which you can't explain" (qtd. Yard 143). Greenberg too urged submission to the intuitive. "When it comes to art," Greenberg said late in life, "watch out for thinking. Let your eye or your ear, your taste, take over. Don't think too much" (qtd. Shiff,

"Watch" 75). This expresses loyalty to the "aesthetic idea," Kant's anti-concept. Indeed Greenberg admired Kant as the "first real modernist" (for his powers of "self-criticism"—he "used logic to establish the limits of logic") (4:85). As Richard Shiff puts it, "art is the context in which thinking becomes problematic" ("Watch" 77).

With the advent of abstract expressionism, thinking, it seemed, might be purified out of existence. Largely free of mimetic obligations, artists could now immerse themselves and viewers in the immediacy of paint: we are "left alone with shapes and colors," Greenberg wrote in 1959. The "purity" (Greenberg's word, which he usually set in scare quotes to remind us that it was only a "useful illusion") of abstract art is "an arch-example of something that does not have to mean, or be useful for, anything other than itself," an autonomy that is a "relief" from the domination of the instrumental (4:94, 80).

Lest this last remark suggest that Greenberg is a romantic anti-capitalist bemoaning modernity, in fact his sense of formalism is acutely historicist. This is worth pointing out since many of his critics, says de Duve, "stubbornly continue to see him as a kind of Platonist of pure painting" (*Clement Greenberg* 71). Greenberg remarks that "there is nothing in the nature of abstract art which compels it to be so. The imperative comes from history," which by the late nineteenth century was, with the rise of kitsch and mass culture, threatening ambitious art's survival. In response, the avant-garde emerged to preserve art as art. History, in Greenberg's influential essays, had "hunted back" the arts "to their mediums, and there they have been isolated, concentrated and defined. It is by virtue of its medium that each art is unique and strictly itself. To restore the identity of an art the opacity of its medium must be emphasized" (1:37, 32). Pictorial art's uniqueness was the flatness of its surface, so "modernist painting oriented itself to flatness as it did to nothing else."

Greenberg's stress on the medium, then, is grounded in "historical justification" (4:87; 1:37). Hence his repeated claim that his advocacy of abstract art is contingent: it is the best art "at this moment in the history of art" (3:189). That moment's embattled quality is revealed if we hear in the phrase "hunted back" its undertone—hunted down. In being "isolated and concentrated" painting has suffered "a certain impoverishment in renouncing image and object," Greenberg acknowledged in 1954. Asking himself, "May not an abstract painting, even when it is very good, still leave us somewhat dissatisfied in a way that an equally good representational painting wouldn't?" he answers "yes" (3:189). The best art of our time is a "necessary impoverishment" inseparable from its "excellences." This paradox reflects, Greenberg speculates, not that "the abstract is invariably a sign of decline" but the possibility that "art in general is in decline," unable to "match the past no matter how it paints and sculpts" (3:190).

Respect for the "opacity" of the medium demanded that the gap between art and life be respected. Greenberg condemned those like Duchamp (and conceptualists and minimalists who had revived his reputation by the sixties) who defied the art/life boundary and substituted ideas for aesthetic experience: "Art as Idea is for those who don't ask enough from art" (qtd. de Duve, *Clement Greenberg* 121). Greenberg was inclined to what he candidly called a "bland, large, balanced, Apollonian art . . . in which an intense detachment informs all. Only such an art, resting on rationality but without permitting itself to be rationalized, can adequately answer contemporary life." We have had "enough of the wild artist" and instead need poised "men of the world . . . not at all overpowered by their own feelings" (2:168).

The Apollonian Greenberg championed wild Dionysian man of the west Pollock because he regarded him as the best painter of his generation, not because Pollock's physical movements when "*in*" his painting could be allegorized as existential affirmation. This latter move was Harold Rosenberg's influential effort to make the act everything and the artifact secondary, merely "the solipsistic record of purely personal 'gestures,'" as Greenberg derisively described Rosenberg's account (4:136). In his 1952 essay "The American Action Painters," Rosenberg declares: "A painting that is an act is inseparable from the biography of the artist" (191). Self-consciously in the American grain, Rosenberg invokes Melville and Whitman in his hymn to the "Open Road of risk" that tempts the action painter (194). Despite sharp differences, both critics would concur that from its inception non-figurative painting has dreamed of "attaining immediacy, . . . of escaping from

words into seeing and being" (T. Clark, *Farewell* 253). The dream generated dissent and "it was possible for artists to believe and not believe
in it at the same time" (and sometimes the same artist held opposing
convictions): abstraction became an "eternal war between the discursive and the immediate" (254).

In three years Pollock titled four paintings *One*. Evidently "abstraction seemed to mean priority in Pollock's case: the possibility of
making the first painting again" (*Farewell* 333). Pollock's multiples
of *One* enact something akin to the quest for "raw unverbalized life"
that left William James, he himself admitted, a "foolish little" child
"in the eyes of reason" (*Writings* 2:755). Both are in the grip of an
Adamic fantasy of a fresh start. Hence the "psychic automatism"
preached by Surrealism appealed to Pollock for it involved abandonment of consciousness—at least at the start—for "free-association,
in the specific form of doodling," as Robert Motherwell put it. He
regarded painting's appropriation of automatism as "the most powerful creative principle . . . consciously developed in twentieth-century art" (qtd. Danto, *Philosophizing* 22, 30). T. J. Clark speaks of the
"quality of renunciation" in the "fierceness of Pollock's abstraction"
that marks his effort to be rid of "a parasitic relation to likeness" and
finally to be wholly "in" and "of" the "world" by squatting on the
floor flinging paint, feeling the ground, rather than upright, bound
within the space of the frame and border of an easel. He has departed
the cloistered domain of figural painting (*Farewell* 332–333). Pollock,
in other words, uses his body (not only fingers, wrists, and elbows
traditionally exercised by putting a brush to canvas) to depart art's
sanctuary. For him, the habits and mannerisms produced by devotion
to the ideal of deliberate "madeness" are the enemy; he felt "revulsion . . . from the look of the intended and arranged and contrived and
trimmed." Instead, he made "crucial decisions" based on intuition
rather than "manual skill," implying that without inspiration, discipline is irrelevant (Greenberg 4:247–248).

Pollock's generative renunciation is embodied in the supple darting movements he made at his East Hampton studio, a performance

that has become iconic thanks to the 1951 Hans Namuth film of the painter at work. Dispensing with the easel's verticality, prowling the canvas nailed to the ground, darting on and off it, leaving handprints, discovering "the power of an explosive line without outline or contour" that "delimits nothing . . . continually changing direction," eye subordinated to hand, optical to haptic (reversing the traditional hierarchy), hand liberated to work up a "heavy impasto" coarsened with "sand, broken glass and other foreign matter," including his cigarette butts, the "painting having a life of its own," Pollock seems already poised to exit culture. He has "destroyed painting." Back to square one (Deleuze, *Francis Bacon* 85, 87; Pollock 139–140; Kaprow 2). Not so fast: one isn't so easy. By 1998 art historians, digitally enlarging Namuth's pictures, discovered what had long been suspected—that Pollock's process was more cautious and complicated: he began not with abstract splats but with deliberately dripped human and animal figures that he buried in a cascade of splattering, only to then repeat the alternation of figures and splats. Precisely this "interaction" between imagery and the "all-over, all-absorbing web" is the source of his unique "rhythmic energy" (Karmel 129). More recent discoveries show that Pollock set the canvas back on the easel for final reworking.

Even if Pollock's drip paintings are not quite the blazing liberation from nature and the figure they were reputed to be, the artist's hunger for "priority" is undeniable. As is what rouses the hunger—the imperative to renounce culture—that accumulated repository of the "secondhand." No one has described this impulse more memorably than the phenomenologist Merleau-Ponty in his classic essay "Cézanne's Doubt" that appeared in *Partisan Review* (1946). Cézanne, he writes, "is not satisfied to be a cultured animal but takes up culture from its inception and founds it anew: he speaks as the first man spoke and paints as if no one had ever painted before. What he expresses cannot, therefore, be the translation of a clearly defined thought, since such clear thoughts are those that have been already said. . . . 'Conception' cannot precede 'execution.' Before expression, there is nothing but a vague fever. . . . The artist launches his work just as a man once launched the first word, not knowing whether it will be anything more than a shout" (69).

In reconstructing the birth of advanced art, Merleau-Ponty stages a purging of the prior, washing away ancestors, precedents, traditions, and speech. Even "clear thoughts." "I would like to see like a newborn," said Cézanne. (Monet envied the blind man just restored to sight.) The scene is almost Emersonian and Nietzschean in its ruthless evacuation of history; Merleau-Ponty's Cézanne in effect poses Emerson's brusque question: "Why should not we enjoy an original relation to the universe?" (*Essays* 7) The Frenchman is without Emerson's exhilaration, shadowed instead by a sense of precariousness, of irreducible fragility and doubt. "We hardly dare say Cézanne lived; he [only] painted," said a friend; and Merleau-Ponty says his obsessive "devotion to the visible world" represents "a flight from the human world, the alienation of his humanity" ("Cézanne's" 61).

"Cézanne's Doubt" honors the fact that the battle against culture is waged every time the artist confronts the unprimed canvas. Because that bareness is an illusion: there are no empty surfaces, no fresh beginnings. They are already brimming with what lodges in one's head, in one's studio—the second-hand cultural detritus of the routine and familiar, the figurative and narrative and illustrative "givens" found in photographs, newspapers, television. Such givens are, in sum, the "readymades" that Duchamp would offer as art. *"They are what is seen, until finally one sees nothing else."* These swarms of already-known images must be destroyed before painting may begin. To begin requires, paradoxically, the absence of deliberation. "The moment you know what to do," declares Francis Bacon, "you're making just another form of illustration." Hence the preciousness of "making marks without knowing how they will behave." Only then "suddenly there comes something which your instinct seizes on as being for a moment the thing which you could begin to develop" (qtd. Sylvester 54, 58).

"The painter," writes Gilles Deleuze, "does not have to cover a blank surface but rather would have to empty it out, clear it, clean it" (*Francis Bacon* 71). He quotes D. H. Lawrence on Cézanne's war against cliché: "After a fight tooth-and-nail for forty years, he did succeed in knowing an apple, fully; and not quite as fully, a jug or two. That was all he achieved. It seems little, and he died embittered."

Actually his accomplishment, Lawrence insists, is immense: when he escapes cliché and "really give[s] a complete intuitive interpretation of actual objects . . . he is inimitable." What he creates is "the real appleyness, and you can't imitate it. Every man must create it anew and different out of himself: new and different. The moment it looks 'like' Cézanne, it is nothing" (qtd. Deleuze, *Francis Bacon* 72–73).

Because the proliferation of cliché has only intensified since Cézanne ("even the reactions against cliché are creating clichés," says Deleuze), great painters feel "hunted back" (again), forced to become relentlessly "severe with their work." Like Cézanne, Francis Bacon "ruined" or "renounced" many of his paintings as soon as the "enemy reappeared" (73). "Great painters know that it is not enough to mutilate, maul, or parody the cliché" (73). Purgation is imperative: Before one commences one must "empty it out, clear it, clean it." *The Lord Chandos Letter* performed this necessary renunciation for Hofmannsthal; each artist or writer needs to find his own version. Broch suggests this conclusion when he says of James Joyce, who also started writing as a lyric poet: "Joyce too probably had his *Chandos* experience, for the destruction of expression that he undertook in his prose work in order to create, from its sentence fragments and word particles, a new and more genuine expression of reality points to a positively wild anger and contempt, to a disgust with traditional and impoverished language, with its clichés petrified in both vocabulary and syntax" (*Hugo* 126).

■

The emptying out—the counter-violence pushing back the violence of culture's suffocating ubiquity—does not remove the doubt Merleau-Ponty dramatizes. Doubt shadows the launching of one's work into the unknown, an anxiety that shapes the conspicuous reticence or studied inarticulateness of many artists when asked to reflect on their practice (Robert Irwin being an exception). The invitation to reflect demands words, precisely the medium of the "second-hand."

An example: in the film *Gerhard Richter Painting* (2012), Richter at one point faces the critic Benjamin Buchloch, who wants to know about the logical relation between Richter's original "planlessness" and the moment he feels confident "making the judgment 'Now it's a painting.'" Distrustful of "clear thought" (the exhausted realm of the "already been said," in Merleau-Ponty's words) Richter calls into question the whole point of talking: "To talk about painting is not only difficult but perhaps pointless too. You can only express in words what words are capable of expressing, what language can communicate. But painting has nothing to do with that . . . painting is another form of thinking. . . . What interests me in general, and this also applies to painting, are things I don't understand. It's like that with every picture: I don't like the ones I understand." His preference for opacity insulates Richter from the pressure to rely on the "already been said." In a journal entry Richter once wrote of his "profound distaste for all claims to possess the truth" and quotes approvingly evolutionary scientists "who say that our sole hope of survival lies in the 'gropings of human self-doubt'" (Richter 171).

"That one hides," Richter says admiringly of one of his own paintings. Hides what? He doesn't say, letting us infer his fondness for its refusal to be understood other than by its sheer frontality. Richter's fencing with Buchloch (which has occurred a number of times in various contexts) stages for the painter a necessary ritual of renunciation: of explanation and of words and capital M Meaning. Let life or painting "teach the lesson," as a similarly frustrated William James said. Not surprisingly, Richter's fondness for what hides and his wariness of language extends to being adamant about ridding his canvas of accumulated clichés: "the things you can't help seeing a million times over, day in and day out: the impoverishment. . . . I paint all that away, out of myself, out of my head, when I first start on a picture. That is my foundation, my ground. I get rid of that in the first few layers, which I destroy, layer by layer, until all the facile feeblemindedness has gone. I end up with a work of destruction" (177).

■

The root issue here—the "eternal war between the discursive and the immediate," to re-invoke T. J. Clark's phrase—is important to clarify, since it animates the standoff between artists and critics and the turn from books back to life basic to many of the renunciations considered here. To a prominent strain of postmodern theory talk of presence and pure perception, of "immediate experience" or of "the living, moving, active, thickness of the real" is, at best, poignantly naïve, at worst, embarrassingly incoherent. Identifying insight with demystification, postmodern theory tends to be skeptical of the unmediated in any form, be it body or nature. When "presence" is invoked it seems inevitably prefixed by "nostalgia for." In 1971 Paul de Man wrote that literature is the "only form of language free from the fallacy of unmediated expression" (17). This became orthodoxy, reappearing, for instance, a dozen years later when art theorist Hal Foster began an essay on what he called the "expressive fallacy" (abstract expressionism's naïve claims to immediacy, presence, and a unitary self) with de Man's sentence "Unmediated expression is a philosophical impossibility" as part of his epigraph (Foster 59).

By 2004 Hans Gumbrecht, a comparative literature professor, aptly remarked that "it has long been a symptom of despicably bad intellectual taste in the humanities" if one dares use such words as "presence" or "reality" or "being" (53). He calls this censorious attitude the "soft terror" practiced by deconstruction (54). Stressing the ubiquity of the "constructed" and making the natural synonymous with the naïve, postmodern theory inadvertently reinstates the dualisms it ostensibly decries—the gap between nature and culture, body and mind, emotion and reason—and leaves the first term under suspicion. The concept of "experience," of course, was an early casualty, doomed by its fatal entanglement, for instance, with assaults of feeling on a self-present subject. In Jacques Derrida's *Of Grammatology* (1976) the verdict is clear: "'Experience' has always designated the relationship with a presence" and "a plenitude, whether it be sensory simplicity or the infinite presence of God." However, Derrida does make convenient exceptions: he retains the concept for the "'experience' of *différance*" and especially "the experience of aporia, or the impossible" (qtd. Gasché 354).

Forms of intellectualism pervade postmodern theory, among them belief in the primacy of textualism (the early Derrida), of rhetoric and figurality (de Man), of interpretation (Stanley Fish), of intention (Walter Benn Michaels). Most egregious is Rorty, given that he was a self-proclaimed pragmatist in the tradition of Dewey, who nonetheless ignored his predecessor's stress on the human as "live creature."

Instead, Rorty posited a "linguistic transcendentalism," to borrow
Frank Ankersmit's description of Rorty's belief that human beings are
simply the vocabularies they possess. Hence Rorty not only skews
Dewey but also pays minimal attention to William James, reducing
A Pluralistic Universe to "Bergsonian nostalgia for the rich, whooshy,
sensuous flux we bathed in before conceptual thought started to dry
us out" ("The Pragmatist" 32). Rorty sees James as setting up a "metaphysics of feeling in opposition to the metaphysics of cognition,"
hence violating pragmatism's commitment to "no views about what is
real 'in the completest sense of the term'" ("Some" 92).

In *The Nick of Time* (2004) Elizabeth Grosz lucidly frames the postmodern bias toward the primacy of knowing. When discussing Bergson
she notes that a recurrent theme in his writing—"the inadequacy of
intelligence, science, and thus epistemology" to address "central questions of existence"—has always drawn fire, from both early rationalist critics like Bertrand Russell who affirmed "logic in explaining and
ordering the real," to contemporary deconstruction which collapses
"ontology into epistemology," that is, being into knowing. What both
"otherwise antagonistic" positions, early and recent, share is the
premise that "representations, whether mathematical (for Russell) or
discursive (for Derrida) are our only means of access to the real" (Grosz
191). Defining Western philosophical self-consciousness is Socrates's
response that thinking is the answer to the question of what is it to be
a human being. He conceived thinking as accurate representation or
correspondence to the way things are—"rationality as representation"
(another way to put James's "vicious intellectualism") (Edwards 20).

The primacy of rationality, says Charles Taylor, assumes that "we
have contact with the real in knowledge only through some interme-
diary depiction or category" and defines knowledge as justified, true
belief that gives reasons, grounds, criteria ("Retrieving" 72). To this
disengaged and disembodied stance (which he calls "mediation theory") Taylor contrasts "contact or immersion" theory. It posits: "Truth
is self-authenticating. When you're there, you know you're there."
This sense of stable orientation is not an assumption or a belief needing justification, but an unquestioned, taken-for-granted framework of
our lives—what Wittgenstein calls "a form of life"—"in relation to
which we go about the things we're doing, including the things we

question and argue about" (75). We have confidence that these forms or frameworks are not open to doubt for they are inseparable from "our general grasp of the world" and reflect "our sense that by operating within them we are in contact with reality" (76). When something unpredictable occurs, our confidence will prove "misplaced" and require revision, "but never totally, because we will be only able to cope with these errors within an amended framework." Within it we cope with change by giving reasons and criteria "but all this goes on within a larger context of presumed contact with reality" (76). Taylor names Wittgenstein, Merleau-Ponty, and Heidegger as among the early framers of the contact or immersion theory; he might have added William James. All concur regarding "a basic move which gives rise to this theory"—"a re-embedding of thought and knowledge in the bodily and social-cultural contexts in which it takes place" (73).

Antipathy between renunciation and "rationality as representation" (mediation theory) was established early: Diogenes the Cynic, who refused to convene any philosophic school or transcribe any wisdom into books, wandered Athens alone, performing histrionic self-exposure as hands-on mockery of the metaphysical abstractions his philosophical colleagues lived by. When Zeno "declared there was no such thing as motion, he got up and walked about" (Diogenes Laertius 41). After Plato defined man as "an animal, biped and featherless," Diogenes "plucked a fowl and brought it into the lecture room with the words, 'Here is Plato's man'" (43). Diogenes dubbed himself a "Socrates gone mad" (55). Finding capital P Philosophy infected by theoretical speculation, Diogenes turned it into spiritual exercise or therapy, a way of life. As a "mode of existing-in-the-world," his philosophy sought "wisdom itself. For real wisdom does not merely cause us to know: it makes us 'be' in a different way," says Pierre Hadot (*Philosophy* 265). "In antiquity one historian wondered whether Cynicism could be called a philosophical school—whether it mightn't be instead, only a way of life" (*What Is* 109).

In Diogenes's antagonistic relation to philosophy James finds a model for his own anti-philosophy. James's pragmatism ultimately

renounces itself, lets life have priority. "To my readers," I present pragmatism as a theory of truth "to be verified *ambulando*, or by the way
in which its consequences may confirm it" (*Writings* 2:933). James's
Latin refers to the tag *"solvitur ambulando"*: "the problem is solved
by walking." Announcing kinship with Diogenes licenses James's
exit from closed theoretical systems and descent to the horizontal.
Scorning the "refinement" of the classroom, the pragmatist takes to
the "street" and delights in finding it "multitudinous beyond imagination, tangled, muddy, painful and perplexed" (494–495). Elected poverty
(a life James extols in *The Varieties of Religious Experience*), perpetual
journeys, and willed homelessness—this estrangement marks renun-
ciating thinkers in the Cynic spirit, above all Nietzsche and implicitly Wittgenstein, ascetic and itinerant anti-philosopher (Nietzsche,
Untimely 194). Something of Diogenes's scoffing finds expression in
Wittgenstein's "Don't think, but look!" The anti-novelist W.G. Sebald
lets this Cynic spirit of deracinated wandering suffuse his literary universe, culminating in *Austerlitz* (2001), whose title character, we learn
early on, possesses a personal and physical similarity to Wittgenstein.
A close-up of the philosopher's penetrating gaze stares at us from the
third page.

Postmodern intellectualism does not reign unopposed. The previously
invoked Yves Bonnefoy, for instance, critiques the "textualist revolution" that in reducing poetry to a strictly "intellectual . . . game" thereby
misses that we are turned by a poet's "very words toward something that
escapes them"—presence beyond or prior to representation ("Lifting"
796, 798). Jean-Francois Lyotard is another exception: a postmodernist
skeptical of "the language men" (Lacan, Derrida), he values unassimilable otherness, what he calls "the unharmonizable" (*Inhuman* 4). Some
regard his esteem for difference as a late romantic strain of postmodernism. Germane here is Lyotard's depiction of the "sublime" of avant-
garde art (Barnett Newman) as an insistence on making a painting an
"occurrence" in the "here, now" of its happening, to which the "best
gloss" is a "feeling of 'there' *(Voilà)*" (79, 93, 80). He shares a commitment to singularity or haecceity—a thing's *thisness*—with the Deleuze

of *Francis Bacon: The Logic of Sensation* (quoted earlier), a book whose premise is that "we do not listen closely enough to what painters have to say" (81). So Deleuze bases his book on *The Brutality of Fact*, the painter's remarkable interviews with David Sylvester. Before returning to Lyotard, a brief look at Deleuze's Bacon.

"Presence, presence . . . this is the first word that comes to mind in front of one of Bacon's paintings," says Deleuze (44). Here presence is neither silence nor the immaculate tautology of autonomy—be it the "rose without why" or Valéry's tiger who is "magnificently what he is, just as he is, whatever he is." Instead it is aggressive physicality. Presence is visible on the flesh—of spectator and of the depicted figure—as "sensation," that which, says Bacon, "acts directly upon the nervous system" (rather than first passing through the brain), and becomes the "agent of bodily deformations" while avoiding "the detour and boredom of conveying a story" (32). (Bacon acknowledges that he paraphrases Valéry here). That is, Bacon retains the figure but strips it of figuration—that which provides representation, narration, and illustration. A Bacon portrait often depicts a body in the throes of disintegrative pressure, flesh undergoing violent transmogrifying distortion, while the painter carefully deletes any traces of what might place the sufferer in a familiar narrative context. "I wanted to paint the scream more than the horror," in Bacon's oft-quoted remark about his famous series of screaming Popes (after Velazquez's Pope Innocent X) (qtd. Deleuze 34). Deleuze adds: "The horror is multiplied because it is inferred from the scream, and not the reverse" (34).

Unassimilable to cause or motive, the painting's unleashing of the scream as bodily sensation is a source of "excessive presence" in Bacon's work and reveals, for Deleuze, "the special relation between painting and hysteria." He runs with this last word after finding it in Bacon's description of the sitter for the Popes—he was "very neurotic and almost hysterical" (44). In fact, says Deleuze of a 1955 Pope painting, "the whole painting . . . is hystericized," by which he means it fractures representation by making "presence or insistence . . . interminable": it displays "the insistence of the smile beyond the face and beneath the face. The insistence of a scream that survives the mouth. . . . Everywhere there is a presence acting directly on the nervous system, which makes representation . . . impossible." Painting "is hysteria, or converts hysteria, because it makes presence immediately visible" (44–45).

The body, as both subject and object, gives and receives sensation, is the "unity of the sensing and the sensed." Here Bacon is an heir of Cézanne. By denying himself contours and outline to contain color and without consistent perspective, Cézanne "was abandoning himself to the chaos of sensation," Merleau-Ponty says in "Cézanne's Doubt" (63). He paints the sensation, giving it "unprecedented status" in the experience of viewing a painting. Deleuze adds that "as a spectator I experience the sensation only by entering the painting" and recovering my body, "the unity of the sensing and the sensed" (Deleuze, *Francis Bacon* 31). Whereas Impressionism located sensation in the weightless play of light and color, for Cézanne "it is in the body, even the body of an apple. Color is in the body, sensation is in the body, and not in the air. Sensation is what is painted. What is painted on the canvas is the body, not insofar as it is represented as an object, but insofar as it is experienced as sustaining *this* sensation" (32–33).

Like Bacon, Bridget Riley, quoted earlier, relishes the violence of sensation and describes the release of "wild" sensation when "visual elements are *not* asked to do something which is against their nature— not asked to serve concepts or to represent" (qtd. Shiff, "Sensation" 77). Bacon speaks repeatedly of painting as an effort to record "one's own feelings . . . as closely to one's own nervous system as one possibly can" (qtd. Sylvester, *The Brutality of Fact* 43).

Some art historians are frustrated with both the distancing discourse of postmodern skepticism and the analogous bias of iconology against perception ("there is only representation" since perception "will already have flowed into a system of signification"). In response, some have sought to "rend" the image, release its opacity, confront its visceral charge (Didi-Huberman 100, 143). James Elkins devoted a 1998 book to "pictures and the words that fail them." He starts with the claim that "first and last, pictures are not the narratives of art history"—that is, not "aggregates of signs and symbols"— "they are stubbornly illegible, weirdly silent, 'meaningless' artifacts where all our best attempts at understanding fall apart" (*On Pictures* xii). Elkins is tacitly dissenting from an intellectualism that in effect has made it the art historian's job to tidy up the artist's allegedly naïve trust in the priority of feeling and sensation born of grappling with obdurately palpable materials. "Cézanne as Greenberg describes him, sounds almost scholarly, in fact, a critic with a brush," remarks the literary critic Philip Fisher in his book about the effacing of art in a "culture of museums." The implication is that "the critic might be a more interesting, because more profoundly historical and philosophical, commentator than the artist. . . . Is this a passing, accidental arrogance? I think not" (35).

A museum culture is necessarily a monument to tidying up, of intellectual control, built on suppressions and silencing and the stripping away not only of contextual webs (the crucifix, when seen in a museum, no longer means "genuflect!": now we "just neutrally stand in its presence") but also of "sensory values" and "sensory harmony" that formerly organized the arrangement of artifacts. Tactile experience is forbidden: museums encase most of their holdings in glass. Fisher is not offering an anti-modern lament against institutions or "disenchantment": to reach the "territory of art" *requires* these acts of coerced renunciation, what he calls "violent resocialization," wherein objects, including sacred relics, are "stripped of their worlds and resettled chronologically in the land of art" (19, 10). (Hans Belting makes an analogous argument, mentioned later, in describing the historical emergence of the art collection.) The museum effaces but also converts and preserves the energies of objects, which retain "enigmatic presence," if, inevitably, of a different kind. Observes Fisher: "A highly trained profession of observers and critics now delivers nearly instantaneous anchoring, philosophical defense, grounds of explanation and orientation for new work." The artist no longer needs to produce a manifesto; it has already been supplied by this "climate of saturation" (Fisher 89, 90–91).

Amid this verbosity, wordless "faith" becomes a way out. Silence has long served artists. "Nothing gets closer to muteness than the wisdom of the painter," remarks Roberto Calasso of Edgar Degas, "who abhorred those who claimed to *explain*." He let suffice impenetrable, vaguely vacuous epigrams. "The more we move forward in the history of painting," notes Calasso, "the more we perceive its fundamental hostility to the word" (174, 172). (Yet hostility can generate considerable verbal energy, as the example of Ad Reinhardt will attest.) The aesthetic ideal of mute intensity tends to irritate the critical sensibility, as evident in another, earlier exchange between Buchloh and Richter. At one point the painter mentions Barnett Newman: "He painted some magnificent pictures":

> Buchloh: "So it is said. But magnificent in what way?" Richter: "I can't describe it now, what gets to me in them—I believe they're among the most important paintings of all." Buchloh: "Perhaps that's a mythology that needs re-examination . . . because in the encounter with paintings, acts of faith are not enough." Richter: "Acts of faith are unavoidable. They're part of us." Buchloh: "Do your paintings invite acts of faith, or analyses? Which matters more to you?" Richter: "Either would be fine with me. In your case they invite you to analyse, others find them an invitation to perform acts of faith." Buchloh: "So you would be quite happy if—as Rothko demanded of his own work—someone were to fall on their knees in front of one of your paintings and burst into tears?" Richter: "Unfortunately painting can't produce such an effect. Music is better off in this respect."
> (*Daily Practice* 158–159)

No wonder Valéry, a close friend of Degas, said: "A painter should always imagine he is painting for someone who has no gift of articulate speech" (12:87).

The Richter/Buchloh exchange is an emblematic standoff: "acts of faith"—akin to de Duve's "faith" as willingness to be touched by painting—collide with acts of analysis, as if a Kantian allegory where intuition and concept do battle. Both painter and critic likely know better—that the dichotomy will not suffice—but seem compelled to act out an impasse. (Though in this case Richter turned his frustration with Buchloh into a subject, painting the critic's portrait.)

■

You'll have to see for yourself: this is what an act of faith implies and is the unspoken directive of many acts of modernist renunciation, especially of texts that sabotage their own authority. The phrase echoes more broadly, entering the culture as the all-but-uttered motto of the ritual of non-communication that unfolds whenever we hear writers or artists evade interrogators intent on pinning them down as to what they mean by their work. This standoff is renunciation's public face, its most familiar manifestation of refusal to embody masterful authority, to give answers, to guide us. The Richter/Buchloh impasse stages the "aesthetic idea" colliding with the "workaday world of conceptual determinacy" impatient with subjective experiences where the norm is less than what is "completely intelligible." The confrontation between painter and theorist is another front in the larger campaign—"art at war with culture," to borrow the words of Leo Bersani and Ulysse Dutoit about Beckett, Rothko, and others who practice an "art of impoverishment" (8–9).

A famous episode in the championing of aesthetic autonomy by refusing to explain is the painter J. M. Whistler's 1877 libel trial against the eminent art critic John Ruskin. The latter had accused Whistler of "flinging a pot of paint in the public's face." The painting in question was a near abstract *Nocturne,* in black and gold, that seemed to depict Battersea Bridge by moonlight. In cross-examination the prosecutor asks the painter about another nocturne—in blue and silver:

> "Do you say that this is a correct representation of Battersea Bridge?"
> "I did not intend it to be a 'correct' portrait of the bridge. It is only a moonlight scene. . . . As to what the picture represents, that depends upon who looks at it."
>
> . . .
> "The prevailing color is blue?"
> "Perhaps."
> "And those figures on the top of the bridge intended for people?"
> "They are just what you like." (qtd. Dayan 15–16)

Whistler's coyness about intention and color suggests that in an important sense Ruskin's accusation had been just. "Divesting" his work of any "outside anecdotal interest" to focus on "artistic interest alone," Whistler had indeed directly immersed the viewer in what he called "an arrangement of line, form and color"—hence the accusation of flinging paint in the viewer's face (qtd. Merrill 144). While Ruskin's description was an apt metaphor, painter and critic assigned it different evaluations (Dayan 13). The jury sided with Whistler but awarded him a single farthing.

Laconic or gnomic or perversely inadequate, the non-response of creators releases a quality of anonymity, letting the work rather than maker take the lead, letting the object speak for itself. This was the point of Whistler's friend Mallarmé announcing his own "death." The object speaks to us, paradoxically, on the condition that, like the maker, we too dissolve. A viewer's subjectivity is disarmed when "you [the beholder] become all attention, which means that you become, for the moment, selfless," as Greenberg says of this emptying out (4:81). It is a version of ecstasy. Whistler calls this impersonal, rapt vision looking *at*, not *through* the painting. Its best chance of occurring is when viewers, left on their own, relax into an encounter with the object. They become alive to the paint and see with their own eyes, not taking shelter in intention, reference, meaning, or representation. "All pictures of quality," remarks Greenberg, "ask to be looked at rather than read" (4:55).

The viewer's aesthetic release into anonymity is one thing; self-effacement when performed by an artist in public acquires its own notoriety. Think of the fame that Glenn Gould and Salinger reaped from insisting on reclusiveness. Or of Thomas Pynchon's rigorously maintained public self-erasure—he performed it on *The Simpsons*. A version of this pattern—refusal of celebrity conferring it—has figured in the enthusiastic posthumous reception accorded the gifted Chicago street photographer Vivian Maier. She never exhibited in her lifetime and earned her living as a nanny; after her death her vast archive of work was fortuitously discovered at auction and saved from oblivion. Hence an aura of the enigmatic and eccentric attached to her. One presumption that guides a 2014 documentary on Maier, according to a *New York Times* article, is that "gifted people who don't seek celebrity have something wrong with them: if you don't maximize your celebrity potential, you have a character flaw" (J. Anderson, "Mystery Woman").

A self-invented American Rimbaud would experience his own craving for an exit from the public glare: "truth was I wanted to get out of the rat race" and was in a hurry to leave. Bob Dylan's motorcycle crash in the summer of 1966 ushered in an eight-year hiatus from touring (*Chronicles* 114). He had grown weary of dueling at press conferences with journalists who demanded he explain his surrealist collages of imagery or the politics his folk or protest songs recommended. I am a song and dance man was his typical response. And he mocked efforts to make him representative: "The big bugs in the press kept promoting me as the mouthpiece, spokesman, or even conscience of the generation. That was funny. . . . I had very little in common with and knew even less about a generation that I was supposed to be the voice of. . . . My destiny . . . had nothing to do with representing any kind of civilization" (*Chronicles* 115). Dylan's resistance to being locked into a representative identity and his intractable disengagement communicated his disdain for the literal-minded press corps, and were witty homage to the elite high modernist stance of deliberate inscrutability in the face of public scrutiny. "He's sure got alot of gall / to be so useless and all," his tormentors might have muttered, taking a line from "Visions of Johanna." Dylan's stance is the first popular culture appropriation of this high art move, bringing it into unprecedented public visibility.

His gesture of opacity has a precise genealogy, beginning with Dylan's hero Rimbaud. Before Rimbaud, poetry had to make sense, an imperative of meaning that vanished with his breakthrough to radical linguistic autonomy. Dylan himself resented, he said, the way his "lyrics had been extrapolated, their meanings subverted into polemics" rather than regarded as embedded within "songs that floated in a luminous haze" (120, 116). This last phrase, insisting on respect for the refusal of clarity, merits context: "I really was never any more than what I was—a folk musician who gazed into the gray mist with tear-blinded eyes and made up songs that floated in a luminous haze" (116). Dylan's sentence neatly enacts his slipperiness: what begins with the simple sincerity of a tautology of self-identity turns out to be a feint, suddenly swaddled in hazy and maudlin symbolist imagery—"tear-blinded eyes" and "gray mist."

■

Dylan's song title "I'm Not There" (made famous by Todd Haynes's brilliant Dylan film of that name) suggests the singer's own lability and nods to Rimbaud's "I" as an "other." The phrase "Je est un autre" appears twice in his "Lettres du voyant" of May 1871; the poet proposes to renounce the sovereign subject of authorship, what he calls the "false meaning of the Ego"—the fiction that we are originators (*Complete* 307). A song, for instance, "is so seldom a work, that is to say, a thought sung and understood by the singer. For *I* is someone else. If brass wakes up a trumpet, it is not its fault. This is obvious to me. I am present at this birth of my thought: I watch it and listen to it: I draw a stroke of the bow: the symphony makes its stir in the depths." Earlier he had declared: "I is someone else. It is too bad for the wood which finds itself a violin" (305). Rimbaud recasts the poetic self as both medium and spectator. *"I"* becomes an onlooker witnessing the playing of an instrument—himself—by another. So far as meaning or intention is concerned, the poet is as unknowing as anyone in the audience. Rimbaud thus builds evasion of authority into the ontology of the visionary poet; his only goal, appropriately, is *"the unknown"* (307).

"Lettres du voyant" comprise a kind of manifesto—full of directives and goals for the future, including an Esperanto-like "universal language" (309)—but a manifesto for a party of one. Rimbaud had not a grain of literary entrepreneurship. His *"unknown"* germinated, eventually helping to inspire André Breton's Surrealist Manifesto of 1924, which celebrated language pouring forth uncontrolled. By then a number of modernist movements had been launched with the help of a torrent of hectoring, self-promoting avant-garde manifestoes on behalf of, among others, Dada, Futurism, Suprematism, and Vorticism. If we place on a continuum these aggressively explanatory projects, often to forge artistic and political solidarity, they are at a far end from the individual performances of anonymity sketched above. Somewhere in the middle are explanatory efforts undertaken by master modernists seeking to set the terms of their reception. Late in life Henry James wrote prefaces to the New York Edition of his collected work. Yet rather than usefully identify figures in carpets, the prefaces plunge the reader into an account of literary composition as evolving and shifting formal strategies. More straightforward was James Joyce who helped his friend Stuart Gilbert to publish a handbook on *Ulysses*'s Homeric structure. Seemingly straightforward: Eliot's "Notes" that he appends to *The Waste Land* dutifully supply citations but whether they prompt clarification has never been clear. Mallarmé was a public man of letters in Paris, his name ubiquitous in the press, and a daily morning newspaper, *L'Echo de Paris*, interviewed him in 1891. He used the occasion to clarify his aesthetic strategies—precisely by stressing that "there must be enigma in poetry, and that is the end of literature" (qtd. Candida-Smith 37).

Most of these writers simultaneously explained and evaded. Readers of William Faulkner confronted his own elaborate cat-and-mouse game when he was asked to explain his narrative experiments. Faulkner had perfected the mask of enigma and evasion by the late fifties when questioned at graduate seminars at the University of Virginia (sessions that became canonical when published). Asked about, say, *The Sound and the Fury,* Faulkner would opine: you would have to ask Quentin, referring to his novel's main character. It is tempting to write off a Dylan, a Faulkner's public performance of estrangement before his own creations as a quintessentially American pose that pledges allegiance to our most enduring native tradition: anti-intellectualism. "Sophistication and taste hiding behind clowning and crude manners," says Ralph Ellison, is the "American joke"; it is "Hemingway when he pretends to be a sportsman, or *only* a sportsman . . . Benjamin Franklin when he pretended to be a 'child of nature'" (Ellison and Murray, *Trading* 167, 165).

If we turn anti-intellectualism from the familiar philistine sense to a less familiar one—philosophical anti-intellectualism—we will be more accurate. The deadpan understatement of Dylan and the Southern gentleman misdirection of Faulkner also enact artists' refusal to enthrone themselves as transcendental knowers in sovereign control. Both favored an anonymity that protects art's aura, part of their inheritance from the French symbolist tradition in which each was steeped. Faulkner loved Mallarmé (his first published work was a version of "L'après-midi d'une faune"). Novelist and songwriter preserved mystery by draping their early history in elaborate legends: Faulkner claimed he was a fighter pilot, Dylan a circus performer. Beginning with his assumed name—the reasons for which themselves vary— Dylan has crafted mask upon mask; indeed "his refusal to be known" is a "passion that has shaped his work," as Ellen Willis once wrote (4). He has also refused to be a knower. Such is the way of genius, according to Kant: "Where an author owes a product to his genius, he does not himself know how the ideas for it have entered his head" (137). The genius incarnates the verbal shrug of a Dylan or Faulkner.

John Ashbery might enroll Faulkner and Dylan in his group of "brilliant know-nothings" (along with Emerson, Thoreau, Dickinson, and Stevens, among others) who "at intervals have embodied the

American genius." They, like the painter Fairfield Porter, another "know-nothing" according to Ashbery, dismiss any artist who "treats art," said Porter, as though it were the "raw material for a factory that produces a commodity called understanding" (*Reported* 314–315). Ashbery's own poetry is staked on the same dismissal. When a critic offered a reading of his "Litany," two long poems printed in parallel vertical columns, to be read simultaneously, Ashbery found it intelligent but "arbitrary," a "way to deal with the poetry" by enlarging a small thematic pattern into the figure in the carpet. Yet to produce critical flailing was precisely Ashbery's intention. Expert in French poetry and a translator of Rimbaud, Ashbery describes his effort "to write something so utterly discursive that it would be beyond criticism. . . . This would somehow exemplify the fullness, or, if you would, the emptiness, of life, or, at any rate, its dimensionless quality. And I think any true work of art does defuse criticism; if it left anything important to be said, it wouldn't be doing its job" ("Art of Poetry"). To recall Valéry: "The thing is to see that something 'understood' is something falsified." Ashbery's way of putting his effort to defeat critical appropriation is to say that his poems offer a sort of "environment" and, like our relation to any environment, we do not, and cannot, take notice of every aspect ("Art").

Hiding in plain sight, Ashbery implicitly raises the question: how are we to approach works of art that "hide," to recall Gerhard Richter's word of praise for one of his own paintings. "Hide" suggests Heraclitus's dictum "nature loves to hide." These words, Pierre Hadot tells us, provide "a glimpse of what may be the beginning of reflection on the mystery of reality" (*Veil* 1). How does a reader or that professional reader, the critic, respect mystery, avoid the demystifying posture of the detective in pursuit, accept renunciation of explanation rather than imposing it? Since critics, like any analysts, necessarily traffic in the conceptual, how do they honor works brought into being by hunger for the non-conceptual? Don't even bother, was James McNeil Whistler's tart answer. He sought, in the words of Henry James, "the absolute suppression and extinction of the art critic and his function" (*Views and Reviews* 211). "Let work be received in silence" was Whistler's recommendation: language and painting are simply irreconcilable (*Whistler* 59).

Sontag is of Whistler's party. He would likely have welcomed her given that she inveighs "against interpretation," calling it the "revenge of the intellect upon art" and "upon the world." Interpretation displaces "*the* world" with a "shadow world of 'meanings'" that de-eroticizes art (*Essays*14). Sontag's confessed predecessor is Whistler's rival Oscar Wilde, the source of her essay's second epigraph. In the dialogue "The Critic as Artist" Wilde has one voice declare that the goal of the critic as interpreter is not always to "explain the work of art. He may seek rather to deepen its mystery, to raise round it, and round its maker, that mist of wonder which is dear to both gods and worshippers alike" (372). For all his archness, Wilde discloses a familiar transit: the move that banishes explanation for mystery ends by embracing spiritual reverence.

Theodor Adorno, whom Sontag also admired, urged that we "renounce understanding" in the intellectualist or Enlightenment sense and replace it with immersion in art's "immanent movement" which demands the reader or viewer "recompose" or "repaint" in an act of "co-execution" (*Notes* 2:97). This kind of "follow-through" on the part of the recipient "renounces understanding, which would constitute a non-understanding that did not recognize itself as such" (97). What "intelligibility in art actually means . . . deviates in essential respects from interpretive understanding as the rational grasping of something in some sense intended. One does not understand a work . . . the way one understands concepts, judgments, and conclusions" (96). Here distilled, if implicitly, is the lesson of Kant's "aesthetic idea."

The "harsh light of the incomprehensible" cast by modernist works exposes as "shallow" a reader's habits of "customary comprehensibility" (*Notes* 1:243, 2:95). What differentiates customary understanding from a richer engagement with modernism's strangeness? The question reminds us that "understanding is in want of understanding," as Werner Hamacher notes, elaborating on Adorno's thinking. By its very nature, understanding "stands off from itself" at a distance "because it refers to something uncomprehended. Otherwise it would not be understanding at all: it would be knowledge" (1–2). Understanding's

difference from itself is an aporia that precedes and propels philosophy. Philosophy begins from wonder and astonishment—"an impasse,
something incomprehensible" that arouses the desire to comprehend
(5–6). We impose understanding, but at a price, "by turning away from
that which, as incomprehensible, first demands comprehension. . . . It
is thus understood at the cost of not understanding the very excitation
to which the further course of understanding owes its impetus. . . . If
understanding understands itself, it has already forgotten the devastation, the astonishment, the wonder" that sparked it in the first place
(9–10). Thus something is "understood" in every case only because
it is not "understood" (10). Awareness of this paradox defines "free"
understanding ("only an understanding that was free of understanding
would be a *free* understanding") as a turning toward "muteness," in
effect a dwelling with the originary, inciting astonishment (21, 35). To
be immersed in the incomprehensible rather than anxiously to impose
the "self-securing of cognitive reason" is to live the temporal experience of change and alteration, possibilities of something new and "non-
anticipated," something "still incomprehensible" (5). This exposed
("free') understanding submits to time. In his essay's concluding words,
Hamacher notes Celan's remark that "poetry no longer imposes, it exposes itself," adding "and so too, does understanding. It ex-poses itself," that is, it abandons *pos*iting and im*pos*ing and *pos*itions (43).

Ex-posed understanding withdraws from its very identity to face the
unanticipated: this suppleness is what modernist difficulty demands
of readers as they grapple with the "crisis in intelligibility" (Adorno).
Not confined to modernism, the crisis is neither socially imposed nor
a symptom of art's "fate in society," but rather an "internal necessity,"
says Adorno, rooted in the "double nature of language"—its primary
function of communication (sign) and its capacity to express. The error is to ignore one for the other. Dadaism, for instance, risks killing
art by forsaking sign for expression. Dadaists deliberately dispensed
with language's "significative moment, with concepts and meanings," since their "aim was not art but its assassination." Meanwhile,
"the Expressionists . . . tried to jump over their own shadows. They

championed the primacy of expression without regard for other considerations." Adorno throws some useful cold water on the dream of word liberated from world, painting from resemblance: "Perhaps no optical configuration can be imagined that would not remain tied to the world of objects through some resemblance to it, however distant" (*Notes* 2:98).

Seeming to acknowledging this, Pollock filled a two-hundred-and-seven-inch-wide canvas with black, brown, and white splattering and entitled the thing *Autumn Rhythm*. Its world of somber, exhilarating, cascading swirls of motion summons the titular frame of reference. "Analogously, everything linguistic, even in its most extreme reduction to expressive values, bears the trace of the conceptual. . . . Even a stammered sound, if it is a word and not a mere tone, retains its conceptual range" (99). As always for Adorno the best works abide in antinomic friction, in tension "with what is heterogeneous to it": "Literature gropes its way toward making peace with the conceptual moment without expressionistic quixoticness, but also without surrendering to that moment" (99). Failure to perform this double move results in "vulgar aesthetic irrationalism" where "feeling is to be everything" and artistic experience "turns into a bad, passive irrationality of consumption": instead of "co-execution" there is a "mere babbling along with the stream of language. . . . The passivity of that mode of response is mistaken for a praiseworthy immediacy" (97). He has in mind John Cage's intentionless art of chance that seeks to merge with life.

Heidegger, Adorno's despised rival, flirts with passivity, albeit not of the vulgar variety. He is not interested in having the reader recompose the text or maintaining antinomies; such acts smack of a willfulness that fails to respect poetry's resistance to paraphrase, its self-sufficiency. Hence, says a commentator, Heidegger adheres to the "hermeneutic ideal of a perfect transparency of commentary with regard to the plenitude of the work" (Schaeffer 260). "For the sake of what happens as a poem," writes Heidegger, "the interpretation must seek to make itself superfluous. The final but also the most difficult step in all interpretation consists in the latter's disappearance along with all its explanations before the pure presence of the poem" (qtd. Schaeffer 260). The "critical mimeticism" Heidegger implies between critic and poem is the opposite of Adorno's participatory sort, for the former's relies on willed passivity: one must let the poem speak by coming to hear what is unspoken in it (265). The hushed mood of suspended will starkly contrasts with another route to presence: the violence of Bacon's "hysteria" that Deleuze evokes.

In his reverence for "the pure presence of the poem," Heidegger implicitly revives a central tenet of German romanticism: "The difference between prose and poetry," said Friedrich Schlegel, "resides in the fact that poetry seeks to present, whereas prose seeks only to communicate. . . . It is the indeterminate that is presented so that each presentation is something infinite; inversely only what is determinate can be communicated. The sciences as a whole seek not the indeterminate but the determinate" (qtd. Schaeffer 314). Poe, a reader of Schlegel, would endorse this distinction. While prose's primary task is direct transmission of Meaning, says Poe, poetry presents the sheer musicality of language as acoustical event, beliefs that will also become basic to Valéry's thinking.

Only the poet, says Schlegel, has access to the absolute unity of pure presence, which overcomes the subject/object dualism that structures re-presentation. "If the poet can present the One and All, it is because he himself has already attained it, in the sense that he is outside his empirical ego (that is, of the subject to which an object is opposed)." Novalis calls this the "exit from ourselves" (anticipating Rimbaud's equally dispossessed self) that is also an entrance into "the depth of ourselves," an "essential interiority" where we are at one with the universe (85, 80). These dialectical gymnastics constitute the experience of ecstatic knowledge exclusive to Art; they are born from the blunt binary of Schlegel's statement. His dualism suggests other pairs: concept versus intuition, understanding versus imagination, each opposition inherited from Kant; Schlegel also nods to his "aesthetic idea" (the infinite indeterminacy of presentation). The stature Schlegel accords presentation anticipates the French symbolists but also looks far ahead—to that hoary creative writing motto, "show, don't tell." But we will defer this to 1939, when J. D. Salinger takes a writing class.

When Schlegel endows the poet, poetry, and presentation with a superiority to prose, science, and communication, he creates a hierarchy that would help define the "Western art world's aesthetic horizon of expectations" for over two centuries (12). For better and for worse, most of the figures in my pages subscribe to this elevation of Art. But this puts it too intellectually; more precisely, they, like most lovers of literature and art, internalize the logic (probably at an early age) even as over the years, like Sontag or Adorno, they revise its tenets. Art's stature is affirmed by a celebratory and compensatory discourse (Schaeffer names it the "speculative theory" and offers a critique in *Art of the Modern Age*) that regards the aesthetic as a path to recover an authentic, organic life that might redeem degraded profane capitalist modernity (61). Seeking to reverse the secularizing thrust of the Enlightenment, this idealization functions as a conservative force that makes Art a religion; the belief that Art transcends the mundane and occupies an exclusive domain reserved for itself implies "that beyond our world there exists another, truer world. . . . That is indeed what the theological ontology of romanticism asserts. It is therefore impossible to accede to Art without placing oneself within this theological worldview" (9, 92). Not coincidentally Novalis worshipped the medieval Church and yearned for the restoration of a supreme papacy; Schlegel converted to a militant Catholicism (68, 96).

Unlike Europe, the United States has never possessed a recognized philosophical lineage to secure the exalted status of Art. Hardly surprising given that our Puritan origins encouraged suspicion of art and the few serious American artists were either trained in Europe or took its traditions as a model. Aesthetic thought here was left to be improvised by such mavericks as Poe, Emerson, Thoreau, and Whitman and, before them, the powerful aesthetic implications of Jonathan Edwards's theological works. By the last quarter of the nineteenth century Harvard had become the institutional home of late-Victorian aesthetic idealism embodied (embalmed?) in the anti-democratic genteel tradition. Leading figures included the cosmopolitan Brahmin-aesthete

Charles Eliot Norton, who promulgated his close friend John Ruskin's ideals of the inseparability of the beautiful and moral. Artworks are to edify rather than ornament (Ruskin's terms), to be judged by the "clearness and justice of the ideas they contained and conveyed" by the maker's intention (Ruskin, qtd. Merrill 291). By 1911 Santayana had anatomized the genteel tradition—arguing that it grew from the clash of Calvinist ("agonized conscience") and transcendental (solipsist) impulses—and laid it to rest. Though its ghost lingered for decades as tweedy gentlemen, WASP aristocrats of culture strode English department halls. Art (and the aesthetic) in America has never really shed the fact (or fantasy) of its class and racial bias.

An epochal challenge came as early as 1903 when a dapper black man with a Harvard doctorate, a student of James and Santayana, invoked a "kingdom of culture" open to all as a model of (and step toward) racial equality. To democratize the traditional patrician sanctuary was one aim of Du Bois's *The Souls of Black Folk*. In the early 1890s, Du Bois had received his aesthetic education firsthand in the great museums of Europe where for the first time he enjoyed "unhurried thought and slow contemplation." Before he had been impatient: "I wanted a world, hard, smooth and swift. . . . Now at times I sat still. . . . I looked long at the colors of Rembrandt and Titian. . . . Form, color, and words took new combinations and meanings" (*Writings* 587). In the leisure granted by a traveling fellowship, Du Bois cultivated a relaxed absorption in sensuous surface and appearance, feeling no obligation to leave the enchantment of form and color in search of subject matter or moral message.

Du Bois dramatized his aesthetic awakening in the figure of John Jones, the protagonist of his short story '"The Coming of John," the penultimate chapter in *The Souls of Black Folk*. By its end Du Bois splices together renunciation and aesthetic experience: the last scene features Jones, after killing a white man who was trying to molest his sister, abandoning any effort to save his own life as a lynch mob swoops down upon him. Instead, he stands musing about the overture to *Lohengrin* he had once heard in New York. "And the world whistled in his ear" is the tale's final sentence, as aural memory transforms the incipient violence of external reality into pure sound—a whistling. Is the final tableau a perverse tribute to the power of art, or a warning of the calamity that awaits the black intellectual seeking aesthetic bliss? Jones is as wrapped in enigma as his opposite number and fellow renunciator of 1903, Lambert Strether in *The Ambassadors.*

Like Du Bois in Europe, New Critics were committed to slowing down the hurried pace of modern life, the better to perform careful close reading. Many of them had been raised in small Southern towns, and their wariness of modernity included a strong anti-capitalist tilt, but Agrarian rather than Marxist. Though its theorists tended to be racially unenlightened, New Criticism of the 1940s and 50s proved a democratizing pedagogical movement and one more intellectually robust than the genteel tradition. Making the emblematic high modernist move, New Criticism emphasized poetry rather than prose fiction and aesthetic autonomy rather than art as moral statement. The public shrug of a Faulkner embodied that renunciatory autonomy—the creator of the work effaces himself in the act of offering the artifact to the public. New Criticism was at one with Valéry's emphasis that "once published, a text is like an apparatus that anyone may use," the author having no unique authority. This removal of authorial control inevitably made meaning the reader's responsibility. There was no better place than the classroom to fulfill it. Immersion in the verbal life of the poem—not its history, not its reception—became the new basis of literary pedagogy. This scene of instruction grounded New Criticism's decisive success in the academy.

By taking the focus off the author, New Criticism's "intentional fallacy" was designed to discourage reducing literature to a moral message. Which is to say New Critics would have sided with Whistler. Message, not medium, is a Ruskinian priority, one that Whistler in his 1885 lecture "Ten O'Clock" lamented for encouraging "the habit of looking . . . not *at* a picture, but *through* it, at some human fact that shall or shall not, from a social point of view, better their mental or moral state" (*Whistler* 81). Whistler, as we have seen, scorned art critics for looking "through" and treating paintings as novels with plots to be followed. New Critics rejected sociological or historical approaches for ignoring the primacy of the literary medium. Linking painter and critics was Whistler's friend Mallarmé, who translated "Ten O'Clock" into French and whose authorial self-erasure informed New Criticism via his antecedent influence on Eliot's doctrine of "impersonality."

Staying "at" the surface, New Criticism gave to literature, especially lyric poetry, the unique task, in the words of the movement's architect, John Crowe Ransom, "to present things in their thinginess" and to "contemplate things as they are in their rich and contingent materiality." The image is the bearer of this density for "it cannot be dispossessed of a primordial freshness, which idea can never claim. An idea is derivative and tamed." "Presenting images so whole and clean that they resist the catalysis of thought," the art of poetry "is pure exhibit; it is to be contemplated; perhaps it is to be enjoyed." Against this commitment to the particularity of the "world's body," New Critics set the universalizing abstractions of science (Ransom, *The World's Body* 116, 115, 113, 116, 118). Implicit (sometimes explicit) in this aesthetic stance, many of whose proponents were men of faith, was a poetics of incarnation antithetical to secular modernity's reliance on the exchange principle, which enthrones the fungible and the prepackaged, the already known.

New Critics contest secular disenchantment by combating this "societal abstraction with artistic abstraction"; the latter, in the form of the autonomous poetic artifact, abstracts from—negates—"known conceptualities." The poem becomes the domain of the sensuous, material particular by obstructing the reader's effort to contain it under a concept (Bernstein *Against* 151, 62, 63). New Critics made paraphrase a "heresy." Hence, modern poetry's notorious difficulty, which is also "a condition of its authenticity." This reversal of abstraction from rationalist tool to locus or preserve of "meaningfulness without meaning" (59) orients both New Criticism and a slightly later and more urban movement—Abstract Expressionism.

Indeed Ransom adumbrates a general link; in 1941 he observes that the "abstractionist paintings of many schools . . . have tried to abandon direct representational intention almost as heroically as music. They exist in their own materials." For Ransom, "any poetry which is 'technically' notable is in part a work of abstractionist art"—existing in its own "material textures" and structure. He locates the "value" of poetry and "abstractionist painting," their "will and intelligence," in the "act" of "structure or composition itself" ("Criticism" 651). New Critical formalism, in other words, coexists with a commitment to a poem as an action in itself rather than a statement about action. "A poem does not say something—it *is* something," Eliot reminds us in 1948, finding it a view characteristic of recent times ("From Poe" 634). It is suggested as well by Cleanth Brooks in *The Well Wrought Urn* (204).

At least one Abstract Expressionist dissolves the distinction between a painting saying something and one that "*is* something." Mark Rothko declared: "My art is not abstract; it lives and breathes" (qtd. Breslin 276). In doing so it communicates. "I'm interested only in expressing basic human emotions." If a viewer "is moved only by" the "color relationships" on my canvas, "then you miss the point!" (qtd. Elderfield 101). Rejecting formalism—I am "*not* an abstractionist"—he remained an expressionist. By eliciting a flood of feeling he disrupted the spectator's reflex effort to convert images into ideas: "The people who weep before my pictures are having the same religious experience I had when I painted them" (qtd. Elderfield 101). The layered, uneven density of Rothko's horizontal bands of color creates the much remarked on quivering or pulsating quality of his brooding art of "presence." This last word is Rothko's for the haunting, lingering quality he wanted his paintings to radiate: "a presence so when you turn your back to the painting, you would feel that presence the way you feel the sun on your back" (qtd. Breslin 275). His admirer, Agnes Martin, would concur. Unlike the force of sensations provoked by Bacon's assaultive imagery, Rothko's felt presence, like Martin's, is less palpable—his enveloping imagery leads an afterlife in remembered sensation, in the silence of memory. Regarding language as irrelevant and obtrusive where art was concerned, Rothko calls to mind T. J. Clark's recent remark that "the distance of visual imagery from verbal discourse is the most precious thing about it. It represents one possibility of resistance in a world saturated by slogans, labels, sales pitches" (*Sight* 122–123). As Rothko's biographer remarks: "Any kind of writing about his work—by critics, by curators, or even by Rothko himself—fixes the artist" in what the painter called "premature entombment" (Breslin 276). He wanted to manage his own burial, which he hastened by suicide in 1970.

Rothko's sometime friend Barnett Newman had no bias toward reticence. Indeed he came to his mature style through first writing theoretical essays. Sharing Rothko's unease with received, dogmatic notions of formalism and abstraction, Newman articulated with passionate precision an aesthetic in the renunciatory American grain of Emerson and James. Though without referencing his predecessors, Newman, like James, a self-described anarchist, was steeped in the New England intellectual tradition. He visited Walden Pond with his wife on their honeymoon. As a philosophy major at City College, Newman admired the legendary Morris Raphael Cohen, who studied with James at Harvard. Newman regarded his own art as "embodiments of feeling, to be experienced." He spoke of political/existential implications—his work asserted "freedom" and repudiated "all dogmatic life," including "state capitalism and totalitarianism"—as well as spiritual, transcendent ones, though "without working from a set of a priori mystical precepts" (Newman 251, 162). This last remark was crucial. Just as carefully as William James emphasizes the phenomenological moment—reminding us that "intellectual operations" are "interpretative," occurring "after the fact" of "immediate experiences"— Newman too banished the a priori. He tells an interviewer he is "an intuitive painter, a direct painter" who doesn't work from sketches or plans, has "never 'thought out' a painting" (James 2: 389; Newman 248). Unlike European modernists, who lead us "into their spiritual world through already known images," American artists, Newman argued in 1947, do "without the props of any known shape": "they start with the chaos of pure fantasy and feeling . . . and they bring out of this chaos of emotion images that give these intangibles reality" (164, 163). The aim is to make contact with mystery (108).

Rosenberg emphasized existential and spiritual meanings and he called Abstract Expressionism "essentially a religious movement" (193). Whereas Greenberg found talk of the mystical "archaic" and "half-baked" but granted that if it stimulated "serious painting" it should be "left aside" (2:188–189). Both admired Newman. Although Rosenberg links the "religious" with "Whitman's mysticism" ("he wanted the ineffable in *all* behavior—he wanted it *to win the streets*") (195), Emerson seems more germane, for he makes the impatient American demand for "a religion by revelation to us, and not the history of theirs," as he says at the start of "Nature." In short, religion becomes a gateway to the immediate, founded on refusal to "grope among the dry bones of the past" (*Essays* 7). This renunciatory belligerence, the motor of American romantic individualism, is echoed in Newman's commitment to "Now," to a new beginning, that propels his strikingly Emersonian essay "The Sublime Is Now" (1948). The aftermath of Hiroshima has left us with a "new sense of fate," one severed from Greek ideals of beauty and refinement, one that demands we confront the world with a "sublime . . . sense of being aware" in the here and now (169, 167, 258). This awareness requires, Newman wrote, emancipation from "the impediments of memory, association, nostalgia, legend, myth," which "have been the devices of western European painting." To renounce them clears a path for "revelation, real and concrete," inspired not by "making *cathedrals* out of Christ" but simply by "our own feelings" (Newman 173). He was inspired by those as if outside history—the Kwakiutl artists of the Pacific Northwest, specifically by how they regarded shape: "Rather than a formal 'abstraction' of a visual fact, with its overtone of an already-known nature," shape, for the Kwakiutl artist, was "a living thing, a vehicle for an abstract-thought complex, a carrier of the awesome feelings he felt before the terror of the unknowable" (108). The emotion of terror becomes a universal linking primitive and modern man, though only the latter has seen it embodied in mass destruction.

A year after stating his felt affinity with the "primitive art impulse," a quintessential modernist move, Newman in 1948 made his breakthrough painting. *Onement I* depicts a single narrow vertical stripe—of intense reddish orange, heavily impastoed—that bisects in half a (comparatively) smooth and even painted field of Indian red. Abandoning such traditional European pictorial conventions as figure ground relations or a background setting off a foreground, Newman sets the vertical single band (or "zip" as he called it, made with a strip of masking tape) on top of the painting surface. Eliminated is depth and reference: no "already-known nature," no anthropomorphism, distract from an "openness" that is one's stark confrontation with the dark field and ragged zip, the latter betraying the uneven motions of the painter's palette knife. Just as the painter was there, "the onlooker in front of my painting knows that he's there" and this shared "sense of being aware" is also a "sense of place"—a being there that is both a sublime "mystery" and a "metaphysical fact" (257). Up until making *Onement I*, Newman would later say, "I was able to remove myself from the act of painting, or from the painting itself," but now the "painting itself had a life of its own" (256). At-one-ment. Atonement.

In "The Sublime Is Now" Newman says that the "real and concrete" image of revelation his paintings produce "can be understood by anyone who will look at it without the nostalgic glasses of history." Accepting Newman's offer, Lyotard took off the glasses. Dissenting from the postmodern fetish of the textual and the mediated, Lyotard was inspired by Newman's essay to grasp avant-garde painting as a willingness to bear witness to the "indeterminate," yet not in the traditional Kantian sense of the boundless sublime but as rooted in the *here and now.*

Recalling a surmise originally made by the painter's friend Thomas Hess, Lyotard (in a 1984 essay "The Sublime and the Avant-Garde") links Newman's "now" to the Hebraic tradition of the Unnameable Lord—the *there,* the *site,* the *place* are some of His approximations. Though none of us "know enough about *Now,*" Newman's *now,* for Lyotard, is simply "that something happens," "just an occurrence"— not a *"what* happens or *what* this might mean"—but a mute but moving presence, a *"something there,"* as James calls the "reality of the unseen" in mystical experience (*Writings* 2:59). This happening is a blind spot in consciousness, what it "cannot formulate." "That which we call thought must be disarmed," says Lyotard, the more intensely to dwell with the "it happens" which in pictorial art is the paint and the canvas; "here and now it happens that . . . there is this painting, rather than nothing, and that's what is sublime. Letting go of all grasping intelligence and of its power, disarming it, recognizing that this occurrence of painting was not necessary and is scarcely foreseeable . . . guarding the occurrence 'before' any defense, any illustration, and any commentary, guarding before being on one's guard, before 'looking' under the aegis of *now,* this is the rigor of the avant-garde" (*The Inhuman* 90, 93). This rigor is also, for Lyotard, the rigor of "presentation"— what is "implied and forgotten in representation" (111). Like Merleau-Ponty, who spoke in "Cézanne's Doubt" of the artist "not knowing whether" one's work "will be anything more than a shout," Lyotard strikes a note of anxious wonder (a sublime affect) at the fragility of art having come into being at all. What happened could just as well not have happened: surprise defines the event as a perpetual possibility rather than a fact.

■

The renunciatory imperative implied in Newman's 1948 phrase "the sublime is now" points ahead to Sontag in the sixties. She shares something of his Emersonian impatience, including an urge to renounce reigning pieties, which for her include mimetic representation and extractable Meaning. She becomes the most influential American celebrant of immediacy, what she calls "transparence." With impeccable Emersonian logic, Sontag launches her project by dismissing reigning authority, which she finds embodied in—Emerson! He is, she alleges, one of the cultural critics of nostalgic anti-modernist lament whose retirement is urgent. These "literary men" (she names Emerson, Thoreau, and Ruskin), having "abhorred and deplored" the alienation inflicted by science and technology, "are inevitably on the defensive. They know that the scientific culture, the coming of the machine, cannot be stopped" (*Essays* 276). To clear the ground here, Sontag has blatantly reduced Emerson to an anxious Luddite (in fact he was fascinated by and knowledgeable about natural history). The (alleged) "defensive" stance of Emerson et al. is not only regressive but assumes that science is changing while literature stands still, "fulfilling some perennial generic human function" such as "consolation." But avant-garde art, Sontag argues, has "developed" and is now as experimental and as "abstruse" as science, open, like science, only to those who can understand "a specialized language" (276).

This forced convergence of art and science (here made synonymous with innovation and freedom from the past) not only confirms Sontag's sense of the emptiness of the "two cultures" debate then raging, but, more important, announces the advent of a "new (potentially unitary) kind of sensibility" "rooted" in "new" experiences in "the history of humanity" (277). Especially liberating is that this anti-sentimental "new sensibility" is a "non-literary culture" comprised of philosophers and painters but also "social planners," "neurologists, electronics engineers" (and a few poets), none of whom have any special allegiance to the traditional centrality of literature, "above all, the novel," as the "model" art form (279).

Although her essays of the 1960s mention Pollock, Reinhardt, and Rothko only in passing (28, 40, 276), Sontag might have been sympathetic, even to Rothko's ambition to move spectators to tears as they feel the precarious presence of *Now*. She admired Kaprow's "Happenings," their "freedom from time" since "always in the present tense" (250–251). Sontag stresses the precarity of "now" as reflecting the perennial paradox of the artist's spirit "seeking embodiment in art." The struggle between art's materiality, especially "the treachery of words," and the creator's bid for transcendence is irresolvable given that "the artist's activity" is "cursed with mediacy." Hence art "becomes the enemy of the artist" and "every age has to reinvent the project of 'spirituality' for itself" (292). In the modern era art is a key "metaphor" for this project. So begins "The Aesthetics of Silence," the opening essay of *Styles of Radical Will* (1967). By this date Sontag had already established herself as the principle importer to the US of avant-garde European aesthetic thought and perhaps at last the person to provide art in America with something of the philosophical enfranchisement it had long enjoyed in Europe. With a graduate degree in philosophy, an instructorship in religion in 1960 at Columbia, creator and critic of literature and film, possessed of a freelancer's insouciance about scholarly detail and documentation, she met the demands of the moment.

Sontag's account of the "new sensibility" sketched above as a rapprochement of the arts and sciences has striking parallels with Greenberg's famous essays of 1939–1940 that chart the birth of European modernism, "Avant-Garde and Kitsch" and "Towards a Newer Laocoon." "The birth of the avant-garde coincided chronologically," says Greenberg, "with the first bold development of scientific revolutionary thought in Europe"; and music would dethrone literature as the "paragon art" (1:7, 25, 31). Whether by reading Greenberg or not, Sontag had come to grasp that postwar American high culture was in some ways repeating with a difference the emergence of aesthetic formalism and impersonality in France, Germany, and England of the last quarter of the nineteenth century. Accordingly,

she looked to figures of that epoch (and its descendants, particularly Barthes) to help her create a mode of criticism answerable to the
"new sensibility."

Concluding her 1963 manifesto-like "Against Interpretation" with
a march of portentous monosyllables, Sontag declares: "The function of
criticism should be to show *how it is what it is*, even *that it is what it
is*, rather than to show *what it means*" (*Essays* 20). In other words, another demand of the moment was to renounce Meaning, as she import-
ed to Puritan America—uneasy with art unless freighted with moral
purpose—Valéry's symbolist aesthetic of presence. To this she added a
bit of the *épater le bourgeois* glee of Wilde's fin-de-siècle aestheticism,
dedicating to him her "Notes on 'Camp'" (1964). The essay reveals the
legacy of his sensibility in the then closeted region of "camp," a world
of gay taste and wit largely ignored by New York intellectuals. "Notes
on 'Camp'" was her debut in *Partisan Review*; its longest piece that issue was a symposium on Barry Goldwater's candidacy.

For some, Sontag's embrace of reverential tautology and disdain
for content and meaning announced an indifference to logic that was
less exciting than merely incoherent. To declare "the work already
is just what it is" is to beg the question "because 'just what it is' has
not been established yet. . . . The work already is just what it is (how
could it be anything else?)" remarked the art critic Thomas McEvilley.
Her formalism, he argued, relies "on a kind of pre-logical incantation
masquerading as reason." "Perhaps a stone can be without meaning"
but cultural objects exist "in a web of intentions and meanings" (*Art
and Discontent* 38, 41). True enough, but Sontag's tautologies could be
said deliberately to refuse articulateness as a response; this is her way
to imply "the poverty of those systems through which such a response
might be formed—primarily language, but also processes of logical
thought according to which we parse, analyze, literally come to terms
with experience." Craig Owens wrote this of the analogous refusal
performed by a work Sontag loved, *Einstein on the Beach* (7). Robert
Wilson's 1976 experimental opera with music by Philip Glass bathes
the spectator in mobile images linked to musical and verbal repetition, as one relaxes into the rhythms of dispersed attention or improvises coherence by intuitively sensing motifs and echoes. In her essays
Sontag achieves something of this presentational immediacy: bursts of

aphoristic insight in short paragraphs that do not linger for analysis or argument; once the surgical observation is made, she moves on.

Without explicitly making art a religion, Sontag emphasized the avant-garde's demands, at once austere and hedonic. "So far as the best art defines itself by essentially 'priestly' aims," she writes, "it presupposes . . . a never fully initiated, voyeuristic laity," an audience that is ultimately "sent away." Such distance is entailed by the defining desire of the avant-garde—"to be *unacceptable* to its audience" (*Essays* 296, 295). Thus a paradox, one she kept tacit, defines Sontag's effort to enlarge the audience to be initiated into pure art. She reveled in works born of the deliberate collapsing of language and sound into expressive silence, of depth and meaning into sensuous surface. As opposed to "discursive or scientific knowledge," works of art "give rise not to conceptual knowledge . . . but to something like an excitation . . . judgment in a state of thralldom or captivation" (27). Here departing from her effort to reconcile the two cultures, Sontag revives the romantic elevation of Art as approximate to revelation, or to an "erotics" of revelation, to use her word for what interpretation should celebrate.

While retaining Greenberg's formalism and his fondness for French symbolist autonomy, Sontag enlarged his range, widening what counted as American cultural sophistication to include science fiction films, conceptual art, and homosexual sensibility. Like her favorite film critic, Manny Farber, opening the hushed sanctuary of high culture to the pleasures of "termite art," his phrase referring to the eager, unkempt artistic vitality of American genre films, Sontag replaced the bland moralistic American diet with a taste for "scathing originality." She also had a fondness for self-sacrificing "culture-heroes"—Kierkegaard and Nietzsche but also Cesare Pavese and Simone Weil, Jean Genet and Heinrich von Kleist. Of Weil's "fanatical asceticism," Sontag admits: "No one who loves life would wish to imitate her dedication to martyrdom. . . . Yet so far as we love seriousness, as well as life, we are moved by it, nourished by it. In the respect we pay such lives, we acknowledge the presence of mystery in the world—and mystery is just what the secure possession of the truth, an objective truth, denies" (54). Lionel Trilling in 1951, celebrating John Keats as a "hero" and praising his idea of "negative capability," was basically making the same epistemological point while affirming the tragic sense of life.

Sontag raised the stakes: she turned respect for renunciation as "the presence of mystery" into the first step on the path to a higher consciousness founded on aesthetic rapture.

Part 2

"THE AESTHETICS OF Silence" invokes such culture heroes as Rimbaud, Wittgenstein, and Duchamp for their "exemplary renunciations of a vocation," but is silent about Salinger. Wholly understandable, since by 1967 Salinger had ceased publishing only two years before. Yet Sontag might as well be describing him when she says by silence the artist "frees himself from servile bondage to the world, which appears as patron, client, audience, antagonist, arbiter, and distorter of his work" (*Essays* 293). Directly pertinent to Salinger as well is her invoking of negative theology—Zen, Tao, and Eckhart are among her examples—which has "always recognized, in Norman O. Brown's phrase, 'the neurotic character of language'" (308). Regardless of the clear connections, and even if Salinger had become a renunciant long before "The Aesthetics of Silence," Sontag still would not have been interested; she wouldn't get past his chatty domestic realism depicting a middle-class world. The senior Glasses were an (unironic) vaudeville team, for crying out loud.

She was hardly alone. Not taking Salinger seriously as an artist defines his critical reputation. Which is most remarkable for its non-existence. Granted—he achieved global fame with *The Catcher in the Rye*, which has sold far more copies (65 million) than any other literary American novel. All his books continue to sell, but America's most notorious renunciant remains invisible in the academy. Casebooks on *Catcher* proliferate but his later fiction draws almost no attention. Reviews were largely hostile or reductive and gave later critics an excuse to stay away. Salinger's rare combination of genuine literary gifts and a vast audience has always seemed to chafe the critics and provoke "envy" among his peers, (as Norman Mailer admitted in the late fifties), provoking an irresistible impulse to deflate this object of worship—"everyone's favorite" (467–468). Salinger's decision to end his publishing career in 1965, after issuing just five long short stories in the years since *Catcher* (1951) and *Nine*

Stories (1953), deepened a general sense of disappointment. Three are preoccupied, via his alter ego, Buddy Glass, with grieving and pondering the meanings of Seymour's shattering suicide. The final one, "Hapworth 16, 1924," dispenses with Buddy as narrator to present Seymour speaking for himself.

Salinger can partly be blamed for the critical retaliation against his post-*Catcher* work, given the frequent rants of his fictional Glass clan against the New York literary establishment and the English professoriate. By the early sixties the die was cast: here is Irving Howe in 1963 laying down the literary law: "Among contemporary novelists, Saul Bellow commands literary influence, Norman Mailer an intellectual following, and James Baldwin an intense audience. Only J. D. Salinger can be described as the priest of an underground cult" (4). Mary McCarthy had already finished him off with a similar verdict in 1962. Whether "closed circuit" of narcissism (McCarthy) or "cult," the point was to mark off a fanatical readership of "well-scrubbed," apolitical rich kids, too self-involved to rebel or conquer, merely "bright, 'cool,' estranged" (Howe). The alleged key to Salinger's success is that the Glass family, a hothouse of scornful brainy underachievers, offers a flattering mirror to his audience. Howe's judgment, shared by many, has never really been disputed (with the notable exception of Janet Malcolm, whose "Justice to J. D. Salinger" fulfills its title and definitively assesses the critical animosity). One hesitates to call Howe's an aesthetic judgment since it centers on the sociology of literary reputation. That sociology is indeed important but hardly synonymous with Salinger's literary accomplishment.

Regarding the precise ground of Salinger's fame the *New York Times* is instructive. "J. D. Salinger, Literary Recluse, Dies at 91" ran its headline of January 29, 2010. Ignoring what made him celebrated in the first place, the obituary's opening paragraph makes reclusiveness, not authorship, the keynote: Salinger "turned his back on success and adulation, becoming the Garbo of letters, famous for not wanting to be famous." Only in the third paragraph are his books mentioned. The reordering of priorities implies that Salinger's self-fashioning as a "literary recluse" counts as his major achievement. This is well put by the obituary writer: he "turned silence itself into his most eloquent work of art" (McGrath).

The silence of renunciation is where life and art intersect for Salinger: the same year—1953—that he frames *Nine Stories* with the deaths of Seymour in "A Perfect Day for Bananafish" and of Teddy in the story of that name, he initiates his public withdrawal, as he moves from New York to tiny Cornish, New Hampshire. Once he bolted New York, attention shifted gradually but decisively from the renunciations his alienated characters perform to his own secluded and increasingly misanthropic life. Appetite for information and gossip about it has never been lacking, fed by books from neglected children, spurned lovers, stymied biographers, including a relentlessly snide and censorious oral biography in 2013. Scandalously disregarded in this noisy ongoing cultural melodrama of grievance is his post-*Catcher* fiction.

With the final work, *Seymour: An Introduction* (1963), now a half century old the time seems promising for a rereading of his later work that recognizes Salinger as a novelist of ideas who enacts them in risky experimental forms, ambitions largely erased by the defensive reflex condescension that his cultural presence once aroused. Any re-engagement should try to take Salinger on his own demandingly digressive terms: digressive because Salinger works from inside his characters' eccentricities and spiritual beliefs. What they share is a refusal of "compactness"—an aesthetic built on the assumed value of shapeliness, hierarchy, and narrative momentum. The refusal manifests itself as what Seymour, a master of haiku, calls "indiscrimination" which he will "champion" "til doomsday on the ground that it leads to health and a kind of very real, enviable happiness. *Followed purely*, it's the way of the Tao" (*Raise* 74). Yet, he adds, "for a discriminating man to achieve this, it would mean that he would have to dispossess himself of poetry, go *beyond* poetry." In other words, spiritual enlightenment asks us to dispense with a literary form built on compression; the haiku form requires that one work "inside attractive restricted areas" (*Seymour* 127). By the logic of a renunciatory paradox dear to Salinger, if to embrace "indiscrimination" means going "beyond" the *writing* of poetry, one thereby grows attuned to "the main current of poetry that flows through things" (*Raise* 72).

To stake so much on "indiscrimination"—to make it an aesthetic and ethical ideal—obviously risks, indeed *courts* alienating one's audience; and indeed the critical fallout was harsh. Salinger, though, had no choice, given that for him the only thing that counted was writing "*on his own terms,* not anyone else's," to quote Zooey's advice to Franny (199). Being true to this advice would also allow him to keep faith with Seymour's to his writer brother, Buddy. Speaking of Flaubert, Seymour regrets that friends convinced him to write *Madame Bovary:* "they got him to write a masterpiece" but "they killed his chances of ever writing his heart out. He died like a celebrity, which was the one thing he wasn't" (*Seymour* 160). Salinger died the most celebrated of anti-celebrities. But in renouncing the publishing world and the literary life, in refusing to write another masterpiece after his first novel but rather only five pieces of prose fiction, none of novel length, none like anything seen before, all at once obsessively concentrated and diffuse, Salinger kept to his "own terms." Critics received this brazen act of integrity largely as a personal affront. They have taken revenge with a half century of (at times willful) critical incomprehension or indifference, by and large preoccupied instead with the mirror of their blankness—Salinger's own zealously enforced isolation.

The critical impasse can begin to be dislodged by coming to understand and appreciate Salinger's "*own terms.*" Alertness to clues helps. Salinger offers one when his fictional alter ego defines the "beautiful" as an ideal production of the *Cherry Orchard* "where Chekhov's talent is matched, nuance for nuance, idiosyncrasy for idiosyncrasy, by every soul on stage" (*Zooey* 61). To tap the implications of nuance Roland Barthes's *The Neutral* (2005) is helpful. There he describes his own "guide to life (ethical project)": "to live according to nuance. Now, there is a teacher of nuance, literature; try to live according to the nuances that literature teaches me" (11). For Barthes, living according to nuance is inseparable from finding ways to respect its delicacy and fragility (etymologically "nuance" is related to *nuage*, clouds and mists and fog). So one needs to choose approaches that avoid the aggression of mastery: hence the critic will display and describe ("in a

non-exhaustive manner") rather than define, explain, or conceptual-
ize: "I don't construct the concept of Neutral, I display Neutrals" (11).
In sum, though he leaves Salinger unmentioned, Barthes shares the
novelist's commitment to nuance as indispensable for aesthetic living.

Nuance brings seeming opposites into proximity, among them
Mailer and Salinger. The former praises (in 1959) the hipster's effort to
"get into the nuance of things" because "he lives in a state of extreme
awareness, and so objects and relations that most people take for granted
become terribly charged for him; and living in a state of self-awareness,
his time slows up. His page becomes more filled" (379). Salinger shares
the hipster's commitment to slowness and to a page filled with the density of nuance funded by "extreme awareness," an affinity that the ri-
valrous Mailer repressed, calling *Seymour* perhaps "the most slovenly
portion of prose ever put out by an important American writer."

Salinger's precocious eccentrics—"psychopathic prodigies," as a
friend of Zooey's remarks in a Mailerish phrase—are steeped in Eastern
thought, which sharpens their alertness to nuance (*Zooey* 132). A
"ringding enlightened man, a God-knower," Seymour finds divinity
everywhere; his fiancée's "frozen cream-cheese" dessert brings tears to
his eyes (*Seymour* 106; *Raise* 67). Aggravating and worrying his family,
Seymour never stops looking "in the queerest imaginable places—e.g.
in radio announcers, taxicabs . . . literally everywhere," reports brother Buddy. Even "investigating loaded ashtrays with his index finger,
clearing all the cigarette ends to the sides—smiling from ear to ear as
he did it—as if he expected to see Christ himself curled up cherubi-
cally in the middle" (*Seymour* 108). So we learn not only the contents
of ashtrays but of Mrs. Glass's robe pockets and of medicine chests; a
page-long inventory of the latter is found in *Zooey*.

If Taoism teaches "the art of being in the world," Seymour's art of
being is also Whitmanic in its paratactic reach, and thus a challenge
for the would-be portraitist. When that portraitist is writer and brother
Buddy Glass who is grieving, but also "ecstatically happy," the plan to
contain Seymour's "Heinzlike variety of personal characteristics" in a
plot and to build narrative momentum, must remain only that—a plan
(108). A "poet," "artist-seer," and "heavenly fool," alongside a damaged war veteran (corporal in the Air Force), an "unhealthy specimen,"
a "Sick Man": Seymour contains multitudes. He is, after all, cycling

in and out of multiple lives, a believer in Vedantic transmigration of souls (101, 104–106, 108). As readers of *Seymour* soon discover to their delight and irritation, the intrinsic failure—indeed impossibility—of plot is enacted in Buddy's garrulous diffuseness. He defeats such narrative mainstays as the carefully distributed telling detail and the use of pacing to maximize tension and climactic power. Such devices are antithetical to Zen, to Seymour's holy "indiscrimination," to Buddy's own ambivalences, and to his "ecstatic happiness," all of which thrive on digression and deferral. These modes enact for Salinger "the utopian promise" of the aesthetic, to recall Adorno—the glimpse of uncoerced forms of thought. In short, Buddy frustrates expectations to open space for alternative ways of thinking and acting.

∎

"Aiming but no aiming," says the Zen archery master that Buddy quotes in describing Seymour's brilliance at marbles (207). "The Tao man does everything not to exercise an authority, not to fulfill a function," Barthes reminds us (*The Neutral* 148). Nuance is the medium of this anti-authority, for attunement to the ubiquity of the holy requires promiscuous attention; Zen has us break "inveterate habits of relevance" (118). "We're required only to keep looking. Seymour once said, on the air, when he was eleven, that the thing he loved best in the Bible was the word WATCH!" (*Seymour* 152). Nuance, then, registers openness and watchfulness and is, appropriately, an aesthetic and ethical imperative blessed by both Eastern and Western mystics. As is already evident, Salinger (like the younger Glasses) was eclectic about his spiritual inspiration, taking from Chinese and Japanese, Indian, Christian and Jewish, among others.

In making nuance a mode of aesthetic living that is insouciant about calculation and striving, Seymour and his siblings inevitably ignite suspicion in a society anxious to discipline the wayward. When young, the seven Glass children, especially Seymour and Zooey, gained national fame for polymathic brilliance on the hit radio show *It's a Wise Child*. Their success incited an army of explainers to scrutinize them—psychiatrists, mothers-in-laws, fiancées: indeed, "every *summa-cum-laude* Thinker and intellectual men's-room attendant in the country had been having a go" at Seymour, remarks Buddy, since he was ten years old and a child celebrity, host of the show (*Raise* 59–60). At thirteen, Seymour was examined "by a reputable group of professional Freudians for six hours and forty five minutes. . . . They stopped just short of taking a brain smear from him" (*Seymour* 102). Zooey, second only to Seymour in "super-precocity," was also a frequent subject for testers and researchers intent on locating the "source" of his wit. As a writer, Buddy has his own bêtes noirs—he loathes a "new breed" of literary critic—the "clinician"—"bursting with good mental health" and "free of any inherent morbid *attrait* to beauty"—who specializes in analyzing "aesthetic pathology" (101).

Buddy's satirical jabs at dour American scientism disclose that Seymour and Zooey ignited a barely sublimated collective rage, becoming targets of the culture's defensive compulsion to label and control (*Zooey* 139). A version of this intolerance provokes Barthes's "neutral" into being in the first place: it responds to what Barthes calls the "arrogance" of the paradigm devised by Saussure that says meaning is diacritical, i.e. produced by the difference between terms. The paradigm's arrogance is in forcing us to choose one meaning over the other. Hence there is "always a sacrifice made to meaning, to produce meaning, to offer it to be consumed." Renouncing this renunciation, the neutral is "everything that baffles the paradigm," that outwits the paradigm's "menacing pressure" (7). Far from neutrality, Barthes's "neutral" is structural and nuance is one of its tools.

With the "neutral" Barthes brings together high modernism's regard for polysemic richness and the divestments of ego and desire found in Zen. While not, like Salinger, a practicing Vedantist, Barthes infuses *The Neutral* with an Eastern sensibility—"I am outside mastery," "I never interpret" (64–65). Of Buddhism, Taoism, and negative theology he says: "I know nothing" "insofar as they are doctrinal, systematic . . . these objects are altogether absent from my discourse" (64). In presiding over a similar marriage of East and West, Salinger shares Barthes's premise, the refusal of the "sacrifice" demanded by "implacable binarism." Relaxing the pressure to produce Meaning, Salinger fashions improvised, meandering narratives of philosophical and spiritual questing conducted on the Upper East Side in the sharp, cutting banter of "Manhattanese" (*Seymour* 112).

Happily, for Salinger, his distaste for explaining and explainers found support in the reigning literary models of the day. As a student in Whit Burnett's Columbia short story writing seminar in 1939, Salinger ingested the Henry Jamesian imperative to "Dramatize, dramatize!"—father of the now ubiquitous workshop tag, "show, don't tell." The other presiding spirit was Hemingway, by 1939 *the* minimalist master of the genre, tempering Jamesian excess with tautness. Having perfected the form in *Nine Stories*, Salinger by the late fifties renounces it and remakes his aesthetic with *Franny and Zooey*. He abandons the reigning laconic template perfected by Hemingway for a reflexive and discursive style while remaining committed to the concreteness of "showing" via density of detail. Blending Proustian elongation with an intimacy of address to the reader, Salinger calls his new form "prose home movies," as Buddy describes what he is about to present in *Zooey* (49).

Amid melancholy memories, career frustrations, his sister's spiritual crisis, and his mother's comic intrusions, Zooey Glass, television and stage actor, struggles to impart "wisdom." Franny craves it, having found wisdom in short supply in her college courses, its dearth precipitating her emotional breakdown. Zooey's effort however is inevitably flawed and compromised given that it occurs in a secular postwar America of striving careerists and given that the Glasses are self-confessed "freaks"— unkind, intolerant, scornful; "we've got 'Wise Child' complexes. We've never really gotten off the goddam air" (*Zooey* 140).

Salinger paints loving portraits while making the Glass children not particularly lovable. He is unsentimental about them. This is crucial; otherwise he would fail to disclose that their lavish intellectual gifts—their education in wisdom literature East and West, their infinite IQs and "freakish" high "standards"—have left them adrift in the search for spiritual enlightenment. The very notion of "search" is the problem. Indeed the two youngest Glasses, Zooey and Franny, may have to disinherit themselves from their intellectual endowment, for only then might they embody rather than know wisdom. As Buddhists say, knowing is one thing but realization is another. The latter involves feeling for themselves the force of the conviction that guided their education—Seymour's insistence that it should begin not with a "quest for knowledge at all but with a quest, as Zen would put it, for no-knowledge," a "state of pure consciousness" (*Zooey* 65).

In other words, Salinger places his characters directly inside the perennial paradox of spiritual instruction—how is the ineffable transmitted? Lao-tzu faced this dilemma as he pondered the demand of the Gate Keeper. For Wittgenstein the question runs up against "the inexpressible"—what only *"shows"* or manifests itself. "It is the mystical" (*Tractatus*, 6.522). The question's implied assumptions are part of the trouble: the very notion of transmission is self-canceling, for it assumes that "wisdom" is an entity and the telos of a project. We begin to surmount this reification, the limitations of "knowing," by not confusing intellectual mastery of a body of knowledge with spiritual living. Grasping this is the first step for Franny in making *"use"* of their "freakish education," as Zooey implores her to do. To "use" it is to come to grips with its limits and learn "detachment" while shooting "for some kind of perfection" on one's own terms, "not anyone else's" (198–199). "Detachment," we shall see, opens a rich vein of intellectual history. Here let it suffice that detached devotion is not achieved wisdom, nor a recipe or goal for achievement, but a stance of receptivity to the poetry of life's indiscriminate flow.

■

Internet pockets of the Salinger cult flourish—one site (deadcaulfields. com) imagines each reader journeying, "like the Glass family itself," in search of "something of comfort and elevation in an otherwise callous and ego-filled world." The yearning and poignancy of this attachment to the Glasses is nothing if not sincere but for that very reason has little to do with the tonal and emotional complexity of Salinger's voice on the page. One of the most familiar voices in postwar American literature, Salinger makes the love of his characters a subject in itself by showing how vexed is the relation of love and happiness to language—vexed by the wayward propensities of all three. *Seymour: An Introduction* is a novel about a writer, at the very brink of beginning an introduction, running up against the limits of saying.

Hence the self-reflexivity is organic, which renders inseparable formal and thematic motives. Both are filtered through the freely confessed ambivalence of Buddy the narrator. Manically self-conscious yet also a Zen adept, he is an unsettling mix of spiritual happiness and compulsive loquacity; and he is the lens—blurring subject and object—that introduces us to his brother Seymour: saintly mystic poet and *"non-stop talker*—which is a pretty vile thing to call somebody" (110).

Seymour's tracks are everywhere, in family lore, mementoes, letters, anecdotes, his diary, and his bedroom door full of quotations from his favorite mystical reading. "This whole goddam house stinks of ghosts," says Zooey (103). It is as if Seymour never died. And he never does; "all you do is get the heck out of your body when you die," says another wise boy-man, the child savant Teddy: everybody does it thousands of times without knowing it (*Nine Stories* 193). Another brother, Waker Glass (later a monk), addresses Buddy's puzzlement that some of Seymour's haiku apparently allude to details with no relation to his actual life by reminding him that "Seymour, in many of his most effective poems, seems to be drawing on the ups and downs of former, singularly memorable existences" (133). In Seymour's last published work, "Hapworth 16, 1924," he is seven, writing his parents from camp, and makes repeated reference to "previous appearances." From Seymour's viewpoint, individuality, like ownership, or any sense of firm possession, is merely a manner of speaking. He feels guiltless when he borrows Buddy's tie carefully stored away in cellophane. "Is it so important for us to keep in mind which is whose? That time two summers ago when I was out so long, I was able to trace that you and Z [Zooey] and I have been brothers for no fewer than four incarnations, maybe more. . . . The membrane is so thin between us" (*Seymour* 158).

Seymour's death is not only an emotional burden on Buddy but also a formal pressure on the novel's composition. As a writer, Buddy is proud of his "professional passion for detail" and describes his "highly inclusive account" of Seymour's wedding day in 1942, in which "the details were served up with a fullness possibly just short of presenting the reader with a sherbet mold of each and every wedding guest's footprint to take home as a souvenir, but Seymour himself—the main course—didn't actually put in a physical appearance anywhere" (112). This statement of discrepancy—abundant dessert without the "main course"—defines the novel's structural irony: a density of detail that can never encompass what incites it and would give it transcendent meaning—namely, Seymour. *Nomen est omen:* his name predicts perpetual imbalance—to always "see more" is at once excess but also privation that defeats attainment of clarity or precision or adequacy. Seymour is not only an epistemological abyss but a psychological one. Buddy calls him "our rather notorious 'mystic' and 'unbalanced type,'" for "by every logical definition he *was* an unhealthy specimen." When his "cries for help" were heeded, he refused to "say in perfectly intelligible language where it hurt" (106, 104).

Seymour is both ungovernable muchness and an empty center that continually elicits words that never contain him, instead revealing language's precariousness. This recognition prompts Buddy to turn to what is more reliable: the mute compensatory testimony of things—here sherbet molds as a "souvenir" of the silence Seymour embodies. Early on, Buddy offers another. Addressing us "privately," Buddy proffers a gift: "Please accept from me this unpretentious bouquet of very early blooming parentheses: (((( )))). I suppose, most unflorally, I truly mean them to be taken, first off, as bowlegged—buckle-legged—omens of my state of mind and body at this writing" (98). The bouquet as "omen" is several things at once: a textual icon of the empty space of grief at the center of Buddy's book, of his family, and of his psyche, a kind of shrine to Seymour and his irrecoverable absence. The icon also gives shape to the gap that instigates language—the endless effort to be at one with what it names. At the same time, the bouquet of parentheses announces the novel's stylistic and affective principle: the digressiveness of "ecstatic" happiness. The first is the compositional principle of the second.

Buddy explains how this works three pages into *Seymour: An Introduction.* "Professionally speaking," he informs us, he has been "seized" for the first time not by a "reasonable" happiness but by a "large and consuming . . . happiness." Having been "seized" he admits he doesn't have "any real choice of behavior in decent company" so he warns us that "an ecstatically happy prose writer can do many good things on the printed page" but "he can't be moderate or temperate or brief. . . . Worst of all, I think, he is no longer in a position to look after the reader's most immediate want; namely to see the author get the hell on with his story. Hence, in part, that ominous offering of parentheses a few sentences back" (99). "From this point on," he warns, his "asides" will "run rampant" and "speed, here, God save my American hide, means nothing whatever to me" (99–100). Instead, he will defer and digress, scattering parentheses with abandon, even sprinkling the occasional footnote with them. Indeed, abandon is what he revels in. Recalling a moment when Seymour bounded up the stairs to greet him, Buddy says: "I'd love to pursue this stair-bounding business for a minute—that is, pursue it blind, without giving a great damn where it leads me" (189). And he does so. In deserting cardinal American literary values—mainly speedily efficient storytelling—Buddy's priority is living within ecstatic happiness, the Zen state of acceptance.

Preceding his interest in Zen, Buddy was hostile to boundaries, especially temporal designations. Since boyhood he had torn up dozens of his stories "simply because they had . . . a Beginning, a Middle, and an End" (212). Later Buddhism will teach him how trivial these markers are, that death is only the start of one's next incarnation. Given that Seymour's "character lends itself to no legitimate sort of narrative compactness," Buddy's happiness, his subject matter, his literary style, and his balking "at any kind of ending" are in synch. Tempted to "pursue it blind," Buddy and his creator are improvising a literary artistry that is their own version of Allan Kaprow's portrait of Pollock—his act of making propelled by a "Zen quality" and a "certain blindness" that dispenses with the "reasoning faculties" to create an art that "gives the impression of going on forever. . . . To follow it [his form], it is necessary to get rid of the usual idea of 'Form,' i.e. a beginning, middle and end" (5). Startlingly, Salinger made the *New Yorker* of the fifties an outpost of the New York avant-garde.

Before digression relaxed the form of Salinger's Glass fiction, there was the crystalline tautness of his 1948 *New Yorker* debut, "A Perfect Day for Bananafish," an ostentatiously enigmatic story. The detachment of its prose maximizes the disturbance of its concluding shock: "He glanced at the girl lying asleep on one of the twin beds. Then he went over to one of the pieces of luggage, opened it . . . he took out an Ortgies caliber 7.65 automatic. He released the magazine, looked at it, then reinserted it. He cocked the piece. Then he went over and sat down on the unoccupied twin bed, looked at the girl, aimed the pistol, and

fired a bullet through his right temple" (*Nine Stories* 18). Salinger will
let this "without why" stare back at us for years, forcing readers to wait
until he fills in particulars of the Glass saga and then only to defer the details of Seymour's death. The motive of the suicide is as unfathomable as
the sources of Bartleby the Scrivener's lethargy. This blank is his way—
Buddy and his creator's—of outwitting or baffling the arrogant paradigm
of meaning production with its "menacing pressure" to generate a legible
identity for consumption, to recall the strategy of Barthes's Neutral (7).

■

Given the spectacular abruptness of that suicide, Buddy's fervent declarations of "ecstatic happiness" have a hysterical edge. His *Introduction*
stages the interaction between the imperturbable happiness and the ongoing grieving, both authentic expressions of Buddy's "state of mind and
body at this writing"—a "paunchy and very nearly middle-aged man."
The morass of emotions he is coping with inspires his other interest—
dramatizing how high modernism and Zen teachings respond to language's inadequacy in representing feeling. This commences with his
two epigraphs to *Seymour: An Introduction*, both of which insist on the
difficulty of communicating. It presents Kafka's diary entry describing
his efforts to render in words a troupe of characters he loves: "The actors
by their presence always convince me, to my horror, that most of what
I've written about them until now is false. It is false because I write
about them with steadfast love (even now, while I write it down, this
too, becomes false) but varying ability, and this varying ability . . . loses
itself dully in this love." To express something even as direct as love is
to become trapped in the betrayals of language. *Seymour's* second epigraph, from Kierkegaard, is even more severe: perhaps an author's "slip
of the pen," his "clerical error," "was no error but in a far higher sense
was an essential part of the whole exposition . . . as if this clerical error
were to revolt against the author, out of hatred for him, were to forbid
him to correct it, and were to say, 'No, I will not be erased, I will stand
as a witness against thee, that thou art a very poor writer.'" These quotations—first presented unidentified, to maximize our disorientation—are
not exactly inspiring testimonials to hang over one's writing desk. Yet,
Buddy uses them precisely as such, telling us: "I've reproduced the two

passages to try to suggest very plainly how I think I stand in regard to the over-all mass of data I hope to assemble here" (101). These authors, he adds, are two of the figures "whom I most often run to—occasionally in real distress—when I want any perfectly credible information about modern artistic processes."

Buddy chooses as guideposts two epigraphs about language taking on a recalcitrant life of its own; they sponsor the simultaneous making and unmaking of a monologue by a grieving forty-year-old writer who keeps sabotaging his goal of writing a portrait of a beloved sibling. To complete it depends on finding "those lucid intervals" when he can force himself to "sit down and be reasonably quiet," wracked as he is with an "inner, incessant elation" that verges on hysteria and threatens to turn "this whole composition into a fool's soliloquy" (105, 119). Early on in *Seymour* Buddy admits to having scrapped his original plan to write a series of short stories about his brother, and now acknowledges that Seymour is "much, much too large to fit on ordinary typewriter paper—any typewriter paper of mine, anyway" (106, 151).

In his consternation at having gotten in over his head, Buddy confesses that "in this mood I don't go anywhere near the short-story form"; the burden of representing Seymour has reduced Buddy to being "a thesaurus of undetached prefatory remarks about him." Yet he insists, "I am still a narrator, but one with extremely pressing personal needs." These needs crave soothing silence, the silence of presentation rather than representation—that is, the wordless endeavor of communicating by showing us significant objects: "I want to distribute mementoes, amulets, I want to break out my wallet and pass around snapshots, I want to follow my nose" (106–107). Wanting sight, touch, and smell to take over, he yearns to be as removed as his reader: "Oh, you out there with your enviable golden silence" (136). And implicitly he envies that other figure of silence—his dead brother. Even when alive, Seymour the torrential talker turned to art for silence, letting it shape his haiku, which, as Buddy describes it, are "as bare as possible" (129).

■

Buddy Glass's avowed fraternity with K & K, *the* two masters of anxiety, dread, and renunciation, is neither posturing nor pretension but it is risky communion. By choosing these fifties culture heroes as mentors of "modern artistic processes," Buddy learns something about the art of ambivalence and how cross-purposes can release not only anxiety but energy. So Buddy's creator sets his monologue on a knife-edge—the slow-motion panic of someone writing while in the act of trying to renounce writing and efface himself. Or, more precisely, we are presented with the Zen insight into how illusory is the line between writing/not writing, doing/not doing. In effect, *Seymour: An Introduction* plays a variation upon Barthes's famous reminder of the "death of the author," which reasserts a move (initiated by Mallarmé) to the primacy of the text, the reader, and the autonomous life of language, what Buddy's epigraphs also announce. The death of the author writ large is enacted in Salinger's other work—renunciation, his public absconding, leaving only his words behind. Barthes's "The Death of the Author" appeared in the same 1967 issue of *Aspen* as Sontag's "The Aesthetics of Silence."

In his essay Barthes speaks of a text as consisting of "multiple writings, drawn from many cultures and entering into mutual relations of dialogue" ("Death" 148). *Seymour* achieves an approximate polyphony: the epigraphs generate a literary/philosophical meditation concerning the paradoxical status of mastery. This subject acquires an Eastern resonance late in the book when Buddy discusses his relation to Zen. He approaches the topic circuitously, returning in memory to 1927 when ten-year-old Seymour counsels his eight-year-old brother absorbed in "curb marbles" to, as we saw earlier, "try not aiming so much." (Salinger is riffing on a popular book of the day, Eugen Herrigel's *Zen in the Art of Archery*.) What ensues is a feast of nuance. Buddy had admired Seymour's "unbeatable" skill founded on his unique casual "sidewrist . . . flick, vaguely like someone scaling a stone over a pond" (201). Naturally Buddy imitates Seymour's side flick "technique" but the results are disastrous: "to do it his way was to lose all chance of *any* effective control over the marble." *That* is the point young Buddy misses—relaxing effective control of the marble is just what makes Seymour's casual flick effective; hence Seymour's advice. Let "luck" and "accident" play their part, he suggests. When Buddy turns that flick into a "technique" of use he violates its spiritual principle. Buddy grasps this now, thirty-two years later. "When Seymour was coaching me . . . to quit aiming my marble at Ira Yankauer's . . . I believe he was instinctively getting at something very close in spirit to the sort of instructions a master archer in Japan will give when he forbids a willful new student to aim his arrows at the target; that is, when the archery master permits, as it were, Aiming but no aiming" (207).

Falling into his inveterate restless anxiety, Buddy immediately regrets comparing Seymour's advice with Zen archery because "I am neither a Zen archer nor a Zen Buddhist, much less a Zen adept." And no sooner has he distanced himself then he collapses the distance:

> I'm profoundly attracted to classical Zen literature, I have the gall to lecture on it . . . one night a week at a college, but my life itself couldn't very conceivably be less Zenful than it is, and what little I've been able to apprehend . . . of the Zen experience has been a by-result of following my own rather natural path of extreme Zenlessness. Largely because Seymour himself literally begged me to do so. (208)

Buddy crowns these passages on Zen with one more anecdote: he parallels Seymour's "sheer intuition" of the best way to shoot a marble with the "fine art of snapping" cigarette ends into wastebaskets across a room, an art "of which most male smokers are true masters only" when they are indifferent about succeeding or the room is empty of "eyewitnesses, including, quite so to speak, the cigarette snapper himself." That self-absenting puts Buddy in mind of one final fact about Seymour and marbles: when his flick would meet a "responsive click" it "never appeared to be clear to him *whose* winning click it was" and someone "invariably had to pick up the marble he'd won and *hand* it to him" (209). Again, Seymour devalues ownership: "Is it so important for us to keep in mind which is whose?" (158).

This late excursion into Zen reveals its capacity to disturb our Western assumptions with a logic that dissolves dualisms, conjoins opposites. So renunciation—relinquishment of one's will—is joined to mastery, a paradox that the Zen archer's riddle "Aiming but no aiming" clarifies. It shows how mastery works by implicitly juxtaposing the difference between two acts: "aiming" in the second sense ("no aiming") is the executive will of sovereign subjectivity; the other path, first "Aiming," empties out these qualities and is exemplified by Buddy's "natural path of extreme Zenlessness," which has given him, virtually unwittingly, his intimacy with Zen. That intimacy is not to be achieved by any sort of effort. Analogously, Seymour excels at marbles precisely because he is not determined to do so, and in the intensity of his pleasure of casual wrist flicking doesn't even recognize that he is engaged in a ritual with winners and losers. Playing but not playing, Seymour enjoys marble shooting for its own sake, which is to say he has an aesthetic relation to the activity.

■

The aesthetic is where Zen and Western thought meet, a place where mastery is grounded less in self-assertion than self-absenting. The overthrow of our habits of rational deliberation may take the form of visionary blindness—recall Kaprow on Pollock—or, less grandly, can restore our capacity "to simply *see* things," notes Thomas Merton. Rather than rely on words and formulas, "Zen uses language against itself, to blast out these preconceptions. . . . Zen is saying, as Wittgenstein said, 'Don't think: Look!'" (Merton, *Zen* 49). Salinger's scenes of self-absenting—Seymour at marbles and the dissociated expert cigarette flicker—align with the self-effacement—disinterest—basic to Kant's faculty of taste. Aesthetic judgment of a beautiful form in nature "presupposes that the mind is in restful contemplation" (*Critique* 78). Such impartiality is based on indifference to the utility of the thing observed, which ensures that one's purely subjective response is also capable of "subjective universal communicability" (49). What Kant calls "free beauty" elicits a "pure judgment of taste" because that beauty is an end in itself, "pleases freely and on their own account" (for Kant, such things as ornaments, parrots, humming birds, and "marine crustacea"). "Free beauty" differs from "merely dependent beauty" which has a defining purpose—a horse, a person, a house, for instance (60). Neither logical nor cognitive ("contributes nothing to knowledge") aesthetic judgments of taste are grounded upon the perceiving subject's pleasure of feeling, expressed in what Kant calls the "free play" of the imagination (36). It is free, as noted earlier, because enjoyed in the absence of a determinate concept to pin down meaning (37, 49). "Something there is about you that strikes a match in me," as Dylan puts it.

But Kant's portrayal of aesthetic experience is not limited to judgments of taste about the delight of beautiful form. Nor do disinterested judges always retain their poised impartiality and sense of free play guided by taste. There is a less rigidly rationalist and formal side to Kant, the sublime side that inspired romantic poets and thinkers to exalt the freedom of the imagination after reading *Critique of Judgement*. This is the Kant of "aesthetic Ideas," who depicts aesthetic experience as a mode of non-discursive intelligibility, eluding our capacity to frame it coherently, stirring the imagination into receptivity and pleasure in excess (Kneller 105). These subjective claims of *Critique of Judgement* will concern us later. Pertinent here is that this "romantic" Kant also shows the agitating effect on us of the power of the uncontainable, what he calls the terror of the "sublime." Perhaps contrary to his intention, he does not keep disinterested taste and sublime boundlessness strictly apart; rather they meet in his notion of "genius." (William Desmond makes this case in an essay on Kant's "terror of genius.")

With Kant's "genius"—a force of nature, indifferent to taste and to rules, its free play of imagination "lawless"—we circle back to Zen's suspicion of intellectual deliberation. Genius discloses its own kind of disinterestedness that exceeds simple impartiality and instead embodies an absence of self-command that unravels any rules of mastery, including its own. At marbles the genius of Seymour is specifically Kantian.

Four years after *Seymour* the Zen adept John Cage in his "Lecture On Nothing" (1959) will allude to the futility of intellectual control that is basic to Zen and implied in Kant's aesthetics. He writes that "disinterestedness . . . is a proof that our delight lies in not pos-sessing anything . Each moment presents what happens ." Cage finds absence of possession liberating and the basis of poetry (in the large sense of making): "our poetry now is the reali-zation that we possess nothing. Anything therefore is a delight (since we do not pos-sess it) and thus need not fear its loss" (110–111).

The force of *dis*possession, if in a less buoyant key, informs the opening epigraphs of *Seymour*; they suggest that language is not overpowered so much as unreliable. We cannot render it transparent to our aims. At the mercy of context and contingency rather than based on strict rules, language escapes our intentions as frequently as it serves

as our trusty instrument. We tend to repress the first fact and live
by the second. But literature undoes what we repress, a truth Buddy
points to as he draws his "semi-diary" to a close: "I'm finished with
this. Or, rather, it's finished with me" (*Seymour* 211). Student of Zen,
of Kafka and of Kierkegaard, Buddy has learned to live in paradox. And
his creator makes renunciation productive, weaving it into the novel
in ways at once biographical, aesthetic, and spiritual. The result is a
tacit dialogue between West and East that commences with European
high modernism and concludes with Zen while never leaving the
womb of family memory.

Salinger and Seymour Glass preside over this dialogue, presences at
once full and empty, embodying mystery, "that which shows itself and
at the same time withdraws" (Heidegger *Discourse on Thinking* 55).
Both are absorbed by and into the horizontal panoply of particularity,
those "dumb beautiful ministers" of Whitman (307) (whom Salinger
mentions) serving (ministering to) what Salinger, via Seymour Glass,
calls the "current of poetry that flows through things." He embodies
the silent force of the "Now" in the image of the "fat Lady"—what is
present with no metaphysical backing. Metaphysical thinking, says
Heidegger, is born in the distinction between *what* beings are—their
essence—and *that* they are—their existence. This Platonic opposition
breeds suspicion of appearance—thatness—and elevates essence, reducing being to an object for a subject. When one lives within the lyrical flow this split in Western consciousness dissolves, as do invidious
binaries (non-dualism is the heart of Vivekananda's Vedantism) and
we grow open to "releasement toward things." Eckhart's phrase is distilled in his admirer Heidegger's remark that "to allow a being to be as
it is" in its inscrutability is at once the easiest and most difficult task
("Origin" 12).

Salinger seems to associate publication with violation of the lyrical current that lets be the mystery of being. In *Seymour* we learn that
Seymour declined to publish the 184 short poems he wrote in the last
three years of his life. Buddy ratifies this decision by refusing family
pressure to bring out a posthumous collection. Publication risks not
only celebrity but pumping up an author's ego with "pride." Once, after reading a story of Buddy's, Seymour tells him: "for your own sake,
don't make me proud of you. . . . Give me a story that just makes me

unreasonably vigilant" (*Seymour* 159). Vigilant attention to the world dissolves the ego of author and reader into the "lyrical flow," into becoming one with a "passion for detail": this objectivity is what counts in literature (130).

■

A certain hermeticism hovers around Salinger's Glass chronicles, given the intense inwardness of his characters and his near Proustian elongation of time, with scenes in tight spaces (cars, bathrooms) stretching on for dozens of pages. Absorbed in this absorption, the reader may forget the wider literary and sociological realities in which Salinger is embedded. He works from an ironic position within nouveau-riche postwar urban America, at once the darling of the *New Yorker* (in 1965 they devoted nearly an entire issue to his final story) and satiric mocker of the cultural and spiritual limitations of its upper-middle-class readership. Mocker, but also guide: his intimacy of address to his reader—Buddy, in *Seymour*, calls us "you" and "old confidant"—is part of his way of insinuating that we are or may be among those with the potential to unlearn old habits and see the spiritual light.

At the same time, Salinger, as noted earlier, has been a prisoner of that plush milieu, commanding a huge readership at the expense of not being taken seriously as a high modernist sensibility. Evidently the Kafka and Kierkegaard epigraphs just didn't earn him credit with the militant highbrows. Sontag, eager to inter the "Matthew Arnold idea of culture" as stern moral "criticism of life," regarded the realist novel as hopeless and put "outraged humanists" on notice. Moral conscience is "only one of the functions of consciousness," she announces, and urges instead that we "experience the luminousness of the thing in itself, of things being what they are" (*Essays* 283, 281, 282, 19). Glass captures this light, which is to say Buddy Glass had the same intuition as Sontag when he passed around old snapshots, seeking the silence of presentation. This aesthetic ideal—minimizing language's curse of "mediacy" (Sontag) to reach a condition of "transparence"—is deep in the modernist grain and in American precursors of Sontag and Salinger. However, in the 1967 context of programmatic overhaul, communing with ancestors was not the point: in Sontag's hasty redrawing of the cultural map, the *New Yorker*, like the old fogey New York intellectuals (read Lionel Trilling for Matthew Arnold) was allotted only a small corner: she labeled it, with outrageous simplification, "bourgeois-rationalist culture," remnant of a bygone world. Case closed (*Essays* 318).

Those precursors—including Emerson and James, exemplars of the American philosophic anti-intellectual tradition—would applaud Seymour's remark that education should begin with a quest for "no-knowledge." All three authors also share the impatience of intellectuals with those embodying institutional authority. What could be more American than Salinger's contempt for psychiatrists and for professors of literature (though that is Seymour's profession and Buddy teaches writing), or Professor James grousing that most philosophy is "merely reiterating what dusty-minded professors have written about what other previous professors have thought" (*Writings* 2:752). Emerson scorned preachers oblivious to the real. Recalling his attendance at a church when the pulpit had been "usurped by a formalist," Emerson noted that a snowstorm swirled outside: the storm was real, "the preacher merely spectral" (*Essays* 84). The soulless formalist, whether he presides over a literary text, a philosophy classroom, or a congregation, ignores what James's pragmatist successor John Dewey calls the "felt quality of an experience" that makes thinking inextricable from feeling, from intuition and tacit knowledge. Art, for Dewey, expresses this embodied thought.

The philosophic critique of intellectualism allies with Eastern esteem of "no-knowledge" and with the aesthetic against a shared enemy—scientism. The rejection of scientism, P. M. S. Hacker clarifies, is "not a form of irrationalism. It is not to deny reason the power to understand both nature and man. Rather it is to insist that the canons of understanding in the study of nature and in the study of man differ, that the forms of explanation appropriate for the one are typically inappropriate for the other." Scientism, then, "is the illicit extension of the methods and categories of science beyond their legitimate domain" (Hacker 66, 73).

A consequence of this illicit extension is a reductive understanding of the place of the aesthetic, a diminishment familiar since Plato. Aesthetics (especially in the Anglo-American world) has largely been regarded as a playpen or vacation for the unserious, the realm of mere feeling or the non-cognitive, "pseudo-statements" (I. A. Richards) in which claims of truth or falsity are irrelevant. Condescension has been especially acute from those who inhabit the "serious" world of facts and knowledge and logic—the realm of science or some branches of analytic philosophy. Yet the founder of modern aesthetics, seeking legitimacy, defined it, we noted earlier, as "the science of sensual cognition" (a phrase of Baumgarten's whose *Aesthetica* of 1750 gave a name to the discipline). The aesthetic revived Aristotle's "aesthesis" and was understood as a faculty of perception founded on spontaneous feeling and touching. Alas, Baumgarten's phrase was misleading; his sensual "science" did not posit a distinctive and self-governing mode of experience but only a corporeal knowledge inferior to the findings of cognitive science.

At the same time Baumgarten endowed philosophic dignity upon the notions of the "obscure" and "confused," the products of that lower—bodily—knowledge. Challenging the rationalist regime of clear and distinct judgments, Baumgarten did not relegate perception's "confused" ideas to the realm of error, to be submitted to the clarity of rational correction. Rather, he makes confusion the *basis* upon which our ordinary apprehension of truth draws. As a commentator explains: "When we refer to aspects of phenomena not clearly distinguished from one another, we begin to orient ourselves in the world. Nature does not leap from murkiness to clear and distinct thinking" but passes through what Baumgarten calls the "dawn." As opposed to the "intensive clarity" of rational concepts, aesthetic objects possess, says Baumgarten, their own kind of clarity, one founded on "fecunditas," a pregnant excess and abundance that can't be subsumed under an abstract concept (Schulte-Sasse 354).

Treating Baumgarten as a respected foil, Kant formed in *Critique of Judgment* (1790) his own account of the aesthetic. However, Kant repeated the traditional move of making aesthetic reflection irrelevant to cognition and to desire, lodging the aesthetic in a niche of pure disinterested delight in the appreciation of Beauty. He thereby blunted Baumgarten's promising move to assimilate the aesthetic into ordinary experience. In 1934 Dewey summed up the complaint against Kant's segregation: Kant made Beauty "'pure' in the sense of being isolated and self-enclosed; feeling free of any taint of desire. . . . Thus the psychological road was opened leading to the ivory tower of 'Beauty' remote from all desire, action, and stir of emotion" (*Art* 253). (We have earlier noted broader understandings of the aesthetic in Kant and will do so again later).

Only with the late-nineteenth-century rise of *Lebensphilosophie* (life philosophy) was the philosophic scaffolding set in place for integrating the aesthetic fully into human experience. Aiming to view "life without metaphysical prejudice," in the words of its theorist Dilthey (115), life philosophy counted among its proponents James and Bergson, with Nietzsche a forerunner, as was Gustav Fechner, the physicist, philosopher, and poet whom James admired for his refusal of science's trust in abstract rationalism. They perceived, against scientism's blindness, the fact that "reality, life, experience, concreteness, immediacy, use what word you will, exceeds our logic, overflows and surrounds it," in the excited words of James in 1908 (*Writings* 2:725). That overflow was helping to wash away *the* pillar of rationalism, the dualist premise (which Kant inherited from Descartes) that thinking precedes and defines experience. James had delivered an earlier blow, co-developed with physiologist Carl Lange—a theory of emotion that insists on the primacy of the body: we are afraid because we tremble, rather than the common-sense opposite.

James's embodied perspective shared Dilthey's critique of scientism, part of the latter's effort to discriminate the humanities from science without drawing invidious distinctions. Explanation is the province of science while understanding is the aim of humanities, to invoke Dilthey's terms (170–184). In going beyond a "logical treatment of understanding," James and Dilthey depart from Kant to ground it in empathy and intuition attuned to individual particularities without subsuming them under general laws (230). We nurture the empathic state of mind in the reading of a poem, in which "every line is re-transformed ["re-experienced"] into life. . . . Potentialities of the soul are evoked by the comprehension—by means of elementary understanding—of physically presented words" (226). In sum, says Dilthey, "the problems of poetry are the problems of life" (114).

Making literature pivotal in the philosophic defense of "life," turning aesthetic experience into a model for empathic understanding,
Dilthey concluded that "all understanding contains something irrational because life is irrational" (230). He clears a path Dewey eventually
would take—to embed aesthetic living within a natural world where
"live creatures" (in Dewey's phrase) undergo—*suffer*—experience before knowing it. "Our natural relation to the world's existence," Stanley
Cavell writes, is "closer, or more intimate, than the ideas of believing
or knowing are made to convey" (*Themes* 192). What we must hope
for, Cavell says (writing of how Wittgenstein and Kierkegaard "take
seriously the fact that we begin our lives as children"), "is not that at
some stage we will possess all explanations, but that at some stage we
will need none" (232). Art glimpses this possibility. In our initial encounter with visual art we need no explanation, or, rather, explanation
is irrelevant. "'Stuff' is everything," says Dewey of our pre-reflective
experience of painting before "discrimination inevitably sets in" and
imposes form; prior to this is the object's "undefined pervasive" "felt
presence" comprising "matter . . . unified and massive"; this "perme-
ating quality" has no name, it can only be "emotionally 'intuited'";
hence a string of monosyllables will have to do: "it is just that which it
is and not anything else." The object here is preponderant, overwhelming the viewer's capacity for linguistic amplitude (*Art* 191–192, 194).

This "felt presence," which Dewey says is the enlivening "spirit
of the work of art," is in effect a "quest for no-knowledge." Another
James, William's novelist brother, pursued this quest. Though famously refined, Henry James practiced aesthetic living when he
was least so, when he reveled in the pre-cognitive—"sights, sounds,
smells, even the chaos of confusion and change" that greeted him
upon his repatriation to New York in 1904. To his delight, his arrival
demanded "a certain recklessness in the largest surrender to impres-
sions . . . leaving no touch of experience irrelevant." Not long after,
James found himself in a "pushing" Wall Street crowd, "moving in
its dense mass—with the confusion carried to chaos for any intelligence, any perception; a welter of objects and sounds in which relief,
detachment, dignity, meaning, perished utterly" (*American Scene*
1, 3, 83). Rather than safely anchored to detachment and meaning,
Henry James "surrender[s]," carried along by the rush of a mob in

motion with "the will to move, move, move as an end in itself," for once reduced to monosyllables (84).

A year before, in fiction, James had staged an analogous unraveling of mastery, narrating a "quest for no-knowledge." The phrase nicely describes what sparks the happy fiasco that entangles the hero of *The Ambassadors*. Though his mission's success depends on it, Lambert Strether perversely renounces explanation, that prime instrument of knowing. The "heart" of Strether, James's subtlest renunciator, "always sank when clouds of explanation gathered. His highest ingenuity was in keeping the sky of life clear of them" (114). At lunch in Paris alone with the enchanting Marie de Vionnet, the very woman who had been typecast as his opponent, he feels the "warm spring air" begin to "throb," his senses liberated not least because he has dispensed with "explanations": "It was at present as if he had either soared above or sunk below them—he couldn't tell which. . . . How could he wish it to be lucid for others, for any one, that he, for the hour, saw reasons enough in the mere way the bright clean ordered water-side life came in at the open window" (220).

Under the clear open sky of "transparence," Strether experiences— rather than knows—a rapt receptivity toward the ordinary ("water-side life," the "intensely white table-linen") that imbues it with the "luminousness of the thing in itself." "I'm incredible. I'm fantastic and ridiculous—I don't explain myself even *to* myself," he exclaims near the novel's end (355). What he wants, he says, "is a thing I've ceased to measure or even to understand," as he wraps himself in the ineffable. And the enigmatic; he renounces Paris and a friend's offer of companionship to return to his bleak New England town. Strether has banished explanation so he can "take things as they come." Though an "impossible, unattainable art," as the narrator reminds us, Strether approximates this art of the undefended in his aesthetic life lived according to nuance.

In the thirty-one years Seymour Glass is alive he comes to embody aesthetic living as (horizontal) spiritual transcendence. He habitually lies on the floor, as if echoing Whitman's posture of concentrated looking at leaves of grass. Indeed, this relaxed stance orients the education for "no-knowledge" that Seymour and Buddy impose upon their youngest siblings. Since "a state of pure consciousness" lets one "be with God before he said, Let there be light"—before human beings impose distinction and hierarchy—the brothers decide "it might be a good thing to hold back this light" from Franny and Zooey. After all, religion, for Seymour, is about "unlearning the differences, the illusory differences" (*Zooey* 68). The reading list comprises those who had known this "state of being where the mind knows the source of all light"—"Jesus and Gautama and Lao-tse"; they were assigned "before you knew too much or anything about Homer or Shakespeare or even Blake or Whitman, let alone George Washington" (66).

We gain insight into Seymour's spiritual and aesthetic sensibility—his freedom of feeling and freedom from calculating consequences—when he alludes to being suspended as a sixteen-year-old from *Wise Child* for the controversial "Lincoln broadcast." He was misunderstood as having criticized the Gettysburg Address as "dishonest." Seymour clarifies what he actually said: "I'd said that 51,112 men were casualties at Gettysburg, and that if someone *had* to speak at the anniversary of the event, he should simply have come forward and shaken his fist at his audience and then walked off—that is, if the speaker was an absolutely honest man" (*Raise* 74). Seymour has been discussing the Lincoln broadcast with yet another psychiatrist (Mrs. Fedder's analyst) who replies that Seymour has a "perfection complex of some kind." What this remark ignores is Seymour's trust in silence as its own form of expression. To lecture about the slaughter distances the reality of the dead by imposing inevitably factitious meaning. Instead, a silent gesture of emotional urgency, a shaken fist, and then abrupt departure, announces a visceral feeling beyond conceptual determinacy—perhaps it is a gesture of helpless outrage, perhaps of accusation or of shame— that demands we acknowledge the carnage.

What Seymour's would-be Lincoln broadcast suggests is what also concerns Buddy in *Seymour: An Introduction:* as potent as language's power to communicate is its capacity to betray. Though we cannot think without explanation and conceptualization, they are not the "sole avenue to truth," insists William James (*Writings* 2:755). James is so adamant about eluding what he calls "the conceptual decomposition of life" that he prefers silence or pointing "to the mere *that* of life, and you by inner sympathy must fill out the *what* for yourselves" (747, 762). His logic is close to Seymour's: the silent shaken fist in this context is posing provocative mystery in tense fleshly expression. The suitably baffled audience must first experience the fist's *thatness* before being ready, by an act of "inner sympathy," to bring the horror of human slaughter into cognitive focus ("the *what*"). Seymour calls this spirit of pure receptive sympathy the "Fat Lady." As noted earlier, she both embodies and presides over the sheer *thatness* of life before metaphysical binaries propagated "vicious intellectualism."

We hear about the origins of the Fat Lady in *Zooey*. Years ago when he was about to appear on *Wise Child*, Zooey was "bitching one night before the broadcast" that the studio audience were a bunch of "morons." In response, Seymour tells him to shine his shoes "for the Fat Lady." Since no one could see his shoes, Zooey "didn't know what the hell he was talking about, but he had a very Seymour look on his face, and so I did it." And every night after that he shined them all the years he was on the show. When Zooey tells this to Franny, she recalls that Seymour gave her the same command: "He told me to be funny for the Fat Lady" (200–201).

Discerning just *what* Seymour is talking about forms the climax of *Zooey*: "I'll tell you a terrible secret—Are you listening to me?" implores Zooey to his spiritually lost sister (201). The "secret" Zooey imparts is that *"there isn't anyone anywhere that isn't Seymour's Fat Lady"* (201). Maligned and mocked—Franny had imagined her with "very thick legs, very veiny . . . she had cancer *too*"—the Fat Lady in effect is "with God before he said, Let there be light": undifferentiated oneness, as democratic and anti-hierarchical as Whitman's sprawling paratactic catalogues. She is the "current of poetry" that flows through "all things" (*Raise* 72). Honoring things being what they are, the Fat Lady in her living is also dying, vulnerable to ravage. She incarnates charity and forgiveness toward all things; as Zooey reveals to Franny at the end, the Fat Lady really is "Christ himself" (*Zooey* 202).

The sentimentality of this ending often distracts critics from noting the less obvious, more important point—that *Zooey* insists on the distance between the spiritual ideals the main characters articulate and the pettiness of their behavior. Both younger Glasses freely confess their reflex cynical suspicion of people, a move that merely augments their smug self-congratulation. Zooey's blanket scorn for Franny's boy-friend, the pompous literature major Lane Coutell ("this Lane pill" is a "charm boy and a fake"), is exposed as unmerited, since readers of *Franny* know he is also sincerely worried about her and makes frequent concerned calls to Mrs. Glass (96–97). Showing Zooey's dismissiveness of Lane's complexity becomes Salinger's way of revealing Zooey's love of his own nasty judgments and puts his self-absorption on parade. "You're not kind," his mother tells him twice. Gazing into his shaving mirror, his eyes are "neutral territory, a no man's land in a private war against narcissism he had been fighting since he was seven or eight years old" (92). This "war" is clearly an ongoing campaign, likely unwinnable, as we discern from the amount of space devoted to Zooey's assiduous bathroom primpings.

Zooey's own narcissism makes him keenly aware of Franny's: "You're beginning to give off a little stink of piousness," he tells her, "all this hysteria business is unattractive as hell" (160). Zooey admits that his own brand of piety—"being the heavy in everybody's life" by always scolding his writer friends for selling out—is equally soul killing (143). Making vivid Glass frailties, Salinger also suggests their resilience by having Zooey show Franny that their contempt for the earnest and ambitious strivers of the world is ultimately snide and self-indulgent. Narcissist Zooey turns out to be an agent of spiritual redemption, a development whose point is not irony but an index of human mystery. Spiritual illumination doesn't arrive on angelic wings; it is beyond our control and understanding in a terribly mixed world where we are "running back and forth forever between grief and high delight" (161, 145, 62). By the ending of *Zooey*, the memory of Seymour's expansive letting be of that world with its absurdities and sheer recalcitrant density becomes an imperative for Franny to *live* empathically, to move beyond "piousness." *How* one does so is a matter Zooey pursues, we shall see, via the radical critique of instrumentality or attachment found in Eastern and Christian mysticism (60).

Seymour's sense that the "current of poetry" already flows everywhere, encompassing all things, tallies with William James's mystical belief that "every bit of us at every moment is part and parcel of a wider self" (*Writings* 2:762). Quoting in *Varieties* Vivekananda (one of Salinger's spiritual guides) whose Vedanta hymn to "Oneness in the universe" shows "we all have some ear for this monistic music," James concludes: "We all have at least the germ of mysticism in us" (552–553). "The membrane is so thin between us," says Seymour of his sense of brotherly closeness: "For us, doesn't each of our individualities begin right at the point where we own up to our extremely close connections?" (*Seymour* 158). His own membranes are equally permeable. Thus touch is Seymour's most immediate language; his epidermal sensitivity connects him to others; "certain heads, certain colors and textures leave permanent marks on me," he tells his diary, and he recalls grabbing "a yellow cotton dress" of a girl he loved: "I still have a lemon-yellow mark on the palm of my right hand" (*Raise* 75).

According to Buddy at the start of *Seymour*, however, it is not the tactile but the visual that is the mark of genius: The "eyes" of a seer "take the most abuse" (105). "I say that the true artist-seer, the heavenly fool who can and does produce beauty, is mainly dazzled to death by his own scruples, the blinding shapes and colors of his own sacred human conscience. My credo is stated" (105). This is an enigmatic passage; the puzzle of it may derive from Buddy's effort to compress the spiritual ("sacred human conscience"), the aesthetic ("beauty"), and the ethical ("scruples") into a single "credo." Drawing all three uneasily together is the phrase "blinding shapes and colors"—itself a burst of brilliant obscurity that suddenly emerges only to be hemmed in syntactically by "scruples" and "conscience." "Blinding shapes and colors"—the phrase suggests overwhelming haptic immediacy, as when we move up close to a painting and no longer see forms but only intensities and textures.

A turn from being dazzled to death by "blinding shapes and colors" to being pleasurably immersed in aesthetic experience occurred two months after *Seymour* appeared in the *New Yorker* of June 6, 1959. In the *Saturday Evening Post* of August 1959 Clement Greenberg noted that the "purity" and immediacy of abstract art was due in no small part to the banishing of illusion, leaving us "alone with shapes and colors" (4:80). Salinger and Greenberg's sharing of those three words (and a magazine; Salinger published in the *Post* a decade earlier) is notable, not as a means to build a bridge between them (Greenberg's opinion of Salinger would likely resemble the one we have imagined Sontag held), but as an occasion for making vivid the renewed status of the aesthetic in 1950s America, especially as it blurs with the spiritual and becomes a model of aesthetic living. Greenberg urged readers of the *Saturday Evening Post,* in effect, to live with skies clear of explanation, for it heightens receptivity, as we have seen Seymour Glass and Lambert Strether discover. Turn from the familiar, Greenberg suggests, from the comfortable hold of illusion promoted by realist fiction and Norman Rockwell, and savor the new—the immediate pleasures of abstract art. In doing so they would enjoy the rush of blind intuition—the defeat of the cognitive in what Greenberg calls the "bewilderment" one feels before a painting, as if swept up in a "sudden revelation" (4:84, 81).

Aesthetic education in the fifties invited one not only to taste the new but also to taste words; Salinger's proposal to "see more glass," with a name made new in the mouth of a prepubescent girl, found its lascivious counterpart in *Lolita* (1955). (Nabokov admired "A Perfect Day for Bananafish.") Nabokov's novel commences with a seduction: the title name is stripped of its reference, parted into sensuous syllables, each caressed sonically by the tongue—"the tip of the tongue taking a trip of three steps down the palate to tap, at three, on the teeth. Lo. Lee. Ta" (9). Staying with the pre-lingual, renouncing meaning for a few sentences, our narrator (soon to be revealed as aesthete and pedophile) makes us experience the specificity of the medium—language's materiality—conducting a ritual initiation into aesthetic experience that the course of the novel will both repeat and interrogate. Nabokov, Salinger, and Greenberg helped make the fifties in America the democratic heyday of what the émigré called "aesthetic bliss" (Nabokov, "On a Book" 315).

An impetus for the renewal of the aesthetic in the fifties was fascination with Zen, concentrated in Suzuki's weekly seminar at Columbia (1952–1957), which drew, among others, Philip Guston, Agnes Martin, John Cage, Arthur Danto, and, possibly, Salinger. "Artists came as pilgrims and left as converts," Danto recalled (*Philosophizing* 166). They all would likely have concurred with Thomas Merton that "the taste for Zen in the West is in part a healthy reaction of people exasperated with the heritage of four centuries of Cartesianism: the reification of concepts, idolization of the reflexive consciousness. . . . Descartes made a fetish of the mirror in which the self finds itself. Zen shatters it" (*Conjectures* 260). By then (Merton wrote this in the early sixties) Zen had been linked with avant-garde art for some time; indeed, Cage first heard of it in a 1938 lecture in Seattle on the flouting of logic found in Dada and in Zen.

The centrality of the aesthetic in Eastern thought was spelled out for Americans in an influential 1946 book, *The Meeting of East and West* by Yale philosopher F. S. C. Northrop. Repurposing in effect a turn-of-the-century nationalist discourse of purported Japanese uniqueness (a project to which Suzuki was also dedicated) (Sharf 25), Northrop argues that "the modern Lockean, Galilean, Newtonian, Protestant, Anglo-American West . . . has tended to leave the modern Anglo-American man in the state of aesthetical and emotional blankness and starvation" (304). The antidote—and "complement" to the Western bias toward the theoretic, which reduces the aesthetic to "a mere appearance and a mere handmaid"—is the East's "attention to the nature of all things in their emotional and aesthetic, purely empirical and positivistic [by which he means "pure fact"] immediacy"— "colors, sounds, fragrances and flavors in the aesthetic continuum" (375, 377). In the West "continuum" tends to be understood as strictly "differentiated," comprising atomized particulars, as in Hume's empiricism. Northrop names William James as one of the few Western thinkers to conceive of a continuum as indeterminate and "undifferentiated by atomic sense data." James's radical empiricism, says Northrop, "provides a basis for understanding the Orient" (117). That fluid indeterminacy is congenial with the ineffability of "aesthetic immediacy": "when the Oriental designates the *Tao* or Nirvana . . . to be something which is not given through the specific senses," he means something that is "not speculatively arrived at by the logical scientific method of hypothesis, but which is immediately experienced" (377).

Kerouac on the road, following his bliss, his way (his *"tao"*), distills this immediacy into one kinetic syllable: "kicks," felt most intensely in the jazz scenes of rhythmic delirium (with George Shearing and others) that thrill the ecstatic Dean. This barely effable aesthetic bliss breaks the melancholy of what remains the most popular novel of the time, *On the Road*. Abstract art is the other fifties art form that allows one to mainline this bliss since its absence of figuration means no distractions. One is "alone with shapes and colors" on a canvas, says Greenberg in 1959, the "whole" of which we take in "at a glance; its unity should be immediately evident. . . . It is all there at once, like a sudden revelation" (4:80–81). In grasping this "at-onceness" "you are summoned and gathered into one point in the continuum of duration. . . . You become all attention, which means that you become, for the moment, selfless and in a sense entirely identified with the object of your attention" (4:81).

"Presentness is grace" is how Michael Fried would put it less than a decade later. His essay's final word, "grace" brings forward the theological implication that had been present from the start, in his epigraph from Perry Miller quoting Jonathan Edwards's remark that "the world exists anew every moment" (214). "Being lost in the object" is how Schopenhauer put it, to recall how he describes the beholder of the beautiful. This emptying out of self achieves "disinterested contemplation"—when we look at something in and for itself (as when we search the sky for its beauty and not to see what the weather is like, to take a Greenberg example); this is the purity of aesthetic judgment of "free beauty" earlier noted in Kant, Greenberg's master.

Yet for Greenberg, "disinterested contemplation" is not only spiritual but also political, a "challenge and a reproof to a society that . . . exaggerates the intrinsic value of purposeful and interested activity" (4:80). The "liberation" and "concentration" of attention that "detached contemplativeness" demands is not an obstacle but the very cause of abstract art's "growing popularity"—there is a "hunger for this particular kind of experience" that does not cash out in the "workaday world of conceptual determinacy." Indeed, Greenberg concludes "The Case for Abstract Art" (1959) with a hymn to the force of intuitive feeling aroused by contact with the unintelligible: "I don't know what there is in that painting, but I can't take my eyes off it," writes Greenberg, imagining a response many people make about abstract art. He adds: "This kind of bewilderment is salutary. It does us good not to be able to explain, either to ourselves or others, what we enjoy or love; it expands our capacity for experience" (4:84). These passages help refute the familiar charge that Greenberg's formalism eliminates or ignores content. Rather, here he clarifies what content is. He shows how the phenomenology of intense looking—the bewildering encounter with the "strictly optical"—acquires ethical "effect"; in the process content becomes an aspect of form. "You know that a work of art has content because of its effect": effect is content. Since form and content can never be "adequately distinguished," he finds the term "formalism" "stultifying" in assuming they can be separated (4:269–270).

■

In his *Saturday Evening Post* article Greenberg could be said to offer Kantianism for the common reader, and he does so in the most concrete terms, free of condescension. His portrayal of aesthetic experience looks to *Critique of Judgement,* whose author, said Greenberg late in life, "came closer to describing what went on in the mind when experiencing art than anyone before or anyone after him" (qtd. de Duve, *Clement Greenberg* 108). A barest sketch of the Kantian context would note that the first *Critique* (of pure reason) had concentrated on the objectivity and rationality of human thought and the system of logical rules that organize thinking. In *Critique of Judgement* (the third *Critique*) Kant takes up our subjective response to experience. Though he had no great interest or taste in art per se, Kant found in aesthetic experience—our spontaneous feeling for the beautiful—a model for the workings of subjectivity. It is in this sense that commentators remark the paradox that *"The Critique of Judgement* is not primarily or fundamentally a work in aesthetics at all." Only if one possesses imagination and "something like an aesthetic response" to one's experience can one "possibly think coherently about, or pass judgment on," either oneself or one's environment. This capacity attests to the "'subjective' aspects of our cognitive capacities" (Bell 232, 222, 244). (This approach, which tallies with the German romantic appropriation of the "aesthetic idea" as a new—non-discursive—way of making sense, is one way to counter Dewey's complaint that Kant confines the aesthetic in an enclave of beauty.)

I will take up the broader construal of Kant's project sketched above and briefly track what the "aesthetic idea" sponsors—subjective experience, that is, judgment unfettered from understanding's zeal to classify particulars under concepts, and forced to judge spontaneously, without rules in place. The imaginative intuition that is the "aesthetic idea" amounts to Kant's revision of his first *Critique*'s claim that "intuitions without concepts are blind"—that intuitions can only be experienced *after* concepts have been applied. However, this "ignores that, at some point, we have to learn concepts, that we go on learning new concepts routinely" and that there will be occasions, such as the sensory encounter of aesthetic experience, when we engage with objects "prior to having the concepts they will later fall under" (Bernstein, *Against* 328). Because writing about the sublime pushes Kant to venture beyond the rationality of the "understanding"—the master enforcer of determinate rules—he sees that concept and intuition are separable and indeed that "blind" intuition is a crucial actuality in and of our subjective experience, for which the aesthetic is the model.

The potential for encountering the contingent and unsettling when we confront the sublime is built into what Kant calls *reflective* (aesthetic) judgment, which, unlike *determinative* judgment, is free of the responsibility to subsume a particular object under a universal—a concept, rule, principle, or law (Kant 15). The work of subsumption is the work of *determinative* judgment and defines the very activity of thinking as guided by reason and understanding. (Moral judgments differ by responding to commands, categorical imperatives.) By these standards, reflective aesthetic judgment's *not* forming or acquiring concepts makes it something other than discursive thinking. This "other" searches for a concept to render the uncanny intelligible, but the search must fail if the "free play" of imagination vital to aesthetic experience is to flourish. Decisive for reflective aesthetic judgment is "the character of the search, and the unusual results we will find it to have, rather than its completion in a concept" (Pillow 26).

Although lacking conceptual closure, reflective aesthetic judgment is more than mindless rapture. In judgments of taste, pleasure is the free play of imagination harmonizing with—yet not being determined by—the understanding. The variety alive in nature—bird songs, rippling brooks, a rolling meadow—represents nothing, has no "intrinsic meaning," but stimulates and freshens imagination (60, 73–74). In encounters with artworks or obscure objects, the hold of understanding is loosened and imagination is free to be stirred by images, feelings, memories, ideas, as it tries to relate and connect parts to a whole, treating the object *"as if* its various parts do cohere as a unity informed by a purpose or intention" (32). But this experience is necessarily difficult to put into words, eluding as it does a determinate concept (hence its "unusual results"). Recall Greenberg's example: "I don't know what there is in that painting, but I can't take my eyes off it."

If a beautiful *form* has sublime *content,* then reflection moves from "restful contemplation" to agitated exploration of meaning, as "the mind abandons itself to the imagination" and the latter finds itself destabilized: "This excess for the imagination . . . is like an abyss in which it fears to lose itself" (Kant 86, 88). (Here I am following the argument of Kirk Pillow's *Sublime Understanding.*) (78, 93). The abyss opens, for instance, when we see a "bewildering" (Kant's word) work of ornate architecture—St. Peter's in Rome is Kant's example. Sublime content is conveyed via "aesthetic ideas." While not relevant to a formal judgment of taste, "aesthetic ideas" possess the spirit of "genius" and override (at least for a time) the formal discipline of taste (Kant 171). In the presence of the ungraspable multiplicity of "aesthetic ideas," the relaxed self of disinterested judgment has trouble finding its cognitive balance, as an artifact (painting and sculpture but also poetry and rhetoric) provokes the mind into "more thought than admits of expression in a concept determined by words." An aesthetic idea, notes Kant, "cannot become a cognition, because it is an intuition (of the imagination) for which an adequate concept can never be found" (170). Although Kant grows anxious regarding genius and eagerly domesticates it ("taste . . . severely clips its wings" and thereby helps support a "continually progressive culture"), clearly its recalcitrant energy also stirs him (148).

Greenberg not only respected blind intuition, he relied on it in his relish of visual experience over any kind of theorizing about aesthetics. For him aesthetic judgments are "immediate, intuitive, undeliberate, involuntary, they leave no room for conscious application of standards, criteria, rules." These operate "subliminally" and their auditory articulation is the grunt, as noted earlier (4:265). An account (Jules Olitski's, by way of Arthur Danto) of how Greenberg confronted a painting shows his openness in action. In his studio visits he would first keep his back to the new painting, "then wheel abruptly around to let his practiced eye take it in without giving the mind a chance to interpose any prior theories, as if there was a race between the transmission of visual stimuli and the speed of thought. Or he would cover his eyes until it was time to look. . . . Greenberg would say very little other than grunt a kind of approval or disapproval" (Danto, *After the End* 89).

Asked in an interview to name criteria to distinguish good from lesser art he said that "there are criteria, but they can't be put into words. . . . Works of art move you to a greater or lesser extent, that's all. So far, words have been futile in the matter. . . . You just wait and see what happens—what the artist does" (qtd. Danto 90). Even while, as Danto comments, "Greenberg could hardly have achieved his tremendous reputation as an art critic by grunts and grimaces," Greenberg acknowledged that his precepts, standards, and criteria were activated as a "subliminal operation . . . hidden from discursive consciousness" (4:265). Gertrude Stein had the same passion for a seeing that defeated knowing, purged of remembrance, anticipation, and prior conviction. She achieved this empty vision and "really began to realize that an oil painting is an oil painting" only when, on the "long benches" in art galleries during a hot summer in Florence and Venice, she started "sleeping and waking in front of all these pictures" (231–232). Stein's moment of waking, like Greenberg's of sudden turning, enables the freshness of aesthetic looking.

Greenberg's gift was for translating the visceral response to "the instantaneous shock of sight" into descriptive (rather than explanatory) prose that kept in touch with his initial studio encounter. According to Greenberg in 1967, his trust in the intuitive allowed him to relish the fact that "art can get away with anything because there is nothing to tell us what it cannot get away with," a recognition that had long ago liberated him from having to take a "line" or "position." To adhere to such would mean never acquiring what Greenberg deems precious: "an appetite not just for the disconcerting but for the state of being disconcerted" (2:34; 4:267). Hence he confesses impatience with

being labeled a "formalist," a reduction that he also found intellectually incoherent, as noted earlier. Predictably, Greenberg's admirable
openness was greeted as disingenuous by skeptics who charged him
with making form autonomous, thus perpetuating the dualism of form
and content basic to idealist aesthetics (4:272). The postmodernists of
the eighties would indict Greenberg from other directions—his friend-
liness toward "modern science" as a model of "consistency" and "self-
criticism" for "modernist art" (4:90–91) and, especially, his stress on
the optical that was said to devalue the tactile, erase the human body,
and hygienically purify art. Caroline Jones's title (2005) summed up
the verdict: *Eyesight Alone: Clement Greenberg's Modernism and the
Bureaucratization of the Senses.*

◼

In "Avant-Garde and Kitsch" (1939) Greenberg points out that the very
purity of the avant-garde remains dependent on the patronage of the
ruling class, "from which it assumed itself cut off, but to which it
has always remained attached by an umbilical cord of gold. The paradox is real" (1:10–11). In its own way Salinger's career confirmed this.
The Glasses pursue ascetic spiritual ideals while nestled amid glossy
New Yorker ads for Cadillacs and cashmere. A more interesting irony
is that Salinger's fastidiousness and eventual renunciation were actually consonant with an "unconscious but profound . . . ethic of silence" emanating from the *New Yorker*'s long-time editor (1951–1987),
the "incorruptible" William Shawn. "Indifferent" to fame, fashions,
trends, prizes, "and even the preferences of readers," as Renata Adler
describes him in *Gone,* her angry elegy for Shawn's magazine, Shawn
is a kind of ego ideal for the younger Salinger (23, 21). Shawn's eccentricities included the acceptance of pieces that he would postpone
running, sometimes permanently. "The magazine's ambivalence in
precisely the matter of publication was remarkable. There began to
be a feeling that it was vulgar, perhaps morally wrong to write. . . .
The aversion to personal publicity for editors and writers, the increas-
ing respect for privacy of subjects were turning into a reluctance to
publish at all" (23). No wonder Salinger was regarded at the magazine
as the model of artistic and ethical integrity. If Adler is right the *New*

Yorker's advertised hedonism was merely a way to pay the bills so that scrupulosity and silence might reign between the published lines, ineffable music heard only by the subtlest ears. Salinger's turn to silence makes public the magazine's inner logic—his act is the exfoliation of its editorial devotion to an ideal of renunciation.

If aesthetic living is not consumer hedonism, neither should it be equated with fin de siècle withdrawal into Axel's castle; this "purely contemplative aesthetic attitude" that rejects life "on account of art" becomes the "only justification for life." This "fatal romantic renunciation," as Arnold Hauser terms it in *The Sociology of Art,* is usually "compensation for the disappointments we have suffered" (307). Think of that minor scholar of French symbolist poetry and consummate aesthete Humbert Humbert. What I am calling aesthetic living has a less resentful or compensatory tone because it is unattached to material comfort but is alive to a tacit dimension, the elusive and ineffable in art and life.

■

One scientist with a deep attraction to the tacit built a theory around it. He articulated it in 1958 as an alternative and (in effect) aesthetic account of scientific objectivity—one marked by the crucial but overlooked "tacit dimension"—the simple and consequential fact that we know more than we can say. This form of knowing characterizes Kant's notion of poetic genius, as earlier noted, and is here extended to the work of scientists. Much of their experience turns out to be "groping" and "feeling" their "way" amid "inarticulate manifestations" (Polanyi, *Personal* 150). This sounds more like a description of Lambert Strether (indeed "groping" is a key word in James's preface) than a scientist in a lab. Michael Polanyi's *Personal Knowledge,* from which I have been quoting, has always been in the shadow of a work it anticipates by four years, Thomas Kuhn's *The Structure of Scientific Revolutions* (1962). Kuhn saluted it in passing and the book has never lacked admirers, including many artists. Polanyi, a distinguished Hungarian chemist who renounced science for philosophy, writes with fervor, intoxicated, it seems, with aesthetic bliss: "True discovery is not a strictly logical performance" but requires "plunges" and "leaps" across logical gaps

(123). "Tearing away the paper screen of graphs, equations, and computations, I have tried to lay bare the inarticulate manifestations of intelligence by which we know things in a purely personal manner" (64). Neither subjective nor objective but transcending their opposition, personal knowledge in "science is not made but discovered, and as such it claims to establish contact with reality beyond the clues on which it relies. It commits us, passionately and far beyond our comprehension, to a vision of reality. Of this responsibility we cannot divest ourselves by setting up objective criteria of verifiability. . . . For we live in it as in the garment of our skin. Like love, to which it is akin, this commitment is a 'shirt of flame,' blazing with passion and, also like love, consumed by devotion to a universal demand. Such is the true sense of the objectivity in science" (64). Science joins art and mysticism in breaking "through the screen of objectivity," drawing on "our pre-conceptual capacities of contemplative vision," capacities shared, he repeatedly shows, by infants and chimpanzees (199).

William James would have welcomed *Personal Knowledge* as confirming a vision of science he had long championed. New thinking in contemporary neuroscience suggests that William James and Polanyi have been right all along. They certainly had the right enemy, one they share with revisionary approaches in neuroscience: intellectualist orthodoxy. Seeking to replace the view that reduces mind to brain and thinking to computation (deliberate calculation) with a holistic approach to consciousness, new thinking shows that "meaningful thought arises only for the whole animal dynamically engaged with its environment. . . . Consciousness requires the joint operation of brain, body and world. Indeed, consciousness is an achievement of the whole animal in its environmental context." "I deny, in short, that you are your brain," writes a philosopher of science, Alva Noë (10). Counting William James an ally, Noë critiques the intellectualist paradigm governing neuroscience, a model that construes "our distinctive nature" as thinking beings of calculative efficiency: "we perceive, we evaluate, we decide, we plan, we act" and thereby "rise above mere habit and act from principles" (98).

This intellectualist portrait is undeniably flattering. As Charles Taylor notes, its depiction of "modern disengaged agency continuously generates a discourse of self-congratulation" because it is seen as "inseparable from freedom, responsibility, and self-transparency" (79). Such agency and judgment, though, depend on an account of the mind as both pristine and a void, assuming "deliberation and judgment all the way down" and that mental life can exist without presuppositions. This intellectualist fantasy reflects the still entrenched Cartesian belief that human beings are at bottom thinkers. This ignores that we are creatures of habit, which helps us acquire the taken-for-granted background practices, skills, and customs by which we are at home in the world and not perpetual beginners carefully exercising judgment. "Thinking and deliberating are themselves the exercise of more basic capacities for skillful expertise," says Noë. "And the hallmark of expertise is fluency: it is engaged and, precisely, nondeliberative" (99). Expertise in intellectual activities—such as "chess, mathematics, talking, and reading"—is not based on rigorous calculation: "Expertise requires precisely the absence of care and deliberation that the intellectualist wrongly takes to be the hallmark of our mental lives" (Noë 101). In coping with the world, "infants, animals and experts" all rely on non-linguistic, non-conceptual discriminations, and upon this ground is built our linguistic, conceptual capacities, notes the Heideggerian phenomenologist Hubert Dreyfus, a key influence on Noë (see also the papers collected by Joseph K. Schear, in *Mind, Reason and Being in the World*).

Intuition is even granted standing in the social sciences, whose methods and standards have little to do with phenomenology and other philosophical critiques of intellectualism. The influential experimental psychologist and behavioral economist Daniel Kahneman sums up his research by noting the "balance" humans achieve between the "marvels and the flaws of intuitive thinking." Because our judgments are rife with biases and cognitive illusions due to ignoring the logic of probability, "humans are not well described by the rational-agent model" propagated by the Chicago school of economics. Their libertarian assumptions enshrine faith in the human capacity for rational choice as the basis of public policy. But life, says Kahneman, is "more complex for behavioral economists than for true believers in human rationality" (411–412). Impulses and intuitions—when we know without knowing how we know—guide what he calls "fast thinking" which operates as a "machine for jumping to conclusions" (85). Fast thinking is "the origin of much that we do wrong, but is also the origin of most of what we do right—which is most of what we do" (411).

What if, though, far from the optimistic precincts of social science, the "world-involving" quality of habit shrivels to a defensive gesture and absence of deliberation is not fluency but anomie and one's refusal to explain or even to desire leaves the self a vacancy? Behold Melville's hollowed out, ghostly Bartleby, American literature's iconic renunciant. A perverse incarnation of the "radical purity" basic to Greenberg's formalism, Bartleby's opacity is analogous to the "flat picture plane" surrendering to the "resistance of its medium," which consists in the plane's "denial of efforts to 'hole through' it for realistic perspectival space." The "picture plane itself grows shallower and shallower, flattening out the fictive planes of depth" (1:34–35). Greenberg is describing the "destruction of realistic pictorial space" but his words are apt for Bartleby's depthless, hence "impenetrable," surface. He drains away all the vivacity and intensity that such pictorial purity achieves. His notorious verbal signature, the flat, affectless "I prefer not to," seems to emanate from nowhere, a shield of a greeting that repels human contact. The phrase is what Sontag calls "'bad speech,' by which I mean dissociated speech—speech dissociated from the body (and therefore from feeling)" (*Essays* 307). Human detritus in the frenetic capitalist time-is-money world of New York ("A Tale of Wall Street" is Melville's subtitle), Bartleby is also compelling, or at least contagious. Before long, his flat phrase has insinuated itself into the idioms of his fellow office mates. He seems to get under the skin and into the speech of all who meet him, especially the narrator, who is moved to compose "Bartleby" as a memorial to his opaque employee. Hence, for all his minimalism, Bartleby performs a generative renunciation.

Like Seymour Glass, he is another spectral, doomed New Yorker. Whereas Seymour draws an army of explainers, Bartleby is brought into being by just one. His former boss, a rather melancholy lawyer, brings Bartleby before us as a gnawing riddle and his efforts to solve it are for naught—Bartleby remains as fugitive as his vague speech and even vaguer personal circumstances. He denies the lawyer's efforts to carve out some depth and dimension that might disclose a realist figure. By the end, the narrator is so desperate to "hole through" the flat monochrome canvas of Bartleby "for realistic perspectival space" that he offers up a scrap of humanizing rumor—that he once worked in a dead-letter office. The plangent rhyme that ends the tale—"Ah Bartleby! Ah humanity!"—is emotionally powerful but its forced lyricism seems designed to muffle the failure of the narrator's compulsion to explain.

The canvas Bartleby embodies is discernible in Allan Kaprow's description of Robert Rauschenberg's once scandalous work *Erased de Kooning* (1953) (an admirer of de Kooning, Rauschenberg asked him for a drawing in order to erase it). Kaprow notes: "Symbolically the erasure functioned like, say, the renunciation of worldly life by a hermit-saint, but now exercised within the profession of painting and drawing." Kaprow links Rauschenberg's act of "esthetic denial" with his earlier large, utterly flat—one all black, the other all white—monochrome canvases of 1951. Made when John Cage was an influence on him, each is painted with a roller, the color thus evenly distributed across the canvas. Though first regarded as a joke, they are pivotal, says Kaprow, "for in the context of Abstract Expressionist noise and gesture, they suddenly brought us face to face with a numbing, devastating silence," leaving "viewers with themselves and the void in front of them. Their shadows moved across the blank screen, which mirrored the stammering images of their own unwilling minds, because such 'nothing' was intolerable." Everything was "thrown back at" the viewer as "their responsibility, not the picture's" (70–71). A more precise account would be hard to find of that intolerable nothing, Bartleby, and the claims he makes on the baffled, empathic narrator and on us.

Seymour and Bartleby are emblems of their creators' public withdrawals; the former is a poet who prefers not to publish—he thinks his work "too un-western, too lotusy," turned against the American world in which they were written (*Seymour* 124). The latter simply and solely prefers not to; his inertia forecasts Melville's ceasing to publish fiction thirty-four years before he died. And each character is an emblem of art itself, its inscrutable silence. This limit to knowing—entangled for both authors with spiritual meaning—shapes their formal strategies. Melville enacts his Calvinist skepticism of man's capacity to know Truth by fashioning epistemological riddles sentence by entangling sentence, as readers, for instance, of *Benito Cereno* discover when they become enveloped, early on, in "shadows present, foreshadowing deeper shadows to come." Seymour's shadow falls over everything even as the character is represented directly only for a few brief pages that narrate the hours before he dies: shadow is his substance, an equation that has a unique meaning in Seymour's case. For deepening his shadowy existence are his multiple lives. No one, not even Buddy, can be certain about where one of Seymour's identities ends and another begins. Reading Seymour's poems about a young widower, Buddy finds it "very hard to believe that Seymour hadn't buried at least one wife that nobody in our family knew about. He hadn't of course. Not . . . in this incarnation, at any rate" (132). He may very well have led "memorable existences in exurban Benares, feudal Japan, and metropolitan Atlantis" (133).

So what happened in a Florida hotel room in 1948 needs to be read *sub species aeternitatis*. Once the cosmic perspective is invoked, the story's enigma and horror dissipate, if not vanish. An ambiguity remains: Buddy says Seymour "tallied with the classical conception" of a "*mukta*, a ring-ding enlightened man, a God-knower," adding, "with or without a suicide plot in his head" (106). The logic here is elliptical but seems to suggest a delicate balancing act on Buddy's part. In the Vedantin view a *mukta* is one released from the endless cycle of reincarnation (*Samsara*) and reaches *Nirvana*. Suicide however is bad karma, an act that is usually cause to cycle perpetually. Just as Seymour refused to "say in perfectly intelligible language where it hurt," Buddy refuses to specify Seymour's spiritual status or affiliations. He prefers to understand his brother as both enlightened and unreleased, his suicide as merely an exit and an entrance (life and death "are merely words," says Buddy). He believes Seymour dies happy; indeed happiness—embodied in his oneness with life's daily details—is what it means for Seymour to exist. As he tells Buddy, "all we do our whole lives is go from one little piece of Holy Ground to the next" (126, 213). Spending the afternoon playing in the ocean with Sibyl is one of those little pieces.

Seymour possesses "the last absolutely unguarded face in the Greater New York Area," one whose openness radiates alertness and acceptance (174). Given that the "membrane is so thin between us," to recall what Seymour says of his relation to his brothers, inevitably Buddy comes to inhabit his late brother's affirmativeness. In the penultimate paragraph he refuses to give in to "an old urban reflex" (bred by the free-floating sarcasm of the Glass household) and say something "mildly caustic" about the creative writing students he teaches in a girls' college near the Canadian border. He finds himself moved by "being conscious of the good, the real" after having written about Seymour: "I can't be my brother's brother for nothing, and I know . . . there is no single thing more important than going into that awful [class] Room 307. There isn't one girl in there, including the Terrible Miss Zabel, who is not as much my sister as Boo Boo or Franny" (213).

"This happiness is strong stuff" and "marvelously liberating" (113). It gives Seymour boundless energy. He is the "most nearly tireless person," says Buddy, who adds he is "wild about everybody in the family and most people outside it" (190, 180). Of his wife, Muriel, Seymour notes in his diary, "How I worship her simplicity" (Raise 73). Of her dominating mother, Seymour's nemesis, Mrs. Fedder the culture vulture, Seymour confides to his diary: she "might as well be dead." "And yet she goes on living, stopping off at delicatessens, seeing her analyst. . . . I love her. I find her unimaginably brave" (72). In "Hapworth" he finds all of us poor humans "brave" as we stumble along within this vale of tears or, more precisely, Veil of Maya, of earthly illusion and deception.

This final story, the first to give us Seymour plain, without Buddy's supervision, reveals there is no Seymour plain. His transmigrating soul has made him a kind of ceaseless time-traveler, permanently in transit. Overlap and digression, in other words, have become his very being and "Hapworth" is the final defeat of formal "compactness." Filled with exuberant "happiness" while acknowledging a bad temper, sexual lust, and some emotional instability, Seymour is, as usual, a precocious monologist, here a seven-year-old writing a letter home from summer camp. Specificities of time and space are of little relevance given that Seymour possesses the atemporal perspective of a soul who has enjoyed a number of "appearances," as he calls his reincarnations. He fondly remembers, for instance, his friendship ("purely by correspondence") with William Rowan Hamilton (Seymour leaves out that Hamilton was an Irish child prodigy who became, in the mid-nineteenth century, a distinguished physicist, mathematician, and astronomer).

Whereas in the *Introduction* the horizontal was Seymour's typical posture, now this little boy-god looms above; he seems benignly to look down from the heavens, regarding everyone, especially his parents, as adorable children ("you are not old enough, sweetheart," he tells Bessie). Salinger gives Seymour an occasionally gushing vocabulary, for which he apologizes more than once in his endless letter. It includes a request that his family pray for his prose style to improve; he vows to rid it of "fustian." He blames his verbosity on the fact that he is "writing at a swift, terrible rate of speed" since he feels the "in some ways scrawny amount of time left in this appearance." His creator steers clear of dwelling on the potential pathos of the situation; "Hapworth" is another testament to Salinger doing it his way, the way of immanence, as he places himself and his reader inside the (idiosyncratic) spiritual dictates of Seymour's world(s). In his twentieth-century New York "appearance," Seymour, seven-year-old loquacious savant, possesses comically precocious (and precious) literary ambitions, reminding his folks to send the work of his beloved Marcel Proust—"this uncomfortable, devastating genius of modern times"—in its "entirety."

Seymour lives on in death, in the shadows, *is* the shadow at the threshold of transition between life and death. The Seymour of Buddy's narrations dwells in something like satori, the Zen state of "pure consciousness" that escapes "the competence of language, thus of definition, and almost that of description; thus, literally untranslatable" (Barthes, *The Neutral* 173–174). When it is explained at all, "either in words or gestures, its content more or less undergoes a mutilation," says Suzuki (103). Satori abides in the ineffable, refuses to "tame the event by making it enter into a causality, a generality, which reduces the incomparable to the comparable" (*Neutral* 174). And following Suzuki, Barthes observes the "key word of satori—the exclamation: *Ah, this.*" Like Greenberg's grunt, or James's "that," these visceral monosyllables attest to passionate presence that defeats explanation.

■

Salinger has taken remarkable care in making this Glass at once transparent and opaque: Seymour, dead and in transit, is forever safe from the prying eyes of skeptics and lovers alike. Fellow traumatized war

veteran, Seymour is a fantasy of Salinger's own psychic need for absolute safety. "The war, as something not really over, pervaded" life
at home, notes his daughter in her memoir (Margaret Salinger 44).
Achieving safety became the condition of his creativity which he defined as writing exactly *"on his own terms"*—producing not master-
pieces but "prose home movies" as if for friends and family and then,
narrowing the circle, for decades writing only for himself. "There is a
marvelous peace in not publishing. . . . I love to write. But I write just
for myself and my own pleasure" is the closest thing to an explanation
he ever offered of his renunciation (qtd. Fosburgh). All this control,
all this centripetal banking of energies to insure the self's sovereignty
over a community of one, a *reductio ad absurdum* of the symbolist
poet's disdain of the public at large, satisfied "with a single reader of
superior merit," to recall Valéry (8:221). Salinger made himself that
reader, at peace in the solitude he had so assiduously devised, angry
when strangers intruded, which was often.

This world-famous recluse remains a magnet for our clever ironies
and cynical paradoxes and psychological theories (most are variations
on "the privacy-for-profit angle," as Wilfred Sheed once wrote derisively of a Salinger biographer convinced the novelist's withdrawal was a
strategic courting of riches and attention): so much frantic spinning
to fill the void of his compelling indifference to our expectations of
how a beloved author should behave. Indulging our defensive need to
explain is hard to resist (as the above paragraph attests). However, this
writer's uncomfortably simple demand is that we enter into, inhabit,
the challenge of his renunciation: "Please don't simply see it; feel it,"
as Buddy implores us (*Seymour* 170). That is, feel the force of its happiness and preciousness (in both senses), its pain and detachment. To do
so requires some Zen acceptance of "no-knowledge" or Keatsian negative capability—resting in doubt, foregoing the anxious striving after
certainty—and letting be the conundrums of his art and life.

To literature students the fatality of explanation is familiar given the
wariness of modernist writers and theorists toward the ubiquity of instrumental rationalism. "Show, don't tell" is a modernist mantra not

irrelevant to the final movement of the *Tractatus*. Feeling is the domain of showing and both are part of modernism's fascination with mute being: "A poem should not mean/ But be." Archibald MacLeish's always quoted words neatly distill French symbolist and New Critical aesthetics. These formed the intellectual foundation of mid-century college literature courses housed in institutions of "bourgeois-rationalist culture" (Sontag's phrase). In other words, the classroom was shaped by the radical assaults on the stature of cognitive knowing found in Zen and the European avant-garde. This commerce might be less than welcome to Sontag since her relentless sophistication requires the foil of a blinkered, anxious academy. Her modernism is maximally rarefied. Its emblem might be Mallarmé, the first, she reminds us, to use words "to clean up our word-clogged reality by creating silence around things." (*Essays* 309). Language, though, is notoriously promiscuous and worldly, stubbornly referential, too busy conveying, like it or not, so won't stay pure for very long. All a poet can do is try.

According to Franny Glass, however, they aren't even trying. The poems written by her undergraduate poetry professors "don't leave a single solitary thing beautiful." At best they "get inside your head and leave *something* there . . . it may be just some kind of terribly fascinating, syntaxy *droppings*—excuse the expression" (*Franny* 20). Franny's disappointment in the absence of beauty is part of the malaise that seizes her in the middle of lunch with Lane and only deepens in *Zooey*. By then Franny seems depressed enough to join Seymour. An aspiring actress but ashamed of her thirst for applause, Franny finds herself in a dilemma: "just sick of ego, ego, ego" yet also "sick of not having the courage to be an absolute nobody." Her self-awareness is part of her pain; as she tells her brother: "Just because I'm choosy about what I want—in this case, en*light*enment, or *peace*, instead of money or prestige or *fame* . . . doesn't mean I'm not as egotistical and self-seeking as everybody else" (*Franny* 29–30; *Zooey* 149). Franny's dislike of striving and strivers ("I'm sick of everybody that wants to *get* somewhere") is a protest rampant in fifties American literary culture—recall such dropouts as Bellow's Augie March, Ellison's invisible narrator, Kerouac and Ginsberg's "angel-headed" hipsters. By the next decade renunciation goes mainstream in the sixties counter-culture. Franny is too exhausted even to withdraw.

What makes Franny's spiritual torpor, her acedia, unique is how rich it is philosophically. Her crisis has a long foreground: she grew up on the great spiritual works but, as noted earlier, without really grasping how to *live* their demand to empty the soul of desire. Recall Eckhart saying that to understand his teaching of being as "releasement" one must first of all have a released existence. One must be "equal," as Eckhart says, to the truth of which he speaks. Franny needs a new relation to spiritual teachings, one that will lift her beyond her contempt. Beloved brother Seymour turned out to have a fatally literal understanding of the "courage to be an absolute nobody"; his absence only sharpens her sense of desolation. To find a saving middle term is the burden, we will see, of Zooey's interrogation.

A fellow New Yorker, a woman of around Franny's age, was caught in a similar irony: obsessively introspective while also eager to extinguish the ego. Eva Hesse (b. 1936) first assaulted the self in a series of self-portraits she began in 1960 that are brutal in their frontality, as they disclose a swollen, magnified face and forehead rendered in heavy, thick brushstrokes and discordant colors. She eventually would become a pioneer of post-minimalist sculpture of disturbingly sensual, sticky, visceral forms (made often of latex, rubber, fiberglass), achieving eminence even before dying at thirty-four of a malignant brain tumor in 1970. In a 1969 statement that recalls a declaration by Ad Reinhardt (quoted below), Hesse writes of seeking to create "non art, nonconnotive [*sic*], non anthropomorphic, non geometric, non, nothing, everything, but of another kind, vision, sort, from a total other reference point" (qtd. Lippard 165). Or, as Franny puts it—what she seeks is "an absolutely new conception of what everything's about" (*Franny* 37). Hesse's radically "other" vision that embraces contraries is evident when she describes the early piece *Hang Up* (1966), an empty six-by-seven-foot frame set on a wall, from whose top horizontal section is attached a ten-foot steel cord that hangs to the floor, its other end plugged into the bottom horizontal. Its very emptiness can be read as full of "nothing" and of "everything," hence "absurd." (She loved Beckett.) She praises *Hang Up* (its title a nice pun) for being "so absurd. . . . It is the most ridiculous structure I have ever made and that is why it is really good. . . . It is framing nothing" (qtd. Lippard 56). In her notebook (later the catalogue statement) Hesse puts in language

her logic of contraries as she faces the paradox of rendering renunciation. She asks herself "how to achieve by not achieving? how to make
by not making? / it's all in that. / it's not the new. it is what is not yet
known, / thought, seen, touched but really what is not. / and that is"
(qtd. Lippard 165). "How to achieve by not achieving?" This riddle
reverberates for this shell-shocked generation.

A version of Hesse's Zen-like query preoccupies the youngest Glass
children. Franny hopes to resolve it by confining achievement to interiority, where one reaches spiritual transcendence. She reveres the
Greek Stoic Epictetus, and tells Lane and later Zooey how deeply affected she is by *The Way of a Pilgrim*, a prayer book in which a Russian
peasant learns to pray without ceasing. Gradually by repetition the
prayer acquires a "self-active power of its own" and becomes "automatic in the heart": the person praying "is supposed to enter into the
so-called reality of things" (*Franny* 38; *Zooey* 113). Much of the final
fifty pages of *Zooey* concerns her brother's stinging, if well-meaning,
critique, not of the prayer itself, but "why and how" Franny is "using
it" (169). Zooey thinks she has made the prayer the basis of a theatrical martyrdom—"this little snotty crusade you think you're leading against everybody"—that is really an "attack" on "higher education"—and most everything else—as rife with ego (161). Franny's error
is using the prayer as a "crusade"—a means to an end—"to lay up
some kind of . . . spiritual treasure," an error that repeats the original
pilgrim's conception of spirituality as a project: He "begins his pilgrim-
age to find a teacher . . . who can teach him *how* to pray incessantly,
and *why*" (148, 111).

   Zooey's intimation is that the "wisdom" or authentic spirituality
that Fanny craves is not a means or a technique or a project or knowledge, but motiveless, a mode of living without why. Rejection of the
"why" is especially conspicuous in Meister Eckhart, who appears on
Buddy and Seymour's recommended reading list. Abjuring pursuit of
"why" opens one up to the possibility of spiritual inwardness via self-
abandonment. To ask "why" is to regard God as one would a cow:
"you love it for the milk and the cheese and for your own profit. So

do all people who love God for the sake of outward riches or inward consolation. But they do not love God correctly, for they merely love their own advantage," as Reiner Schürmann paraphrases Eckhart (99). In sum, because asking "why" is the path to "possessing and having" it must be blocked—and by nothing less than the soul forsaking "all things, God and all creatures." Eckhart notes the extremity of this charge: "Of course, it sounds astonishing to say that the soul should forsake God" but the "soul must exist in a free nothingness. That we should forsake God is altogether what God intends, for as long as the soul has God, knows God and is aware of God, she is far from God" (*Writings* 244).

Franny's regret at lacking "the courage to be an absolute nobody" points to Eckhart's famous sermon (#52) on what it means to be poor in spirit. Reading is not the same, though, as living the words. Zooey hopes Franny will ponder how being poor and "nobody" might become integrated as a "daily duty," or "whatever the hell your duty is in life" (*Zooey* 169). As noted earlier, this is how you *"use"* your "freakish education." Offering a clue is a passage from the *Bhagavad Gita* printed on Seymour's beaverboard still nailed to his bedroom door: "Desire for the fruits of work must never be your motive in working. . . . Renounce attachments to the fruits" (177). Using terms conspicuous in Eckhart, Zooey implores Franny to realize that "the only thing that counts in the religious life is de*tach*ment. . . . Detachment, buddy, and only detachment. Desirelessness" (198). Franny's rage against peers and teachers and friends is inflated by ego and ambition; such animus is "too damn personal, Franny. I mean it," says Zooey while admitting he has the same problem (162–163).

The emptying out of the "personal"—of will and intention and motive—so as to live without why is required, says Eckhart, for union of human and divine. Possessing and having must be eradicated: "Here the soul forsakes all things, God, and all creatures." Extending this logic, Eckhart says: "We should practice virtue and not possess it. That is the perfection of virtue—to be free of virtue" (243). The Tao poses the same paradox: "High virtue is non-virtuous; / Therefore it has virtue" (qtd. Merton, *Mystics and Zen Masters* 75). The just human being does not possess justice, for Eckhart, but rather *is* the principle of justice.

"He is his own principle or 'principle without principle'" (Hollywood, *The Soul* 141). Even the devout, those who will to do God's will, are not yet empty of possession: "the more one wills to abandon her will, the more one is willing and is caught up in her will" (Sells 166). Recall Hawthorne's version of this trap: monomaniacal black-veiled Reverend Hooper. As Eckhart says to the nuns he addresses: "All those who with attachment cling to prayer, to fasting, to vigils, and to all kinds of exterior mortifications," such "attachment to any work . . . deprives you of the freedom to serve God in this present now" (*Writings* 160). In Eckhart's rigor of renunciation (which he shared with and partly borrowed from Marguerite Porete, whose *The Mirror of Simple Souls* was burned in 1306, four years before she herself was burned along with it) attachment weighs us down while detachment lightens the soul, empties it of the habit of possessiveness. Then it enters a state of "virginity" or receptivity that launches one on a path Eckhart calls wandering joy (Sells 118). This wandering is not a drifting into quietist withdrawal or unworldliness (not a Platonic elevation into cosmic contemplation), but rather a living in the world, an embrace of "this present now" (Schürmann 45–46).

Eckhart's idea of detachment endorses faith as the way to salvation while critically interrogating the other traditional route—of works and rewards. For Eckhart any act done as a means or a use is a "work" and thereby enslaves the will. "The soul that gives up all will and works is no longer concerned with poverty or riches, honor or dishonor, heaven or hell, with self, other, or deity" (Sells 118). In what commentators call his boldest sermon, on the "blessed are the poor in spirit," Eckhart situates this emptied self of "releasement" in radical spiritual poverty: "We want to go further and say: whoever is to be so poor [as I am describing the condition] must live so that he does not even know himself to live, neither for himself, nor for truth, nor for God. He must be bereft of all knowledge to the point of neither knowing nor recognizing nor perceiving that God lives in him; even more: he should be devoid of all knowledge that lives in him." This is the "way to be poor of one's own understanding" (qtd. Schürmann 212–213). The final step to complete emptying out is what Eckhart calls "breakthrough" and it brings man into a kind of vast inner "desert" (Eckhart's word) of solitude:

I stand devoid of my own will and of the will of God and of all his works and of God himself, there I am above all created kind and am neither God nor creature. Rather, I am what I was and what I shall remain now and forever. Then I receive an impulse which shall bring me above all the angels. In this impulse I receive wealth so vast that God cannot be enough for me in all that makes him God, and with all his divine works. For in this breakthrough it is bestowed upon me that I and God are one. . . . Now God no longer finds a place in man, for man gains with this poverty what he has been eternally and evermore will remain. Now God is one with the spirit, and that is the strictest poverty one can find. (qtd. Schürmann 215)

The extremity of this "breakthrough" beyond God is disquieting. No wonder the Inquisition brought charges against him, and the Pope judged him a heretic. In the passage above we can discern what Eckhart means by his statement: "I pray God to rid me of God." This paradoxical yearning for riddance brings him to the positive declaration "I am what I was." A strange claim (derived from the Platonic doctrine of the preexistence of the soul), it points to the freedom one embodies before coming into the world, the pure receptivity and affirmation of a form waiting to be filled. For Eckhart "this original freedom appears not as lost, but as something to be discovered: it is ahead of us as the goal of a liberation" (Schürmann 12–13).

Schürmann makes explicit how far Eckhart takes us: "At the outset of his odyssey of detachment, man did not expect that much. His path appeared as voluntary poverty, but now it has led him to a region beyond God, where he no longer recognizes himself. ["I am above all created kind and am neither God nor creature"]. He feels he has reached that point of wandering that Japanese Zen masters depict by a canvas totally covered with black: God, man, and the world are no more" (117). This migration into self-transcendence then produces a thrust outward. The highest contemplation engenders heightened activity, a "mysticism of everyday life" (Hollywood, *The Soul* 169). Hierarchies voided, man now feels "playful" and "asks no more for meanings and goals," returns to his trade, lets God be, is indifferent to seeking Him. That is the way to find him: "There is no higher attestation of God than this diffidence" (Schürmann 117, 110). It would not be difficult to read an incipient atheism in Eckhart if one tore single statements from the weave of paradox comprising his apophatic logic. The inquisitors did just this—ignored Eckhart's double discourse—to secure a conviction (Sells 178).

Refusing all unequivocal or positive claims of identity, the apophatic opens a space for the non-conceptual. Abraham, for instance, in order to see God, achieved a faith that was said to be "'unmixed and pure of any concept.' The knowledge that he achieved was to know that God cannot be known, a knowing by unknowing" (J. P. Williams 29). Some versions of apophasis negate the negation—Abraham's "knowing by unknowing"—refusing to accept the adequacy of either negative or positive claims, leaving the mind to "hover between the poles of the contradiction, affirming both and neither, negating both and neither." The logic is this: "Language that is writhing in paradoxes is perhaps in labor, undergoing the birth pangs of a nonconceptual experience of the divine" (8, 35). Engaging with Eckhart's writhings involves, he hopes, reproducing in oneself the disposition willing, in his phrase, to "run the danger of detachment." "For Eckhart the first and last word of his preaching" is the moral obligation to expose his listeners to "risk" —the risk of freedom from attachment and from obedience to authority (Schürmann 82, 46, 45). The risk commences in his rhetoric. As Michael Sells has emphasized, many in his audience were nuns, "yet instead of telling them how they should live, his sermons subverted the question . . . by turning to a discourse of 'living without a how' or 'without a why.'" He thus dismantled his ministerial authority into "radical equality" (203).

The risk Eckhart propagates includes breaking our attachment to his words. Eckhart concludes his sermon on the blessed poor by warning us not to worry if we "cannot understand this speech. . . . For as long as man does not equal this truth, he will not understand this speech," a remark whose logic is conspicuous as well in Emerson and Nietzsche. They affirm the priority of life over texts: to know releasement "one must first of all have a released existence." In this final turn, Eckhart calls into question the very enterprise of sermonizing: how can one communicate experiences that can only be lived, not theorized? "Each line of Meister Eckhart testifies to an uneasiness about the fundamental inadequacy of language when confronted by the joy without a cause" (Schürmann xxi).

How does one live up to Eckhart's "breakthrough" and live in wandering joy, a way of life in which being (in Schürmann's Heideggerian accent) becomes the very "act of passing beyond beings, as well as beyond knowing, willing, and having"? (Schürmann 209). Ceaseless movement seems the demanding lot of being without why, a prospect that would have profoundly intrigued Emerson with his love of transitions. In the context of Eckhart's rigor—in effect his own "freakish standards"—the lament of Salinger's Teddy's that "it's very hard to meditate and live a spiritual life in America" loses its air of self-pity to crystallize a general truth (*Nine Stories* 188). Franny's self-indictment is resonant at any time: who indeed has "the courage to be an absolute nobody"? In postwar triumphalist America the question was acutely pertinent, especially haunting to one who lived the oxymoron of being the most famous monk in America.

■

Thomas Merton entered the contemplative Order of the Cistercians—the Trappists—at the Abbey of Gethsemani in the hills of Kentucky in 1941, restlessly residing there (and in a nearby hermitage) until his death at 53 in 1968, accidentally electrocuted at a theological conference in Bangkok. He entered the monastery, taking up its vows of silence and hand-signals, aware that the "logic of the Cistercian life" was the "complete opposite to the logic of the world." In Gethsemani "excellence" "was in proportion to obscurity: the one who was best was the one who was least observed, least distinguished." There "less" and "more" exchange places: "the monk in hiding himself from the world became not less himself, not less of a person, but more of a person, more truly and perfectly himself," perfected in union with God (*Seven Storey* 362). Merton was frank with the authorities that he was bringing with him "all the instincts of a writer" into the monastery—a great lover of literature, he taught for a time at a university after finishing a master's thesis on Blake. The abbot granted permission and encouragement (which would vary through the years) based on the Thomistic principle of *contemplata tradere*—share with others the fruits of contemplation (428, 456). After some hard years of emotional pain in which he ceased writing because it seemed to violate his vows of silence, fruits eventually were abundant. Merton published over sixty books and had a large and loyal readership, becoming a noted poet, literary and spiritual essayist, critic, and diarist, as well as social critic and pacifist. His most fascinating creation was himself.

A number of Merton's books were published by New Directions, the pre-eminent US imprint of international modernism—publishers of Rimbaud, Pound, Henry Miller et al.—whose owner, James Laughlin, was a close friend and literary adviser. Indeed, Merton's strong sales, along with those of Tennessee Williams, helped fund Laughlin's avant-garde list (D. D. Cooper 66). Merton noted his proximity to his pagan fellow authors but elected to remain among them, even though as a group they embodied the secular decadence he railed against most stridently from the forties through the fifties. By then his anti-modernism had run its course and he had grown frustrated by the "damnable abstractness of 'the spiritual life'": he began to open his monastic life to the seething world (*Conjectures* 280). Merton moved from suffering contradictions to embracing them: he came to see they were not only internal to his complex temperament but part of the very air he breathed as a monk of modernity.

His refuge, Gethsemani, was not untouched by change either. Merton's book royalties helped fund the Abbey's expansion projects, work requiring the clamor of trucks and jack hammers that shattered monkish tranquility, a distraction which Merton often protested (D. D. Cooper 6). He mocked as well the thriving capitalist enterprise ongoing under the Abbey roof—the production of cheese in Gethsemani. Where once Trappists ate the food they made themselves, now they supplied "Trappist cheese" for the Catholic holiday market (Elie 395). The long historical view however reveals the entwinement of monasticism and disenchantment: fifteen hundred years before the industrial revolution began to rationalize daily life, the monastery, which incorporated the individual hermit—an eremite—into a community of cenobites, was an inaugural disciplinary site, a template for future institutions, like the military and factories, devoted to systemic control. A monk's day was ruled "for exclusively moral and religious ends" by a "temporal scansion" that turned life into a clock, with duties arranged hour by hour. Monasteries were run with a strictness that exceeded the schemes of Taylorization (scientific management) at the turn of the twentieth century (Agamben 19).

Merton's own entanglement with modernity became apparent in the decades after *The Seven Storey Mountain* (1948), which concludes with his decision to enter Gethsemani. A surprise bestseller that won him fame, the memoir exerted a powerful emotional hold on many young readers (especially returning G.I.'s) who followed his example and made Merton's the most influential act of renunciation in mid-century America. *The Seven Storey Mountain* likely spoke intimately to the Army veteran Salinger, despondent after the carnage and combat of the war, and whose *The Catcher in the Rye* appeared three years after Merton's book (Sheed). Salinger and Merton shared an eclectic attraction to various modes of Eastern and Western mystical thinking, moving easily among them. Both were drawn to the apophatic strain in the Christian tradition of negative theology, the *via negativa* which has a "parallel development" within Eastern mysticism (J. P. Williams 35). Merton, for one, noted this: "Whatever Zen may be, however you define it, it is somehow there in Meister Eckhart" (*Zen* 13).

One of Merton's correspondents, Suzuki, had been reading Eckhart for fifty years. In a published dialogue Merton and Suzuki located common ground between Zen and Christian mysticism. Eckhart, said Merton, "was trying to point to something that cannot be structured and cannot be contained within the limits of any system. He was not trying to construct a new dogmatic theology" (*Zen* 13). Finding parallels between the "no-self" of Zen and the "perfect poverty" Eckhart extols, Merton urged Zen enthusiasts to read Eckhart, something John Cage had been doing since the forties. All were following in the steps of Schopenhauer, who first made the link to Eckhart and Buddhism, noting their shared emphases on breaking the will in resignation, voluntary poverty, and indifference to all worldly things (*World as Will* 1:387).

■

Upon a young priest's urging Merton started both "Franny" and *Zooey*. Although other things got in the way of Merton finishing them, he had read enough to say he "thought the people were alive, and I could see where one could get deeply absorbed in their concerns" (*Road To Joy* 325). Merton's comment makes a great deal of sense, for Franny's

dilemma is remarkably proximate to his own. Though living a monastic life, Merton, like Franny, questioned his own courage to surrender all attachment. Doubt had been there from the start: he ends *The
Seven Storey Mountain* admitting: "By the time I made my vows, I was
no longer sure what a contemplative was, or what the contemplative
vocation was, or what my vocation was." All he knew was that solitude was the one thing that closed his distance from God (460–461).

Merton's doubts persisted, the seed of self-revision decades later.
A candid assessment in a 1963 letter begins with his reverence for
Eckhart: "I think more and more" of Eckhart, "he towers over all his
century." A few paragraphs later, perhaps with Eckhart's rigorous standards in mind, Merton takes up the frustrations of "spiritual life":
"What I object to about 'the Spiritual Life' is the fact that it is a part,
a section, set off as if it were a whole. It is an aberration to set off our
'prayer' etc. from the rest of our existence." Integration of spirit and
body never emerges, stifled by one's "comfortable and respectable existence"; comfort is "to a great degree *opposed* to the real demands of
the Spirit in our lives." Merton finds the very idea of the "spiritual
life" impoverished if restricted to the interiority of mental life. He faces the unsettling consequence: "In actual fact, if we could really let go
of everything and follow the Spirit where He leads, who knows where
we would be?" The question's "if"—its hypothetical status—suggests
what prompts it—the stubborn fact of attachment. "We cannot simply say that our bourgeois existence is purely and simply the 'will of
God.' It both is and is not. Hence the burning and the darkness and
the desperation we feel." Letting go of everything would demand leaving "the tame setting where we do not suffer the things that the poor
and disinherited and the outcast must suffer." He draws the unsparing
conclusion that "we are not in the fullest sense Christians because we
have not fully obeyed the Spirit of Christ." All we can do is "understand more and more the paradoxes in which" we "must live" (*Hidden
Ground* 357–358).

Anxiety regarding spiritual insufficiency is a standard trope of the
religious life. Yet it seemed especially to preoccupy this monk devoted
to a life of contemplative silence and celibacy. And devoted to much
else. Insatiably curious, (hetero) sexually ardent (in the sixties he had
a love affair), ambitiously epistolary, voluminously self-reflective

(nearly ten published volumes of journals), Merton's energy is reflected in the scope of his correspondence. It spans Boris Pasternak to
Lawrence Ferlinghetti, Henry Miller, Joan Baez (who visited him and
danced and sang at his request) to Ethel Kennedy and Louis Zukofsky.
No wonder that in a 1961 chapter entitled "Detachment," Merton
wrote: "We are left helpless, knowing very well that we are asked to
give up everything, yet not knowing how or where to begin. . . . If we
resolutely face our cowardice and confess it to God, no doubt He will
one day take pity on us, and show us the way to freedom in detachment" (New Seeds 213).

Six years later he seems to have fashioned some provisional relief
from his "desperation": "I am now convinced that the first way to be a
decent monk is to be a non-monk and an anti-monk . . . but I am certainly quite definite about wanting to stay in the bushes." He calls the
anti-monk a "hermit" and the "bushes" likely refers not to his monastery but to his hermitage, a cottage built for him less than a mile
from Gethsemani after his abbot officially granted him "hermit" rank.
(For years Merton was permitted to stay only several hours a day, but
gradually gained permission to live there.) For Merton hermit status
was significant, a stimulus to thinking, paradoxically, about living a
more integrated spiritual existence, "a resolution of all alienation": it
means, he writes, a "non-categorized man, a plain simple man: not as
an ideal status or a condition of 'striving for spiritual perfection,' but
a reduction to the bare condition of man as a starting point where everything has to begin" (Hidden Ground 511, 508). Here an exemplary
modernist, Merton flirts with renouncing renunciation to start afresh.

Franny has yet to reach Merton's version of hermit minimalism
and his realism, which renounces the quest for spiritual perfection.
Buddy and Zooey have seen—in Seymour—the dangers of the pursuit.
Maybe Mrs. Fedder's analyst, who urged on Seymour "the virtues
of living the imperfect life", was on to something. Indeed, Seymour
agreed with him, "but only in theory" (Raise 74). Buddy and Zooey's
way of resolving the torment of spiritual imperfection is to improvise
a bridge from the religious to the aesthetic. "Act," Buddy implores
his younger brother, "but do it with all your might"; do something
on stage "nameless and joy-making, anything above and beyond the
call of theatrical ingenuity" (Zooey 68-69). In turn, Zooey implores

Franny that "the only re*li*gious thing you can do is *act*. Act for God, if you want to," just do it on your "*own terms*, not anyone else's" (198–199). Because the art of acting demands mimetic receptivity, the actor surmounts the nagging ego by entering into and animating otherness. Pursuing one's art with creative abandon, insisting on the "nameless" and the nuanced rather than the soothingly familiar and ingenious, is a "religious thing" because it is an act of faith—work without a why—and so offers a taste of detachment's joyous freedom in a world of entrapping attachment.

Merton's way of experiencing detachment's wandering joy was on his "*own terms*" and simultaneously a "gift from God": "The life that I represent," he said near the end of his life, "is openness to gift" (*Asian* 307). The writer Guy Davenport shows this openness in action. "I wonder," remarks Davenport, who lived in nearby Lexington and came to know Merton in his last years, "if there has ever been as protean an imagination as Thomas Merton's? He could, of an afternoon, dance to a Louisville jukebox to Bob Dylan, argue an hour later with James Laughlin about surrealism in Latin American poetry, say his offices in an automobile headed back to Gethsemani, and spend the evening writing a mullah in Pakistan about techniques of meditation" (*Hunter* 45). This is what an "anti-monk" does and what "a resolution of all alienation" looks like. By 1964 Merton writes of "leaving behind the renunciations of yesterday and yet in continuity with all my yesterdays": he reconciles with secular modernity without submitting to the ego-driven selfhood it encouraged. I must "change," he wrote at the time, but added: "not that I must undertake a special project of self-transformation" (qtd. D. D. Cooper 172, 174). After years of self-torment, this mid-twentieth-century American hermit begins to integrate spiritual life into the whole of life, insists on *living* "change," living hour by hour his "protean" range of impulses even if it means flirting with spiritual disaster. "A free-floating existence under a state of risk" is how he described his "new approach" two months before he died (*Asian* 308, 307).

Merton now understood himself as propelled by a free curiosity rather than adherence to a "special project"—inevitably monolithic and deliberative. In sum, as Davenport shows us, the anti-monk improvises his own form of Eckhartian "freedom in detachment":

appropriating nothing, perpetually doing, entirely receptive in the moment—"free and new in each now" as Eckhart says of those detached.
In contrast are the attached, who live not in the instant but in duration, "stretched between a 'before' and 'after'" (qtd. Schürmann 14).
Avoiding embedding himself in larger ends or projects, Merton's "virgin" soul lives in the perpetual transit of transitions. He is true to the
spirit, if not the letter, of Eckhart's releasement, which, as Schürmann
reminds us, "carries a mark of 'worldliness,' since it designates a being
among things, without restraint" (15).

■

Merton's 1960s remaking of a medieval role exemplifies what his close
friend Ad Reinhardt noted of art:

> Art cannot exist without permanent condition of being put into ques-
>   tion
> Explores itself
> Path of razor's edge, balancing, sharpest, thinnest line. (*Art* 111)

Merton is, we have seen, balanced on the brink of a precipitous absurdity, almost falling but not quite. This is the edgy path the "anti-monk" shares with Reinhardt, the "last" painter. They share too
a startlingly analogous commitment to extremity—and to history.
Historical awareness is at one with the belief that "Art cannot exist
without permanent condition of being put into question."

The habit of interrogation will lead Reinhardt to Merton's ideal —
nothing less than "a resolution of all alienation." The painter's stance
has been called "the strongest position in this century against any kind
of instrumentalization of art" (Bois, "Limit" 25). This passion to defy
the instrumental also shaped his prose statements where, we shall see,
he develops a rhetoric—a back and forth movement between assertion
and denial—that his canvases formally embody. Hedging and suspending come to co-exist with categorical certitude, with the resulting tensions the very point.

Unlike Merton, who turns his life into a canvas of improvisation,
Reinhardt confines his renunciations to the realm of painting. Always
the goal is "Make something out of nothing, that would stand alone / Not

have to lean on anything external to work" (*Art-as-Art* 111). They met as Columbia college students working on the campus humor magazine in the late thirties. A Communist Party member, Reinhardt would gradually, after the war, channel his political idealism into aesthetic idealism. Uniting them was an abhorrence of the capitalist exchange principle, which reduces everything to a means to an end (*Art* 55). What Reinhardt had once envisioned as "the absorption of the imaginative artist in a more collective and anonymous job of creating better spaces for people to live in" would evolve into an aesthetic ideal of freedom enacted in paintings that insisted on being "unmarketable"—beyond the reach of the logic of the fungible (qtd. Corris 72; *Art* 83).

The effort to purify painting into a radical self-sufficiency can't help but acquire the mystical intensity of a yearning for the ineffable. We have seen this with Mallarmé, whom Reinhardt saluted as a predecessor "master of voidness" (*Art* 106). Harold Rosenberg captured the spirituality of the painter's venture in dubbing Reinhardt "the black monk" of negativity. "Monk" summons Merton of course, with whom Reinhardt also shared both an enthusiasm for the Eastern mystics—"the Tao is through and through mysterious and dark," he noted—and for Eckhart, whose praise of "divine dark" the painter would also invoke (108, 105). The aesthetic attraction of Eckhart's theology is obvious: the evocation of faith as demanding annihilation of will, means, and use, culminating in the experience of releasement, speaks to Reinhardt's emotional need to make icons of uselessness.

Need aside, the painter didn't bring art to Eckhart; the mystic explicitly invokes art as an analogue to God's "existence" which is "Sufficiency Itself." In his "Commentary on Exodus," Eckhart writes: "Every effort of nature and of art pursues, desires, and seeks" this state of "achieved existence" where "turbulence and conflict" are "stilled" (qtd. Franke 1:302). Yet to call him an influence would be imprecise; Eckhart for Reinhardt is closer to a climate, if not quite habitable, or to an oasis, if not quite reachable. Besides, Reinhardt said emphatically religion was irrelevant to his art, though, he added, "I know I can sound religious" (Reinhardt, "Oral History"). To this we will return. In sum, Eckhart's purgation of the instrumental is an exhilarating ideal against which Reinhardt, like Salinger and Merton, feels at once inadequate and inspired.

Though he had tried to persuade Merton against joining a monastery, Reinhardt too craves ascetic rigor: his artistic premise is "Art begins with the getting rid of nature" because "art is separate from everything else, is related to nothing, and so is one thing only, only itself" (*Art* 205, 216). This is a first taste of Reinhardt's compulsive negations and tautologies that keep art free of positive content. Reinhardt found serenity in the traditions of Asian art, steeped in "standard forms and identical patterns repeated and refined for centuries" (217). Loving what he saw as the quiet dignity, the timeless, universal, disinterested quality of Asian art, Reinhardt became an authority on its painting and sculpture and a Zen devotee. So when Reinhardt visited his old friend at Gethsemani they had much to discuss. Their talks helped enlarge Merton's aesthetic sensibility to include abstract art. Where once he had denounced it as a fraud and scandal, in 1964 Merton wrote that such art had spiritual richness and allowed communion with "our own time" (D. D. Cooper 129). After Reinhardt's death, Merton reprinted as a tribute his friend's "Art as Art" manifesto in his self-published magazine. He described the painter as a "rigorous contemplative" and a "prophetic" figure for a new generation (120). Some years earlier, Merton had asked Reinhardt to paint an "almost invisible cross on a black background" as an aid to his prayer—the cross of renunciation would not be readily apparent but discernible only after intense contemplation, waiting in the deep recesses of blackness.

"Not 'see' it but 'oned' [sic] with it" is how he describes the viewer's intimacy with a painting—to see *in* rather than to look *at* (*Art* 113; Simonds 19). Reinhardt's "own terms" of praise—he admires "art or painting" for being "detached," "empty," and "immaterial"—thus echo Eckhart's vision of releasement (*Art* 55). His black paintings in effect reach "that point of wandering that Japanese Zen masters depict by a canvas totally covered with black," recalling Schürmann's words that unwittingly summon Reinhardt.

In reaching this far, Reinhardt knows that the unconditional self-emptying that enables one to wander without purposiveness—without why—is now a vanished ideal (though "there must be one or two" untethered by any attachment, Merton wryly observed) (*New Seeds* 203). As Merton remarked, we can never "really let go of everything and follow the Spirit where He leads." So to register this dissonance between spiritual aspiration and historical reality, Reinhardt enacts a double move: in his apophatic prose he insists on an unsparing poverty—"a fine artist has no use for use, no meaning for meaning, no need for any need"—while he honors and undermines this absolutism in his black paintings, which only first *appear* impenetrably black. Recall the "almost invisible cross on a black background" that he painted for Merton.

Reinhardt's "almost invisible" shapes bind him in contradiction, the double logic of apophatic utterance ("pray God that we may be free of God"). In unpublished musings he displays this tension:

> Painting that is almost possible, almost does not exist, that is not quite known, not quite seen
>
> To be detached from all forms, not to take hold of anything, not to be determined by any conditions, not to have any affections or hankerings (*Art* 109).

The first statement discloses that the *practice* of painting is conducted within the realm of limits, the "almost possible," while the second implies that the *theory* of utter detachment occurs in the realm of ideals, and is therefore realizable only as ideal. Hence the need to put quotation marks around Reinhardt's "not quite" black "black" paintings: the "not quite" testifies to our secular historical moment with its anxious relation to faith. "In the 'almost' lies his art," as Dore Ashton said of Reinhardt in 1967, playing off of his statement above regarding "Painting that is almost possible." Yves-Alain Bois salutes and enlarges her insight a quarter century later in an essay on "The Limit of Almost" (qtd. 33). The "almost" or "not quite" I invoke here marks, on the macro level, the loss of divine grounding; this is reflected, on the micro level, in the interplay I have constructed among Salinger, Merton, and Reinhardt: all three work to, at best, approach the renunciatory rigor of Eckhart's depiction of released man's risky detachment.

■

Just as Zen was mediated to Cage via Dada, Cage, Merton, and Reinhardt encountered Eckhart not through a Christian context but an aesthetic one, from Ananda Coomaraswamy's chapter on him in

The Transformation of Nature in Art (1934). This pioneering study
aimed at recovering a "time when Europe and Asia could understand
each other very well" (3) and building upon this fact the "possibility
of a renewed *rapprochement*" (4). In noting the soul's "two powerful
faculties, intellect and will," Coomaraswamy summarizes Eckhart's
aesthetic thinking. The intellect, as a "means of understanding and
communication," works with the "imagination": "It is here that
things are known in unintelligible multiplicity and must be realized
in intelligible unity, here that the use of things is understood, and that
renunciation of all uses must be made." He quotes Eckhart: "'to find
nature herself all her likenesses have to be shattered. . . . ' Such renunciation and such shattering being of the essence of art, in which
all things are seen alike without any sense of possession, not in their
nature but in their being, quite disinterestedly" (64). Coomaraswamy
has intuited that the religious and aesthetic intersect as forms of dis-
possession; hence he adroitly marries Eckhart to Kant, "releasement"
to disinterestedness.

Implicitly confirming Coomaraswamy, recent scholarship has explored Eckhart's influence on Baumgarten. The founder of aesthetics
refers to the mystic's phrase "the ground of the soul" and employs it
to mark a realm of possibility and receptivity free of the instrumental, a freedom Baumgarten compares to a leisurely stroll without plans
or goals (Largier, "Plasticity" 539). One commentator has remarked:
"The aesthetic realm took on many of the affective and figurative traits
associated with the mystical life in early and medieval Christianity"
(Hollywood, Introduction 31). Yet this "does not indicate a religious
turn" in Baumgarten, but an "attempt to retrieve something contemporary philosophy did indeed not have a term for—namely the plasticity of the soul and its utter freedom to take shape in an aesthetic experience." The "ground of the soul" is the "virtual basis of all possible
experiential intensity that is not pre-framed by reason and that can be
explored in aesthetic enthusiasm" (Largier, "Plasticity" 551).

Reinhardt's renunciation is formal; he restricts abandonment to the
canvas, refusing interplay between art and life, abiding by one of his

best-known mantras: "Art is art and life is life" (*Art* 54). Not surprisingly, he was thoroughly at odds with Cage's opposite effort—his perennial campaign to bring life and art together. Agnes Martin, we will see, seeks to effect a stance between her mentor Reinhardt and Cage; she says "the artist tries to live in a way" that will open herself, her canvases, and the viewer to "the sublimity of reality" (*Writings* 93). For Reinhardt the distinction between art and life is foundational, and emanating from it is a mystic "oneness" diffusing calm. Here, as we have seen, Asian art's impersonality inspires him: its "preformed and premeditated" "sacred procedures" abolish any "grasping or clinging to anything." Only a "formula-ized art can be formulaless. . . . Finally there is nothing in the purest art to pin down or point out. Nothing is attached to any miserable creature or jolly soul, or to any special place" (*Art* 218).

Contemporaneous with Reinhardt, the French painter and provocateur Yves Klein made purely blank blue monochrome canvases, erasing any "almost." Klein's logic is one Reinhardt (and Barthes) would have found congenial: "Why not two colors in the same painting? Well, because I refuse to provide a spectacle in my painting. I refuse to compare and put in play, so that stronger elements will emerge in contrast to other, weaker ones. Even the most civilized representation is based on an idea of 'struggle' between different forces . . . a morbid drama by definition, be it a drama of love or hate" (qtd. Bois, *Painting* 299). Or, as Reinhardt puts it, "art that is a matter of life and death is neither fine nor free" (54). Preserving the "almost," Reinhardt draws back from Klein's pure monochrome.

From the mid-fifties until his death in 1967, he concentrated on the cycle of almost imageless black canvasses, each sixty inches, and spoke of "my making a painting that can't be seen"—"the last painting which anyone can make" (*Art* 23, 13). Critics called them "invisible paintings." The tension embodied in the paradox of depicting what can't be seen becomes a source of energy that Reinhardt distills into his black canvases. In stark contrast to the "invisible" aspirations of his painting is Reinhardt's often noisy prose—chants of negation that he regarded not as a bid for pathos but as a barrier to interpretation, a way "to keep the painting free." For one thing free from the existential histrionics he disparaged in the more popular abstract expressionists

Pollock and Rothko (14). Technically, he kept his art free by using extremely thin paint to create layer upon layer of color, effacing all traces of texture, brush, or hand, thereby defeating "spontaneous expression" (his consistent enemy). "There are no gymnastics or dancings over paintings or spilling or flinging paint around" (13). He saved the theatrics for his percussive manifestoes. Vigilant against concepts as the enemy of aesthetic experience, Reinhardt unleashes them on the page, eager to announce, as did Eva Hesse, the creation of "a free, unmanipulated and unmanipulatable, useless, unmarketable, irreducible, unphotographable, unreproducible, inexplicable icon. A non-entertainment, not for art commerce or mass-art publics, non-expressionist, not for oneself" (83). He also has a less hectoring mode, comprising elliptical exploratory musings, some quoted below.

Reinhardt's barrage of negation could not release his art from use, only make it maximally defiant of its inevitable fate: the reduction to commodity status in the art market. Reinhardt did, though, defeat reproducibility—even the best photographs of the black paintings fail by making the contrasts all too readily visible, betraying their actual fugitive status and the time required to discern even this. Reinhardt staked all on an immaculate tautology: "The one reality of art is just the reality of art, not the reality of reality" (57). The severe, indeed cloistered, autonomy of his painting—a "clearly defined object, independent and separate from all other objects and circumstances"—focuses our attention by confining it: "We cannot see whatever we choose or make of it anything we want." Its "meaning is not detachable or translatable" (83). Reinhardt is the kind of artist Franny Glass would respect. Richard Serra calls him "some sort of moral barometer" (2) while others found him overbearing. Elaine de Kooning, for one, made fun by dubbing him "Mr. Pure" (qtd. Bois, "The Limit" 33) (a play on *Rein*, German for "pure").

Reinhardt's negativity extended to a ban on commentary about his work: "I give them no encouragement"—the critics and viewers—"I'm a responsible artist . . . and they drop it after a while" (14). Their "need" for "translatable" "meaning" exposes a yearning to rely on some prearranged thematic drama heavy with portentousness to guide the viewer's experience. One of his favorite examples was the abstract expressionist Robert Motherwell's series of elegies for the Spanish Republic. Not surprisingly, viewers outside the cognoscenti felt frustrated by

Reinhardt's contempt for anything ingratiating and reacted with anger, striking back at an asceticism they found punishing. At shows in Paris, London, and New York spectators tried to deface the seemingly impassive canvases, frustrated they had nothing "to latch on to" (Crow 119; Reinhardt Art 15). They were impatient with the time the shadings of blackness demanded to be seen. But "seen" is optimistic, for even if viewers do slow down, they are not rewarded with legibility. The shapes that the blackness surrenders—the nine-square grid forming a cruciform—and colors—blues, maroons, and grays—are phantom, teasing, flickering, and contingent. Quality of light matters, as does stance.

The paintings empty us of the will to possess, but only after we stop grasping and let go of the presumption of "detachable" meaning, an expectation bred by the hungry ego's impatience to "get it" and move on. The black paintings' indifference to our understanding brings us into Eckhart's realm of calm emptied of epistemological ambition, where we accept that we "should not wish to understand anything about God, for God is beyond all understanding" and "the finest thing that we can say of God is to be silent concerning him" (Writings 237). Reinhardt's art induces an analogous silence. It nurtures detachment. We grow aware that, like the artist, we too have "no need for any meaning"; "Any meaning is a demeaning" (Art 142, 77). One needs words but only "to prove the uselessness of words," Reinhardt wrote, quoting an ancient Buddhist sage (qtd. McConathy 146).

This experience of breaking down attachment "so we can become poor in knowing" (Eckhart), releases us into more capacious vision, from "less" springs "more." This last word appears in notes called "Oneness" (the leitmotif of Neo-Platonism, a prime influence on Eckhart) in which Reinhardt invokes Eckhart's "the Divine Dark," and then tracks what evolves:

... "luminous darkness"
First, light, then cloud, finally dark
Yearning for further vision—> vision beyond vision . . .
Always seen as something new, strange, wonder
Never exhaust desire to see more . . .
Awareness of hidden things, look toward what is hidden
Avest for that which has no dimension, no time
Nothing to take hold of . . . (105–106)

The ungraspable "hidden" Reinhardt calls the "One"—it "does not contain any difference, always present"—is the

> Sum of all enigmas, deliberately thwarts every system of inquiry and
>   interpretation
> Pervasive presence (107).

Out of the "Divine Dark" emerges "Pervasive presence." In front of the black paintings after an (always insufficient) amount of time, we are left beyond understanding, detached from knowing, released into "Pervasive presence" void of "why." Eckhart call this the "single Oneness, the pure being of the Soul, resting in herself," "when all images are removed from the soul" (since all images are imperfections) (*Writings* 235).

Given Reinhardt's fascination with Buddhist and Islamic art, inevitably some critics ascribe a mystical content to the black paintings. McEvilley notes that the Taoist mandala of sixty-four squares is "virtually identical" to the "internal quadrature" of the black canvases (McEvilley, *Art and Discontent* 35). Given that the mandala carries "a weight of metaphysical content with it," the black paintings "could be hung in the manner of icons in a church as readily as in the manner of pictures in a gallery. They are saturated with content" (35). Reinhardt, as noted, denied any connection between his spiritual interests and his art, relying instead, like Sontag, on a tautological fable of purity—"the one object of fifty years of abstract art is to present art-as-art and as nothing else"—that discourages interpretation, especially the religious (*Art* 53). Ironically, the religious persists, for what the tautology of purity protects—art as pure sensory presence—is easily read as a "desire for the sacred in a secular age" (McEvilley, *Art* 26).

This is to say that Reinhardt is less opposed to the religious than he admits. The "almost" has a way of slipping in, complicating his denials. The equivocalness of "I know I can sound religious" deepens in his Smithsonian interview (circa 1964): I "have a kind of faith in art or whatever it is or your own art but the minute you start to make it positive it sounds terrible, you know. I've always talked negatively anyways. That sounds religious too, the negative kind of theological approach where you never especially in the Hebraic and

Islamic where you wouldn't pin down God, or the minute you make him a thing its not Him or not it, or it's a vulgarization" (Reinhardt, "Oral History"). Here in the very effort of trying to distance himself from the "religious"—it "sounds terrible" when you make "positive" claims for faith in art but talking "negatively" about it "sounds religious too"—Reinhardt abides with it. This sticky relation to the religious (affirming as he denies) is a model of the double status of his black paintings. Reinhardt on another occasion admitted that religion might be "the best analogy today" for approaching his art and acknowledged "what he had wanted to achieve in his art immediately calls to mind 'negative theology'"—which incarnates the "almost" (qtd. Bois, "The Limit" 29). "What Reinhardt means," says Bois, "is that his negative language, and art, are naturally condemned to look religious—almost" (29).

■

In Reinhardt's plunge into the unfathomable, in his drive to make "an inexplicable icon," a "painting that can't be seen"—"the last painting which anyone can make"—renunciation is poised between art and its extinction. In his seven-year cycle of black paintings, Reinhardt made his impossible objects over and over again, each sixty inches high, the scale of a man. This implicit concession to the human undoes any fiercely proclaimed imageless purity. Cruciform becomes crucifix: recall the "almost invisible cross on a black background" that he had painted for Merton years before. The cross is "as though immersed in darkness and trying to emerge from it," perennially seeking the light. As Merton notes: "You have to look hard to see the cross. One must turn away from everything else and concentrate on the picture as though peering through a window into the night. I should say a very holy picture—helps prayer . . . and to help set aside trivial and useless images that wander into prayer and spoil it" (Merton, *Journals* 3:139–140).

Merton was not alone in remarking the contemplative intensity that the black paintings elicit. David Antin, the poet and art critic, offers a vivid account of how the black paintings trigger ocular struggle:

They are composed of very dark blue and very dark red but so close to black it takes intense looking to reveal it [if you look at them in a fully lit room with white walls] but when you try to see into one of the dark paintings your pupils start to dilate but are afflicted by the glare of reflected light spilling into your field of vision from the white walls which stimulates your pupils to contract so you find yourself struggling to keep looking into the pool of darkness willfully struggling to keep your pupils dilated against any stimulus from the gallery light after a while this produces a kind of intense strain and you become slightly feverish from the strain and the feverishness of your feeling resulting from the eye strain produces a weird exaltation that becomes an analog for a kind of transcendence . . . this is effective and powerful. (*Radical Coherency* 129)

One is tempted to use the word "meaning" to describe what gets generated in this encounter, where the pressure of physical sensation in turn mimes a spiritual sensation. "Meaning" *malgré lui*—given Reinhardt's disgust for the word. "Most artists" and curators "just love all these meanings," especially grandiloquent existential ones. Impatient with inflation—something he shares with Cage—Reinhardt mockingly asks: "What curator has not thrilled to the strains and old refrains of 'Art is a style of living, so to speak' (de Kooning, 1951), 'Painting is voyaging into the night, one knows not where . . . ' (Motherwell, 1959). 'There is no such thing as a painting about nothing' (Rothko and Gottlieb, 1947), and 'Let no man undervalue the implications of this work, or its power for life, or for death, if it is misused' (Still, 1959)?" (*Art-as-Art* 61). Reinhardt was a biting satirist and caricaturist of the art world in his work as an art cartoonist from the late forties to early sixties, a self-styled Diogenes of merciless witty deflation (Storr, "Diogenes").

Reinhardt's alternative—the unrehearsed, unprotected encounter between viewer and canvas—is punishing, as Antin attests, a trial to win a moment of grace, as Merton might put it. And give some credit to the hostile museum crowd, who in their urge to deface the black paintings testified to the ordeal that awaited them and said no. Their negativity, attesting to the intensity of the art's visceral disturbance, seems a not inappropriate response, one that Reinhardt might (almost) appreciate.

These testimonies to his paintings' aesthetic and affective life, their forceful, even painful, capture of body and mind, exist in uneasy tension with the negativity of Reinhardt's extraordinary evocation of the artwork as a kind of airless realm, a virtual tomb or mausoleum: "The one thing to say about art is its breathlessness, lifelessness, deathlessness, contentlessness, formlessness, spacelessness, and timelessness. This is always the end of art" (*Art-as-Art* 56). "This" in the final sentence evidently refers to the multiple negations piled up in the preceding sentence. But the meaning of "this" depends on clarifying "end." "The end of art" could mean art's aim or cessation; the pun puts in play the uncomfortable proximity of both. The aesthetic life of a black painting—the viewer's rapt contemplation of it—could be said to occur in the frail margin of the work's passage toward extinction.

Reinhardt came to see the frailty of his conviction—that purity frees art from "the ceaseless attempt to subserve it as a means to some other end or value" (*Art-as-Art* 55). To exist perpetually as an end in itself depends on absolute privacy. Spectators inevitably drag in the impurities of their worldliness—"the life of life" and "the nature of nature"—and their defensiveness, aroused by the demand to surrender to darkness. He faces the impossibility of his project—an art of silence—in a brief passage from a series of elliptical notes:

Push painting beyond its
 thinkable, seeable, feelable
 limits, graspable
Not a joke, jest, gesture
Invisible, silent, empty
Transcend "system"
No such thing as emptiness
 or invisibility, silence
Own nervous system
Own eyes, own learning (*Art* 104).

Here Reinhardt affirms his intention to render the "Invisible, silent, empty" by pushing painting beyond its "feelable . . . graspable" limit—but only to confess its impossibility: "No such thing as emptiness or invisibility, silence." John Cage too discovered there was no such thing as silence when he entered an anechoic chamber and heard his blood beating. *4'33"* taught the same lesson. "Always ideal, and illusory," silence, Cage showed, is a "dialectic between" theory and practice, which posits "the promise of pure silence and the minute particulars of surface and system noise" (Dworkin 134, 133). Exposing this discrepancy between theory and reception, Reinhardt acknowledges that emptiness, silence, and invisibility are, finally, fictions, since his art must submit to the grossness of public display and transaction, the encounter with the viewer, whose own body and brain—eyes and nervous system and learning—are all aroused in the act of contemplation. Knowing his art of renunciation—to push painting beyond its graspable limits—was literally impossible (or impossible to literalize), Reinhardt regarded the effort as sacred, as what counted. "An artist-as-artist, / *Has always nothing to say, / And he must say this over and over again, / Especially in his work.*" Beckett had his own version: the artist must fail again and fail better. A meditation of Reinhardt's called "End" begins with a question: "End of painting as an art?" and concludes: "Last word must always be secretly the first" (*Art* 142, 113–114). "A denial made on behalf of a deeper yes," as William James put it, about the apophatic rhetoric of mysticism (*Writings* 2:375–376).

■

"*Say this over and over again*": this is how one says Franny's Jesus Prayer—repeatedly. And we thereby might fuse with God's grace. Franny's theory, if not her practice, of the prayer is cogent: If you keep saying the Jesus Prayer over and over "something happens, and the words get synchronized with the person's heartbeats, and then you're actually praying without ceasing . . . [you] purify your whole outlook" (*Franny* 37). The change Franny describes here is of spirituality and expression fused, as prayer and heartbeat, word and body, are "synchronized"; abstraction is defeated and a "purified outlook" attained, a harmony of inner and outer life.

To "get synchronized," as Franny puts it, is to defeat intellectual distance. "Profundity," writes Kierkegaard, "is not an utterance, a statement, but an existing" (*Book on Adler* 164). The deep thinker is one who not merely has profound thoughts but whose life exemplifies his thoughts. For American intellectuals in the forties and fifties Kierkegaard's *existenz* philosophy, the fount of twentieth-century French existentialism, was regarded as a beacon of integrity in a philistine world of compromise.

"Meaninglessness became very respectable" after the war, Reinhardt noted; "everybody was reading Kierkegaard" (Reinhardt, "Oral History"). Including Mark Rothko; in 1958 he extolled not the meaningless but the refusal of transparent meaning, which he found exemplified in Abraham's willingness, in *Fear and Trembling*, to sacrifice Isaac. "What Abraham was prepared to do was beyond understanding. There was no universal that condoned such an act. This is like the role of the artist" (Rothko, qtd. M. Taylor 95). For Kierkegaard "faith begins precisely where thinking leaves off" (*Fear* 82). But that leap into silence is intolerable in the public world, "the present age"— mid-nineteenth-century Copenhagen—of "reflection" and of chatter, an age of piety without "passion." "Talkativeness is afraid of the silence which reveals its emptiness" and even a suicide "deliberates so long and so carefully that he literally chokes with thought" ("On the Difference" 33, 68). He was determined not to speculate about faith—neither to explain, theorize, nor even *know* it—nor to send forth disciples, but to *live* a life of faith. Kierkegaard said he was a Christian insofar as he knew he was not Christian (Hadot, *What Is* 266). Modeling himself on Socrates, who lived rather than wrote, Kierkegaard's existentialism (explored in his scores of books) takes as foundational the priority of existence to thought, rejecting the traditional privilege accorded Reason and Intellect. To affirm the priority of existing and becoming Kierkegaard practiced renunciation—he flirted with but spurned the demands to identify required by the institutions of marriage, the church, and academic philosophy. "The great Kierkegaard was never a Kierkegaardian, let alone an Existentialist," shrewdly remarks Buddy Glass at the start of *Seymour*. The philosopher's contempt for affiliation and careerism, says Buddy, "cheers one bush-league intellectual's heart no end, never fails to reaffirm his faith in a cosmic poetic justice" (100).

Part 3

KIERKEGAARD'S USE OF renunciation affirms not only his philosophic anti-intellectualism but revelation as well—the religious experience of mystery that "surpasses human understanding" (*Book on Adler* 23). Because it destabilizes the control afforded by deliberative rationality, revelation is inherently disturbing. As the philosopher Leo Strauss noted: it is "not a kind of self-experience, of the actualization of a human potentiality, of the human mind coming into its own, into what it desires or is naturally inclined to, but of something undesired, coming from the outside, going against man's grain" (146). Kierkegaard calls it "being jolted" (*Adler* 104). The proximity of revelation's spiritual power to aesthetic experience concerns George Steiner in *Real Presences* (1991). He asks us to respect what revelation exposes—"irreducible 'otherness,'" the mystery of "real presence" at the heart of aesthetic encounter. Becoming "answerable" to that mystery, according to Steiner, is the needed antidote for our culture of the secondary (journalism and electronic media) which "craves remission from direct encounter" (39). One of Steiner's examples of salutary otherness is the autonomy of literary character we witnessed in Faulkner's shrug disowning authority. Though he does not mention the example of Faulkner, Steiner's larger point is germane: "When artists and writers tell us that they are not regents over the complete or latent meanings of their own devisings, it is to this 'otherness' that they testify." He continues: "In most cultures . . . the source of 'otherness' has been actualized or metaphorized as transcendent. It has been invoked as divine, as magical, as daimonic. It is the presence of radiant opacity. That presence is the source of powers, of significations in the text, in the work, neither consciously willed nor consciously understood" (210–211).

The prehistory of this power occurs "before the era of art," as Hans Belting tells us in his great work known in English as *Likeness and Presence* (1994). In the medieval world, until the early sixteenth century, the image was prized not for its beauty or fidelity to nature but for its life-altering effect on the beholder: "the image *was* the person it represented," was sacred talisman or relic in a cultic practice, exuding a supernatural power "more important to the believer than were abstract notions of God or afterlife." "Kissed and venerated with bended knee" as if "personages," these icons, not surprisingly, alarmed Christian theologians, for here was an experience that bypassed Church authority. Theologians, Belting notes, "were satisfied only when they could 'explain' the images" (47, 6, 1). For in jeopardy was the status of God's written word in the Gospels as the sacred and exclusive channel of revelation and redemption. It was now threatened by what, according to church tradition, was "dead matter," the "pictorial effects of paint" and wood (150, 152). In response, an invidious hierarchy was imposed: the power of icons was deemed to be limited to those easily aroused by the senses—the mad, children, women, and the illiterate.

Art before the era of art is the experience of the visible manifestation of an icon's sacred presence. In the Renaissance this pictorial revelation is replaced, as the work of art becomes for the beholder an "object of reflection"; and with the emergence of art collections "form and content renounce their unmediated meaning in favor of the mediated meaning of aesthetic experience and concealed argumentation" (16). Even though the "image was now the work of the artist and a manifestation of art" (471), "the lost way of experiencing images" was never wholly lost: beholders still remain compelled by the mysterious power of images to grip them as if a force of revelation (the *as if* marks secular distance from the holy). Aesthetic experience asks us to feel the tremor of wonder that eludes the flight to explanation. So argues David Freedberg in *The Power of Images* (1989). In a remark whose import we have heard before in these pages, he says: "Much of our sophisticated talk about art is simply an evasion. . . . The obstacle is our reluctance to reinstate emotion as a part of cognition" (429–430).

Evading the force of feeling emerges as a theme in Kierkegaard's own analysis of the status of revelation. In *The Book on Adler*, his study of a minor Danish cleric (Adler) who claimed a revelation of Christ and wrote a few books about it, Kierkegaard argues that the need to explain and domesticate revelation is the fetish of idealist or speculative philosophy which employs the "objectivity and disinterestedness of abstract thinking" to distance experience. Uneasy in the grip of the immediate, speculative thought steps out into reflection: in the case of Adler "exegesis got busy" and "Hegelian philosophy actually explains away the revelation." The only way truly to understand a revelation, says Kierkegaard, is to "stand by it, argue on the basis of it, act in accordance with it," and to "transform [one's] whole existence in relation to it" (*Adler* 34, 100, 84–85). The "revelation is that there is no revelation apart from his living it out," as David Walsh notes (452).

What fascinates Kierkegaard about Adler is his "comic" quality of playing "both sides"—participant and analyst. His ambition is "to be in every way the man for everything, the man with the revelation and the man with the explanation" (103). In an age of "reflection and common sense," of "distraction," where most people are "never at home" but "continually out," Adler's "excellence" was his openness to revelation in the moment of its impact. This made his experience spiritual, for "all religiousness lies in subjectivity, in inwardness, in being deeply moved, in being jolted, in the qualitative pressure on the spring of subjectivity" (104, 105). The majority of Adler's fellow citizens, church-going Christians all, Kierkegaard accuses of being absent-minded and preoccupied, eager to defer acting in the present. Unlike Franny Glass, most people "never in self-concern sense each his own *I* and the pulse beat and the heart beat of his own self. They live too objectively to be aware of something like that, and if they hear mention of it they tranquilize themselves with the explanation that such things are hysteria, hypochondria, etc." (103). To be shaken in the religious sense is to jostle a man until he wakes up and becomes himself—in his inwardness (112–113).

This effort to rouse the good Christian sleepwalkers around him is Kierkegaard's project. At the same time he is also concerned with the means that will bring his reader into a heightened experience of actuality. Upon hearing F. W. J. Schelling's second Berlin lecture in 1841, Kierkegaard recalled in his diary that "when he mentioned the word 'actuality' in connection with philosophy's relation to the actual, the babe of thought leapt for joy within me. . . . This one word, it reminded me of all my philosophical pains and agonies" (*Papers* 145). The challenge is how to get "actuality" to live on the page. Although only an approximation of "actuality" is possible, our desire for the literally impossibile testifies to what he regards as the "ultimate paradox of thought: to want to discover something that thought itself cannot think." So he trusts in paradox, calling it "the passion of thought" (*Philosophical Fragments* 37). Kierkegaard trusts as well in the art of representation. His passion for "actuality" is matched by his virtuoso skill in invention; in his numerous works of pseudonymous authorship he fashions characters as effortlessly as Dickens. Unlike a William James, Kierkegaard does not regard writing as a betrayal that freezes the flowing "present" on the inert printed page. Instead, his style registers the excess and overflow of actuality (*Adler* 110).

Hence Kierkegaard salutes Adler's prose for being full of "confusion," "imperfection and unruliness." These qualities mark Adler's being in the moment, which denies him the leisure to shift to a more poised address. What Kierkegaard calls "an almost audible lyrical seething" marks Adler's style; above all, it has the merit of "assaulting the reader" (*Adler* 110). This phrase as well evokes precisely Kierkegaard's own stylistic pressure on his reader. It is a verbal assault that finds energy in flaunting an unsolvable paradox: his torrential flow of words is in the service of extolling the silence of inwardness. This dissonance is what keeps the reader in the grip of Kierkegaard's obsessions; his characterization of Adler's stylistic presence serves as self-description: "He is quite able to . . . stimulate, to grip the reader" because "what he has to say is not . . . fetched from far away; no, he *is in* the haste, *in* the danger, *in* the struggle" (110). This limns the immersive aesthetic that later authors share with Kierkegaard. He distills his modernist bequest in a pithy line that William James quotes admiringly in *Pragmatism:* "We live forward but understand backwards" (*Writings* 2:584). Bergson too found this a watchword and Faulkner, admirer of Bergson, would internalize Kierkegaard's logic as an aesthetic premise of his own literary experiments that plunged readers into disordered consciousness.

Not surprisingly, Kierkegaard has compelling affinities with that other man of paradox, his contemporary Emerson. Also in pursuit of actuality, if not essences, Emerson too disturbs his readers as he sets sentences in motion to mime the "fugitive" nature of words and of experience (*Essays* 410). He upends even his pet phrases; hence Emerson is at once proponent of self-reliance and its subtlest critic. Both thinkers are consumed with the question of what counts as "true" religion; they share reverence for inwardness and contempt for institutionally mandated piety, which shapes their attraction to renunciation of official, external form. In a journal entry, Emerson wonders: is "religious form impertinent" when one "speaks the truth, follows the truth, is the truth's; when he awakes . . . to the faith that God is in him, will he need any temple, any prayer"? (*Selected Journals* 337). "Is not the Church opened & filled on Sunday because the commandments are not kept by the worshippers on Monday?" He hastens to insist on a distinction: "Now does this sound like high treason & go to lay flat all religion? It does threaten our forms but does not that very word 'form' already sound hollow? It threatens our forms but it does not touch injuriously Religion. Would there be danger if there were real religion?"

Kierkegaard would have delighted in Emerson's contempt for "pasteboard religion," for rationalism and its instruments of explanation, as well as his relish of contraries. These attitudes culminate in Emerson's belief that "in order to be a good minister it was necessary to leave the ministry" (193). Both men extend this impatience with formal constraint and love of being un-housed into a stylistic principle.

Kierkegaard's excited response to Schelling's use of the word "actuality" in his Berlin lectures is worth pausing over. A predecessor in rejecting the primacy of rational cognition, Schelling for a time inspired Kierkegaard, who shared his impatience with the fixity of the page. The effort to escape the power of life-obstructing texts is conspicuous in Schelling's career. At the age of sixty-six, he was called in 1841 from the provinces to Berlin to combat the atheistic Hegelian influence sweeping up German intellectuals and the general public. Schelling delivered a course of lectures on revelation as critique of Hegel (lectures attended by Kierkegaard, Karl Marx, and Friedrich Engels). He proclaimed a "positive" philosophy of freedom (in contrast to the "negative" philosophy of Hegelian a priori Reason) grounded in the priority of actual existence, what is wholly other to Reason and which makes thinking possible in the first place. Prefiguring William James, existence for Schelling is the sheer "thatness" of things that precedes meaning—the "whatness" of abstract essence (Toews 420). He compared the way idealism deals with the world of lived experience to "a surgeon who promises to cure your ailing leg by amputating it" (Schelling 23).

A recent commentator speaks of Schelling opening up self-reflection and consciousness to "the abyss of pre-reflective, 'blind being,' the pure

existence that preceded language" (Toews 7). Schelling insisted on taking this "extra step beyond rational thought," while rejecting charges
of irrationalism (6). Revelation—that which "exceeds reason"—is compelling, he said, not least because Hegel's system cannot account for it:
"If revelation contained nothing more than what is in reason, then it
would have absolutely no interest" (Schelling 189). In response to the
ideal of totality found.in Kant and Hegel, Schelling locates "the entire
dignity" of philosophy "in the fact that it will never be completed. In
that moment in which he would believe to have completed his system,
he would become unbearable to himself. He would, in that moment,
cease to be a *creator*, and instead descend to being an instrument of his
creation" (3).

Apostle of the open and incomplete, Schelling lost faith in the
printed word, regarding books as a betrayal of his central tenets: that
being—existence—precedes thinking and that inwardness, the goal of
philosophy, was inexpressible. Recovering in effect a Greek Socratic
tradition of philosophy as conversation rather than writing, Schelling
in Berlin told his audience that he would not be providing a textbook
transcript of his lectures, as was the custom, because "the content of
these lectures is just not suited" to such a thing, for they do "not con-
sist of a series of finished propositions" but rather are "generated in a
continuous but thoroughly free and animated progression and movement, whose moments" are captured not in "memory" but solely in
"spirit" (103). So "philosophy could no longer be contained in books"
and though his son edited his works, Schelling was largely unread for
decades, falling into obscurity.

Schelling's ideas helped Kierkegaard formulate his critique of Hegel's
closed conceptual universe. Eight decades later this critique attained
new currency in 1920s Weimar. Gaining notice was the "new thinking"
of a young German-Jewish philosopher, Franz Rosenzweig. Working
through Schelling and Kierkegaard, he offered a turn from Hegel's ab-
solutist metaphysics of "unreal forms, essences, or concepts that can
never be more than . . . objects of mere thought." A contemporary
admirer, Leo Strauss, dubbed the "new thinking" an "'experiencing

philosophy.' As such it is passionately concerned with the difference between what is experienced . . . by the present-day believer and merely known by tradition. . . . As experiencing philosophy it starts in each case from the experienced, and not from the nonexperienced 'presuppositions' of experience" (Strauss 147, 151). Idealism, always inquiring into the inner essence of things, insists on the priority of knowledge at the expense of experience.

The futility of this choice was brought home to Rosenzweig during his combat duty in the First World War. He mocks the insulation of Idealism at the start of the book he began writing at the Balkan Front. His *The Star of Redemption* begins, unforgettably:

> Philosophy presumes to cast out the fear of the creature, to rob death of its sting, hell of its pestilential breath. All mortal things live in the fear of death. . . . The womb of the tireless earth incessantly creates new beings, and each is doomed to die. . . . But philosophy denies these terrestrial anxieties. . . . It abandons the body to the abyss, but the free soul soars above. What does philosophy care that the fear of death knows nothing of this division into body and soul? (qtd. Glatzer 179–180)

For Rosenzweig, the prospect of death does not defeat man but only sparks his determination to *"remain"* in life—"he wants to live." The prospect of burrowing into a scholarly career, a world of books, now became intolerable. Fueling the logic of his renunciation was his "new thinking," particularly what he dubbed (after Schelling) its "absolute empiricism." "'The' truth," declared Rosenzweig, "must be converted into 'our' truth. Thus truth ceases to be what 'is' true and becomes a verity that wants to be verified, realized in active life" (qtd. Glatzer 206–207). Rosenzweig called *The Star* "only a *book*" and he "did not attach any undue importance to it" (*Understanding* 13). It concludes with the command "INTO LIFE." He followed suit, turning from what would have been an illustrious career in the world of books to spreading the living word of Judaism. In 1920 Rosenzweig renounced an academic career in philosophy by embracing *"das nichtmehrbuch"*—the no-longer-book—stepping into "midst of the everyday" by working for a Jewish adult education center (*Philosophical* 136–137). This turn from a world ruled by abstraction (in Rosenzweig's case

Hegelian idealism) and intellectual understanding was a long journey, marked by an early transitional stage of absorption in aesthetic
feeling as a mode of vision. Here is Rosenzweig in a remarkable 1906
letter, written at twenty, reporting on a trip to Venice where he saw
Giorgione's *Famiglia*:

> You sit there for a few minutes on a rococo chair, and the miracle
> happens . . . you look without knowing what it is you are seeing; you
> simply turn into eyes. Without passion or emotion, without thought,
> empty of awareness, including self-awareness: pure vision. This is ab-
> solute art in the sense that one speaks of absolute music, the kind of
> music that represents nothing whatever . . . that music that is noth-
> ing but music and can only be *heard*. It is something so mysterious
> that one might found a religion on it. (qtd. Glatzer 11)

The aesthetic and spiritual crystallize in a moment of bliss; receptivity relinquishes cognition as a goal and experience is burnished
to a gem-like Paterian intensity. It is an initiation into mystery and
revelation, yet not redemptive or compensatory so much as engulfing, routing the intellect as it unleashes fervent looking. Rosenzweig's
account of ecstatic self-transport—indeed self-effacement—has more
than a touch of fin de siècle "Art for Art's sake" (down to the "ro-
coco chair" and the salute to music as the "absolute art," an aesthetic
commonplace since Schopenhauer and Nietzsche). His last sentence
yoking the mystery of music and religion proved a portent: in renouncing an academic career, he sought to make divine Revelation a living reality, neither a doctrinal remnant of an old tradition, nor part of
progressive liberalism's optimistic vision of historical progress (Moyn
117–121). Acknowledging that he is no longer "under the spell" of his
once "omnivorous aesthetic appetite," he declares his relish of the
daily "demand of the day" (he borrowed Goethe's phrase)—"I mean
the nerve-wracking, picayune, and at the same time very necessary
struggles with people and conditions, have now become the real core
of my existence" (qtd. Glatzer 96–97).

Leo Strauss was also pondering the tension between revelation and
reason. In his vivid account of revelation cited earlier (from his retrospective 1965 preface to his 1930 book on Spinoza) Strauss is recalling
his fascination as a philosophy student in Weimar with questions of

theology and in particular with Rosenzweig's views of secular reason. Notes Strauss, paraphrasing Rosenzweig: this reason "has reached its perfection in Hegel's system; the essential limitations of Hegel's system show the essential limitations of reason and therewith the radical inadequacy of all rational objections to religion" (Strauss 147). Revelation, said Strauss, is a "present experience, which every human being can have if he does not refuse himself to it" (146). Strauss would eventually temper his enthusiasm for Rosenzweig, finding his thought too comfortable with the irrational. Yet philosophy for Strauss would forever be shadowed by its inability definitively to deny the possibility of revelation; philosophy is not grounded on rational necessity but "is as arbitrary as it accuses religion of being" (qtd. S. Rosen 151). Philosophy cannot, finally, explain or account for itself. Thus revelation, whose "very *boast*" is to be a "*miracle*, hence most improbable and most uncertain," exposes a crack in a foundational principle of philosophy—the principle of sufficient reason ("everything which is incapable of being made manifest, is suspect") (qtd. Meier 175–176). For Strauss, finally, philosophy rests on a leap of faith. This, in effect, is Rosenzweig's legacy.

■

A less noted but unmistakable influence on Rosenzweig was William James, who is invoked in *The Star. The Varieties of Religious Experience* (translated into German in 1907) helped inaugurate the German field of religious psychology. *Varieties* helped to challenge the rationalist reduction of God to a concept (Moyn 123). The American thinker's critique of intellectualism and emphasis on philosophy as the testimony of subjective experience—what James, after Emerson, calls "temperament"—are equally compelling to Rosenzweig: "To achieve being objective, the thinker must proceed boldly from his own subjective situation" (qtd. Glatzer 179). James is also a clear influence on Rosenzweig's "The Little Book of Healthy and Sick Understanding" (1921) (the literal translation of the German title published in English in the 1950s as *Understanding the Sick and the Healthy*) which was meant to introduce his "new thinking" to a lay audience. Rosenzweig's comic rendering of the absurdity and futility that ensues when we ignore our everyday uses of language and our "ordinary common sense" for the metaphysical search for essences has clear affinities with James and, as Hilary Putnam has argued, with Wittgenstein. Consumed in wonder and reflection about "what actually *is*," the philosopher embarks on a quest for "the 'essential' nature of things" that only a philosopher finds reasonable: "No one but a philosopher asks this question or gives this answer. In life the question is invalid; it is never asked. . . . The terms of life are not 'essential' but 'real'; they concern not 'essence' but fact." He "separates his experience of wonder from the continuous stream of life, isolating it. . . . He does not permit his wonder . . . to be released into the stream of life. . . . Wonder stagnates, is perpetuated in the motionless mirror of his meditation" (40–41). Rosenzweig warns that "any man can trip over himself and find himself following the trail of philosophy" (42).

Rosenzweig's *Understanding the Sick and the Healthy* attracted notice among New York intellectuals, including an admiring review from Philip Rieff. However, Rosenzweig never achieved the fame of a Kafka or Kierkegaard. Indeed, despite a brave battle in the last years of his life with the ravages of ALS, as he—while paralyzed—collaborated alongside Martin Buber on a new translation of the Bible into German, Rosenzweig failed to make the cut on a list of heroic intellectual martyrs drawn up by Rieff's former wife. "For the modern consciousness, the artist (replacing the saint) is the exemplary sufferer," wrote Susan Sontag in an essay of 1963. We need writers [Kierkegaard, Nietzsche, and Simone Weil] "for their personal authority, for the example of their seriousness, for their manifest willingness to sacrifice themselves for their truths." Such extreme lives—"absurd in [their] exaggerations and degree of self-mutilation"—are "exemplary." Yet, Sontag warned, they are less to be imitated than to be "regarded from a distance with a mixture of revulsion, pity, and reverence" (*Essays* 54).

Rieff—no surprise—implicitly disagreed with such accounting, since he did not keep his distance, coming close to making Kierkegaard, including his "self-mutilation," an exemplary model of his own sacrificial career. The extremity of Kierkegaard's tutelage for both Rieff and Salinger in their exits from public life is evident at the start of the final entry of his *Journals* (at least the first American selection translated in 1959) where he had answered the question of how to live in faith by asking: "What is 'spirit'? (for Christ is spirit, his religion that of the spirit). Spirit is 'to live as though dead' (dead to the world)" (254).

■

Rieff and Susan Sontag married after a ten-day courtship in late November 1950 at the University of Chicago: she was a seventeen-year-old student and he a twenty-eight-year-old sociology instructor. "I marry Philip with full consciousness + fear of my will toward self-destructiveness" are the ominous words Sontag jotted in her diary (*Reborn* 62). The marriage would produce a son in 1952 (David Rieff) and would formally reach a miserable end in 1958. The year before Sontag left by herself for England to take a fellowship at Oxford. After a few months, she escaped to Paris and there resumed an affair with a former female lover and experienced an intellectual awakening to what she deemed new standards of beauty and style that by 1965 she would christen "the new sensibility."

Her vitality and adventurism—"*I can do anything! . . . I am infinite*—I must never forget it" she declared in early diary entries (37)—stood in sober contrast to Rieff's gloomy temperament. He resembled more than a little his depiction of another of his heroes—Freud. His "tired wisdom" and "stoic rationality" assure us of nothing "except perhaps, having learned from him, the burden of misery we must find strength to carry will be somewhat lighter" (*Freud* 327, xi). It seems something of a miracle that the marriage of this perhaps oddest couple of intellectuals lasted eight years. One spouse would write about the aesthetics of silence; one simply lived it, enacting her remark that "so far as he is serious, the artist is continuously tempted to sever the dialogue he has with his audience."

After thirty-three years between books, Rieff published in January 2006 the first of a trilogy, *Sacred Order/Social Order.* He died seven months later, and the second and third volumes were issued in 2008; a book he wrote in the early 1970s on Max Weber and charisma appeared in 2007. The first of three volumes of Sontag's journals and diaries, this one covering the years 1947–1963, also appeared in 2008, four years after her death. We can use Sontag's most telling reflection upon Rieff to understand his strange trajectory. In a 1958 diary entry made in Paris, his soon-to-be-ex-wife noted: "P is a bleeder in fact physically, and emotionally, too. He won't die of this grief [of divorce] but neither will he ever recover from it" (*Reborn* 193). Of course on one level Rieff recovered quite nicely—not only remarrying but making a distinguished academic career and publishing two famous and influential books: *Freud: The Mind of the Moralist* (1959) and *The Triumph of the Therapeutic* (1966). But Sontag's early prediction that he would forever hover between death and recovery in some ghostly purgatory proved uncannily accurate. "Some humiliations may serve us well; others make us ill," Rieff once remarked (*Fellow* 138). What fascinates is how he made humiliation serve his career: he turned his wounded, liminal status into an elaborate, highly allusive and self-conscious project of worldly renunciation that became the measure, for him, of the intellectual's integrity.

Rieff's long goodbye began with the fierce, disgusted, but also mordantly witty torrential internal monologue, *Fellow Teachers: Of Culture and Its Second Death* (1973). The tense, crowded pages of *Fellow Teachers* survey the cost incurred when a society dedicates itself to an unprecedented "conclusive freedom": the United States "has been the revolutionary place" to escape the sacred and its prohibitions but lacks "the disciplinary means to install meaningful interdicts as character" and thereby transform the "endless self-expressional quest into culture" (88–89). Amid this promiscuous flood of expression (Rieff's own torrent of words mirroring and admonishing) he raises an inevitable question: "Why publish?" (162). In a culture addicted to faddism and glibness, to the cult of the intellectual guru mesmerizing the young, why bother to compete? He outlines his logic with lapidary precision: "The moral life begins with renunciation; the therapeutic life begins with the renunciation of renunciation. So it is that certain contemporary false prophets [read Norman O. Brown and R. D. Laing] call upon us to become ahistorical infants that is, to act contrary to our historically achieved renunciations. . . . I, for one, will not choose sides nor be chosen; I will stay out; and I will not be guruized, in my attempt to stay out. . . . To teach ourselves how not to be played in the ideas market, perhaps the best we can do is practice the art of silence, especially in this period of over-publication" (208).

He wasn't kidding about public silence. Following *Fellow Teachers* he withdrew for nearly three decades to the seminar room, a teacher of legendary rigor who deemed the page "sacred" space inside which one must live: a semester devoted to a close reading of several pages of, say, Max Weber was not unheard of. "It would be better to spend three days imprisoned by a sentence than any length of time handing over ready-made ideas" (2). He opted to teach "an inhibiting subtlety, to think in something like late Jamesian sentences" (52). Rejecting the "more" of "sheer productivity," he opted for the "more" of taking one's time, a luxurious affordance which he regarded the academy as uniquely able to provide: "Within our strict discipline, we are the freest of creatures" (95, 191). From this unhurried stance to public effacement was a short step. Rieff began a 1985 preface to a reissue of *Fellow Teachers* by describing the book as a "postmortem letter to the dead, myself self-addressed among them. Addressing fellow teachers, I do not exclude from readership or resurrection any who discover that they, too, are as good as dead. . . . In my dual office, as fellow corpse and coroner, the death I have in mind is not the first, which is of the teaching body, hyperactive as it remains, but the second: of the teaching soul" (vii).

Rieff's "art of silence" has itself been interpreted as one of his major works. "Our most eloquent and effective critic of the therapeutic style asks us to consider the possibility, in effect, that the most telling form of criticism, in a culture in which the activity of criticism has itself been assimilated to therapeutic purposes, may turn out to be silence," commented Christopher Lasch, whose anatomy of the "culture of narcissism" Rieff had decisively influenced (220). That silence has acquired texture and density thanks to the flood of posthumous Rieff work—his public silence turned out to be hiding private production—and in light of Sontag's diary which makes their marriage available to public scrutiny and offers clues to his eventual self-erasure.

"Today, a wonderful opportunity was offered me," Sontag noted in 1950, "to do some research work for a soc professor named Philip Rieff" (*Reborn* 56). Her initial terms resonate, for the marriage would be, on some level, a mutual research opportunity, field-work in alien territory that gave each an intimacy with the enemy. It is easy to regard them as nearly antithetical figures. Rieff not only sought the cloister of the university but scorned "that ruinous fantasy, the life of a free-lance intellectual," a remark that the career of his ex-wife resoundingly disproved (*Fellow* 190). It is not too perverse to say that what proved of value to them in their marriage was that each came to embody most everything the other loathed, a mutual contempt that doubtless added urgency and vividness to their subsequent writing.

In *Against Interpretation* Sontag made an implicit slap at Rieff by rejecting his portrait of Freud as grim survivalist in favor of Norman O. Brown's ecstatic Freud who teaches that "we are nothing but body; all values are bodily values" (243). She salutes the commanding imperative of appetite: "We must learn to *see* more, to *hear* more, to *feel* more" (20). As if in answer, Rieff declared in his own work of 1966: "Quantity has become quality. The answer to all questions of 'what for?' is 'more'" (*Triumph* 65). ("In one word, *more*, you have our civic religion," he later remarked.) He recommended reverence for and constant relearning of the single word that a culture requires: No (*Fellow* 89, 136).

The Triumph of the Therapeutic: Uses of Faith after Freud collides head on with the anarchy and restlessness of the new sensibility, which Rieff knew not as an abstraction but as a visceral, wounding force. I rest my case might have been his response to *Against Interpretation:* here is exhibit A in my argument that we are witnessing nothing less than the "impoverishment of Western culture" and the "bankruptcy of super-ego energies," portentous phrases that resound in his book (48, 259). It not only laments the modernism that Sontag celebrates but can be read as judging her championing of an aggressively anti-intellectual—in the philosophic sense—sensibility as symptomatic of the emergence of a culture unprecedented in its absences—of moral limits, nature, community, and any integration of reason and faith. This lightness leaves us liberated to enjoy what Rieff characterized as "the gaiety of being free from the historic Western compulsion of seeking large and general meanings for small and highly particular lives" (59).

In dogged pursuit of its self-interest, the therapeutic mentality has an ascetic element but has stripped itself of the "principles" of the "ascetic ideal": obedience, faith, a sense of sin and of the sacred. These are the interdicts that define culture (until now) as a "moral demand system" of prohibitions and limits (*Triumph* 30). With this indifference to larger meanings and attachments, "the ascetic becomes the therapeutic" (60). This transition could be said to inform Sontag's embrace of the "new sensibility" and unloading of the "heavy burden of 'content,'" a divestiture that shares with the therapeutic a chilly affect and minimizing of vulnerability and inwardness. Rieff links the therapeutic sensibility to "a new character type" or "myth" that he dubs "psychological man" (an ideal type preceded by three others: religious, political, and economic man) because it has internalized the cool detachment found in both Freud's "analytic attitude" and de Tocqueville's individualism (61). That attitude teaches us how to become unsentimental about ourselves and to grow adept at "self-contemplative manipulation" premised on the belief that "to live on the surface prevents deep hurts" (60).

This new type externalizes inwardness "so as to live in the bright, sober light of the present, where, ideally, the moment is always high noon" (60). Whereas Sontag applauds the receptivity of the new sensibility as evidence of a defiant pluralism—"the voracity of its enthusiasms . . . is very high-speed and hectic"—Rieff finds in the therapeutic an "unprecedented . . . plasticity and absorptive capacity" that is open to the point of emptiness: "It stands for nothing" (Sontag, Essays 285; Triumph 65). He lays blame for this vacancy at the doorstep of Freud's rationalism—his hostility to religion, which dismisses faith as escapist consolation or as fanaticism. Freud's attitude encouraged a hollowed-out, instrumental mode of being whose "terminal sin is immobility" and whose "one virtue is growth" (Fellow 178).

The Triumph of the Therapeutic made its mark; like "against interpretation," the title itself became part of the lexicon of intellectuals. One reason for such success is Rieff's aphoristic style, with its penchant for making pronouncements rather than arguments. He shares this pithiness with his ex-wife. Distilled from a depth of learning, their slightly intimidating aphoristic compression (that Rieff will take to a punishing extreme in his posthumous works) has the effect of dramatizing the intellectual as sage, displaying their sensibility. Here a pointed irony intrudes, for Rieff regards such display as a signature of the therapeutic. He asks: "Why should the therapeutic feel anything deeply when he can exhibit his sensibilities?"—by which he means "pseudo-sensibility." The therapeutic "demands, he appeals, he does whatever needs to be done . . . to assert himself" (Fellow 45).

Loathing this thirst for self-assertive exhibitionism but evidently not immune, Rieff seeks to mitigate it with his pedagogical ideal of "true objectivity" as "positionless understanding" (4). It is our duty as teachers "not to be public men," for they traffic in "messages and positions" which are "the death of teaching" (17, 6). Instead, the goal is to try to cultivate distance from all "social struggles": Colleges provide breathing room for sustained thought that may "help save this society from its cruel infatuations with one damnable simplification after another. The most complex analyses grow brutally simple as they become public objects" (5). The imperative of objectivity is to "escape for a time the success that will transform it into publicity—dead knowledge—making it over, thereafter, into one of the techniques of power and modern commerce."

For Rieff, then, success is a kind of pathology inseparable from the corruption of publicity that the therapeutic craves. How ambivalent, then, he must have been to win success, even fame, to find himself a public intellectual, if not a guru; such visibility was tantamount to the death of the soul, the "second death" in his subtitle of *Fellow Teachers*. His discomfort is immediately palpable; at the start he recounts that the book was prompted by an invitation from the editors of *Salmagundi* to conduct a public interview. He soon regretted accepting: "as a teacher, positionless, I had no business allowing myself to be interviewed" and he ends the book pledging (accurately, it turned out) not to have "another public episode" (6, 217). Applying a kind of penitential logic, he will permit *Fellow Teachers* to be published as a text, which means, inevitably, as a commodity replete with messages and labels, only if he makes clear that regret and disavowal are the conditions of its birth. To reduce, if not defeat, the aggressive self-display of publication, Rieff's opening gambit is a ritual of disaffiliation: he asks rhetorically of those who issued the invitation, "Did you imagine that I am a herald of the therapeutic? I am neither for nor against my ideal type. Nor am I a Freudian or anti-Freudian, Marxist or anti-Marxist, Weberian or anti-Weberian" (1).

Instead, he names himself generically as a "scholar-teacher" whose unshakeable duty is "the enforcement of intellect, upon ourselves and reluctant students." To live the intellectual life, in Rieff's exalted but still compelling idealization, is to practice humility and self-effacement: "I have never had an original thought in my life. I owe every thought to some predecessor"; indeed being an intellectual amounts to assuming a "priestly"—a mediating—role (vii). Teachers must understand themselves as "links in a chain of interpreters, keeping a cautious distance from the political order, as from a vicious animal, more than apologists, more than critics." Only then "can we teachers achieve our ineluctably privileged and dangerous knowledge, favored neither by officialdom nor revolutionaries. . . . My argument against taking sides is one of principle not prudence" (19).

Suiting his actions to his words, Rieff by 1973 had permanently entered the "temple of intellect," the "secret life," emerging rarely over the next thirty-odd years. Looking out at the (pseudo) religiosity of the counter-culture, he pondered a paradox: how has inwardness, the discipline of faith, been lost in an epoch that is putatively awash in spirituality. The medium is the message for Rieff—the era is crowded with zealous charismatic hucksters hawking their spiritual wares, announcing new paths and new revelations. "The world is fuller than ever before of people who look like charismatics and try to act the part . . . they insist on wearing sandals, some even in winter" (*Charisma* 3).

Charisma: The Gift of Grace, and How It Has Been Taken Away from Us is a counter-intuitive argument about Weber's disenchantment thesis. Weber extolled the power of the charismatic to subvert a principal manifestation of that disenchantment, the disciplinary rule of bureaucratic routine. However, argues Rieff, by construing the charismatic as a heroic individualist, Weber in fact "became one of the midwives attending the birth of the therapeutic": his romantic, secular emphasis severed charisma from its original creedal moorings and made it anti-institutional, a "cult of infinite personality" (120, 119). Weber fails to respect its root meaning in the gospels, where "charisms" are God's gratuitous gift or favor of grace, a "gift or capacity for right action" for the benefit of a creedal community. God's deputy, Christ, is at once the pre-eminent giver and receiver of charisms on behalf of all others. "Each time the word 'charism' occurs in the gospels"—and it appears seventeen times—"its use is the practical embodiment of the interdictory form—against the freedom to do anything, a practical opposition to transgressive conduct" (82–83).

The antidote to the therapeutic and the way to recover grace, Rieff declares, is "holy terror"—not the fear of a "mere father," as Freud would have it—but "rather fear of oneself, fear of the evil in oneself and in the world. It is also fear of punishment. Without this necessary fear, charisma is not possible. To live without this high fear is to be a terror oneself, a monster. And yet to be monstrous has become our ambition, for it is our ambition to live without fear. . . . A great charismatic does not save us from holy terror but rather conveys it. One of my intentions is to make us again more responsive to the possibility of holy terror" (6).

Having announced this ambitious, almost Calvinist mission, Rieff promptly tabled it. Over three decades earlier, in *Fellow Teachers*, he mentions he is working on the charisma book to make it "tight as a drum" and will likely fail; but this is "the one thing the academy is for" (162). He would later remark that "there was no constituency for the book. Something in America had changed. We live in an anti-theologic age" (x). He changed his mind four weeks before his death, as he helped his editors assemble the manuscript.

Charisma continues Rieff's identification with "the divine Kierkegaard," who, as the "last and greatest virtuoso of faith in the Protestant tradition," also suffered (and resolved) an anxious relation to publicity. Whereas the secularism of Weber and Freud made them, finally, inadvertently complicit with the therapeutic, Kierkegaard is the passionate upholder of faith as inseparable from the sanctity of inwardness and of truth as subjectivity. The vexed relation of inwardness to a public intellectual career is a consuming interest of Kierkegaard's. He is obsessed with the delicate and precarious passage of faith as it is translated into external representation. To protect inwardness from betrayal by publicity and other forms of the instrumental, the philosopher devised various modes of what he calls "indirect communication"—the panoply of devices, including pseudonyms, he used to undermine authorial reliability. Strategies of indirection to rouse readers to think for themselves were imperative in a mid-nineteenth-century Copenhagen suffering not only spiritual sloth but also a leveling of distinction by rampant "advertisement and publicity," and the swallowing up of Christianity by Christendom—the Established Church.

The enemy of the inwardness of faith, Kierkegaard tells us, is nothing less than "the admired wisdom of our age" which insists that it is "the task of the subject increasingly to divest himself of his subjectivity in order to become more and more objective." The objective tendency of speculative abstract thought, engrossed in constructing "universal history" (he says in *Concluding Unscientific Postscript*), "proposes to make everyone an observer and at its maximum" to turn them almost into "ghosts" (118). The objective perspective, passionless and dogmatic—associated with Descartes and above all Hegel—"translates everything into results" and favors "direct communication" on the assumption of achievable certainty (68). This spirit of the age has made men forget what it means to exist and to have faith—to understand that one never reaches results nor is ever finished. One is always in the process of coming to be.

As early as his first book, on Freud, Rieff had invoked Kierkegaard as an alternative to Freud's subordination of religion to culture, the realm which blurs faith into its churchly incarnation, precisely what Kierkegaard's attack on Christendom is meant to undo. Before long Rieff imagined a more intimate relation, taking the philosopher as a model for his own sacrificial career. At the same time Rieff marked the difference: "we remoter Kierkegaards: we cannot live in faith for a moment except under the paradox of an historically distant authority." To bridge some of that distance requires, says Kierkegaard, renunciation of worldly connections, which is the ground of kinship Rieff stakes out. The importance of renunciation for Kierkegaard is evident in his opening salvo against the recently deceased primate of the Danish state church. The philosopher finds preposterous the claim that this man be regarded a "witness to the truth" since his "preaching soft-pedals, slurs over, suppresses, omits" what "would make our life strenuous, hinder us from enjoying life, that part of Christianity which has to do with dying from the world, by voluntary renunciation." To "take away the danger" is merely "playing Christianity," as a child "plays soldier" (*Fellow* 212; *Attack* 5, 8).

Kierkegaard reiterates the ascetic imperative when he lambastes the vulgarity of the public, who use publicity to "destroy everything that is relative, concrete and particular in life," an emptying of subjectivity into abstraction that defines the "diabolical principle of levelling" of "the present age" (this last phrase, until recently, was the English title for Kierkegaard's extraordinarily prescient 1846 essay portrait of modernity) (*A Literary Review* 96). The few people of distinction and authority who have understood this dilemma and remain pledged to leap into God's embrace must train themselves in the discipline of becoming "*unrecognizable,* like plainclothes police carrying their badges secretly and giving support only negatively—that is, by repulsion." The "unrecognizables," who "serve in suffering and help indirectly," have a "twofold task": they have to keep working "and at the same time strive to conceal the fact that they are still working" (96–97).

This notion of the *unrecognized* had considerable charm for Rieff given his own decision by the mid-seventies to escape the public while offstage maintaining a furious industry. Near the end of *Charisma* he hailed Kierkegaard's "the unrecognized one" as the true charismatic (244). Greatness "must be poised against publicity," and the question persists: how, despite the vast "celebrity machines," does a culture "create again the possibility of inwardness?" (223). In *Charisma* Rieff quotes Kierkegaard's "Spirit is 'to live as though dead' (dead to the world)," which is clearly a seed of his own self-image as "corpse and coroner."

Rieff's sacrificial election "to live as though dead" to the public world enacted his faith and became his mode of "indirect communication." What this entails acquires some clarity when set in the context of Kierkegaard's depictions of faith—via his pseudonymous author Johannes de Silentio—John of Silence—in *Fear and Trembling.* To have faith is to live happily every moment "on the strength of the absurd" and to discover "how monstrous a paradox" living thus is. The absurd paradox means, finally, a commitment to that which cannot be comprehended; "faith begins precisely where thinking leaves off" (*Fear* 79, 82). In short, keeping faith demands an exit from philosophy into life. "No way of communicating the message of Christianity is available other than the witness that is borne in life," notes a recent commentator (Walsh 447). More pointedly, how does one bear witness to inwardness in public? Kierkegaard's answer was that one takes care to be misunderstood, at least by the public. And one must also endure "the pain of being unable to make himself intelligible to others but feel no vain desire to show others the way," says the Knight of Faith, Silentio. Those "unable to bear the martyrdom of unintelligibility" instead choose "conveniently enough, the world's admiration of their proficiency" (*Fear* 107). In bearing the martyrdom, Kierkegaard made sure he never attained worldly admiration. "What is great about me, if there is indeed greatness," he wrote in his *Journals,* is that "in spite of all my endeavours," I "achieve nothing all along the line"; I "do not make money, do not get a position, am not decorated." And he added: "I am despised in the bargain" (171).

Paradoxically, the martyrdom of being misunderstood must be made visible, dramatized: a sacrifice must be enacted in life. Kierkegaard's notorious botched marital engagement served this purpose. He ended a thirteen-month pledge to his young beloved, Regine Olsen, because of his self-confessed "melancholy bordering on craziness" and offered her an either/or: "Either I become yours or you will be allowed to wound me so deeply, wound me in my melancholy and in my relation to God, so deeply that, although parted from you, I will yet remain yours" (qtd. Hannay 156). His life "will be forever dedicated to the memory of their failed association" and it will echo in book after book, comments a recent biographer, Alastair Hannay (156). As has often been noted, Kierkegaard appeared to have revoked his engagement to Regine as a way of enacting his sacrifice of bourgeois happiness—love and marriage—which he must abjure to remain a man of faith. The philosopher called this episode a "religious collision"; the last word, Hannay notes, is "the dramatic category under which Kierkegaard liked to grasp the meaning of his life" (387). Indeed, Kierkegaard "came increasingly to regard the actual events in his life in the light of dramatic categories" (157).

In *Fellow Teachers* Rieff comments on Kierkegaard's broken engagement to Regine as dramatizing the "sacrifice built into the success" of his first book, *Either/Or,* which confirmed his decision to become "an author rather than husband and family man." Of this sacrifice— his "highly personal effort[s] to signal fresh obediences to a distant yet final figure in authority"—Rieff notes the irreducible contradiction: the philosopher's compulsive meditations upon his willed "collision" "excluded the one thing that Kierkegaard protested . . . would be unambiguously superior to any and all published workings-through of his obedience: a piety of silences" (26–27). From Rieff's point of view, the Dane's ceaseless stream of books until his death at forty-two "may be said to constitute Kierkegaard's greatest failing," the betrayal of his genius, a category of being the philosopher defines (in his essay "On the Difference between a Genius and Apostle") as living withdrawn and satisfied within itself, always developing "industriously," while making sure that "none of its achievements have any exterior *telos*" (107).

Rieff tells us he is "not embarrassed to refer, in the respect I hold him in his work, to the divine Kierkegaard. This respect raises its own questions. A genius lives in his work. In the case of Kierkegaard, how can authorship be excluded from the authority he found recognizing his life in his work?" (*Fellow* 26). It cannot be excluded, and it is hard to resist reading Rieff here as (unwittingly) inviting us to probe his identification—his "respect" for the "divine" philosopher "raises its own questions"—by posing analogous questions about the relation of his own authorship to "his life in his work." We are tacitly invited, in short, to read his attention to the symbolic play of Kierkegaard's canceled engagement to Regine Olsen as a way to grasp Rieff's own use of his broken marriage to Sontag, the most publicized of all American intellectuals. Rieff perhaps came to regard his painful marriage as the "collision" that inflicted the enabling mutilation spurring his monastic turn from public life. "Some humiliations may serve us well," to recall his remark. His renunciation of the public would keep faith with the "piety of silences" that the always publishing Kierkegaard failed to achieve.

Stitching together the threads of clues in Rieff's reverence for Kierkegaard discloses a self-justifying narrative of the loftiest self-idealization: faith's resignation from the vulgarity of publication and publicity, a renunciation authenticated by a wounding from a woman of celebrity, a wound that kept them connected forever, for she had always embodied for him what he wanted to deflect from himself: the therapeutic's self-display, appetite, and restless mobility. Wrapping himself in public silence for over three decades Rieff became a martyr of unintelligibility. That martyrdom (if not the unintelligibility) ended with the posthumous works, supplying as they did the latent narrative with a remarkable final chapter—reconciliation. His trilogy's first volume, *My Life among the Deathworks*, is dedicated: "In remembrance: Susan Sontag."

Reconciliation. And mimesis: now that she is gone, Rieff is liberated to incarnate her sixties and seventies relish of modernism.

His trilogy is written at least partly under the sign of Sontag. They share the premise (found in Weber and Kierkegaard) that modernity is the "intellectualization of the world": "ours is the age of under- standing and reflection, without passion" (from the opening page of Rieff's second volume). Amid this aridity the work of art, "vibrant, magical, exemplary," "returns us to the world in some way more open and enriched," to borrow Sontag's words from 1965 (*Essays* 33). Her evocation of modernism has, four decades later, become Rieff's. Like the young Sontag, Rieff surrenders to anarchistic appetite; all manner of cultural artifact, from exalted to degraded, falls under his always rapt, at times disgusted, gaze. What never flags is his avidity. (Another irony: Sontag, by the mid-nineties, had turned from her liberationist stance of the sixties; in a preface to a thirtieth anniversary edition of *Against Interpretation*, she admitted that "what I didn't understand" back then "was that seriousness itself was in the early stages of losing credibility . . . and that some of the more transgressive art I was en- joying would reinforce frivolous, merely consumerist transgressions") ("Thirty" 312).

What Rieff used to call the therapeutic he now in his trilogy dubs "third culture"—our contemporary anti-culture, founded on "fiction" rather than a sacred order; its predecessors are "first" (pagan) culture grounded in "fate" and "second" (Judeo-Christian) whose watchword is "faith" (*Sacred Order* 1:12). What I called his surrender to appetite places Rieff on the "remissive" or "horizontal" axis of third culture. This is not his sole or definitive stance, for the horizontal is embedded within the "vertical in authority" or *via*—his acronym "for order that is in its vertical structure immutable and therefore reasonably called 'sacred.'" We each shift for ourselves in the *via*, are "free to choose which way to go. Human life takes on the shape of a cross. We can go up, down, or sidewise" (12). Posthumously, Rieff never stops moving, occupying all positions.

His commitment is to reproducing something of the tumult of living *in* modernity, which is to live synchronically, if unequally, in all three cultures, "in a world permanently at war within itself" (12). To render this synchronicity Rieff fashions an experiment in cultural criticism as modernist artifact. The book is "broken, like the culture it examines, into a jumble of fragments," and he acknowledges the influence of Ezra Pound's "ideogrammic" method of juxtaposition (21). By presenting the image as a fused intellectual and emotional complex, Pound, like Eliot, sought to heal the split between thought and feeling. Rieff works by an analogous logic. To combat "disenchantment, the sin of sheer intellect" and its corollary that "one can, in principle, master all things by calculation" (tenets that Weber made famous), Rieff writes an unmasterable text. He signals a predecessor by making the trilogy's opening words a quotation from *Finnegans Wake*, and fills his text with "image entries"—"crystallization of real action," enemies of abstract intellect (*Sacred Order* 2:13; 1:32).

Rieff asks us to read these visual, verbal, acoustic, historical nodes of sensuous particularity (including family photographs and autobiographical asides about his father and grandfathers) as "sorties into an otherwise invisible sacred order that is inseparable from our lives in social order. To enter sacred order, we need only read our own lives and the imaginative lives of others, or, alternatively, works of the imagination" (1:20). Sacred order only appears in epiphanies of revelation provoked by our encounter with "some telling detail" of the artwork. Rieff also insists, correctly, that the aesthetic traffics in the low and bodily, the horizontal; and he quotes Goethe on the imagination as propriety's "deadliest enemy," taking pleasure, as it does, in the "absurd" and in the "savagery" of caricature. (9). How the material and ethical messiness of art yields the purity and inviolate truth of the vertical in authority is left unexplained.

Rieff's investment in art is remarkable, given that he squarely faces the fact that the power of the aesthetic, the imagination, has long provoked hostility and refusal by many he most admires (he mentions St. Paul, Plato, Edmund Burke). Rieff gives the term "deathworks" for art that makes "an admiring final assault" on what is vital in the established culture. He calls his trilogy "my own lifework as deathwork," and intends it to "strike a fatal blow at third culture." He fashions his deathwork as a "collage," "bricolage," and "biopsy": "cut a slice from the whirling contemporaneity and hold it under the microscope to see it more clearly" (18).

Here in brief summary is one part of a whirling torrent regarding the "anti-Christian doxa of desire." Rieff begins with Don Giovanni, a "mythic figure of inexhaustibly primal force," who, long before Freud, made "sexuality the mainspring of human conduct." He first appears as a bisexual in an early seventeenth-century play by a Catholic monk and then is taken up in the late eighteenth century by Laclos and Mozart, figured in both as a panther who scents the presence of a woman. Such animality links Don Giovanni to "first world culture" where the panther is a creature who "has the kind of body perfume secreted about itself that is a lure for creatures that are to be its prey." By the time of third-world culture, Don Giovanni as "the panther image of the sexual hunter has been recycled" in white romantic racial fantasies of black primitivism, not only the celebration of orgasm in Mailer's "The White Negro" (the denunciation of which has been a set piece of Rieff's down the decades), but a more recent version—Lou Reed's song "I Wanna Be Black." He quotes Reed's hope to "Shoot twenty feet of jism too / And fuck up the Jews." As Rieff comments, "twenty feet of shot semen is a considerable distance, even in mythic measure. Here recycled are typically third culture inversions of normative identifications" downward to "transgressive depths." Summing up, Rieff declares: "Mozart's aristocratic man of primal sex force and Reed's jism shooting black, the ancient Jewish importance of seed mocked in the age of Auschwitz, are synchronic soul brothers under the foreskin" (2:146). Whether this collage sparks in the reader an epiphany of sacred truth is debatable, but as performance it is clear that Rieff is enjoying himself, as his mock-solemn response to Reed and punning summary make clear. Alas, and yet again, the triumph of the therapeutic: in third culture, there are no truths, only readings and fictions.

One of Rieff's strengths is that his polemics are rooted neither in political advocacy (the therapeutic "knows no political boundaries, neither Right nor Left") nor Arnoldian nostalgia. The *kulturkampf*—the assault on interdicts and their reassertion—is a constant of history. Third-culture art may be unique in the ugliness of its hatred and transgression, but, as Rieff notes, the anti-sacral *Piss Christ* of Andres Serrano, for instance, is not unprecedented; it recalls Hans Holbein's terrifying, putrefying *Dead Christ* of 1521. The loss of sacred wisdom has been proceeding apace since the Mishnah recorded that when great teachers died "so died some virtue vital in their culture." The lesson Rieff draws is that "with the death of every teacher, his culture, liberated from his teaching, lowers itself by that death deeper into its grave" (*Fellow* xii). So the lowering has been going on a very long time.

It didn't start with Woodstock or Robert Mapplethorpe's bullwhip (one of Rieff's image entries).

When, toward the end of volume one of *Sacred Order*, Rieff speaks of Rauschenberg's *Erased de Kooning*, an image of "self-erasure . . . in all its calculated emptiness," as a "great effort at displaying the negational character of the third culture" it is hard not to think of Rieff's own act of self-erasure (1:199–200). That sense is only heightened when he remarks a "certain predicative affinity" between *Erased de Kooning* and second-culture Christian theorizing of self-disposal "as the necessary imaginative act in the procedures of redemption. Those procedures of redemption allow the self to disappear into a highest and better self which is the redemptive *I* of Christ crucified" (201).

Living in a third culture but not of it, Rieff kept faith in inwardness and kept faith with his wound of humiliation until it healed into reconciliation. Pledged as it is in remembrance (and tacitly in forgiveness) of she who wounded, *Sacred Order/Social Order* makes a bid for redemption, whose procedures are inseparable from the rigor his trilogy demands of himself and of readers. Whether it demands too much is not for me to say. That question is for a higher authority. I leave it to Kierkegaard:

> To me it seems better to reach a true mutual understanding in inwardness . . . though this might take place slowly. Indeed, even if this never happened, because the time passed and the author was forgotten without anyone having understood him, to me it seems more consistent not to have made the slightest accommodation in order to get anyone to understand him, first and last so tending to his own self as not to make himself important in relation to others, which is so far from being inwardness that it is noisy externality. If he acts in this manner he will have the solace in the day of judgment, when God is the judge, that he has indulged himself in nothing for the sake of winning someone, but with the utmost exertion has labored in vain, leaving it to God to determine whether it was to have any significance or not. (*Concluding* 247)

■

Rieff no doubt was aware of a predecessor in his identification with Kierkegaard's canceled engagement. Kafka in a diary entry appreciatively notes his affinities with Kierkegaard. "As I suspected, his case, despite essential differences, is very similar to mine, at least he is on the same side of the world. He bears me out like a friend" (*Diaries* 230). (Stach offers additional context, *Decisive* 412–413). Kierkegaard's use of Regine Olsen for his renunciatory ends bears uncanny similarities to Kafka's tangled relations with Felice Bauer; he a Prague insurance official, she a Berlin career woman. Their five-year correspondence, during which they were engaged twice, offers an extraordinary look at Kafka in the act of crafting an "ascetic survival strategy" (Stach, *Decisive* 423). Nearly 600 pages, over 500 letters, *Letters to Felice* was published in Germany in 1967 and in English in 1973. I will look at a few passages to impart a sense of Kafka's simultaneous scorn and courting of bourgeois expectations while staking his deepest commitments on what he calls "a desire and a command to torment myself for some higher purpose"—purifying art into a "higher" calling of crucifying autonomy (*Letters to Felice* 314).

In a characteristically self-loathing refrain Kafka tells Felice: "I am not a human being. . . . You have no idea, Felice, what havoc literature creates inside certain heads. It is like monkeys leaping about in the treetops, instead of staying firmly on the ground. It is being lost and not being able to help it. What can one do?" (288). The unnerving candor of Kafka's vulnerability has its mirror image opposite in his serene belief that he may be an "instrument" for a higher purpose. "If there is a higher power that wishes to use me, or does use me, then I am at its mercy, if no more than as a well-prepared instrument. If not, I am nothing" (*Felice* 21). Kafka is the "instrument" of a higher power that is not God but literature. As he famously puts it: "I am nothing but literature; I can and want to be nothing else" (*Diaries* 230). He becomes both the self-effacing instrument and the active higher power itself.

This double incarnation requires, however, that he surrender his sovereign will to the autotelic power of writing: "the strange, mysterious, perhaps dangerous, perhaps saving comfort that there is in writing: it is a leap out of murderer's row; it is a seeing of what is really taking place. This occurs by a higher type of observation, a higher, not a keener type, and the higher it is and the less within reach of the 'row,' the more independent it becomes, the more obedient to its own laws of motion, the more incalculable, the more joyful, the more ascendant its course" (*Diaries* 406–407). This vertiginous freedom, exempt from masochistic and sadistic impulses (the "murderer's row" that plagues him), comprises the raw "wilderness" of "this other world" of unfettered creativity (the diary entries occur on consecutive days). "In this world it is possible even for the humblest to be raised to the heights as if with lightning speed"; though of course, being Kafka, he adds: "though they can also be crushed forever, as if by the weight of the seas" (407). He seeks both the heights and the crush. As he once wrote Felice: "Simply to race through the nights with my pen, that's what I want. And to perish by it, or lose my reason, that's what I want too" (289).

Writing's untethered, exhilarating ascendancy begins below: "I have often thought that the best mode of life for me would be to sit in the innermost room of a spacious locked cellar with my writing things and a lamp." Absolute solitude of the cellar is required "for writing means revealing oneself to excess; the utmost of self-revelation and surrender, in which a human being, when involved with others, would feel he was losing himself, and from which therefore, he will always shrink . . . even that degree of self-revelation and surrender is not enough for writing. Writing that springs from the surface of existence . . . is nothing, and collapses the moment a truer emotion makes that surface shake. That is why one can never be alone enough when one writes, why there can never be enough silence around one when one writes, why even night is not night enough. This is why there is never enough time at one's disposal" (Felice 156). The presence of another—Felice, in her imperturbable innocence, had asked if she could sit beside him while he wrote—would tempt Kafka "to run back" from the ordeal of "surrender" and self-exposure. So to be "nothing but literature" is, among other things, to be "a cellar-dweller," as he cheerfully describes this fantasy of creative isolation.

Kafka repeats nearly verbatim several times the remark "I am nothing but literature; I can and want to be nothing else." It occurs, for instance, in a letter to Felice after she recounts the opinion of a graphologist to whom she has showed Kafka's handwriting, and who sees in it evidence of being "extremely sensual" and "very determined" and of an "artistic bent." Kafka scoffs at all these conclusions but calls "most erroneous" the belief in an artistic bent: "I have no literary interests, but am made of literature" (Felice 304). "Not a bent for writing, my dearest Felice, not a bent, but my entire self. A bent can be uprooted and crushed. But this is what I am. . . . Not a bent, not a bent!" (309). His exasperated claim that he possesses neither "literary interests" nor "bent" seeks to eliminate a mere *relation to* literature since a relation would demand (at least) a minimal amount of distinction or distance from literature. To be "*made* of literature" is to erase distance and relation in favor of embodiment. Life and art merge.

To be "nothing but literature" is to be hostile to relation itself, is to live in one's writing; hence Kafka's love of maintaining distance by sending letters ("this communication . . . is the only kind of communication in keeping with" his determination to create literature) (197). The "concentration" writing demands confines Felice to largely an epistolary presence (though only an inferred one, since Kafka burned all her letters): "With F. I never experienced (except in letters) that sweetness of experiences in a relationship with a woman one loves" (*Diaries* 329). "My mode of life is devised solely for writing, and if there are any changes, then only for the sake of perhaps fitting in better with my writing" (*Felice* 21). Not surprisingly, face-to-face meetings tended to be painful impasses: "Each of us silently says to himself that the other is immovable and merciless. I yield not a particle of my demand for a fantastic life arranged solely in the interest of my work; she, indifferent to every mute request, wants the average. . . . We were alone two hours in the room. Round about me only boredom and despair. We haven't yet had a single good moment together during which I could have breathed freely" (*Diaries* 328–329).

Even so, Kafka needs the dangling possibility of marriage. Since literature is his way of life, is above all the practice of renunciation, it is crucial that there be something to renounce. Hence the beckoning prospect of marriage that Kafka carefully nurtures in his five years of fitful engagement with Felice. Without the possibility of marriage there is no way to catalyze the torment, and without torment there is no urgency to renounce: "The desire to renounce the greatest human happiness for the sake of writing keeps cutting every muscle in my body. I am unable to free myself. Everything is obscured by the apprehensions I feel at the idea of not renouncing" (*Felice* 315). "Consigned to darkness" by his "inner voice," "yet in reality . . . drawn" to Felice, Kafka feels "this contradiction" tear him apart (314). "How could my writing to you," he rhetorically asks her, "achieve everything I want to achieve: To convince you that my two requests are equally serious: 'Go on loving me' and 'Hate me'" (225). The "two requests" reflect the "two selves wrestling with each other"; this is the combat galvanizing his "incoherent" psyche (438).

Incoherent or no, in 1912, a year before meeting Felice, he wrote in his diary an entirely clear-eyed assessment of his psychic economy. Premised on sacrifice and on indifference to balance, it operates by inverting any normative sense of "development": "It is easy to recognize a concentration in me of all my forces on writing. When it became clear in my organism that writing was the most productive direction for my being to take, everything rushed in that direction and left empty all those abilities which were directed toward the joys of sex, eating, drinking, philosophical reflection and above all music. I atrophied in all these directions. . . . My development is now complete, and so far as I can see, there is nothing left to sacrifice" (*Diaries* 163). Kafka re-imagines "development" as multiple modes of extinction, as the ability to maximize sacrifice: to "renounce a little everywhere, in order to retain just enough strength" (*Felice* 20). Unclear is whether sustenance is figured as what remains, that which is "retain[ed]," or if "just enough strength" is based on the little renunciations themselves, meted out over a lifetime of sacrifice.

Kafka's directive to have his work burned upon his death is the most famous renunciatory intention in modern literature. Yet it is often misunderstood, its ambivalences ignored. "Chances were slim that Kafka's last will would be followed point by point, even though he had spelled out his wishes in detail, because no one shared his strict notion of an author's exclusive power of disposition" (Stach, *Years* 476). He had first appointed Max Brod his executor and instructed him simply to destroy all his writings. Then, after a relatively creative period, Kafka was somewhat more discriminating. A revised will, drawn up around this time, exempted "The Judgment," "The Stoker," "In the Penal Colony," "The Metamorphosis," "A Country Doctor," and "A Hunger Artist" from this sweeping verdict; all other writings of whatever kind were to be cremated as per the prior order. Brod disregarded these instructions. In explaining himself, he not only invoked the immeasurable loss to literature had he followed the letter of the law but also persuasively argued that Kafka, by appointing "as his executor a man whom he knew to be incapable of carrying out this wanton destruction of his work, was in effect sanctioning its publication without compromising his self-critical stance" (Pawel 426).

Walter Benjamin links the ambivalence of Kafka's directive to his aesthetic investment in indecision: he "had a rare capacity for creating parables for himself. Yet his parables are never exhausted by what is explainable; on the contrary, he took all conceivable precautions against the interpretation of his writings. One has to find one's way in them circumspectly, cautiously, and warily. . . . The text of his will is another case in point. Given its background, the directive in which Kafka ordered the destruction of his literary remains is just as unfathomable, to be weighed just as carefully, as the answers of the doorkeeper in "Before the Law." Perhaps Kafka, whose every day on earth brought him up against insoluble modes of behavior and imprecise communications, in death wished to give his contemporaries a taste of their own medicine" (804).

Part 4

"I CAN'T REVOLT against the law of nature—and so hatred again and only hatred." Kafka's anguished frustration (at having the parents he has) could be a line out of Thomas Bernhard's novel *The Loser* (1983), an interior monologue and meditation on Glenn Gould, whom Bernhard regarded as the heroic exemplar of the creative life. Nature is named the enemy in Gould's quest for pianistic perfection: "basically we want to be the piano," as Bernhard has him put it, a remark that parallels Kafka's "I am nothing but literature; I can and want to be nothing else." Harassed by the external world, Kafka and Gould seek immunity and immortality by effacing themselves in their art.

To speak of Bernhard's Gould invites Bernhard's Wittgenstein. Not only does Bernhard's novel *Correction* (and less directly *Wittgenstein's Nephew*) concern a Wittgenstein figure, but the philosopher also joins the pianist at the heart of the novelist's more basic preoccupation with genius. The two men merge into a single figure of such intellectual intensity and concentration as virtually to defeat understanding. What Elizabeth Anscombe, Wittgenstein's student, translator, and later herself an eminent philosopher, once said of him sounds Bernhardian:

> To write a satisfactory account [of Wittgenstein's thought] would seem
> to need extraordinary talent. . . . I must confess that I feel deeply suspi-
> cious of anyone's claim to have understood Wittgenstein. That is per-
> haps because, although I had a very strong and deep affection for him,
> and, I suppose, knew him well, I am very sure that I did not understand
> him. It is difficult, I think, not to give a version of his attitudes, for
> example, which one can enter into oneself, and then the account is
> really of oneself: is for example infected with one's own mediocrity or
> ordinariness or lack of complexity. (qtd. Engelmann xiv)

Anscombe's remarks could articulate the starting point for *The Loser:*
Glenn Gould not only embodies the opacity that Anscombe ascribes to
Wittgenstein but his pianistic genius triggers, paradoxically, a contagion of "mediocrity." Overhearing him play blights the musical ambition of two characters in *The Loser,* including the narrator. Bernhard
himself trained as a pianist and actor, and renounced both careers for
fiction and drama.

In dramatizing the destructive force of his Gould's perfectionism Bernhard might well be drawing on a well-known episode in
Wittgenstein's career: the crushing effect he had on the philosophical
work of his Cambridge mentor, Bertrand Russell, in 1913. The relation starts benignly enough, with Russell urging his student to have
less demanding standards for writing philosophy and thereby actually finish something he had started. Russell explains the problem in a
letter: Wittgenstein's "'artistic conscience gets in the way', so that if
he can't 'do it perfectly' then he would rather not do it at all" (*Letters*
479). The problem of perfection, though, grows more complicated, for
Russell begins to introject Wittgenstein's perfectionism in order to
assess his own intellectual integrity. After asking the younger man to
critique his work, Russell writes in a 1913 letter: "I feel in my bones
that he must be right, and that he has seen something I have missed."
This "has rather destroyed the pleasure in my writing" (459). Russell
worries that if he continues in his work "Wittgenstein will think me
a dishonest scoundrel" (459). When Wittgenstein dismisses as superfluous his mentor's search for a theory of logical forms, Russell press-
es on but leaves his manuscript unpublished, haunted by the verdict of dishonesty he had ascribed to his student. In a letter Russell
admits to a "failure of honesty" regarding his own work, a failure
which though "very slight and subtle . . . spread like a poison in

every direction." "All that has gone wrong with me lately came from Wittgenstein's attack on my work" (462). Three years later Russell assesses the damage done: "His criticism . . . was an event of first-rate importance in my life and affected everything I have done since. I saw he was right, and I saw I could not hope ever again to do fundamental work in philosophy" (qtd. Conant, "Bloody" 105). By assuming in Russell's mind the role of paragon of intellectual rigor ("honesty"), Wittgenstein becomes his mentor's punishing superego. Here is the actual attestation of "infection" (Anscombe) and spreading "poison" (Russell), a power to cripple that in effect Bernhard will incorporate into his portrait of Gould.

Bernhard has his own Anscombe-like statement regarding Wittgenstein (in reply to an invitation to contribute an essay on the thinker):

> Writing about Wittgenstein's philosophy, above all his poetry—for in my opinion, in the case of LW we are dealing with a thoroughly poetic mind (brain) that is to say a philosophical BRAIN, not a philosopher—presents the greatest difficulties. As if I had to write propositions about myself and that's not possible. It is a state of cultural and mental history, which defies description. The question is not: Do I write about Wittgenstein. The question is *Am* I Wittgenstein for one moment without destroying him (W.) or me. I cannot answer that question and therefore I cannot write about Wittgenstein. . . . Wittgenstein is a question that cannot be answered—that puts him on the level that excludes answers (and answering). (qtd. Honegger 155)

Refusing to write *"about"* Wittgenstein: the better to risk inhabiting, becoming, performing Wittgenstein. Honoring this recalcitrant figure who defies answers and understanding, Anscombe and Bernhard perform acts of mediation, she as translator (of *Philosophical Investigations*), he as oblique portraitist, refracting the thinker through the pianist, his demonic double. For both Gould and Wittgenstein, renunciation is the very air—the sustaining medium—each breathes. It is a rarefied, private air. Having advised a young aspiring academic friend "there is no air in Cambridge for you" and to work in the healthier air of the working class, he said of himself: "it doesn't matter . . . I manufacture my own oxygen" (qtd. Monk 334). Philosopher and pianist exist in perfect self-containment. At least this is the image they seek to project.

Before returning to Bernhard's *The Loser*, we need to know more about Gould's career and his essays. He left not only scores of albums but writings on the plight of the uncompromising artist in the modern world. These writings are unusually challenging because Gould refuses the assumption of "plight," and instead of lamenting technology—the familiar gesture of alienated intellectuals, as Sontag tells us in another context—he finds in it salvation.

■

"It avails not, neither time or place, distance avails not," says Whitman in "Crossing Brooklyn Ferry" (308). His confidence in unfettered mobility partly inspires his "hurrah for positive science!" (43), a version of fellow seer Rimbaud's avowal less than two decades later that "we must be absolutely modern." The spirit of transcendence and of limitlessness that guides these visionaries is Gould's as well. He made the "absolutely modern" synonymous with the marriage of music and new technology. This union is the very emblem, for him, of "the *idea* of progress" (*Gould Reader* 331). He had little patience with those reluctant "to accept the consequences of a new technology," calling them time-bound "literalists" who "spurn that elusive time-transcending objective which is always within the realization of recorded music" (341). As instinctively as Rimbaud, Gould embraced "unceasing motion" and "constant variation . . . of a particularly *nomadic* order"—which is how he describes the ideas embodied in the fugue, his beloved Bach's musical form (239). Too, like the poet, the pianist's impatience with the pieties of cultural convention and tradition inclined him to make the future his preferred tense. Rather than be beholden to the limits of the merely human dimension—what he called the "inexorable linearity of time"—Gould pledged himself to an "involvement with the future," which is how he described his preference for recording (316). Ratifying this bid for immortality is the fact that Gould's already considerable album sales at his death in 1982, totaling about one and a quarter million records, have soared since. By 2000 his second recording of the *Goldberg Variations* in 1981 had alone sold nearly two million copies (Bazzana 3). Fifteen years later he continues to flourish.

Unlike nearly any mid-century musician, Gould "seems to have gripped the general imagination and stays there still, more than two full decades after his death," wrote Edward Said ("Virtuoso" 116). Doubtless part of this fascination is with Gould's colorful array of eccentricities and obsessions. They are as much a part of his iconicity as his musical genius. Since the fifties, his native Canada has been revering him as a national treasure, putting his face on a stamp, for instance. But Gould's latest biographer tells us that "he was later rejected for a spot on the new paper currency: according to government polls the public considered him too eccentric, 'neurotic to the point of being damaged'" (Bazzana 6). Psychoanalysts and medical doctors, not surprisingly, have feasted on every detail of his life, starting with the family romance: the anxious, overbearing piano teacher mother (who played music to him when he was in the womb), gruff furrier father (whose shop's animal hides frightened his son), and their phobic, solitary boy genius. One amateur Gould pathologist (a clarinetist) has spent years trying to prove the pianist was a classic case of Asperger's Syndrome. Such approaches can be conceded (or not) and set aside; for surely the most remarkable aspect of Gould's profound strangeness was how little it affected his creativity, perhaps because it was inseparable from it. Grasping how he nearly made his life and art synonymous is what demands attention.

In giving his life over to art Gould was possessed by it, which is already to imply that the relation was a complex mix of self-effacement and willful domination. And a third element: obsession. The line at times seemed precarious between his being in control and being devoured by his need for control. He more often than not erected an immaculate distance between his artistic pursuits and the messiness of "clumsy Life at its stupid work," to borrow a phrase of Henry James (*Art* 121). Distance was vital; proximity was a plague. Gould's hypochondria led him to conduct much of his socializing on the phone; even then, his hair-trigger defenses would compel him to hang up if he heard his caller coughing. If fear of germs—which is to say—human contact often left him anxious in his daily life, his life in art was fearless. There his preternatural ease in the non-conceptual medium of pure (unmediated) form knew nothing of boundaries. The norm there was immersion—in intricate, endless shaping and reshaping of sound, whether in scores or tapes.

After 1964 his musical life became inextricable from his devotion to fulfilling the aesthetic promise of technology. This project, startlingly rare at the time, grew out of the same compulsive need for privacy and control so conspicuous in his behavior. Which is to say his piercing intellect theorized and practiced the theme of renunciation in intricate variations. Rightly insisting that Gould was not simply a brilliant musician but a thinker making an "argument about intellectual liberation and critique," Said offers a promising perspective: he emphasizes "the general nature of [Gould's] overall achievement and mission as an altogether unusual type of intellectual virtuoso" ("Virtuoso" 116–117).

Part of Gould's originality was to reject fidelity to a composer's intentions and to an audience's expectations—and to equate pianism and reinvention. For instance, when he transcribed Wagner's "Siegfried Idyll" for piano, he sought "a realization" rather than a "transcription" that is "faithful to the original": "What I did was to invent whole other voices that aren't anywhere in the score, except that they are convincingly Wagnerian" (Cott 67, 69). Here as elsewhere, Gould ignored the privileged status traditionally accorded the composer's printed score, instead conceiving it as a field of possibility, devising an interpretation steeped in rational coherence while expressed in a performance marked by "ecstasy," which he called "the only proper quest for the artist" (Gould Reader 254).

In demoting the composer, Gould did not put himself center stage. Instead, he literally rejected concertizing, promoting as it did "the self-centered affectations of a performing middleman" (246). He went further: in demolishing the adventurous showcase for the virtuoso to revel in the risky immediacy of live performance, he redefined interpretive prowess, protecting it from the exigencies of temporal pressure by perfecting virtuosity via the studio's technological resources and his own expert sound engineering. The listener would reap the rewards of "editorial afterthought" and even be invited to participate via the latest devices (in 1966 Gould was already speaking of the listener's "tape-edit options") (287, 348).

Scrambling the "hierarchy" of composer, performer, listener
(he rightly predicted the "distinctions . . . will become outmoded"),
Gould's aesthetic democratizing also implies a general deflation of the
ego. He makes this clear when he remarks that "in the electronic age"
"the whole question of individuality" in the arts will undergo "radical
reconsideration." Music of high sound quality will be so accessible
that the listener in daily life can live in and with it. Gould will even
applaud Muzak! "In the best of all possible worlds, art would be unnecessary. . . . The professional specialization involved in its making
would be presumption. . . . The audience would be the artist and their
life would be art" (352–353). Gould called this ego-effaced prospect a
"climate of anonymity," a goal that guides his approach to pianism
and to the other art forms he fashioned, including, we shall see, "contrapuntal" radio (452). Anonymity puts him in synch with a strand of
John Cage's project.

With a Rimbaldian and Nietzschean relish for disturbing compla-
cencies and revaluating values, Gould embraced the "antihuman"
(356) and mockingly described the "humanistic ideal" that "recorded
'live' performances" are said to "affirm": they eschew "splices and
other mechanical adventures, and hence are decidedly 'moral': they
usually manage to suppress a sufficient number of pianissimo chords
by an outbreak of bronchitis from the floor to advertise their 'live'-
ness and confirm the faith of the heroically unautomated" (340). For
Gould, esteem for "'live'-ness," far from being proof of aesthetic morality, amounts to the nostalgia of literalists who value recordings of
live performance because they "provide documentation pertaining to
a specific date. They are forever represented as occasions indisputably
of and for their time" (340). Such historical precision Gould associates
with a cultural fetish that makes identity and authenticity the barren
ground of aesthetic judgment: "Most of our value judgments relate to
an awareness of identity; we tend to be terribly frightened of making
judgments if we're not aware of the identity of whoever is responsible
for a piece of art" (Cott 86).

The promise of studio technology is inseparable from an assault
not simply on "humanistic ideals" of creativity but on the very relevance of identity and linear temporality. Gould called the recording
studio a place where "time turns in upon itself" (qtd. Said, "Music

Itself" 52) and in this atemporal space he achieved an aesthetic autonomy of unprecedented engineered "perfection" untethered to both composer and performer. A recording on Gould's terms may comprise a variety of takes assembled at different times and places—"weeks, months, or indeed years apart." He happily envisions listeners splicing together different movements of Beethoven's Fifth Symphony as performed by different conductors (!) without "alteration of tempo or a fluctuation of pitch. This process could, in theory, be applied without restriction to the reconstruction of musical performance." Predicting the rise of sampling, mix-tape, and the fan edit, Gould speaks of "dedicated connoisseur[s]," acting as their own tape editors, "exercising such interpretative predilections as will permit" them to create their own "ideal performance" (*Gould Reader* 348). Listener verges on creator: such "participational overlapping" and "identity reduction" are decisive steps toward achieving that radically democratic "climate of anonymity" Gould envisions (352).

This vision explains his otherwise peculiar enthusiasm for Muzak, "that most abused of electronic manifestations," he writes in 1966 (350). Against the "new foreground" of listener participation is the new ubiquity of "background sound" circulating, for instance, in restaurants or television commercials, which Gould argues is evidence of the power of recordings, "under the cover of neutrality," to enter the listener's mind subliminally ("its success relates in inverse proportion to the listener's awareness of it"). Potentially able to draw on "all the music that has ever been," a trans-historical grab-bag, Muzak "cunningly" disguises within its "bland formulae" an "encyclopedia of experience, an exhaustive compilation of the clichés of post-Renaissance music," among them the "dregs of Debussy," a "blast of Berlioz," a "residue of Rachmaninoff" (350).

A product of "electronic wizardry" without individual authorship, Muzak, for Gould, signals a salutary departure from the "reverence" and "almost religious devotion" surrounding music, especially the concert hall—"the cathedral of the symphony" (333). Muzak heralds a future in which "the art of music will become much more viably a part of our lives, much less an ornament to them, and . . . it will consequently change them much more profoundly" (353). Though he did not have Muzak in mind, the following statement of Gould's is apt: "I think that the finest compliment one can pay to a recording is to acknowledge that it was made in such a way as to erase all signs, all traces, of its making and its maker" (qtd. Bazzana 266). And this double effacement leads to the next step: "In the best of all possible worlds, art would be unnecessary" (*Gould Reader* 353).

While the general trajectory of Gould's renunciation—from ego-ridden public realm to ego-less utopia—could not be clearer, the logic driving the dichotomy is less obvious: a conviction that the public sphere is inimical to aesthetic experience, which can only flourish in private. Within this logic his notoriously hermetic and eccentric habits make sense. The mittens—on top of gloves—and layers of overcoats and sweaters worn even in July and August; the refusal to shake hands; the telephone as his primary means of social life—all this mediation serves to create the distance necessary for private contemplative freedom. Gould's self-insulation is part of what he calls "aesthetic narcissism—and I use that word in its best sense" (246). Even while concertizing, he had an arsenal of rituals to privatize public performance: the sawed-down low piano chair and the slouching posture, head hovering just above the keys, the removal of his shoes during a performance, conducting to himself when playing with an orchestra or reading a magazine at the piano during a pause in a concerto performance—all these much noted eccentricities—culminating in his uncontrollable humming and singing over his playing—audaciously flouted audience and occasion. Renouncing while on stage the obligations of concert decorum secured in public the margin of privacy in which an "aesthetic narcissism" founded on absorption and introspection could flourish.

That margin expanded to the whole of his life after 1964, when he quit public performing after nineteen years, having debuted in 1945 at the age of thirteen. Always subject to stage fright, he could no longer abide a live audience; it intruded on the concentration required for music making. With their conventional expectations about repertoire, eagerness to be seduced by the virtuoso, and bursts of applause, audiences got on his nerves. Gould found applause a remnant of the thumbs up or down of the bloodthirsty crowd of the Roman gladiatorial arena. He explained his severity in "Let's Ban Applause": "I believe that the justification of art is the internal combustion it ignites in the hearts of men and not its shallow, externalized, public manifestations.

The purpose of art is not the release of a momentary ejection of adrenaline but is, rather, the gradual, life-long construction of a state of wonder and serenity" (246). His "antihumanism" thus turns out to be in the service of inward cultivation, an "aesthetic narcissism" that does not bloat the ego but rather transcends it by nurturing a capacity for creative participation and for "wonder." Gould's equation of the aesthetic and self-forgetting is firmly in the Schopenhauer tradition. Rapt absorption in listening is a merging of self and music outside time, what Gould called "ecstasy." He characterized it in the loftiest spiritual terms: "Through the ministrations of radio and phonograph" we are "awakening to the challenge that each man contemplatively create his own divinity" (246). For Gould, "technology exercises a great charity on our lives," summarizing the thinking of the theologian and philosopher Jean Le Moyne; it is a pacifying instrument, delivering us from the incipient violence of the competitive public realm (290).

Not only is Gould's "antihumanism" to be understood dialectically, as housing its own opposite, so is "aesthetic narcissism," which "in its best sense" works through self-indulgence in the very process of discovering inner "divinity." These tensions recede next to the larger challenge Gould launched when he turned his back on an adoring public to embrace technology as aesthetic salvation. His act unsettles the values of humanist intellectuals brought up on Weber's disenchantment thesis, which regards technology as a prime agent of calculating instrumentalism. Gould's act was not without irony: he bolted the concert business's merchandising of talent to jump into the corporate arms of Columbia Records. Irony permeated his life: his self-delighting anti-individualism, his flamboyant anonymity, and his ecstatic asceticism were his signatures, and he knew it. The interviews he conducted with himself were built on this self-irony.

Given his frantic work schedule with studio engineers, his regular long late-night phone calls to friends, his trips to New York to record, it is tempting to say that Gould theorized solitude more than practiced it (Ostwald 267). Yet the legend of his monkish life persisted until 2007 when the painter Cornelia Foss spoke publicly of her five-year affair with Gould. Long a subject of rumor, and mentioned but sketchily in the three full-length biographies, Foss left her husband and moved to Toronto in 1967 with her two children to live near Gould.

Rather than demystifying anything, the episode suggests the ubiquity of overlap and simultaneity in Gould's life and art—he was monk and lover, semi-secretly balancing both, at least for a time. His deepening hypochondria ("the one aspect of the Gould legend that has never been exaggerated") and need for solitude hastened the end of the affair (Bazzana 352).

■

Gould, writes Sanford Schwartz, "believed that music in which voices overlap was a symbol of the right way to live, and this belief took over his life" (155). The apotheosis of Gould's love of the contrapuntal was his devotion to Bach, that genius of the polyphonic whose *Goldberg Variations* he recorded in 1955. It won him international acclaim at twenty-three and was one of the best-selling classical albums of its era. Writing of the prominence of the contrapuntal for Gould, Edward Said notes that its essence is "simultaneity of voices . . . in counterpoint a melody is always in the process of being repeated by one or another voice," hence any series of notes is "capable of an infinite set of transformations, as the series (or melody or subject) is taken up first by one voice then by another, the voices always continuing to sound against, as well as with, all the others" ("Music Itself" 47). Against and with, "sinuously interwoven": this is the taut intricate logic that nurtured Gould's musicality and by which he shaped his life.

Approaching Gould contrapuntally is to see that he thinks fugally: modeled on Bach's favorite musical form, the fugue is devoted to "a concept of unceasing motion" (*Reader* 239) and overlapping harmonies. When Gould speaks of achieving the "ideal" he construes such a goal not as a static end but as means of sparking artistry. In the "quest for perfection" emphasis falls equally on both nouns (339). The fugue's "tenaciously contrapuntal point of view" expresses a dynamism that coincides with Gould's own core aesthetic assumption: "the only excuse for recording a work is to do it differently" (458).

A passion for overlap found expression in Gould's invention of a new documentary form he dubbed "contrapuntal radio." To this genre he contributed his *Solitude Trilogy*, comprising "collages" of voices addressing life in the desolate far Canadian North. Not surprisingly,

Gould enjoyed the back and forth of interviews (especially when he wrote the questions and answers) and the most spirited and probing are the ones he explicitly conducted with himself ("Mr. Gould, I don't feel we should allow this dialogue to degenerate into idle banter"). His love of self-multiplication extended to delight in other forms of mimetic play: in televised comic impersonations, replete with wigs and wardrobe, he portrayed a gallery of "exotic *Doppelgangers*," among them Myron Chianti, mumbling, motorcycle-jacketed Brando-Beat poet-pianist, and Sir Nigel Twitt-Thornwaite, "dean of British conductors" (Cott 119). "Je est un autre" (Rimbaud, Kierkegaard, Dylan) indeed.

In the radio collages Gould devised a formal alternative to the flat "linearity" of the typical radio format. He had no patience with radio documentary's enthrallment to identity manifested in its "respect for the human voice": why should one voice, he asked, shut "down all other patterns to an appropriately reverential level"; why is it that "the moment any character . . . happens to open his mouth, all other activity has to grind to a halt . . . to ensure respect. It's nonsense. The average person can take in and respond to far more information than we allot him on most occasions" (380). We are at ease with overlap, Gould once noted, because density is a basic fact of our experience of urban life—the simultaneous conversations that comprise a city's soundscape, what we half hear in subways, restaurants, hotel lobbies. In a characteristic Gouldian irony, to revitalize the underused capacity of the urban sensorium, he wrapped the listener in a tapestry of spoken words from and about those living in the farthest reaches from any city.

In the *Solitude Trilogy* Gould enacted a belief he shared with his friend Marshall McLuhan, who remarked in an interview (with the pianist): "the spoken word is music, pure music, at any time. It is a form of singing" (qtd. Bazzana 303). In each installment of Gould's trilogy the sonic texture grows denser, making increasingly greater demands on our hearing. By its final work, "The Quiet in the Land," on the flux of change roiling the closed Mennonite community in Winnipeg ("it could go in fifty different directions," says one speaker), there is no introductory exposition. The listener is immersed at once, at times struggling to negotiate three, even four narratives or pieces of music crossing each other simultaneously, as the subject of "mixed" ethnic "background" and "loosing your moorings" is aurally enacted, fading in and out, frustrating our desire to follow each word of a single strand. After a while the words start becoming sounds, unmoored from reference.

This simultaneity, this oscillation that blurs meaning, these refusals to gratify conventional expectation, are basic to Gould's vision of aesthetic experience as the inducement to learn to hear contrapuntally. He designed "contrapuntal radio" to disorient—to have his listener "caught up, in the old Wagnerian sense, by a work of art" which requires keeping "all of the elements in a state of constant flux, interplay, nervous agitation . . . so that one is buoyed aloft by the structure and never at any moment has time to sit back and say, 'Oh, well, that's going to be the bridge to Act Two,' you know. . . . It seems to me terribly important to encourage a type of listener who will not think in terms of precedence, in terms of priority, and collage is one way in which to do it" (*Reader* 380). In disturbing through "agitation" and "flux" the medium's traditional linearity, his aural collages enact an aesthetics of the Kantian sublime, releasing the power of "aesthetic ideas" by scrambling "complete intelligibility."

Gould reveled in perfecting a "structure through creative deception—to cheat with the help" of technology (282). Turning from authenticity and identity to invention and revision, he was more than happy to name his tutelary spirit: "the role of the forger, of the unknown maker of unauthenticated goods, is emblematic of electronic culture" (342–343). Against the pleasure and trust Gould felt in artifice and invention (Said notes the "overwhelming unnaturalness of his performances") he opposed identity—not simply as manifested in the outsized ego of the acclaimed virtuoso but on more philosophic grounds. Identity for Gould was the sterile realm of the linear, static, monadic, and predictable—all that is deaf to the contrapuntal.

At the same time though we depend on identity as the ground against which artifice is engendered. Gould had another way of putting it: creative birth involves dialectical tension, as identity is opened up to "negation," the world outside music. In this collision is expressed the power of the "antithetical" indispensable for invention (3). Perhaps this dwelling with the negative indicates he had been reading Hegel. Whatever the case, some philosophic impulse inspires Gould to theorize negation in a remarkable address to the graduating class of the Toronto Royal Conservatory of Music in 1964, seven months after his final concert. It is a confused and confusing speech but for that reason an intimate mirror of its transitional moment: in the throes of a momentous midcourse correction Gould is thinking out loud, trying to make sense in public of his dramatic act of negation.

Gould stresses two things at once: the "totally necessary systems which we construct in order to govern ourselves—our social selves, our moral selves, our artistic selves" and the importance of *not* forgetting their "artificiality," their humanly constructed character (4). These are impeccably pragmatist emphases. System (including music which is largely a "product of the purely artificial construction of systematic thought") here functions as identity, and it conditions us—we "are firmly ensconced in system." Gould warns against reifying system into a totalizing, foundational, natural fact: "The trouble begins when we start to be so impressed by the strategies of our systematized thought that we forget that it does relate to an obverse, that it is hewn from negation, that it is but very small security against the void of negation which surrounds it." When people who practice the art of the artificial system that is called music "become disrespectful of the immensity of negation compared to system—then they put themselves out of reach of that replenishment of invention upon which creative ideas depend, because invention is, in fact, a cautious dipping into the negation that lies outside system from a position firmly ensconced in system" (5).

Luckily for his audience, Gould near the end shifts from abstraction to anecdote to illustrate what he is getting at—while practicing one day suddenly a vacuum cleaner "started up just beside the instrument." He can't hear any sound from his playing, but can only imagine it. "But the strange thing was that all of it suddenly sounded better than it had without the vacuum cleaner, and those parts which I couldn't actually hear sounded best of all." For Gould, the accident—as a spontaneous burst of negation from outside—is valuable not for invading the sanctuary of system but only because it revealed that "the inner ear of the imagination is very much more powerful a stimulant than is any amount of outward observation" (7). The lesson he draws here is characteristic: he celebrates interiority rather than seeing it as part of a larger arc of experience initiated by the opposite—the accidental intrusion of "totally contrary noises." In closing he reiterates that the young musician must "remain deeply involved with the processes of your own imagination," but now sets that involvement in a wider dialectic: not as a substitute for "the reality of outward observation" but as a crucial relay between "that foreground of system and dogma . . . for which you have trained, and that vast background of immense possibility, of negation . . . to which you must never forget to pay homage as the source from which all creative ideas come" (7).

To look at the entire address is to see that Gould's theory seems at odds with itself: it urges a balancing dialectical interplay between background and foreground—"the most difficult and most important undertaking of your lives in music" will be to keep in "balance" "systematized thought and the speculative opportunities of the creative instinct" (6). Yet he clearly favors the cultivation of "the inner ear of the imagination" over "opportunities" and "possibility" afforded by contingencies beyond system's control. He privileges the inner even though his theory that thought is "hewn from negation" affirms the precipitating power of what is "outside system." The goal of reciprocity or "balance" seems merely rhetorical.

This suspicion is affirmed by the fact that he had already renounced the stage. Measured by the terms Gould employs in the graduation speech, his act of abandonment fails to heed his own advice: his negation of concertizing for inward cultivation of imagination is a bluntly binary move that neglects to enact the delicate dialectic he outlines to the graduates. That is, he erases the public domain rather than performing the "cautious dipping into the negation" he had recommended. Ignoring "balance," he enters the closed circuit of "system" in the shape of the recording studio. That asylum of engineering precision eliminates openness to the stimulating accidents of "totally contrary noises."

To his forfeiture of "balance," of interplay with the world in which "things are antithetical to our own experience," Gould a decade later would give a name: "prisoner." Half in jest (or not) in his 1974 self-interview he says that he would "like to try" his "hand at being a prisoner" ("on the understanding, of course, that I would be entirely innocent of all charges"): "to be incarcerated would be the perfect test of one's inner mobility and of the strength which would enable one to opt creatively out of the human situation" (326). By way of explanation he blithely remarks: "I've never understood the preoccupation with freedom as its reckoned in the Western world." His fantasy of inner liberation via imprisonment is echoed in his belief that "isolation is the one sure way to human happiness" (qtd. Bazzana 237). Huysmans's monkish aesthete Des Esseintes, in his study lined with Moroccan leather, could not have said it better. But it is not French fin de siècle decadence that stirred Gould's imagination of solitude. Rather, it was the classic Japanese film *The Woman in the Dunes* (1964), about a man who becomes entrapped in a woman's subterranean house of sand. He saw it dozens of times, claiming to study it frame by frame (337). The film's portrayal of isolation is ominous, hardly an affirmation of "happiness," which makes his attachment to it all the more fascinating.

More benign is Gould's other image of imprisonment, the "idea of north." This became, he said, his "handy metaphor" for the salutary power of solitude, which for him did not depend on living in the actual Canadian Arctic. Rather, it was a state of Thoreauvian non-conformity (he often employed this adjective) capable of being experienced anywhere: "There are probably people living in the heart of Manhattan who can manage every bit as independent and hermitlike an existence as a prospector tramping the sort of lichen-covered tundra that A. Y. Jackson was so fond of painting north of Great Bear Lake" (*Reader* 456, 392). His locating of the Manhattanite in a *painted* world underlines the aesthetic status of Gould's north. Being Gould, he also means the opposite—the actual experience of those who "immerse themselves in the north" encourages them to "become, in effect, philosophers" (392). This "purification process" starts when one grows indifferent about what one's neighbors or colleagues might say about seeking solitude (456). More than once Gould vowed to spend a "year in the dark" of Arctic Canada. He never did so. Gould was already there, living his *idea* of north.

The turn to inwardness as a refuge from the assaults of the urban has been an oft-noted response to modernity since Georg Simmel theorized the blasé attitude in his essay "The Metropolis and Mental Life" (1903). Gould's preference for living in the mind is one form of this privatization of experience, which has its material site in the bourgeois

interior space of the home as sanctuary against the social alienation of
the public sphere. For Walter Benjamin, who influentially discussed
this haven for coping with harried life under capitalism, the bourgeois
interior is compensatory, a refuge for imagination and aesthetic contemplation. Gould, though, enacts a striking double role: he *disen-
chants* by abolishing the concert, in effect helping to empty the public
sphere, sending home listeners to reproduce in their dens, with their
own technology, the "womb"-like, atemporal rapture Gould found in
the recording studio. Yet, contrapuntal as always, he simultaneously
re-enchants aesthetic experience—refusing to make it a pre-packaged
commodity easily digested; he instead turns it into an enlivening participatory process.

Ultimately, Gould's renunciation of the public is an unabashed ex-
tremism: in art and life he refuses the salubrious unity envisioned by
many intellectuals as the way to heal the fractures of modernity, a
unity that the previous, less urban, century treasured as "A balance,
an ennobling interchange / Of action from within and from without."
This is how Wordsworth describes the workings of a restored imagination in *The Prelude* (1850) (365). Instead, Gould privatizes artistic
contemplation as an experience of "aesthetic narcissism." The phrase
touches a nerve in our contemporary moment of anxious humanism
that tends to regard the aesthetic, especially when not busy doing political "work," as a guilty pleasure. Hear the note of reservation found
in even one of Gould's most appreciative analysts: "For someone so
self aware, he never reflected on the unflattering complicities of an enterprise such as his, which depended ultimately on giant corporations,
and anonymous mass culture, and advertising hype for its success. . . .
It was as if the real social setting of his work was one of the things that
Gould's contrapuntal skills were not meant to absorb" (Said, "Music
Itself" 53–54).

Gould's blind historical eye should be insult enough, but adding
injury is the fact that he is the first great musician, says Said, "un-
equivocally" to embrace the making of art in what Benjamin called
the age of technological reproduction, exploiting the alienating conditions that trample the delicate "aura" of the artwork, its nimbus
of unique presence and distance as embedded in a tradition. Gould's
dismissal of our romantic humanism amounts to a discordant yoking

together of contraries: championing aesthetic bliss as a product of the recording studio, Gould worships two gods and embodies a double scandal. By the standards of the disenchantment thesis, Gould traffics with the enemy. His act seems perverse, leaving us morally queasy. As well it should. Such are the complexities of allegiance to being "absolutely modern."

The same commitment is manifest in the conduct of his life, which Gould engineered with the same painstaking editing of risk and contingency that ruled his work in the recording studio. If Benjamin's Baudelaire is the heroic martyr of modernity, willingly jostled by the crowd, exposed and defenseless to shocks, Gould is the anti-Baudelaire: "Monastic seclusion works for me," Gould said. When however we recall that Baudelaire (in Benjamin's reading) grasps that the volatile bustle of the crowd hides the actual deadening of the administered public world ("the life of immediate experience is essentially demonic semblance," or mocking simulacrum) Gould's stance acquires historical precision rather than evasion: his late-twentieth-century monasticism registers the truth of the public realm's impoverishment, its pseudo-immediacy (Friedlander, *Walter Benjamin* 152).

Gould's seclusion functioned as the motor of his unflagging creative energy (Bazzana 320). So the obsession to which his eccentricities condemned him was at the same time the instrument of freedom to pursue uncompromising dedication to his art: "He was really living precisely the way he wanted and needed to live," says his biographer Bazzana, in a persuasive effort to redress the fixation on tormented genius prominent in many accounts of Gould (318). (Bernhard, as we will see, shares this redress). Gould's anti-tragic sensibility should be kept in mind even as one sways to the lyrical summary of estrangement that Said offers: "In nearly every sense Gould did not belong," writes Said; "whether as son, citizen, member of the community of pianists, musician, or thinker: everything about him bespoke the alienated detachment of a man making his abode, if he had one, in his performances" (Said, "Virtuoso" 131–132). Though vigilant about solitude ("for every hour that you spend in the company of human beings you need x number of hours alone"), Gould at the same time was raised to believe in music making not only as art but also as civic engagement (Cott 103). The artist is "to be morally useful to the community" rather than to present himself as one of the "seers, spiritual adventurers, and social pariahs," to borrow the distinction and words of Sontag. Not for Gould the outlaw roles taken by modernist figures as they seek to "disestablish themselves": for them art "no longer defines itself as responsible" (Introduction to *Artaud* xviii).

If the "responsible" Gould contrasts with the amoral seer Rimbaud, a resemblance also suggests itself: poet and pianist equate aesthetic rigor with pursuit of the unknown. "Above all, the result [of Gould's endless splicing] had to sound like something never heard before" (Ostwalt 269). The allure of the unknown includes the "idea of north" in sub-Arctic Canada, a quest that finds its mirror image reversal in Rimbaud's literal flight to the tropical ends of the known world. Like their geographical radicalism, their shared commitment to the aesthetic unknown under-writes hostility to the cultural marketplace's fetish of the already made, the prefabricated—the artwork as commodity. Within their "absolute modernity" this animus is an anti-modernist moment.

In "Solde" (usually translated as "Sale" but John Ashbery's "Clearance" is sharper), possibly the last of the *Illuminations*, Rimbaud conducts a going-out-of-business sale of all that is most precious to him—what neither the "masses" nor "time and science" recognize because it escapes material embodiment: "Revived Voices: the broth-erly awakening of all choral and orchestral power and their immediate application; the unique opportunity of freeing our senses!" After sev-eral lines it concludes: "for sale: bodies, voices, the tremendous, un-questionable wealth, what will never be sold." Vendors and traveling salesmen should keep busy; they "won't have to hand in their receipts just yet!" (Rimbaud 254–255; *Illuminations* 125). "The unique oppor-tunity of freeing our senses!" is "what will never be sold" for market consumption because such "awakening," which Rimbaud figures as musical, a surge of orchestral energy, defies reduction to public codes and rituals of intelligibility. The experience of aesthetic nuance is too delicate for that.

A moment when music unchains the senses occurs to the hero of Richard Powers's novel of renunciation, *The Goldbug Variations:* lis-tening in 1955 to Gould's *Goldberg* recording, his ear awakens to the elusive sound of a "variation beyond the variation." What he hears is "the pianist singing, caught on record, humming his insufficient heart out. Transcribing the notes from printed page to keypress is not enough. Some ineffable ideal is trapped in the sequence, some further Platonic aria trial beyond the literal fingers to express. Sound that can only be approximated, petitioned by this compulsory, angelic, off-key, parallel attempt at running articulation, the thirty-third *Goldberg*" (462). Bach gave us thirty-two variations, and Gould's humming sounds the ineffable remainder of what is "just beyond the printed score" and beyond the fingering of keys: humming as acoustic incarnation of the Kantian aesthetic idea (636). Powers has presented a uniquely Gouldian moment of aesthetic intimacy—a thirty-third variation comprising the listener's contrapuntal attunement to the pianist's "unauthorized permutations" practiced on Bach's contrapuntal music (*Reader* 320).

"I don't see why anyone puts up with it," remarked Gould when asked once what function his vocal accompaniment served. "I would do without it if I could." He called the humming question one he was rather afraid of, regarding it as "impotent-making," a "centipedal question," he told John McClure (Gould, *Concert Dropout*). He was referring to a fable borrowed from the composer Arnold Schoenberg: when asked to describe how it moved its legs, the centipede grew paralyzed. Like Kant's genius, Gould "didn't ever want to think analytically about pianistic things. . . . All he knew was that he could do it," remarked a friend (qtd. Ostwald 281). Humming, then, was the sound of the unexplainable, of his refusal to explain, hence an aesthetic signature, hence, as often with Gould, an asocial one. His humming (at least at first) alienated listeners. This aesthetic impulse was a distancing device, one among, as we have seen, an ingenious battery of eccentricities. Another, subtler one: he could "not tolerate being contradicted," said a friend noting his avoidance of engagement in human relations (qtd. Ostwald 14).

■

"Glenn didn't ask any questions at all, I never heard him ask a question, I thought," remarks the nameless narrator of Bernhard's *The Loser*, published a year after Gould's death at fifty in 1982 of a stroke while asleep (87). The novel is an uncannily penetrating portrait that flaunts fictive invention as biographical fact. He calls his Gould "our

American-Canadian genius," saddles him with lung disease, and has him live in the woods, barricaded with bodyguards in an "isolation cage, as he called his studio, in America, close to New York." His Gould speaks fluent German and dies at fifty-one, "collapsing at his Steinway" in the middle of the *Goldbergs* (5, 156).

Bernhard is offering a faux memoir of a fantasized friendship with Gould but that (fairly transparent) conceit is less important than the fact that *The Loser* amounts to an interpretive meditation. It seems as if licensed by the pianist's idea of "realization"—"what I did was to invent whole other voices that aren't any where in the score, except that they are convincingly Wagnerian," to recall Gould (Cott 69, 67).

Bernhard realizes—brings to the surface—as the keynote of his "convincingly" Gouldian invention what had been latent in Gould's genius and his renunciations: creative vitality thriving under the sign of death. Bernhard might have encountered the kernel of his deathly reading in a comment Gould made in his 1974 self-interview: "I think that we must accept the fact that art is not inevitably benign, that it is potentially destructive" (*Reader* 324). We know he found public performance inherently "competitive," breeding "aggression" and envy (325). These emotions permeate *The Loser* and they swirl around Gould, who is at once their catalyst and target without becoming their victim. *His* injuries, Bernhard shows, are generated from within his very perfectionism; without the slightest moralizing, the novel lays bare the self-annihilation inherent in that project.

The narrator dubs Gould "the *refuser*" who lives in an "inhuman state" from which he "didn't even want to escape" (6). Here Bernhard seems inspired by Gould's fantasy of being a prisoner, "which would enable one to opt creatively out of the human situation" (*Reader* 326). Within this "inhuman state" Bernhard's Gould prospers by devotion to "simplicity"—not in itself but as the form of his "arrogance," "the arrogance with which Glenn set about everything" (83). The pure concentration of a titanic will marks the genius's supreme self-confidence whose source is an utter absence of self-consciousness. Although his rigor made him appear strange, "he always talked people out of the idea that he was an unhappy person, he claimed he was *the happiest, the most blessed by happiness*" (40). No impotence-inducing "centipedal" moments of reflection for Bernhard's Gould, who is all decisive, furious action with no interest in reading and diary keeping (which is more fiction). Bernhard plays variations on this bass note of arrogant "simplicity":

> *Glenn and ruthlessness, Glenn and solitude, Glenn and Bach, Glenn and the Goldberg Variations, I thought. Glenn in his studio in the woods, his hatred of people, his hatred of music, his music-people hatred, I thought. Glenn and simplicity. . . .* We have to know what we want right from the start. (75–76)

Setting off these qualities are two foils or doubles—one is the unnamed narrator of this interior monologue, the other his friend Wertheimer. Both are former aspirants for piano virtuosity and are wealthy, anxious, ambivalent, and addicted, like many Bernhard protagonists, to repetitive, crippling self-analysis that sabotages their creative projects. The narrator is forever re-starting an essay "About Glenn Gould," while Wertheimer collects and destroys the aphorisms he is composing for a book entitled *The Loser.* They first meet him at a music school in Salzburg (the school is real, the meeting fictitious) one summer when the three are ambitious students and all become "spiritual" friends. They regard Glenn with envy and awe: "I hated Glenn every moment, loved him at the same time with the utmost consistency," declares the narrator (83).

Hearing Glenn play compels and destroys them: "When we meet the very best, we have to give up," comments the narrator; "we hear a genius play a few bars and are washed up" (9, 85). "I would have had to play better than Glenn, but that wasn't possible . . . and therefore I gave up playing the piano" (8). Wertheimer's reaction is even more extreme—hearing "a few bars of Glenn's playing meant [Wertheimer's] end . . . *he* was *fatally* wounded." Years later Wertheimer commits suicide (85). The *Goldberg Variations* "were originally composed *to delight the soul*" and to ease an insomniac Count to sleep, "and almost two hundred and fifty years later they have killed a hopeless person. . . . If Wertheimer hadn't walked past room thirty-three on the second floor of the Mozarteum twenty-eight years ago, precisely at four in the afternoon, he wouldn't have hanged himself twenty-eight years later" (155).

The deadpan tone of this account, vintage Bernhard in its disconcerting comedy, is also troubling since it rests on a claim—the lethal power of art—that is never explained or justified. Does it emanate from Wertheimer's pathologies? Is it a claim about the nature of all art? The "simplicity" of its iron absolutism simply rules the world of the novel. It destroys Wertheimer and drives Glenn. Evidently "the refuser's" ascetic minimizing of life for the pursuit of the immortality of perfection in art is deathly. But deathly for whom? On the novel's second page the narrator, recalling an early encounter, doubted that "we'd ever see him again, he was so possessed by his art that we had to assume he couldn't continue in that state for very long and would soon die" (4). The worry is not due, however, to Glenn's "hypersensitivity" or his pill popping. The narrator dismisses his reputation as an "absolute weakling of artists": his fans worship a phantom, whereas "*my* Glenn Gould is incomparably greater," "an athletic type" (80).

The lethal quality of art's absolutism remains as a premise; any asking why—however natural—is itself a sign of weakness. The narrator witnesses Glenn's implacability when the pianist reacts to a distracting ash tree outside his window where he plays: "Without even asking the owners he went to the toolshed, grabbed an ax and a saw and chopped down the ash. If I have to spend time asking, he said, I just lose time and energy. . . . Without our help, I thought, he created the perfect order he needed where the ash had once stood. If something is in our way we have to get rid of it, Glenn said, even if it's only an ash. And we don't even have the right to ask first . . . we weaken ourselves that way" (79). As Bernhard's Gould always says: "Basically I hate nature," "*Nature is against me.* . . . Our existence consists in always being against nature and setting to work against nature, said Glenn, setting to work against nature until we give up, for nature is stronger than we are, we who in arrogance have turned ourselves into *art products*" (81).

Looking at Gould's actual life through the lens of these lines permits one to "realize" in a new way his hatred of nature, which is indeed a red thread in his biography. As the decades rolled along after retirement from public performance, dedication to perfection in effect required staving off death by a mimicry of it, reducing life to basically an ambit between two womb-like cocoons, at once sterile and fertile chambers of regression: the recording studio or his always eighty degree Fahrenheit, window-sealed apartment (where heavy drapes kept out the sun, since his schedule turned night into day). From these atemporal spaces he eliminated all bright colors (he particularly feared

red) for a uniform "battleship gray," "a negative color." The logic of its usefulness extended to his donning of blinders when driving in mid-town Manhattan to shut out potentially distracting squalor that his peripheral vision might register (*Reader* 322; Bazzana 322, 456). Carefully neutralizing (when not defeating) the natural world and insulating himself against the human—recall his multi-layered sartorial armor—he did indeed "continue perfecting himself to the utmost limit," which came down to refining away that self into an "art machine," as Bernhard's narrator hazards about Glenn (106, 92).

The envious Wertheimer would reject "refining"; he says Glenn dehumanized himself: he "destroyed" his personality to be a genius, ending up having "nothing in common with human beings anymore" (92). So Glenn's (alleged) destruction of his own personality apparently induces a mimetic contagion that is fatal for Wertheimer's musical ambitions and eventually his life. An "unrelieved *emulator,*" Wertheimer ends up being driven mad by his own frantic parodies of Glenn, at one point playing Bach and Handel "without stopping, *until he blacked out,*" tormenting an audience he has bribed to listen (93, 168). Wertheimer is Glenn's monstrous double, the embodied nightmare of the competitive concert world, the envious figure of death stalking him. Glenn early on dubs him "*the loser* . . . always busy losing, constantly losing out" because insufficiently concentrated and decisive (17). "All his life Wertheimer always wanted to assert himself" whereas "Glenn had never had to assert himself, he simply asserted himself always and everywhere" (94). In the face of Glenn's "ruthless and open, yet healthy . . . manner," Wertheimer is eaten up with barely suppressed resentment that he directs against one and all (146). Controlled by his "deep-rooted loser mechanism," he is determined to "drag" others down "with all his might" (147).

If the loser Wertheimer is Glenn's deathly double, that makes Glenn a loser too. And he is, in his battle against nature. We fight "until we give up, for nature is stronger than we are":

We are the ones who continually want to escape from nature, but can't do it, naturally . . . we get stuck halfway. Basically we want to be the piano, he said, not human beings, but the piano, all our lives we want to be the piano and not a human being, flee from the human beings we are in order to completely become the piano, an effort which must fail. . . . My ideal would be, *I would be the Steinway, I wouldn't need Glenn Gould*, he said, I could, by being the Steinway, make Glenn Gould totally superfluous. (81–82)

This wish for self-cancellation recalls the real Gould's remark: "I think that the finest compliment one can pay to a recording is to acknowledge that it was made in such a way as to erase all signs, all traces, of its making and its maker." According to the narrator, even to "get close" to this ideal of achieved superfluousness is enough to drive one mad. Even the greatest virtuosos are losers in their bid to survive in an "inhuman state" of perfection, to be *contra naturam*. Gould came as close as one could. But "he couldn't continue in that state for very long and would soon die," to return to the narrator's early conviction that Glenn "would destroy himself . . . with his *piano radicalism*" (5).

The narrator has his own account of what ended Glenn's life: "He was killed by the impasse he had *played* himself into for almost forty years, I thought" (5). The "impasse" is the "inhuman state" that Gould, in life and in *The Loser*, never escapes and from which he never wants to escape. From that liberating prison of renunciations Gould tracked artistic perfection, a pursuit indifferent to moderation, to balance, and to the inevitable revenge of nature—his stroke certainly hastened by a hypermedicated hypochondria and the bodily toll inflicted by such punishing hermeticism. From that prison Gould found happiness in the uninhibited creativity produced by obsessive concentration. This ease and this intensity comprises for the rest of us the outrage embodied in genius—the affront to conventional notions of fulfillment, fairness, and even to sense making that *The Loser* dramatizes. Bernhard's novel does this without supplying the (factitious) relief of a clarifying moral authority that teaches a lesson in, say, the perils of excess. Instead it offers the opposite—a morass of untidy passions, "the injustice and exaggeration . . . in a word . . . the subjectivity" that the narrator has always "detested" but from which he has "never been immune" (149).

For the self to melt into the means to an artistic end is the effort to "make Glenn Gould totally superfluous" and to enter an "inhuman state." This logic (of self-effacement) and goal (renunciation) partake of the "worldlessness" Hannah Arendt speaks of in *The Human Condition* as inherent both in "good works" and in "wisdom in antiquity" (76). Like Gould's aesthetic and ascetic denial of the public world, Christian goodness and Platonic thinking, when practiced as a consistent way of life, both possess an "essentially non-human, superhuman quality," which is to say that they resist outward and phenomenal manifestations (76). Good works must be done for themselves; as soon as they become "known and public" they lose "their specific character of goodness, of being done for nothing but goodness' sake" (74). This autotelic logic recalls Meister Eckhart's account of poverty.

When goodness "appears openly, it is no longer goodness, though it may still be useful as organized charity or an act of solidarity" (74). Only when it is imperceptible, even by its "author," is goodness manifest; "whoever sees himself performing a good work is no longer good, but at best a useful member of society." Because they must be "forgotten instantly," good works "can never become part of the world; they come and go, leaving no trace. They truly are not of this world" (76). Lovers of goodness and of wisdom are "essentially religious" figures, pushing purity beyond Gould's ambitions: for unlike him they are without the impulse to fabricate artifacts—they pledge themselves to their vocation as an autotelic activity (76).

Worldless too is the awed, speechless contemplation of "shocked wonder at the miracle of Being" that is the ancient philosopher's highest calling, indeed the beginning and the end of philosophy (302). Arendt hazards that Plato reached these conclusions after observing Socrates "time and again suddenly overcome by his thoughts and thrown into a state of absorption to the point of perfect motionlessness for many hours" (302). Unique among the great thinkers, Socrates never spoiled his "experience of the eternal" by writing about it. Had he done so he would have shattered his state of absorption and entered a new realm—the *"vita activa"* with its path to "permanence and potential immortality" (20). Shunning the ambition of immortality, Socrates contemplates the eternal that exists outside language and outside "the realm of human affairs"; hence he dwells in a "kind of death, and the only thing that separates it from real death is that it is not final because no living creature can endure it for any length of time" (20).

In 1954, four years prior to Arendt's remarks in *The Human Condition*, her mentor Heidegger had depicted Socrates even more dramatically, as an icon of the purest self-sufficiency:

> All through his life and right into his death he did nothing else than place himself in this draft [of thought], this current, and maintain himself in it. That is why he is the purest thinker of the West. This is why he wrote nothing. For anyone who begins to write out of thoughtfulness must inevitably be like those people who run to seek refuge from any draft too strong for them. An as yet hidden history still keeps the secret why all great Western thinkers after Socrates, with all their greatness, had to be such fugitives. (*What Is Called* 17)

This portrait chimes with what Pierre Hadot says of the figure of the ancient sage—in him "wisdom was considered a mode of being . . . a state in which he is a kind of superman" (*What Is Ancient Philosophy* 220). He "appears as a kind of unconquerable, unalterable nucleus of freedom"; and Epicurus says he lives "'like a god among men'" (223). All others are susceptible to buckling under the pressure of thought and taking "refuge" in writing. *Writing* philosophy is figured here as forced retreat from or even a renunciation of a life of thought, writing as already an admission of defeat, a betrayal of the pure act of thinking. A related conundrum emerges: how to write philosophy without it becoming Philosophy.

Part 5

CONSIDER A POSSIBLE exception to Heidegger's sweeping claim that, after Socrates, the great Western thinkers embody a falling off from purity, are "fugitives" in their flight into writing; consider this description of a philosopher thinking in public:

> His behavior was not caused by any arrogance. In general, he was of a sympathetic temperament and very kind; but he was hypersensitive and easily irritated. . . . His point of view and his attitude toward people and problems, even theoretical problems, were much more

similar to those of a creative artist than to a scientist; one might almost say, similar to those of a religious prophet or seer. When he started to formulate his view on some specific problem, we often felt the internal struggle that occurred in him at that very moment, a struggle by which he tried to penetrate from darkness to light under an intensive and painful strain, which was even visible on his most expressive face. When, finally, sometimes after a prolonged arduous effort, his answer came forth, his statement stood before us like a newly created piece of art or a divine revelation. . . . The impression he made on us was as if insight came to him as through a divine inspiration, so that we could not help feeling that any sober rational comment or analysis of it would be a profanation. (qtd. Monk 243–244)

This is Wittgenstein: at once anonymous medium of higher powers and vulnerable human being, his face a map of the strenuous movements of his thinking. When he arrives at speech his language does not annul itself in being understood (the condition of prose, according to Valéry) but rather projects the sensuous palpability of an artwork and the unbidden force of revelation. It is less the meaning of his words than the miracle of their birth that endows them with concreteness: "his statement stood before us." If, to recall Kierkegaard, whom Wittgenstein revered, "profundity is not an utterance, a statement, but an existing," here Wittgenstein's profundity turns statement into an existing. The philosopher Rudolph Carnap has brought Wittgenstein to life in the portrait quoted above; he and his fellow logical positivists have in their midst so compelling a figure that in this Viennese salon of scientists and mathematicians he reduces the possibility of "sober rational" reflection to an impertinence. There is no knowing the precise reason Carnap was jolted, but that is the point of revelation; in flooding us it eludes our rational accounting.

■

The quality of Wittgenstein's genius is restless, defiant, as is his life: the peremptory, oracular address of the *Tractatus*, its concluding imperative of silence, his renunciation of a career in philosophy followed, eventually, by a return to capital P Philosophy at Cambridge, but now remade as small p philosophy, built low to the rough ground,

as investigations of how we use language, a project that banishes explanation and makes description alone admissible. All this severity is
reflected in the monastic austerity of his life and person. He cherished
intense friendships (mostly with men, several of whom he loved), in-
vesting them with the demands for perfection—of self-disclosure and
self-analysis—that he brought to everything in his life. More than
one friend found his "nerves worn to death" by their conversations
(*Wittgenstein in Cambridge* 170). His clenched recalcitrance to any
way but his own way brings into full relief a thread running through
Gould's and Salinger's lives—that one who renounces a career in the
midst of success, who deliberately fades from public view, who prefers
not to, is exercising, however temporarily or parodically, an inscrutable, god-like willfulness.

Wittgenstein was for a time a mathematician, mechanical engineer,
architect, and sculptor. He had first studied at Cambridge as a twenty-
one-year-old undergraduate, working, as we have seen, with Russell in
1911–1913. He soon wearied of Cambridge style—"bright and amus-
ing but brittle," is how his friend J. M. Keynes once summed up the
tone of the elite discussion society, the Apostles, a Bloomsbury enclave
that elected Wittgenstein a member. He found annoying the general
air of superior cynicism and theatricality and kept his distance (qtd.
McGuinness 150). Instead, Wittgenstein preferred to pursue thinking
by secluding himself often in his Norwegian mountain village hut, until the First World War erupted in July 1914. After fighting for Austria
(he was awarded a Silver Medal for valor) and serving a year in an Italian
prison camp, in 1919 Wittgenstein renounced the prospect of a brilliant
career in philosophy. During the war he wrote the *Tractatus* (which,
with Russell's help, was published in 1922).To the bewilderment of
family and friends, he instead spent six years as a grade-school teacher
in rural Austria. After an incident in which he struck an eleven-year-old
pupil, he resigned in 1926. He returned to the family home in Vienna to
help build and design a house for his sister.

By 1929 he had recovered his interest in philosophy and returned
to Cambridge to enroll as a doctoral student, submitting the *Tractatus*
as his thesis. He was appointed a lecturer in 1930, becoming a professor in 1937. Always feeling a misunderstood outsider, Wittgenstein
kept apart, returning for renewal to his hut in Norway and other

remote locales. "Temptations to shallowness are immense unless you live very isolated; and even then they are immense" (*Wittgenstein in Cambridge* 218). One could take this as his watchword. He retired in 1947, dying four years later, all the while ceaselessly writing his escape from philosophy.

Wittgenstein found being a Cambridge professor a "kind of living death" (385). He warned a new professor: "Cambridge is a dangerous place. Will you become superficial? smooth? If you don't, you will have to suffer terribly" (423). The dangers were not unique to Cambridge. No sooner has he congratulated a young friend (Norman Malcolm) on obtaining his doctorate and a Princeton professorship, then Wittgenstein warns: "May you not cheat either yourself or your students. Because . . . *that's* what will be expected from you. And it will be *very* difficult not to do it, and perhaps impossible; and in this case: may you have the strength *to quit*" (326). The option of renunciation looms as the ultimate test of integrity. One way Wittgenstein maintained the "strength *to quit*" while not quitting was to write incessantly but publish little; after the *Tractatus* and a short "Lecture on Ethics" in 1929, he confined his publishing to informal modes. He would occasionally give to those in his circle a packet of duplicated lecture notes he had dictated to pupils, one called "The Blue Book" of 1935; a "Brown" one followed.

A major event in his remaining years was the shifting of his attention from the metaphysical to the everyday, thus radically deflating the pretensions of philosophy, such as his own *Tractatus*, to offer definitive solutions regarding the essential nature of language. Some commentators have recently claimed that he initiates this deflation within the *Tractatus* itself (so-called "resolute readings," to be discussed below). Less contested is that the work is concerned to undermine its own authority. Valuing what can be shown but not said, it invites us to leave the book behind. His own work continued apace. Wittgenstein's *Nachlass* is some 20,000 pages and includes posthumous work that already numbers over twenty published volumes, with scores more expected. As Stanley Rosen has dryly noted: "Wittgenstein lapsed into silence, that is, a silence in which he continued to say what could not be said at ever greater length" (158). This updates the paradox that Russell was the first to note. "Mr.

Wittgenstein manages to say a good deal about what cannot be said,"
he remarks in his preface to the *Tractatus* (22).

Though frequently fretting that no one understood his book,
Wittgenstein actually sought this response. As early as 1912, Russell
had warned that his style of oracular pronouncement left out arguments and reasons: "I told him he ought not to simply *state* what he
thinks true, but to give arguments for it, but he said arguments spoil
its beauty, and that he would feel as if he was dirtying a flower with
muddy hands." He does "appeal to me," adds Russell: "the artist in intellect is so very rare" (qtd. McGuiness 104). For the artist philosopher
beauty demands opacity—"his statement stood before us," to recall
Carnap—and the object he makes is a "flower," a rose "without why,"
a fantasy of self-sufficiency to which its author is deeply drawn.

■

"God has arrived," Keynes wrote to his wife upon Wittgenstein's 1929
return (*Wittgenstein in Cambridge* 7). Already crowned with the hon-
orific of "genius," he is by now, nearly seven decades after his death,
more than a philosopher, or a philosopher *malgré lui*, but a unique
cultural icon, the subject of a film, novels, artworks (best known may
be Eduardo Paolozzi's screenprint series *As Is When* (1965) and Mel
Bochner's drawings accompanying a 1991 edition of *On Certainty*)
and muse of at least two major late-twentieth-century writers—the
Bavarian émigré in England W. G. Sebald and the Austrian Bernhard.
His severity of manner and thought fascinated and unnerved others; "I
believe that most of those who loved him and had his friendship also
feared him," remarked Georg Henrik Von Wright, his literary executor (qtd. F. Sontag 63). A student described him as the "oracle"; we
"wait for" him to speak (*Wittgenstein in Cambridge* 219). Another
remarked: "Wittgenstein is the nearest thing to a prophet I have ever
known. He is a man who is like a tower, who stands high and unattached, leaning on no one. . . . He fears no man . . . but other men fear
him. . . . They fear his judgment" (so testified O. K. Bouwsma, who
became a well-known philosopher in the US) (qtd. Sluga 19–20).

Many have linked Wittgenstein to Socrates, as implied earlier;
both are "*atopos*, meaning strange, extravagant, absurd, unclassifiable,

disturbing," as Hadot describes Socrates (*What Is Ancient Philosophy* 30). Relentless questioning rather than attainment of knowledge is the common passion: the "total naked absorption of the mind in its problem," to borrow the phrase of novelist and philosopher William Gass, who is recalling witnessing Wittgenstein thinking very late in life, in a visit to a Cornell graduate seminar (250). Gass remarks: he "felt philosophy was an activity . . . exactly as Valéry had felt concerning the craft of poetry, where every word allowed to remain in a line represented a series of acts of the poet, of proposals and withdrawals, which, in agony, at last, issued in this one, and how no one word was final, how the work was never over, never done, but only, in grief, abandoned" (248–249).

An ascetic with mystic yearnings to be a saint, yet habitually self-lacerating about his imperfect quest to be decent and modest (his words), Wittgenstein warmly admired William James's *The Varieties of Religious Experience*. In 1912 Wittgenstein had written to Russell: "This book does me a *lot* of good. I don't mean to say that I will be a saint soon, but I am not sure that it does not improve me a little in a way in which I would like to improve very much" (*Wittgenstein in Cambridge* 30). He was moved by its praise of poverty and of those who exercise "the right to fling away our life at any moment irresponsibly." Wittgenstein seemed to take James's words to heart, for in 1919 he disinherited himself from his share of a large family fortune and for the rest of his life lived as an ascetic. At this time, he told a friend he felt "reborn" and spoke of wanting to study for the priesthood (McGuinness 273–274).

Like James, Wittgenstein is a kind of anti-philosopher. Yet they have conspicuous differences. Whereas James's philosophic universe gives priority to experience, and concepts are present as though on sufferance, a necessary evil, Wittgenstein's is centered upon our life with language, which is inseparable from rules and concepts and learning how to use them—the embodied logic that helps form the "grammar" that makes possible "forms of life." "The notion of logic is basically foreign to his philosophy," says Russell Goodman of James. "There is nothing in James's writing to match Wittgenstein's idea of an all-pervading logic or grammar" (28). According to Wittgenstein, James was always too much the empiricist consulting experience while

ignoring "a *logical* view of the self, according to which the self occupies a position in a conceptual framework" (118). James's commitment
to experience led him to rely (too often, implied Wittgenstein) on self-
introspection of the stream of thought in analyzing emotions and other
psychological states. Quoting James's effort in *The Principles* to derive
the self by attending to "peculiar motions in the head," Wittgenstein
found that James's procedure objectified states of consciousness un-
naturally. "I cannot observe myself unobserved" (*Investigations* sec.
413; *Zettel* sec. 592; Meyer 288).

Wittgenstein's emphasis on logic however is not positivist, that is,
he does not treat logic as a science, a system of truths to be justified.
Rather, Wittgenstein says it is nonsensical to ask whether logic is correct or incorrect. The claim of logic "is not that such and such is the
case, but that something *is*; but that is *no* experience. Logic *precedes*
every experience—that something is *so*" (*Tractatus* 5.552). Simply "in
understanding language we necessarily already grasp all that the propositions of logic articulate, but the grasp is practical not theoretical. . . .
To think of the world is already to think according to the laws of logic"
(McGinn 32). So there is no perspective above language to reflect upon
logic, no meta-language in which we might speak about or "say" the
nature of logic: "I cannot use language to get outside language" (qtd.
Sass 128). Immanence rules; "there is no outside; outside you cannot
breathe" (*Investigations* sec. 103).

In the *Investigations* Wittgenstein exposes illusions to which he
was once captive. Among them is the illusion that "thought is sur-
rounded by a halo" of logic that is the essence of thought and language,
and presents an "order, in fact the a priori order of the world" without
"empirical cloudiness." This is an (illusory) "order of the purest crystal"—comprising a "*super*-order" of "*super*-concepts" such as 'word,'
'truth,' 'experience'—yet it appears "as the most concrete" –the "incomparable essence of language" that we pursue as the goal of our
investigations (sec. 97). There are however no "super" words and concepts above and beyond ("outside") our ordinary use of them. If, say,
the words 'language,' 'truth,' 'experience' have a use "it must be as
humble a one as that of the words 'table,' 'lamp' 'door'" (sec. 97).

Wittgenstein's humbling of philosophy took a number of
forms; one was to challenge the priority and prestige of Cartesian

epistemology—which requires that knowledge be grounded on indubitable propositional truth. By his final work, *On Certainty*, Wittgenstein argues for a new kind of proposition, what he calls a "hinge proposition"—our basic beliefs (for instance, that the earth exists, that I have two hands)—that "stand fast for us" without any need for justification or to interrogate their grounds (sec. 341). "If I want the door to turn, the hinges must stay put" (sec. 343). Truth or falsity has nothing to do with it. *On Certainty* treats man as a "creature in a primitive state," guided more by animal instinct than by reason or knowledge.

The book accords with Wittgenstein's larger ambition to move from (philosophical) doubt to (existential) fluency, from text to world, a transit he partly accomplished by making his work "entirely philosophical and literary at the same time" (qtd. Monk 177). This simultaneity suggests a concern not to communicate doctrinal truths but to make philosophy an activity—to spark thinking by showing its limits, fashioning a form that thwarts readers' customary reliance on authority. He traps them in an unreliable text so to force them to do what they are not inclined to do—to let it go. "All that philosophy can do is to destroy idols. And that means not creating a new one—for instance, as in 'absence of an idol'" (*Occasions* 171). In its formal inventiveness, demands upon the reader, and emphatic use of silence, the *Tractatus* resembles high modernist literary works of the same period. For instance, Eliot in *The Waste Land*, like Wittgenstein, audaciously uses shock tactics to unsettle the reader for an ethical purpose—to induce heightened consciousness. For Eliot that means spiritual rebirth (he retains idols) beyond rational accounting, an experience to which language merely gestures. *The Waste Land* concludes with a Sanskrit mantra, "Shantih," triply repeated and which he translated in the notes as the "Peace which passeth understanding." In the case of Wittgenstein, the wager of his text's self-dismantling is to open philosophy to life and reinstate the ineffable, much as William James urged a reinstatement of the vague.

■

Kierkegaard was Wittgenstein's master both in the art of silence and in making philosophy not a theory but an activity. Wittgenstein learned Danish to read him in the original and told a friend that he "was by far the most profound thinker of the last century. Kierkegaard was a saint" (qtd. Schonbaumsfeld 10). Kierkegaard likely inspired Wittgenstein's own ambitions in this direction. He shared Kierkegaard's existential grasp of faith as lived rather than known, and his contempt for explanation, which Wittgenstein regarded as the result of philosophy aping positivist science, with its disregard of the particular and preference for theory. "Man has an urge to thrust against the limits of language," Wittgenstein said in 1930, and added, "Kierkegaard too, recognized this thrust. . . . This thrust against the limits of language is *ethics*" (qtd. Waismann 12–13).

Those limits are visible regarding religious questions; both believed such matters to be unexplainable, not matters of fact. A shared hostility to explanation is made vivid in their similar response to a famous Platonic conundrum. The *Euthyphro* asks: does God will the Good because it is good, or is the Good good because God wills it? Wittgenstein (as did Kierkegaard) believes that the Good is good because God wills it. Wittgenstein calls this the "superficial interpretation," and the other— God wills the Good because it is good—the "deeper" one. He comments (in 1930) revealingly on his choice: "I think that the first interpretation [the "superficial" one] is the deeper one; Good is what God orders. For this cuts off the path to any and every explanation 'why' it is good, while the second conception [the "deeper" one] is precisely the superficial, the rationalistic one, which proceeds as if what is good could still be given some foundation" (Waismann 15; Wisdom 221–226). There are no facts of the matter to appeal to that would ground the source of goodness or happiness and make them rationally intelligible.

Wittgenstein here redefines "deep" as what resists explanation and "the superficial" as what embraces explanation, pursuing its self-defeating inquiry into essence. This counter-intuitive reversal orients all his work and indicates his dismissal of what counts as the philosophically interesting. Philosophy has nothing to offer ethics or religion. And, analogously, it has nothing to offer logic: "Logic must take care of itself," he writes in the *Tractatus,* for "all the propositions of our everyday language, just as they stand, are in perfect logical order" (5.473, 5.5563). Regarding, for instance, the question of value, all Wittgenstein is willing to say is that people have preferences. "Is value a particular state of mind? Or a form inhering in certain data of consciousness?

My answer is: Whatever one said to me, I would reject it; not indeed because the explanation is false but because it is an *explanation*" (qtd. Waismann 15–16).

The seeming perversity of Wittgenstein here—flouting philosophy's responsibility to offer explanation, principles, doctrines, and theories—is not unlike Darwin's dropping talk of ideal types or essences from natural history; both seek drastically to recast their respective disciplines. Trained as an engineer and a research student of aeronautics at University of Manchester, where he built an aircraft engine, Wittgenstein had no animus against scientific explanation per se, only its ubiquity: "The scientific way of thinking (which today possesses the whole world) . . . wants to respond to every disquietude with an explanation" (qtd. Klagge *Exile* 129). If presented with a "*theory*, I would say: No, no, that doesn't interest me. Even if the theory were true that would not interest me—it would not be *what* I seek" (qtd. Waismann 16). What he seeks instead, especially in his later work, are truisms and clarifications, which leave everything exactly as is. This subversive quietism threatens to mock the power of philosophy, the Queen of the Sciences, but such deflation is salutary, for Wittgenstein finds the lofty dignity of philosophy part of what ails it.

After all, he had been similarly afflicted. In its search for the essence of language, the *Tractatus* exhibits the illness of metaphysical speculation and scientism, and seeks to work through these pursuits. The book's passion for abstraction and indifference to particularity and context in part projects his own youthful fantasies of purity and perfection, as Brian McGuinness has argued. In the *Tractatus* Wittgenstein both expresses and exposes the purism that helped inspire elimination of the human contribution to language. What makes the work momentous is that the author's fantasies turn out to be the delusions animating philosophy itself, so his therapeutic working through is meant to relieve both himself and the discipline of confusions.

■

"My work has broadened out, from the foundations of logic to the nature of the world," remarked the author of his then work-in-progress (qtd. Klagge *Exile* 8). By the end of the *Tractatus*, with god-like grandeur, he demolishes his ambitious inquiry, making it stone and rubble. Yet one of the first audiences for the book ignored this last astonishing self-immolating turn and decided the *Tractatus* confirmed its own radically anti-metaphysical scientism. This selective perusal describes how Carnap, head of the Vienna School, the cradle of logical positivism, and his colleagues approached the book. Their misreading distorted Wittgenstein's reputation for decades. The Vienna School greeted his book as brilliant confirmation of their position that, in the words of Schlick, "since science in principle can say all that can be said there is no unanswerable question left" (qtd. Stroll 59). The collection of over 500 numbered, laconic declarations or propositions (there are no arguments) describing the essence of the world, the *Tractatus Logico-Philosophicus,* affirms a strict segregation between fact (nature, science) and value (humans, culture): Given that "the world is the totality of facts" (the book's second proposition) "the sense of the world must lie outside the world. In the world everything is as it is and happens as it does happen. *In* it there is no value" (6.41). Only empirical propositions, purely factual language, can be said. Accordingly, his treatise's final pages consigned "value"—ethics, aesthetics, and religion—"the problems of life" as Wittgenstein describes them—to "outside the world." This is the realm of what can be "shown"—"the inexpressible"—forever separated from the inside, the realm of what can be "said."

This crucial distinction, between what can be said and what can be shown, was uniquely Wittgenstein's and not part of Logical Positivist doctrine, so they tended to pass over it. Or misconstrued it, failing to consider the book as a "*reductio ad absurdum* of the idea that fact and value must not be allowed to *contaminate* each other." So remarks the philosopher and novelist Iris Murdoch, who was at Cambridge in the late forties when Wittgenstein was occasionally there (31). The Vienna School's "reductionist ruthlessness" distinguishes between fact and value so as to "deliberately remove value," whereas "Wittgenstein's silence indicates the area of value" (43). In other words, Carnap and his circle assumed the said/shown distinction was invidious and its purpose was to relegate the inexpressible mystical values to the trivial and nonsensical. The positivists did not grasp that although technically concurring with them, ethically Wittgenstein was wholly at odds, for the domain of the inexpressible contained all he most treasured. These inexpressible things show—manifest—themselves: they are what is mystical (6.522). His point is that we cannot speak of life problems or values because they do not belong to the natural world. They are not quantifiable, and thus not susceptible to scientific investigation.

Thus there was far more regret than triumph in Wittgenstein's late remark: "We feel that even if *all possible* scientific questions be answered, the problems of life have still not been touched at all" (6.52). This grew out of an earlier notebook entry: "The urge towards the mystical comes of the non-satisfaction of our wishes by science" (*Notebooks 1914–1916* 51). In its late propositions, the *Tractatus* turns, emptying out the whole enterprise that Wittgenstein has been patiently erecting. Three propositions before the end he writes: "The correct method in philosophy would really be the following: to say nothing except what can be said, i.e. propositions of natural science— i.e., something that has nothing to do with philosophy" (6.53). In this proposition, quoted earlier, the method of philosophy begins to unravel from within; it seems to say that if we adhere to the text's imperative—restricting ourselves to what can be said—philosophy's method would have nothing to do with philosophy.

Tottering reaches collapse in the penultimate proposition where Wittgenstein invokes his famous ladder. He waits to the end to inform us that his "propositions are elucidatory in this way: he who understands me finally recognizes them as senseless, when he has climbed out through them, on them, over them. (He must, so to speak, throw away the ladder, after he has climbed up on it)" (6.54). To understand me is to understand my utterances as nonsense. A form of the "Cretan Liar" paradox seems to emerge here: is his insistence that he is uttering nonsense just more nonsense? After telling us to climb on its rungs and then throw it away, Wittgenstein gnomically concludes:

"Whereof one cannot speak, thereof one must be silent."

The koan-like tautology that is this final remark—after all, how can we *not* be silent about what we cannot speak—prompts confusion, and thought. The effort to grasp nonsense as nonsense and not to equate it with philosophical insight begins the "ethical" work that Wittgenstein told his publisher was the "point" of the book. The tautology also urges us to wonder what, precisely, do we hold, once we have thrown away the ladder? How do we understand a text which its author informs us is nonsense? Such questions have never stopped absorbing readers of the *Tractatus*. One calls it a fantasy of destroying the work of language, which means that it "is an impossible work. Logically speaking, the *Tractatus* does not exist" (Friedlander, *Signs* 131).

Carnap ignored such quandaries; he "encouraged people to simply ignore the concluding sentences of the book as confused" (Conant, "Putting" 286). Wittgenstein was appalled. In a letter to a colleague of Carnap's, he writes: "I cannot imagine that Carnap should have so completely misunderstood the last sentences of the book and *hence* the fundamental conception of the entire book" (qtd. Conant 286). Carnap failed, says James Conant, to "attend to what the work itself says about how it must be read" (286). Ignoring its form he extracted, he assumed, its content, treating it as conventional philosophy—i.e. a treatise offering a doctrine. But in his preface Wittgenstein had said the book was "not a text book" and on 4.112 states, "Philosophy is not a body of doctrine but an activity."

In his "resolute" account of the "ladder," Conant writes: "What we hold on to is the frame of the text [the preface and ladder]—the text's instructions for how to read it and when to throw it away. What we eventually throw away is the body [everything between the preface and the ladder] of the text—its mock doctrine" ("Putting" 286). Most interpreters—irresolute—regard the nonsense as "deep and metaphysically illuminating nonsense" and "still want to hold on to what (they imagine) the nonsense is trying to say"—ineffable insight into the truth of "certain deep matters that cannot be put into language" (286). This is "chickening out" though, says Cora Diamond: "To chicken out is to pretend to throw away the ladder while standing firmly, or as firmly as one can, on it" (Diamond 20). Resolute readers do not scare: insists Conant, the nonsense "is plain and unvarnished nonsense—words that do not express thoughts" (287). The *Tractatus* "does not delimit profound but unstable truths—it aspires to unmask the pseudoprofundity of the 'truths' of philosophy" (Conant, "Throwing" 341). The resolute dismissal includes the saying/showing distinction, what Wittgenstein regarded as his book's "main point" (as he told Russell) and the basis of the "mystical," for which resolute readers have as little patience as did the Vienna positivists.

In an effort to soften the "resolute" stance, one commentator compares Wittgenstein's nonsense to the humor of Lewis Carroll's *Alice in Wonderland;* Carroll deploys nonsensical dialogues that can be understood—so that the nonsense it displays is at once "real" and "something more, or less" (McManus 51, 54). Dennis McManus finds a place for nonsense and the unsayable in certain contexts; they are confused if treated unconditionally or literally, as when we conflate "showing" strictly with silent action. To treat the inexpressible unconditionally risks fetishizing it as rich in mystic import. This ignores that saying can express ethical conduct, as when we verbally comfort or advise someone. Wittgenstein's larger point is that these specific acts do not result from the application of philosophic principles. They are simply what we do at certain times. Philosophy has nothing to say about such occasions or behaviors.

In his detailed (if less aggressively austere) "resolute" reading, McManus posits continuity, as do Conant and Diamond, between the *Tractatus* and the *Philosophical Investigations.* The earlier work only *seems* to advocate what the later work rejects: "con-formism"— a metaphysical theory of truth as representation of reality, the belief that intelligibility of thought is grounded in an isomorphic fit among language, thought, and world, a fit embodied in objective laws of logic that mark the boundary between intelligible and unintelligible, conceivable and inconceivable, thinking. The *Tractatus* exposes as illusion "anything that would seem to set the bounds of sense, to give 'substance' to the laws of logic" (28). Such laws would exile the human factor in meaning making. *Philosophical Investigations* abandons the verticality of laws and principles and opts for horizontal investigation of our ordinary life with language. This abandonment had begun when the *Tractatus* enjoined us to throw away the ladder of propositions that comprise it.

As McManus puts it, "early Wittgenstein shared the later Wittgenstein's view that philosophical problems—how the world happens to be constituted metaphysically—ought to be dissolved rather than solved, that the appropriate response to a philosophical problem is *not* the formulation of a substantial philosophical theory about the nature of the world, thought or language, but instead an identification of *confusions* that have left us facing this apparent—but *only apparent*—problem" (47). In the *Tractatus* this identification proceeds via a radically immanent method: Wittgenstein works *within* these metaphysical confusions; he accedes to the demands of con-formism, that is, he talks nonsense. Unlike the philosopher, however, he knows he is doing so. At the end of this process, says McManus, "we emerge not with answers to the philosophical questions with which we arrived, but instead with a recognition that those were not real questions after all" (75).

This working through of the demands of the pseudo-logic of "intelligibility as con-formity," as McManus puts it, is intended to help us see that "it is only confusion that gives these demands their apparent sense" (7). To remain blind to the philosophical confusion of metaphysical speculation—belief in logical laws that determine the bounds of sense—encourages us to enchant words—endow them with an independent life of their own (and make them "super" words, as quoted earlier). This is a mystification that ignores that our words, for Wittgenstein, "have as much life as our use of them gives them" (McManus 69). Only after throwing away the ladder do we regain access to what non-philosophers intuitively practice all the time—fashioning and refashioning meanings within the web of agreements, the forms of life, that constitute the ordinary practice of our everyday life.

Succumbing to metaphysical enchantment promises to "spare us the trouble, not only of thinking but of living" (1). It is as though philosophers want to "invent a machine for becoming decent," as Wittgenstein remarked in a letter (qtd. McManus 178). Imagining, for instance, "ethical seriousness as the pursuit of principles to cite in support in our actions," philosophers assume that the theory or doctrine they devise will within itself capture the essence of ethical living. This assumption substitutes the pursuit of principles for "clear understanding of what ethical seriousness requires"—the willingness to take responsibility and speak for oneself—dispositions that reflect common-sense impatience with empty slogans. "Who would ever have thought differently," McManus asks: precisely the philosopher, imagining "that one might entomb responsibility in a sentence, in a string of ink marks on paper" (McManus 177, 224, 209–210).

Not only "logic must take care of itself" but ethics must do the same. Like logic, ethics has no need for philosophy. Ethics cannot be theorized, but only shown. The assumption that being ethically serious is a speculative task to which philosophers should dedicate themselves rouses Wittgenstein's impatience and he urges in a letter "an end to all the claptrap about ethics—whether intuitive knowledge exists, whether values exist, whether the good is definable" (qtd. McManus 178). They exist as enacted in particular situations, but not in the elevated realms of theoretical abstraction insisted upon by philosophy: "The whole thing" about acting ethically "is as plain as a sock on the jaw" he tells a friend (Engelmann 11). That plainness is of a piece with the uncanny simplicity of his later work: "We want to understand something that is already in plain view" (*Investigations* sec. 89). What obstructs this seemingly simple task is the bias, taught by the method of science, which construes logical thinking as ignoring surface in search of explanation or essence supposed to be "purest crystal."

Witness how Wittgenstein fashions ethical action on the occasion of a visit to the Vienna Circle. Reports his biographer: "Sometimes, to the surprise of his audience, Wittgenstein would turn his back on them and read poetry. In particular—as if to emphasize to them, as he had earlier explained to von Ficker, that what he had *not* said in the *Tractatus* was more important than what he had—he read them poems of Rabindranath Tagore . . . whose poems express a mystical outlook diametrically opposed to that of the members" of the Vienna Circle (Monk 243). Here, in a rare moment of theatricality, as Wittgenstein, back turned, performs self-effacement, refraining from, say, delivering a philosophic lecture on poetic value—that would be just more "babbling"—but instead *showing* by example, showing the power of poetry in action. For Wittgenstein, "words are also deeds" (*Investigations* sec.546). In making Tagore's words manifest, Wittgenstein's act of reading becomes an unsaid counter-statement to his hosts' scientism. The poetic presence he brings into being has the silent force of an ethical reproach against intellectualism: "We could not help feeling," to recall Carnap, "that any sober rational comment or analysis of it would be a profanation."

To regard the rational as exclusive arbiter is also a profanation: this could be the motto that presides over Wittgenstein's final work, where he embeds certainty in habitual action rather than explicit rules, a certainty so little to do with language that he calls it "animal." (He is not denying that there is also a certainty that is *justified*, that we *come to* after reasoning and observing. But this is not his concern). The "primitive form of the language game is certainty, not uncertainty. For uncertainty could never lead to action" (*Certainty* sec.475; *Occasions* 397). His late stress on silent action had been there from the beginning. In the final movements of the *Tractatus*, says George Steiner, Wittgenstein turns his back on the Western dictum that man is the language animal, intuiting "an antithesis to the Hebraic-Hellenic definition of man as one endowed with the imperative of speech, as one 'having to speak' in order to realize his humanity. For the *Tractatus*, the truly 'human' being, the man or woman most open to the solicitations of the ethical and the spiritual, is he who keeps silent before the essential (or whose right conduct, the precept Wittgenstein adopts from Tolstoy, is his true mode of statement)" (Steiner 103). Steiner, in sum, hears at the end of the *Tractatus* an intriguing pregnant silence around the ineffable, precisely what "resolute" readings reject.

Efforts to understand what the silence means continue unabated. How could it be otherwise? Silence generates "difficulty"—not in our managing to reach silence but in "deciding what silence *says:* contempt, renunciation, the avowal of impotence, or else the highest honor rendered," to quote Jean-Luc Marion, the philosopher of religion who has the end of the *Tractatus* partly in mind. "The silence concerning silence thus conceals from us that, finally, nothing demands more of interpretation than the nothingness of speech. . . . Silence, precisely because it does not explain itself, exposes itself to an infinite equivocation of meaning" (qtd. de Vries 134).

■

Wittgenstein's penchant for self-questioning and revision, that is his capacity for renunciation and remaking, extended to his psychic economy. He was devoted to rigorous self-examination and confession, returning, for instance, to the mountain village where he had taught school to apologize to the family of the pupil he had hurt. The teaching stint, he realized early on, was a mistake; he was temperamentally unsuited to be a teacher but stayed on because he felt "the troubles" it caused did him "good." He vowed to leave when "it no longer gives me the particular kind of pain which will do my character any good" (*Wittgenstein in Cambridge* 157). Unsparing personal self-scrutiny— what he called "the terribly hard work" of demolishing "the edifice of your pride"—is required for both personal and philosophical honesty: "If anyone is unwilling to descend into himself, because this is too painful, he will remain superficial in his writing" (qtd. Monk 366). Two years after his death in 1951, that descent yielded the publication of *Philosophical Investigations*. It commences by recalling the lofty metaphysical ambitions of the *Tractatus* and reversing them: "The *preconceived idea* of crystalline purity can only be removed by turning our whole examination around" (*Investigations* sec. 108).

Philosophical Investigations is a new form of philosophy, composed with the audacity of an artist or poet. And what it offered was also unprecedented—therapy to cure Philosophy's infection of ordinary language by "chimeras" spawned by the Big Questions. Language will now be regarded as embedded within "forms of life" and its meanings dependent on context and use; to complement his down-to-earth approach, he will populate his text with examples instead of theses. Like Franz Rosenzweig, Wittgenstein was a combat veteran of the First World War—an experience that served for both men a similarly cathartic function: war annihilated idealism's cherishing of the inner Soul and inspired them eventually to stand "in the midst of life" (Rosenzweig) and examine the "rough ground" (Wittgenstein). The latter will proceed piecemeal, without an articulated overarching argument, example by example, expending intense scrutiny on our ordinary uses of language.

Turning its back on venerable topics, the *Investigations* dispenses as well with conventional form, replacing the treatise with an "album" of "remarks" "jumping" from topic to topic, "criss-cross in every direction" (v). This dynamism complements the pattern of stating, revising, and canceling that comprises his mode of advancing claims, a rhythm that begins, for Wittgenstein, with the body: "My writing is often nothing but 'stammering,'" he said of his wayward mode, which his notorious manner of lecturing made painfully vivid (*Culture* 18).

Observers noted that he rarely uttered one complete sentence the entire hour, instead stopping in the middle of a sentence to say: "That's
not what I meant to say" and trying again (qtd. Klagge *Exile* 165). His
"album" retains the improvisatory, unpredictable, and revisionary texture of this "stammering" while artfully mitigating its potential paralysis by displacing it into a flexible structure of dispersal and repetition
amid shifting contexts as well as by orchestrating voices in invented
dialogues and exchanges with imaginary interlocutors. The book has
been described as fugue-like.

Part 6

"PERHAPS THEY WILL have a good influence on me," Wittgenstein
noted in his diary late in the fall of 1914 in Krakow about his recent
purchase and reading of Emerson's *Essays*. Within a month this soldier in the Austro-Hungarian army had also bought several volumes
of Nietzsche, including *Twilight of Idols* and *The Anti-Christ* (Monk
121; McGuinness 225). Whereas the first of Wittgenstein's biographers—Brian McGuinness—remarks that "parallels and faint echoes
are worth looking for in all," the second, Ray Monk, grants the impact
of Nietzsche (he locates it in his view of religion as a practice, a way
of life, rather than a body of doctrine) but closes the door on Emerson:
he "is not mentioned again in his diary. Certainly there is no trace of
Emerson's influence in the work that he wrote at this (or indeed at any
other) time." Monk's confidence in granting the one influence while
denying the other is odd (a point that Gordon Bearn also makes) given
that Nietzsche found Emerson's words so intimate and penetrating he
could not praise them: they are "too close to me," he confessed.

Genius feeding upon genius: even if the spectacle generates results
that can rarely be pinpointed, given the repressions triggered by anxieties of influence, these textual encounters plausibly produced a fertile climate of attunement that helped ideas incubate. The facts, if
not the details, of attunement are easy to establish: Nietzsche said of
Emerson: "The author who has been richest in ideas in this century so
far has been an American" (qtd. Kaufmann 12). In 1938 Wittgenstein
wrote in a notebook that if he wants to teach a "new movement of
thought" (rather than "a more *correct* way of thinking") "then my goal

is a 'transvaluation of values' and I think of Nietzsche, also insofar as in my view the philosopher should be a poet," i.e. someone who writes in a literary fashion (qtd. Klagge *Exile* 21). Worth adding is that Emerson was an exemplar to Nietzsche of the philosopher as poet.

I will not seek to posit or prove influence but to identify and elaborate a cluster of commitments and ideas these three worked through, each on his own terms and with his own distinctive vocabulary. That said, this cluster was shaped to some degree within the generative currents produced by Emerson—Nietzsche's reading and revering of him (in translation) since 1862 and Wittgenstein's reading of both in fall 1914. Now that the Nietzsche/Emerson connection has started getting the attention it deserves, I want to enlarge it by treating Nietzsche as in effect a mediator, a relay, of Emersonian thinking to Wittgenstein and to see how Emerson in his way anticipates some of the Austrian philosopher's concerns. Unbridgeable differences remain. Among the most flagrant: Emerson's moments of transcendental union when he is "part or particle of God," Nietzsche's anti-democratic *Übermensch* discourse, and Wittgenstein's relative indifference to experience, identity, authenticity and to power. What outweighs these differences is their shared commitment to what Nietzsche (in a phrase Wittgenstein quotes) calls a "transvaluation of values" that dethrones the centrality of intellectual deliberation enshrined in Occidental ideals of what comprises human being. Moreover, as philosopher poets, each of these renunciants formally enacts dissent from intellectualist orthodoxy by fashioning texts that flagrantly violate Western expectations of what constitutes reliable authority and authorship. Intuition and improvisation come to the fore.

When Wittgenstein in his notebook remark about Nietzsche cited above writes that if he wants to teach a "new movement of thought" (rather than "a more *correct* way of thinking," a project grounded in a correspondence theory of truth) then his aim is not simply to revise the inner (a better way of thinking) but the external life of readers, to make of philosophy not an academic exercise but a value-altering practice ("a movement") that necessarily breaks down the boundaries between page and world. This crossing over from text to life—or their fusion—virtually defines the figure of the anti-philosopher. As Emerson says of the *Essays* of Montaigne: "I know not any where the book that seems less written. It is the language of conversation transferred to a book. Cut these words, and they would bleed; they are vascular and alive" (*Essays* 700).

Anti-philosophers (among them Montaigne, Pascal, Rousseau, Kierkegaard, Emerson, Nietzsche) move from the shelter of institutions to the risks and freedom of the solitary; they make "their own life the theatre of their ideas" and each insists on exhibiting himself as an "existential singularity," says Alain Badiou in his book on Wittgenstein as "anti-philosopher." The anti-philosopher "climbs in person onto the public stage to expose his thought," rebelling "against millennia of philosophy, in the duty to announce and practice an active salvific break in one's own name only." "Without precedent or guarantee," the anti-philosophical act opposes "the regulated anonymity of science" and the claim by conventional philosophy to speak in the name of the universal (68, 87–88). The recalcitrance of Emerson, Nietzsche, and Wittgenstein is more daring and intimate: in denying readers a stable ground of authority, they confirm that at certain moments the writer hopes the reader "will stop reading him," to recall the words of poet Yves Bonnefoy ("Lifting" 800). In abandoning the book, readers mime the renunciation that first brings the text into being.

■

In Emerson, Nietzsche, and Wittgenstein the power of generative renunciation to serve as a compositional resource reaches an intensity of enactment both formally and affectively: the severance from received ideas they demand is an ordeal by fire. One thing that goads all three thinkers to the restless movement they textually incarnate might be summarized by Kierkegaard's prophetic 1846 observation (paraphrased by Stanley Cavell): precisely because we live in an Age of Knowledge, "we have stopped *living* our lives in favor of knowing them" (Cavell, *Themes* 218). How to recover "living" becomes the goal. Kierkegaard does so with his "indirect method" via pseudonymous authorship that leaves him "without authority" ("in the pseudonymous works there is not a single word which is mine, I have no opinion about these works"), the easier to pose as a patient "servant" of the reader while undermining our confidence in knowing both his texts and our selves (*The Point of View* 25, 151, 28; *Concluding* 551). We know Wittgenstein's regard for Kierkegaard, and Emerson shares the latter's passion to disorient his reader. "I unsettle all things," says Emerson, including, or especially, the reader's dependency on him. "To make you *do* something you won't do" is how Wittgenstein puts it. For Nietzsche the capacity not simply for "wonder," the ancient basis of philosophy, but for "being perplexed" is the origin of critical thought (qtd. Emden *Politics of History* 127).

These three figures of hermit vision devise prose works (Wittgenstein does so in *Philosophical Investigations*) open to and shaped by the darting movement of impulsive thought—hence their appetite for fragment and aphorism—playing havoc with systematic and orderly exposition. Like Valéry, they are drawn to forms of expression that make inseparable the quickening of thought and physiological pressure, forms that defy predictable arrangement because they refuse to rely on covering concepts or categories. Instead of deploying these devices that divide and label in the service of imposing "Meaning," these experimenters make understanding not the enemy of the aesthetic (as it is for Valéry) but a hard-won, indeed bruising experience because they wish "to prevent understanding which is unaccompanied by inner change," as Cavell says of Wittgenstein (*Must* 59). This commitment to inducing change makes their devotion to unsettlement therapeutic, instigating a "return to life" rather than an abiding with books.

The return is to a life, however, stripped of a governing hierarchy: mind no longer precedes and defines experience. "Why do I postulate your mind?" asks William James. "Because I see your body acting in a certain way . . . its gestures, facial movements, words and conduct" (*Writings* 2:1176). Rather than disengaged, invulnerable spectators of experience, we are embodied creatures attuned to what Heidegger calls the "unthought" background of thought—the non-conceptual receptivity and feeling that is under the radar of cognition—blind, intuitive, tacit, as when we "do something without knowing how or why" (Heidegger, *What* 76; Emerson, *Essays* 414); as "when I obey a rule, I do not choose. I obey the rule *blindly*" (Wittgenstein, *Investigations* sec. 219). "Abandonment" or "transition" in Emerson, the "innocence" of "becoming" in Nietzsche, and "certainty" in Wittgenstein: these are strata of the inarticulable where doing without knowing prevails and we must trust our own feelings.

■

"I don't try to make you *believe* something you don't believe, but to make you *do* something you won't do," says Wittgenstein. His intent to change us builds an ethical imperative in to his work, which he makes explicit when he asks: "What is the good of philosophy if it does not make me a better human being?" (qtd. Conant, "Throwing Away" 364). His larger teaching makes us see that to recover our humanity is to liberate our vision from the grip of abstraction. And from textual authority. So the author must model for his reader a certain capacity for self-cancelling. For instance, near the end of "History," Emerson blithely issues a retraction: "I reject all I have written, for what is the use of pretending to know what we know not?" (*Essays* 255). Here he makes good on his often quoted remark in "Circles": "Do not set the least value on what I do, or the least discredit on what I do not, as if I pretended to settle anything as true or false. . . . No facts are to me sacred; none are profane" (412). Emerson seems to enjoy sheer bravado, as does Nietzsche. Tapping into Emerson's vein of rude truth, Nietzsche's calculated effrontery is adroit at making aphorism a weapon of abrupt deflation: granting that philosophers disregard "what has been and becomes," he says they see "only what *is*. But since nothing *is*, all that was left to the philosopher as his 'world' was the imaginary" (*Will to Power* sec. 570). Informing us that "nothing *is*," Nietzsche boasts of being one of the "incomprehensible ones": "Have we ever complained about being misunderstood, misjudged, misidentified, defamed, misheard, and ignored? This is precisely our lot . . . this is also our distinction" (*Gay* sec. 371). He introduces *The Genealogy of Morals* by remarking: "If this book is incomprehensible to anyone and jars on his ears, the fault, it seems to me, is not necessarily mine." He counts no one an authority on his work who has not been "deeply wounded" by each of his words—and delighted too ("Preface" sec. 8).

Even these instances of authorial audacity can't compete with Wittgenstein's throwing away the ladder, which in the annals of the unnerving is hard to top. In his later work he avoids such shock tactics but his aim remains to alter our daily doings with language, by encouraging trust in our intuition. For "instinctively we use language rightly; but to the intellect this use is a puzzle." Not to grasp that "philosophic puzzles are irrelevant to our every-day life" leaves us susceptible to being "bewitched by a word. For example, by the word 'know,'" which insists on the cognitive *(Lectures* 1; *On Certainty* sec. 435). Doing without knowing: this is what Wittgenstein encourages and hence his need to make his written pages accord with the unrehearsed, risky nature of "investigations" (his title points to the hard-boiled detective stories he enjoyed). Those searches proceed according to the "natural inclination" of his thoughts rather than "forced" into a "single direction." We encounter "sketches of landscapes" made "in the course of . . . long and involved journeyings" *(Investigations* v).

Readers of Wittgenstein, Emerson, and Nietzsche are, in short, summoned to "dance," in Nietzsche's word *(Gay* sec. 381). "Intellectual *light feet*" communicate a "subtle thrill" to "all the muscles" *(Twilight,* "What Germans Lack" sec. 7). The point is to make one agile enough to be able, when one wants, to put the book down and stand without its help. "He most honors my style who learns under it to destroy the teacher" is how Whitman captures the violence of the severance (77). Nietzsche called himself an artist of contempt and he seeks to inspire contempt "in us about our present state" (Pippin 40). Impiety about passivity-inducing precedents of all kinds cultivates what Emerson calls "the active soul"—"the one thing in the world of value" *(Essays* 57).

The renunciations that drive these agonistic texts enact the shared need of these thinkers to be "untimely" (Nietzsche's word), "that is to say, acting counter to our time and thereby acting on our time," which includes a willingness to enter into a "hostile relationship with the existing forms and order" *(Untimely* 60, 137). As a way of life the philosophy of all three is premised on the value of "questioning our lives" so as to cultivate the power "to reverse our lives," as Cavell has described Emerson's aims *(Cities* 13, 141). The ability to reverse—which includes the power to renounce—requires we draw on capacities for flexibility and suppleness.

These qualities help author and reader approach the prospect of living in the present. Here a paradox emerges: for all three thinkers the insistence on rudeness, untimeliness, turbulence, the demands of intransigent difficulty are, finally, in the service of instilling fluency, lightness, and peace, so we may come to live *now,* "without why."

Or, as Wittgenstein put it, "Let us be human." We are not the god-like engines of rationality that philosophy would have us believe. Indeed, only when the intellect is liberated, says Nietzsche, does it "contemplate the objects: and now, for the first time, the *ordinary* appears to be *remarkable, as a problem*. This is the true sign of the philosophic drive: the astonishment about that which lies before the eyes of everyone" (qtd. Emden *Politics of History* 128). Here prefigured are Wittgenstein's micro-investigations.

Because they embody philosophy as a way of life (to borrow Pierre Hadot's phrase about the ancients) Emerson and Nietzsche construct a sturdy dichotomy of "Life" versus "Books" (and their institutional incarnations in church and university) that is as simple—and contradictory—as it is inspiring. They in effect sacrifice intellectual subtlety on the altar of Life's exigencies—the urgency of abandoning one's profession. The dichotomy of life versus books, in short, is catalytic; it functions (at least for Emerson and Nietzsche) via exaggeration to produce the emotional momentum needed to renounce. Or, to use an Emersonian word, to make a *transition* from institutional affiliation—the Unitarian ministry, the university department of classical languages—to a less disciplinary place where a genius—he who "wants to augment nature with new living nature"—might thrive (Nietzsche, *Untimely* 174). For the "state can have no interest in the university other than seeing it raise useful and devoted citizens of the state" (191).

"To educate ourselves *against* our age" is Nietzsche's counterstrategy (146). He seeks liberating philosophical exemplars—men of "genius"—those of "unconstrained and unhampered natural being" whose books are less intellectual than "physiological" experiences that produce "the magical outpouring of the inner strength of one natural creature on to another" (145, 136). Reading Schopenhauer produced this rapturous exchange, yet its very medium robbed it of full power: "but I had discovered him only in the form of a book, and that was a great deficiency. So I strove all the harder to see through the book and to imagine the living man" (136). Just as William James will urge his auditors to let life, not his lecture, evoke and invite, Nietzsche esteems what the book cannot encompass—"the outward life" in its corporeal presence, what he calls "the courageous visibility of the philosophical life" (137). This is egregiously absent in Germany, where Kant "clung to his university, submitted . . . to its regulations," and whose "example" has produced only "professorial philosophy" and professors. He "has had a living and life-transforming influence on only a very few men" (137, 140).

"Courageous visibility" is a quality inherited from the ancient Greek thinkers who taught "through their bearing, what they wore and ate, and their morals, rather than by what they said, let alone by what they wrote." The thinker's physical bearing, embodied in "every glance and every gesture," expresses the fused unity of body and spirit. And this dissolving of dichotomy and insistence on "life as whole" undergirds their commitment to visibility and counts as their most valuable teaching (137, 141). Although he taught in the comparatively free-thinking environment of Basel, Switzerland, in 1879 Nietzsche left the invisibility of his professorship in Greek language and literature after ten years of a heavy teaching load and declining health. His contempt for the academy might have a source in rejection: his effort to transfer into the philosophy department had been rebuffed. Thanks in part to a generous yearly pension from the University of Basel he never needed another job, thus fulfilling what he called his public "promise" made five years earlier in "Schopenhauer as Educator," from which the above quotations derive.

In this essay Nietzsche twice quotes from Emerson's "Circles" to inspire his own effort of emancipation from the shackles of professional philosophy. He also sounds remarkably like William James in his own mockery of the profession's insulation in intellectualism: Nietzsche declares that "the only critique of a philosophy that is possible and that proves something, namely trying to see whether one can live in accordance with it, has never been taught at universities: all that has ever been taught is a critique of words by means of other words" (187). To escape the closed circuit of language, Nietzsche embraces life: "I profit from a philosopher only insofar as he can be an example. . . . But this example must be supplied by his outward life and not merely in his books" (136–137). Animus against the bookish goes even deeper, as Nietzsche makes clear: a philosopher is "not merely a great thinker but also a real human being; and when did a scholar ever become a real human being?" (181). Equally blunt is Emerson's disgust for preachers: "I hate goodies. I hate goodness that preaches," he declares of the pre-packaged piety he hears from the pulpit (*Selected* 616). In his conclusion Nietzsche considers Diogenes the Cynic, a man who "when someone praised a philosopher in his presence" skeptically protested: "How can he be considered great, since he has . . . never yet disturbed anybody?" (*Untimely* 194). Nietzsche aligns Emerson with Diogenes as a "dangerous" thinker. This is praise hard to surpass.

■

When one is entrapped within institutional or disciplinary confines and their formulaic discourses, how does one keep language alive, vital enough to disturb? Emerson takes up this challenge. Indeed, a dispute over language partly prompts his resignation from Boston's Second Church. During his dismal tenure (1829–1832) as a Unitarian minister, he encountered firsthand the rule of the "dead forms of our forefathers." What academic philosophy is for Wittgenstein, ministerial preaching is for Emerson: though officially in the business of ethical guidance, of defining the good life and how to achieve it, both institutions instead seal their adherents off from action in the present. Imperative, therefore, is renunciation—of the profession and of approved ways of thinking and of conceiving language. Wittgenstein's concern to combat the inertia of "con-formism"—enchantment by mere words—bears comparison with Emerson's campaign against social conformity as the impoverished psychic state of fearful deference, a shirking of self-trust.

To renounce the Church is to reject its approved mode of preaching: language in the service of received opinion, that is, language wholly indifferent to the task Emerson comes to see as crucial—finding ways to write and speak sentences that approximate the volatility that marks nature and human being. As he decides to quit another ministry (where he had not been pastor but preached each Sunday) his 1838 journal entries are at once blunt and intricate. "I find in me no enthusiasm, no resources for the instruction and guidance of the people when they shall discover that their present guides are blind.

This convention of Education is cold. . . . I hate preaching whether in pulpits or Teacher's Meetings. . . . Preaching is a pledge & I wish to say what I think & feel today with the proviso that tomorrow perhaps I shall contradict it all" (*Selected* 695). Preaching deadens because it stymies the very rhythm of life—to be "sliding," "not fixed," teeming with excess and opposites, dualities and contradiction. "This odious religion" is devoted to arresting the life of language: it "shuts the mouth hard at any remark it cannot twist nor wrench into a sermon" (617). That genre's repressive dependence on fixed Meaning is designed to seduce congregants into obedience, sapping their capacity to think for themselves. The same penalty afflicts he who guides; he makes a "pledge" whose cost is too high—diminished responsibility and responsiveness in the present.

Emerson finds galling not only that moral triteness passes for goodness but that sermonizing is assumed to possess a monopoly on the expression of virtue: "Goodness that preaches undoes itself. A little electricity of virtue lurks here & there in kitchens & among the obscure—chiefly women, that flashes out occasional light & makes the existence of the thing still credible. . . . Goodies make us very bad. . . . We will almost sin to spite them. Better indulge yourself, feed fat, drink liquors, than go strait laced for such cattle as these" (616–617). True to the perverse pulse of life, paraded goodness sparks in us the opposite— the desire to sin. Emerson reprises here his contempt for what he earlier derided as "official goodness" (187), pre-ordained, self-advertised virtue that distracts us from noting unscripted outcroppings of actual virtue (in class and gender precincts out of bourgeois bounds). Hence his reverence for the ordinary (to "sit at the feet of the familiar"), which he will make the heart of his ethical teaching (*Essays* 68–69).

Emerson seems to coincide with Wittgenstein's belief that "what is ethical cannot be taught" (qtd. McManus 179). Is this because ethics is inexpressible, as the *Tractatus* says—"ethics cannot be expressed" (6.421)? Emerson honors silence repeatedly in his writings; in his journal he condemns the present "Age of words" and hopes it is followed by "an age of silence" (*Selected* 694, 696). But in the face of the inexpressible is silence what both men teach? A response depends on what counts as teaching and as the expressible, so we need to interrogate what ethical teaching can be. Like Wittgenstein, Emerson does not make the ineffability of the ethical a final conclusion. His contempt implies only that if *this* ("official" sermons) is what we mean by teaching and by the ethical then, yes, "what is ethical cannot be taught." We will see Emerson's hymns to the inexpressible not as definitive but as if a rung on a ladder to be thrown away. In short, we should treat Emerson's regard for silence as we treat Wittgenstein's "ineffability thesis"—his claim that ethics can only be silently shown—not as a mystical fetish or as unconditional, but as contextually dependent.

Emerson swerves from resting in the inexpressible because his deeper aim is to revise what counts as teaching and as ethical. Teaching, for Emerson, will be the act of turning itself, turning familiar words against their received meanings (the troping that Richard Poirier has emphasized). He will, for example, deny "the name of duty to many offices that are called duties." Analogously, he will teach ethics by inverting its approved form—preaching as a "pledge" to promulgate "official goodness." Instead of this reified speech, impotent in the face of life's careening contradictions, he will preach "counteraction" ("the doctrine of hatred must be preached as the counteraction of the doctrine of love when that pules and whines")—to disrupt expectations and to state the inadmissible (*Essays* 262). These movements and counter-movements of language allow him to put contradictions to work rather than remaining trapped in them. No wonder Emerson said, "I always find that my views chill or shock people," as if the setting of words in motion generates an electrical charge, a "shock," whereas "a minister nowadays is plainest prose, the prose of prose" (*Selected* 590).

Emerson regards language as "vehicular and transitive, and is good as horses and ferries are, for conveyance," not for "homesteading" (*Essays* 463). This is his way of saying language is functional, contingent, not autonomous, and hence "unsettled." Meaning is not intrinsic and static, produced according to precise rules, but is inseparable from how we use words in particular circumstances. *Philosophical Investigations* concurs. Emerson stresses what he calls the "fugitive" quality of "words" to remind us that words live within contexts ("mood," for Emerson, functions as context) and are not to be reified into abstract Truths to worship. Their "fugitive" status underwrites an analogy he makes between language and nature: "This surface on which we stand is not fixed but sliding. These manifold tenacious qualities, this chemistry and vegetation, these metals and animals, which seem to stand there for their own sake, are means and methods only,—are words of God, and as fugitive as other words" (*Essays* 409–410). Even God's words are in motion: Emerson's language plays games rather than housing Truth. He tells us "nothing is secure but life, transition"—i.e. what is secure is precisely what liquidates security. Such riddles offer a mockery of reliable guidance and are within the logic of his more direct surrender of authority: he reminds us not to "value" what he does, for he does not "settle any thing as true or false." With this he leaves us to play the "game of circles" that is life—ceaseless rushing "on all sides outwards to new and larger circles" (408, 404).

Yet "Man is the dwarf of himself" (46) precisely because he balks at playing this game. Rather than embracing transition, he clings to bogus forms of settlement, be they pious sincerity, politeness, or other forms of "official goodness," all "conforming to usages that have become dead" (263). The result, for the conformist, is a loss of "force": one is busy maintaining a "dead church," contributing to a "dead Bible-society" and ends up sinking "under all these screens" of routine (263). In his reliance on dead usages, the blurry, hapless man of conformity mystifies language into a "homestead" to dwell in and loses his sense of immediacy, reveres not "realities and creators, but names and customs." "How easily we capitulate to badges and names, to large societies and dead institutions" (261–262). The conformist robs himself of his own life by in effect enchanting names with a power of their own, ignoring that "good and bad are but names very readily transferable to that or this" (262).

Because Emerson does not rest in a "position"—the very notion of position is as confining as preaching—he continues to flirt with the inexpressible, even though, as argued above, he fashions a way to teach ethics as "counter-diction," to borrow Cavell's term. In "Self-Reliance" Emerson tells us that "when you have life in yourself"—"when man lives with God"—the two conditions seem synonymous—"it is not by any known or accustomed way . . . you shall not hear any name;—the way, the thought, the good, shall be wholly strange and new. It shall exclude example and experience" (271). Here the limits of the expressible seem breached. Indeed, the paragraph that contains these sentences begins: "And now at last the highest truth on this subject remains unsaid; probably cannot be said; for all that we say is the far-off remembering of the intuition. That thought, by what I can now nearest approach to say, is this." In Emerson's Platonic logic here, the "highest" truth is unsayable and our human language at best approximates. It is an "approach"—a way—that expresses hazy remembrance of an inexpressible "intuition."

Prior to "Self-Reliance," Emerson had pursued this line of thought in 1838 journal musings over the inadequacies of language. If, as Wittgenstein remarks, "This thrust against the limits of language is *ethics*," here Emerson reaches these limits: "Speech is the sign of partiality, difference, ignorance, and the more perfect the understanding between men, the less need of words." In a world where "all things cohere & unite," humans are inveterate partialists—"he sides with the part against other parts; and fights for parts, fights for lies, & his whole mind becomes an *inflamed part*." This, Emerson calls "the tragedy of man." Though "within him is the Soul of the Whole," he has no access to it, or certainly not when he speaks or writes (*Selected* 644). "As we advance" out into nature we discover that whereas "you are one thing," nature "is *one thing and the other thing, in the same moment*" (*Essays* 581). Just as nature "runs out into the infinite," so human language, in mimetic response: "If we go to affirm anything we are checked in our speech by the need of recognizing all other things until speech presently becomes rambling, general, indefinite, & merely tautology." This unraveling of coherence can only be halted if "at last" speech becomes "Action such as Confucius describes the Speech of God" (*Selected* 644–645). The ethical is born in silent action that redeems man's fallen language. Salinger would concur. "Act for God," urges Zooey to Franny, to whom a measure of tranquility is restored when she hears in a dial tone a "primordial silence" (*Zooey* 198).

However, Emerson's portrayal of linguistic disintegration rescued by the wordless action of God is a fantasy to which he treats himself; in effect it functions as a disposable rung on a ladder. That is, Emerson pursues it to be purged of it, for when he later revisits these matters six years later there is little trace of the scenario. In "Nominalist and Realist" (1844) he gives up his postlapsarian scenario of man's tragic partiality and the failure of language to encompass nature's excess. Instead, he becomes practical and concentrates on how one can craft language that neither ignores nature's excess and flux (sermons) nor falls victim to it (man's tragic partiality), but is answerable to it. "Nominalist and Realist" concentrates on how to do justice in language to life's incalculability and excess. He invents for this volatility a tutelary deity that he dubs "old Two-Face": "All the universe over, there is but one thing, this old Two-Face." Even as he introduces this impish expression he mimes its slipperiness—calling it the "one thing." Blurring one and two is apt given that Emerson's "old Two-Face"—the world's irreducible doubleness—is the patron of hypocrisy and deception (as when we call someone two-faced), which manifests as the fact of moods and the impossibility of sincerity: "I am always insincere, as always knowing there are other moods" (*Essays* 587). "If we could have any security against moods!" The rest of the sentence is a string of appositives regarding "Two-Face"—"creator-creature, mind-matter, right-wrong, of which any proposition may be affirmed or denied" (585). Emerson then proceeds to do the opposite—affirm *and* deny: "Very fitly, therefore, I assert that every man is a partialist" and he fills this out, but his crisp assertion runs aground: "and now I add, that everyman is a universalist also" and makes a case for this claim. In another twist, he soon wonders: "Is it that every man believes every other to be an incurable partialist, and himself a universalist?" Free of fantasies of language growing incoherent in the face of nature's opulent flow, Emerson insists on making sentences miming that motion. Emerson's anti-conceptualism is, one might say, arrived at through linguistic virtuosity; an interesting paradox—as if artfulness in the medium of sentences could, by some trick, shed the strictures of the general and repeatable, just by the sheer music of one line flowing into the next.

To make language equal to nature's surging puts a writer under enormous pressure. Hence, the temptation to silence: "Good as is discourse, silence is better, and shames it" (408). Silence would reflect a "perfect understanding"—between reader and writer, speaker and hearer (408). Nietzsche tends to think that language's bias against complexity is incurable; "language, so it seems, was invented only for what is mediocre, common, communicable" (*Twilight*, "Raids" 26).

He describes the only adequate philosophy—his own of course—"as an attempt somehow to describe Heraclitean becoming and to abbreviate it in signs (so to speak, to *translate* and mummify it into a kind of illusory *being*") (*Late Notebooks* 26). Emerson is more sanguine about crafting language answerable to life's tumult, as we have seen in "Nominalist and Realist." There he writes: "No sentence will hold the whole truth, and the only way in which we can be just, is by giving ourselves the lie; Speech is better than silence; silence is better than speech;—All things are in contact; every atom has a sphere of repulsion;—Things are, and are not, at the same time;—and the like" (*Essays* 585). This accretive sentence, replacing periods with semicolons and dashes, seems to defy conclusion, a formal resistance that mirrors its refusal to resolve the opposites it poses. Its ending: "—and the like" is ungainly but stubborn testimony of the inextinguishable remainder—the "whole truth" that no sentence can hold but only approach, if we seek to be "just." Justice to language means making sentences move or spin with a self-reflexive torque. That is, only when we solicit the assaults of mood and flux that give the lie to any claims we might wish settled will our language approximate reality's fierce recalcitrance, the tense weave of contraries that defy the logical. Only by consulting context and our needs do we figure out when "Speech is better than silence; silence is better than speech."

Emerson's linguistic volatility underwrites his one loyalty: "I obey my whims," he tells us; "I simply experiment, an endless seeker, with no Past at my back" (412). In a canonical passage from "Self-Reliance," Emerson, having asserted his desire to write *"Whim"* on the "lintels of the doorpost," adds: "I hope it is somewhat better than whim at last, but we cannot spend the day in explanation. Expect me not to show cause why I seek or why I exclude company" (262). In short, self-reliance breeds the self-trust to embrace the recklessness of whim, and to enact whim is to enact indifference to deliberation and caution, including stopping to explain. Emersonian renunciation is synonymous not simply with an energy of insouciance but with the "wonder" making capacity for abandonment. No wonder Nietzsche extolled his predecessor's "cheerfulness" and borrowed his self-description as a "professor of the Joyous Science" (Kaufmann 10).

Emerson's esteem for the unharnessed energy of whim lets him grasp indifference as an aesthetic attribute. He remarks in an 1832 journal entry: "Shakespeare's creations indicate no sort of anxiety to be understood. There is the Cleopatra, an irregular, unfinished, glorious, sinful character, sink or swim—there she is—& not one in the thousand of his readers apprehends the noble dimensions of the heroine." Unconcerned to point a moral, to direct his audience to an elevated "noble" sense of his heroine, Shakespeare radiates self-trust: his great figures are "all done in sport with the free daring pencil of a Master of the World. He leaves his children with God" (*Selected* 192). Something of the Bard's confidence informs Emerson's own attempt to articulate thoughts about renouncing his ministry: "It is the best part of the man . . . that revolts most against his being the minister. His good revolts from official goodness" (187). Like an author's eagerness to advertise a character's nobility, "official goodness" embraces the formulaic, obeys expectations. Cultivating a healthy indifference that encourages the play of antithetical thinking, Emerson redefines "good" as the capacity to "leave" ("I have sometimes thought that to be a good minister it was necessary to leave the ministry") and this renunciation of the received becomes the means of creative turning—akin to Shakespeare's "free daring"—from "dead forms" of institutions (193).

Emerson's commitment to transition, whim, and self-trust intersects with Nietzsche's "revaluation of values." The latter makes ethics a key target for renovation, given that it is a source of psychic petrification, whose agent is the "ethical teacher": a pious fraud who, with his talk of reasons and purposes and commandments, enfeebles men, imposing a guilty conscience (*Gay* sec. 1). Nietzsche hopes to rebuild the psyche that he pulls from the wreckage—the Platonized, Christianized "last man" of late-nineteenth-century Europe, all too content to flourish as a mediocrity, at once anxious, passionless, and complacent, condemned to a condition he calls "nihilism." As always for Nietzsche, this revaluation is aimed at the future; then we will enjoy the "comedy of existence"—"this ultimate liberation and irresponsibility." For now, though, "we still live in the age of tragedy, in the age of moralities and religion," "teachers of pangs of conscience" (*Gay* sec. 1). Philosophy has also played its repressive melancholy part: the intellectualist assumptions of "Socratic culture" decree that the authority of logic and science are without limit; its watchwords are "knowledge is virtue" and "in order to be beautiful, everything must be intelligible."

This is from Nietzsche's first book, *The Birth of Tragedy* (sec. 12). In it he depicts a proud product of that culture, "theoretical man," as not daring "to entrust himself to the fearful, icy current of existence, but instead runs anxiously up and down the riverbank" (*Birth* sec.12, 18). Biased toward control and order, theoretical man is also impatient with surface, with appearance, which he regards as a mere veil over Truth, a veil that must be penetrated and discarded if the "thread of causality" is to be followed "into the deepest abysses of being" and Truth seized (sec. 15). Nietzsche mocks this distrust of appearance and craving for explanation as "sublime metaphysical madness" that "accompanies science." United in fear, theorists, theologians, and philosophers are busy making us forget that "fundamentally" life—which is "drive, instinct, stupidity, lack of reasons"—resists our domination (*Gay* sec. 1).

These inadmissible qualities stand in the shadows, silently mocking that "little changeling, the 'subject,'" stuffed with knowledge, intention, goals, consciousness (*Genealogy* 1:13). This "neutral, independent 'subject'" of responsibility and free will embodies "sublime self-deception" but "has perhaps been believed in hitherto more firmly than anything else on earth." He conceals his weakness by clothing himself in the "self-deception of impotence" (1:13). Hence the "changeling" appears to himself and others as virtuous—calm, quiet, and humble, his weakness seen as freedom. In fact, says Nietzsche, the free will and responsibility that this figure proudly upholds are precisely what open him to the burdens of guilt and bad conscience bequeathed us by the ascetic legacy of Christian morality. "Wherever responsibilities are sought, what tends to be doing the seeking is the instinct of *wanting to punish and rule*. . . . Human beings were thought to be 'free' so that they could be ruled, so that they could be punished—so that they could become *guilty*: consequently every action *had* to be thought of as willed, the origin of every action *had* to be thought to lie in consciousness" (*Twilight*, "Four" 7).

Nietzsche asks how to unburden the centered subject of his paralyzing heaviness, his "anxious stiffness," how to release the instinct of life, of intuition, that is lightness, fluency of motion, part of his "ideal of a spirit that plays naively, i.e. not deliberately but from overflowing abundance and power" (*Gay* sec. 107, 382). Embodying this "floating, dancing, mocking" exuberance is the thought of his master, the hermit Heraclitus: "his regal possession is his extraordinary power to think intuitively." Heraclitus grasped that life is not being but "becoming, passing away and change" such that "being is an empty fiction," akin to the "lie of thinghood, of substance, duration" (*Tragic Age* 52; *Twilight*, "Reason" 2). With Christianity, though, comes a renewed will to truth—"merely the desire for a world of the constant"—and the "innocence of becoming"—what he dubs irresponsibility in its "positive sense"—is "infected with 'punishment' and 'guilt.'" Happiness is now "guaranteed only by being; change and happiness exclude one another" (*Will to Power* sec. 585).

The phrase "innocence of becoming" occurs in a section of *Twilight of the Idols* that poses the question "What can be *our* doctrine alone?" In answer Nietzsche repeats, as an invocation, the word "Nobody." Refusing a name, the word functions as an anti-doctrine of anti-explanation: "that nobody *gives* human beings their qualities, neither God, nor society, nor their parents and ancestors, nor *they themselves* . . . that no way of being may be traced back to a *causa prima*," that "*Nobody* is responsible for being here in the first place, for being constituted in such and such a way" (*Twilight*, "Four" 8). Not human initiative and control but fatality rules: "the fatality of our essence cannot be separated from the fatality of all that was and will be. . . . One is necessary, one is a piece of destiny, one belongs to the whole, one *is* in the whole" (*Twilight*, "Four" 8). With this hymn to the anonymity of fate, Nietzsche mocks the very idea of explanation, the uncovering of causes and logically entailed consequences. He distills this renunciation of rational deliberation in his "formula" for greatness— "amor fati" (love one's fate): one wants nothing to be other than it is (*Ecce* 258).

The antithesis of loving one's fate is *ressentiment*, the brooding over *why* that turns one to the past and devours one's energy, turns all action into reaction, shrinks the self into self-loathing torpor: "someone must be to blame for it [your misery]: but you yourself are this someone" (*Genealogy* 3:15). The ascetic priests burden their parishoners with *ressentiment* by keeping them ignorant of the shaping fact of necessity in the form of natural facts—each of us is born with a physiological, psychological constitution and some "granite of spiritual *fatum*" (fate) that makes us the type of person we are or, as Nietzsche says, "the great stupidity we are" (*Beyond* sec. 231). When man recognizes that he is in some way "*unteachable* very deep down" he recognizes "nobody" is "responsible anymore." This is "*the great liberation*—in this way only, the *innocence* of becoming is restored."

Liberation and stupidity, freedom and fate: each emerging out of or through the other. "See how fate slides into freedom, and freedom into fate," writes another student of Heraclitus—Emerson. Aristotle accused Heraclitus "of the highest crime before the tribunal of reason: to have sinned against the law of contradiction." Emerson is another sinner, inspired by Heraclitus's emphasis on what Nietzsche calls the "strife of opposites": "everything that happens, happens in accordance with this strife" (*Tragic Age* 52, 54–55). Whereas "ordinary people fancy they see something rigid, complete and permanent," in fact the "world itself is a mixed drink which must constantly be stirred" (55). Entanglement, says Emerson, is so "intricate, overlapped, interweaved" that there is no possibility of isolating origin or endpoint (*Essays* 961). Given that "inosculation, and balance of parts" rules, any kind of atomized vision is fatally myopic, since it isolates what it observes. Partial seeing nonetheless comes easy to man. "Through words and concepts," writes Nietzsche, "we are still continuously misled into imagining things being simpler than they are, separate from one another" (*Human* 2:2:11). Only relational vision, however, grasps the simultaneity of flux and fixity; for instance, the "incessant movement" of which all things partake "could never become sensible to us but by contrast to some principle of fixture or stability in the soul" (Emerson, *Essays* 412). "If I have described life as a flux of moods, I must now add that there is that in us which changes not" (485). Nature's contraries are also human's nature. Although "no man can violate his nature. All the sallies of his will are rounded in by the laws of his being," those laws prove plastic. Rather than focused and steady, "my wilful actions and acquisitions are but roving; the idlest reverie, the faintest native emotion, command my curiosity and respect" (265, 269). So we are spectators of our own will, curious where next it will roam. To assume a sovereign unity of selfhood counts as another instance of our imagining things being simpler than they are.

Simplicity, though, has its place and power. The innocence of fatality, our quality of granite stupidity, our irresponsibility: when we are life-affirming we embody such characteristics. They restore the present to the present, allowing us to become creatures of the surface so esteemed both by Emerson and his beloved Greeks. In the words of the former, "the whole frame of things preaches indifferency. Do not craze yourself with thinking, but go about your business anywhere. Life is not intellectual or critical but sturdy" (*Essays* 478). Nietzsche, as we have seen, praised the Greeks for knowing "how to *live:* what is needed for that is to stop bravely at the surface, the fold, the skin" (*Gay*, "Preface" 4).

Inevitably, the skin is mutilated since we are animals bred to make promises; and promises require punishment to mark memory on the flesh. Such marking is repeated, if less painfully, whenever "one has stripped becoming of its innocence" and some alleged virtue—responsibility, for instance—"is traced back to will, to intentions, to acts" (*Twilight*, "Four" 7). This burrowing into the depths is the compulsion, born of fear, to explain and to impute meaning: "our drive to find causes: we want to have a *reason* for feeling we are in *such and such* a state. . . . It is never enough for us just to determine the mere fact *that* we find ourselves in such and such a state." The anxiety produced by the unfamiliar triggers the flight to explanation and any "explanation is better than none" to the frightened human (*Twilight*, "Four" 4–5). Hence explanation is confined to a pacifying function from the start; "the new, the unexperienced, the alien, is excluded as cause."

The defense against risk that motivates explanation "impoverishes" by encouraging us to turn ourselves "into a fortress," "cut off from the most beautiful fortuities of the soul! And indeed from all further instruction!" (*Gay* sec. 305). We seal ourselves off in the belief, for instance, that when we assign cause and effect we are proffering an explanation rather than constructing a "conventional fiction . . . for the purpose of designation and communication" (*Beyond* sec. 21). A "psychology of error" is installed in the realm of morality. The antidote is not to discover Truth but to accept that our self-preserving acts of artifice make error the condition of our existence. "It is *we* alone who have devised" law, freedom, motive, cause, purpose, number, for "we have arranged for ourselves a world in which we are able to live. . . . Without these articles of faith no one could endure living! But that does not prove them. Life is not an argument; the conditions of life might include error" (*Beyond* sec. 21; *Gay* sec. 121).

So Nietzsche grants the saving power of our projected arrangements, our conceptual grids, but at the same time insists on having us see them as man-made, necessary fictions that provide perspectives or maps as need and context demand. Such artifices serve as equipment for living. Concepts are not to be "idolized," as they are by philosophers who, in their terror of change and movement, seek to arrest becoming. Instead, concepts are tools to be used to impose meaning upon the innocent fatality of destiny (*Twilight*, "Reason" 1, 2). As part of their inheritance from Emerson—who wrote that "in all unbalanced minds, the classification is idolized, passes for the end"—William James and John Dewey issue the same warning about the misuse of concepts (*Essays* 277).

A prelapsarian fantasy of wholeness (endemic to German romanticism, we will see, and to which the young Nietzsche was not immune) attaches to Nietzsche's belief that before man was enclosed in society, where his instincts atrophy and he is "reduced to thinking, inferring, reckoning," man "the human *animal*" lived upon the surface of the present moment, innocent of identifiable cause, origin, explanation, responsibility, and meaning. His existence on earth contained no goal; "'why man at all'?—was a question without an answer" (*Genealogy* 2:16, 3:28). We learn in *On The Genealogy of Morals*, however, that man "suffered from the problem of his meaning" (3:28). It was not the suffering itself but its meaninglessness that was intolerable, for man "*needs a goal*" (3:1). For lack of anything better, he adopted the ascetic ideal: it told him that man is fallen, guilty, lost in the unredeemable misery of life, but that if he has faith, redemption will be his in the kingdom of heaven. The ascetic ideal did not end suffering, but at last

made it understandable by placing it "under the perspective of guilt."
Man was saved; he "now possessed a meaning," even if it was imbued
with poisonous hatred of the human, of the body, the senses, happiness, beauty, the animal. The balm of meaning is the consolation of
religion, and to spurn it is to face the unbearable. So we cling to it, for
"man would rather will *nothingness* than *not* will" (3:28). With this
the *Genealogy* concludes.

Is Nietzsche's final image here a salute to man's stubborn existential courage and recovery of a life-affirmative stance? Arthur Danto,
for one, says no, finding a hint of *ressentiment* in man's refusal not to
will meaning. "Meaning is demeaning," a "dubious gift," Danto says
of this passage ("Some" 46). (We have heard Ad Reinhardt make the
same remark apropos of painting). He concurs with what Nietzsche
says elsewhere: one's strength of will can be measured by the "extent
one can do without meaning in things, to what extent one can endure
to live in a meaningless world" (*Will* sec. 585A). Indifference to meaning often draws Nietzsche: recall his envy, in "The Use and Abuse of
History," of the cattle calmly grazing. This "is a hard sight for man to
see" for he is without their happiness in the pure present. His memory obstructs the precious faculty of forgetting. To watch "blissfully
blind" animals or young children at play is to see a "lost paradise"
(*Untimely* 60–61).

Inspired by Spinoza, for whom the world "had returned to that state
of innocence in which it had lain before the invention of the bad conscience" (*Genealogy* 2:15), Nietzsche sought to reveal what Socrates,
Descartes, and Kant had ignored in their preoccupation with the primacy of the cognitive and of the thing in itself: that man had never
lost that paradise. It exists at hand, simply as the capacity to live fully
absorbed in the present, in the everyday. Here Nietzsche escapes the
regressive tug of the romantic project to recover innocence. Recall his
proto-Wittgensteinian remark: "This is the true sign of the philosophic drive: the astonishment about that which lies before the eyes of
everyone." What invariably obstructs this drive, as we have seen, is rationalism's urge to look past the field of the present. And Christianity,

with its anxious eye on the next world, is disinclined to linger on the surface of today.

To live in the present is to live without why amid the "astonishment" of the ordinary. This is where we can locate Wittgenstein's own late depiction of certainty. However, his sense of the "primitive" quality of certainty is unattached to any *Weltanschauung*, any residues of romantic yearning for wholeness found in Nietzsche and Emerson. It results instead from an analysis of language's relation to behavior. Wittgenstein sums up that relation in a line from Goethe's *Faust* (one Emerson and Nietzsche would both find congenial): "Language—I want to say—is a refinement. 'In the beginning was the deed'" (*Culture* 31). For instance, Wittgenstein describes one's empathic response to seeing other people in pain—the impulse "to tend, to treat the part that hurts"—as a "primitive reaction"—behavior that is *"pre-linguistic"* and instinctive; and our language is "auxiliary to" and further extends this primitive behavior. "(For our *language-game* is behaviour.) (Instinct)" (*Zettel* sec. 540, 541, 545).

Our daily lives are embedded in a matrix of "some things [that] stand unshakeably fast," sustained "by what lies around it" and sufficient without gathering evidence, attaining knowledge, giving grounds, (sometimes) without the need of language (*On Certainty* sec. 144). This *"comfortable* certainty" about everyday beliefs and practices would likely arouse the suspicions of philosophers and educators who are busily searching for essences, inflicting their anxious intellectualism upon students (sec. 357). Skeptical educators, notes Nietzsche, have failed to teach "learning to *see*—to accustom the eye to composure, to patience, to letting things come to it; to put off judgment, to learn to walk around all sides of the individual case and comprehend it from all sides." What this patience requires is relaxation of vigilance—"*not* to react to a stimulus right away." This asks for the willpower "precisely *not* to 'will.'" Nietzsche calls this "the *first* preliminary schooling in spirituality" (*Twilight*, "What the Germans Are Missing" 6). The passage anticipates what Heidegger will come to call *Gelassenheit*—"the will-not-to-will."

Nietzsche's emphasis on "learning to *see*" looks forward and back—Wittgenstein would take it up (he owned a copy of *Twilight of Idols*) and Goethe stands behind both. Nietzsche, expert in the science of philology, along with the engineer Wittgenstein, revered Goethe, as did Emerson, that keen student of natural science. Following Goethe's lead, they integrate the aesthetic and the cognitive to produce an enlargement of vision free from the standard erected by Cartesianism's "subliming" of logic and truth into "something pure and clear-cut" (*Investigations* sec. 94, 105). Goethe construed scientific description of nature as founded on human perception at once disciplined and intuitive, not based on experimental observation in the service of extracting general explanatory laws. Learning and seeing both require unlearning utilitarian habits so as to "respect the mystery" of nature.

Wittgenstein asks us to consider, for instance, the concept of "seeing." Seeing "makes a tangled impression. Well, it is tangled." Looking at a landscape, "I see all sorts of distinct and indistinct movement"; and "this is just what is called description of what is seen. There is not *one genuine* proper case of such description" (*Investigations* p. 200). Analogously, in considering how one judges the "genuineness" of a facial expression we may appeal to "evidence" but "'evidence' here includes 'imponderable' evidence . . . subtleties of glance, of gesture, of tone." Although I may be able to distinguish a genuine loving gaze from a false one, "I may be quite incapable of describing the difference" (228). Accepting this "imponderable" is something a philosopher should try to be relaxed about despite the inevitable anxiety of "wanting to make fine distinctions" and identify "*one genuine* proper case." We should try to see this anxiety as a pseudo-problem created by having introjected the foundational Platonic and Cartesian assumption that to define means to offer an essence. This is a "*picture* [that] held us captive" (sec. 115). By relieving us of what he called "philosophic cramps," Wittgenstein seeks a change less in cognition than in living.

The "schooling in spirituality" (recalling Nietzsche's phrase) that redefines will as the power precisely *not* to will culminates in a near mystical reverence, on the part of Emerson and Wittgenstein, for silently observing the ordinary. "All I know is reception," writes Emerson. "I am and I have but I do not get"; he counts as an "apostasy" "that hankering after an overt or practical effect" (*Essays* 491). Because explanation creates the habit of looking past and through in search of causes underneath, Wittgenstein says: "How hard I find it to see

what is right in front of my eyes!" (*Culture* 39). Emerson detects the
same problem via a different emphasis: we habitually forego living in
the present; we are "ashamed before the blade of grass or the blowing
rose" (*Essays* 270). Emerson finds the poised rose an inspiring contrast
to the "timid and apologetic" American unable to "live in the present"
(270). Wittgenstein in effect borrows Emerson's fretful folk and turns
them into "tourists": he compares "people who are constantly asking
'why'" to "tourists who stand in front of a building reading Baedeker
and are so busy reading the history of its construction, etc. that they
are prevented from *seeing* the building" (*Culture* 40). Luckily, he was
spared the smart phone and the mania of "selfies."

"Man does not live in the present" but instead "postpones or remembers," says Emerson, and "he cannot be happy and strong until he
too lives with nature in the present, above time" (*Essays* 270). To live
above time is to inhabit a perpetual present. The roses under Emerson's
window "make no reference to former roses or to better ones; they are
for what they are; they exist with God today. There is no time to them.
There is simply the rose; it is perfect in every moment of its existence. . . .
Its nature is satisfied, and it satisfies nature, in all moments alike" (270).
Such transparency is at one with "the most liberating thought imaginable, that life is without meaning" (Danto, "Some" 46).

Emerson and Wittgenstein are two readers of Angelus Silesius, a group
that also includes Hegel and Heidegger. The first philosopher to read
the mystic was Leibniz, who coined in 1671 the phrase "the principle
of reason" as the "noblest principle"—nothing is without a reason,
which is tantamount to saying nothing is without a why—which might
be construed as a rebuttal of Angelus Silesius (Heidegger, *Principle* 35).
Heidegger takes this up in *The Principle of Reason* (lectures delivered
in 1956) and devotes a number of pages to Angelus Silesius and Goethe
who together, Heidegger shows, offer hints to encourage an alternative understanding—"unsaid" but latent—of the Principle of Reason.
This alternative yields a "reflective" rather than "calculative" mode
of thinking and being. The rose couplet—"the rose is without why;
it blooms because it blooms. It pays no attention to itself, asks not

whether it is seen"—marks the difference, says Heidegger, between the way the rose and humans "are what they are." The difference resides in the fact that humans are busy attending to the world and themselves while the rose's blooming is a pure blossoming. This obvious distinction fades in Heidegger's summing up which emphasizes the "unsaid": "what is unsaid in the fragment [i.e. the couplet]—and everything depends on this . . . says that humans . . . first truly are when in their own way they are like the rose—without why" (38).

Heidegger will stress the precarious status of the "unsaid" in the postwar atomic age, where the Principle of Reason is sovereign and man is regarded as an exclusively rational animal in pursuit of technological perfection. The rule of science makes "standing in front of a tree in bloom" a near impossible experience: "Physics, physiology and psychology display the panoply of their documents and proofs, to explain to us that what we see and accept is properly not a tree but in reality a void, thinly sprinkled with electric charges." As scientific explanation is busy recording the "brain currents, what becomes of the tree in bloom?" To admit we are standing face to face with a blooming tree can only seem "naïve, because pre-scientific" (*What* 42–43).

The anxiety about seeming naïve lingers. More than half a century later many disenchanted postmodernists, schooled by theory masters of suspicion, refuse to be taken in by appearances, wary of perspectives that insist on the bare phenomenal facts. To demystify what appears immediate is the postmodern reflex—and straitjacket. Wittgenstein implicitly exposes the blind spot of this programmatic suspicion of presence by showing that the unmediated is not sought by those nostalgic for presence. It is not sought (or rejected) at all, but rather is the groundless ground of the everyday. Remarks Wittgenstein: "I really want to say that a language-game is only possible if one trusts something" and "My *life* consists in being content to accept many things." Questions and doubts "depend on the fact that some propositions are exempt from doubt" (*On Certainty* sec. 509, sec. 344, sec. 341). Exempt too from foundations, transcendent or logical, for the language-game is "not reasonable (or unreasonable). It is there—like our life" (sec. 559). Merleau-Ponty, analogously, speaks of "faith" in "this unjustifiable certitude" (a "naïve certitude") of a "sensible world common to us that is the seat of truth within us" (*Visible* 3, 11, 13).

All this matter-of-fact acceptance of the groundless, of everyday behavior as comprising pre-reflective, unproblematic certainty, courts charges of flirting with primordialism or worse, especially when invoked in proximity to Heidegger celebrating trees. His rhetoric of "Grund" (ground/reason) when he links it to "Heimat" (homeland) was and is rife with poisonous political implications. But bracketing Heidegger, here is an example of what incites postmodern suspicion: Friedrich Schiller's canonical statement of 1795 about sentimental poetry as yearning for lost unity. Schiller projects a re-enchantment of the world, a vision that a century later Max Weber will renew as the unsaid redemptive obverse of his disenchantment thesis. We moderns, to summarize Schiller, are attached to mossy stones, birds, flowers, running brooks because they embody an *idea* of inner harmony, unity, and self-sufficiency, "their existence in accordance with their own immutable laws." Schiller would allegorize Emerson's esteem for the roses' transparency—"they are for what they are"—as expressing an idea of harmonious self-identity that we envy and seek as an antidote to our fragmented modernist self-consciousness. Says Schiller: "They *are* what we *were*; they are what we *ought to become* once more. We were nature just as they, and our culture, by means of reason and freedom, should lead us back to nature. They are therefore at the same time a representation of our lost childhood." This yearning is "identical" with our love of the Greeks ("On Naïve and Sentimental Poetry").

Wittgenstein's trust in groundless certainty is immune to Schiller's nostalgic project. Emerson, part of the romantic movement, is within Schiller's ambit, but ultimately the author of "Circles" is not looking backward but emphatically attuned to the present tense. And he is not allegorizing. His roses "make no reference to former roses." The young Nietzsche, as suggested earlier, fell under the German romantic spell but eventually emerged from it. As he wrote in a late notebook entry: "German philosophy as a whole—Leibniz, Kant, Hegel, Schopenhauer, to name the greatest—is the most fundamental form of *romanticism* and homesickness there has ever been: the longing for the best that ever existed. One is no longer at home anywhere; at last one longs back for that place in which alone one can be at home: the *Greek* world! But it is precisely in that direction that all bridges are broken—except the rainbow-bridges of concepts!" (*Will to Power* sec. 420).

Nietzsche (and Wittgenstein) will make a virtue of the fact that "one is no longer at home anywhere," whereas Schiller yearns for the Greek world and Heidegger envisions a future found on Graeco-Germanic autochthony (Bambach 218–219). His enthusiasm is tempered, postwar, by his fondness for *Gelassenheit*—detachment—he found in Buddhism and Eckhart. In *The Gay Science* Nietzsche turns upside down the national legacy of homesickness: "we who are homeless" "in a distinctive and honorable sense" comprise the best audience for "gay science" (sec. 377). To be honorably homeless is to be "unfavorably disposed toward all ideals that might make one feel at home in this fragile, broken time of transition"—humanist ideals of liberal democracy, progress, and equal rights. On the other hand, the homeless are equally suspicious of German nationalism with its racial hatred and triumphalism. "We who are homeless are too diverse and racially mixed in our descent" to fit in to the homeland, and so adopt a cosmopolitan spirit found in *"good Europeans"* (sec. 377).

Gay science teaches not only cosmopolitan "untimeliness" in the face of bellicose nationalism but also distrust of the "will to truth," with its impatient "wish to see everything naked . . . to understand and 'know' everything" (*Gay*, "Preface" 4). In other words, gay science seeks to retire the appearance-versus-reality dualism that grounds "this will to truth." Nietzsche seeks truth's integration, what he calls "incorporation": "to what extent can truth stand to be incorporated? That is the question, that is the experiment." When truth is incorporated rather than simply regarded as a product of reason, it shapes one's acts, is lived on one's body, for "the strength of knowledge lies not in its degree of truth, but in its age, its embeddedness, its character as a condition of life" (*Gay* sec. 110). Flattered by the illusion of the sovereignty of Reason, however, we are distracted from "the task of assimilating knowledge and making it instinctive." The task "is still quite new" but crucial to undertake, says Nietzsche, if we are to reverse the "ridiculous overestimation of consciousness" (*Gay* sec. 11).

The naturalist emphasis on the priority of life and instinct is the background upon which Nietzsche describes how one escapes the ascetic ideal's compulsion for meaning and responsibility, which seals man in the deluded assumption that he is helmsman of his craft, the masterful self. This assumption suffers a severe shock in Nietzsche's description of "how one becomes what one is," the subtitle of his autobiography, *Ecce Homo*. He describes his own self-becoming as inextricable from recognizing the "fatality" of his "essence" that "cannot be separated from all that was and will be" (*Twilight*, "Four" 8). What Nietzsche calls "fatality" Emerson calls "temperament": it "shuts us in a prison of glass which we cannot see"; it is "the iron wire on which the beads are strung" (*Essays* 474). We discover our temperament by relaxing the will to know it and letting instinct and feeling guide us.

To relax control requires forgetting; only then do we dare live un-historically, opening ourselves to the present and taking pleasure in surface and in positive irresponsibility. Indeed, this is "how Wisdom wants *us*": "unconcerned, mocking, violent" (*Genealogy* 3:1). These qualities recall those implied in "the healthy attitude of human na-ture" as Emerson describes it in "Self-Reliance," "the nonchalance of boys sure of a dinner, and would disdain as much as a lord to do or say aught to conciliate one. . . . A boy is in the parlour what the pit is in the playhouse; independent, irresponsible . . . he cumbers himself never about consequences." In sum, he possesses an "unaffected, unbiased, unbribable, unaffrighted innocence" (*Essays* 261).

Such brusque casualness drinks from "that source, at once the es-sence of genius, of virtue, and of life, which we call Spontaneity or Instinct. We denote this primary wisdom as Intuition, whilst all later teachings are tuitions. In that deep force, the last fact behind which analysis cannot go, all things find their common origin" (269). As the "fountain of action and of thought," Intuition is also a foe of explana-tion, whose thrusting momentum crashes against its boundary. In ab-sorbing the blows of analysis, Intuition mixes elements of receptivity and passivity, what in "Fate" Emerson calls "impressionability." We are "receivers" of Intuition's "activity. When we discern justice, when we discern truth, we do nothing of ourselves, but allow a passage to its beams. If we ask whence this comes, if we seek to pry into the soul that causes, all philosophy is at fault. Its presence or absence is all we can affirm" (269). Philosophy is "at fault" because in the seeking of causes it takes refuge from life—from change, from impulse (the "involuntary"), from the senses and the body—in fixed concepts, with their illusory discreteness.

Why do we need why? In "Experience" Emerson interrogates our craving for explanation, our need, and philosophy's, "to pry into the soul that causes." His interrogation proceeds immanently, by first submitting to that craving. After declaring that for all his stress on "life as a flux of moods," there is also "that in us which changes not," Emerson seeks to put a name to this unchanging cause, this "that." "Fortune, Minerva, Muse, Holy Ghost—these are quaint names, too narrow to cover this unbounded substance." He then surveys the names offered up by pre-Socratics and later figures to define this "ineffable cause"— (including water, air, fire) and Jesus (love) and Mencius ("vast-flowing vigor") (485). Emerson notes that "the ancients," struck by life's incalculability, "exalted Chance into a divinity, but that is to stay too long at the spark." The implied lesson applies to all the philosophical one-word answers: in seeking causal explanation, one should avoid inflating into a god (or a stable ideal) what is only a "spark." Better the "baffled intellect . . . kneel before this cause, which refuses to be named." Emerson notes that Mencius called his own answer—"vast-flowing vigor"—"difficult" to explain. For Emerson this is precisely its virtue. "We give to this generalization the name of 'Being,' and thereby confess that we have arrived as far as we can go. Suffice it for the joy of the universe, that we have not arrived at a wall, but at interminable oceans" (486). Emerson is pleased with the vagueness because Being is less a name than a "hint of this vast-flowing vigor" that is not arrested in an originating essence (does not arrive at a wall) but flows, swallowed into vast oceans. He has intuited the radical vagueness of the *Tao*. In a later essay, Emerson strips Being of its substantive status and substitutes "To Be," an infinitive suggesting process without end.

In staging the defeat of a quest to find a defining name of our essence, our "First Cause," Emerson anticipates the logic of Nietzsche's and Wittgenstein's emphatic immanence. Nietzsche insists that "there is nothing outside the whole" of life and therefore nothing can judge or compare or measure the whole. Rather than comprehending life, we live within it. For Emerson, too, "The miracle of life . . . will not be expounded, but will remain a miracle. . . . Life has no memory. . . . So is it with us . . . because immersed in forms and effects all seeming to be of equal yet hostile value" (*Essays* 484). To grasp the priority of the whole—of life as a primordial given—is to grasp that there is no space apart from which one might launch a critique of life. Theoretical detachment is not an option; "you are embarked," wrote Pascal, expressing the fact of man's existential immersion. In *The Gay Science* Nietzsche commends Pascal's recognition that "we are already always embarked"—"we have forsaken the land and gone to sea!" (sec. 124; Blumenberg, *Shipwreck* 19). Any critique we make will be immanent—from inside. One consequence is that all our judging and comparing of the whole, all our "value judgments about life, for or against, can in the final analysis never be true; they have value only as symptoms" (*Twilight*, "Problem of Socrates" 2).

Because we are already embarked, we have no means of comprehending life and gaining mastery, that is, coordinating intention and execution: "We design and execute many things, and somewhat comes of it all, but an unlooked for result. . . . It turns out somewhat new, and very unlike what he promised himself." Hence "the individual is always mistaken" (484). This conclusion, which Emerson repeats twice in two lines, is a universal law, what Nietzsche calls life's condition of error, a necessity: to *not* be mistaken and instead to comprehend the whole of life, to master experience, would be to remove oneself from living it. Analogously, Nietzsche insists that even the fiercest immoralist remains a moralist. In *Daybreak*, he declares that what he is writing "does in fact exhibit a contradiction and is not afraid of it: in this book faith in morality is withdrawn—but why? *Out of morality!* . . . there is no doubt that a 'thou shalt' still speaks to us too, that we too still obey a stern law set over us . . . we too are still *men of conscience:* namely, in that we do not want to return to that which we consider outlived and decayed, to anything 'unworthy of belief,' be it called God, virtue, truth, justice, charity" ("Preface" 4).

In transvaluing "conscience" in this last sentence as indifference to the past, Nietzsche casually demolishes the pillars of moral life, virtue and truth among them. Casualness is also in Emerson's rhetorical arsenal; he notes the uneasy proximity of the casual and casualty: "We thrive by casualties. Our chief experiences have been casual," which is to say ungraspable ("all our blows glance") (*Essays* 483, 473). This "evanescence and lubricity of all objects"—"when we clutch hardest" they only "slip through our fingers"— Emerson punningly dubs "the most unhandsome part of our condition." He makes this linguistic and thematic slipperiness aurally present in "lubricity," the keynote of "Experience," his most audacious essay.

"Men have talked about the world without paying attention to the world or to their own minds, as if they were asleep or absent-minded" (qtd. Davenport 7 *Greeks* 158). This fragment of Heraclitus Emerson brings to life in the opening pages of "Experience." At its start he forces us to awareness of our immanence within the whole of life by magnifying it, depicting man living a waking nightmare of passivity, helpless as "all things swim and glitter" (471). "Sleep lingers all our lifetime about our eyes" (471). The name he gives this "lethargy now at noonday," this ceaseless sleepwalking, is: experience. Equally estranging of expectations is what issues from this vertiginous redefinition: "the results of life are uncalculated and uncalculable. The years teach much which the days never know." Starting with the title, stripped of any anchoring preposition or pronoun—neither "Of Experience"— Montaigne—or "My Experience"— "Experience" mocks our capacity to know experience: "If any of us knew what we were doing, or where we are going, then when we think we best know!" (471). This sentence's impregnable concision induces in the reader the flailing that is its subject. "We do not know today whether we are busy or idle," so involved are we in what absorbs us (471). Today is where we live and is all we know, which is to know very little. Make the best of this: "Since our office is with moments, let us husband them." "To fill the hour, that is happiness. . . . Let us be poised, and wise, and on our own, today" (478–479).

Negotiating slippery surfaces, husbanding the moments, filling the hour, Emerson offers relief from our chronic obliviousness and begins to move toward resolving the philosophic urge to name/explain the "deepest cause." He does so by abiding with an immanent logic that finds irrelevant the whole project of nominating an essence. The fluid amorphousness of experience mocks such a metaphysical inquiry as beside the point. That fluidity also exposes the limits of language, its propensity to arrest what is in motion. In "Self-Reliance" Emerson turns against his titular phrase and calls it a "poor external way of speaking. Speak rather of that which relies because it works and is" (271). To speak of the "deepest cause" is also a "poor external way of speaking." His response to this classic metaphysical pursuit is as deflationary and matter-of-fact as Wittgenstein's indifference to justifying certainty against those convinced we have grounds other than in our way of acting. "Shall we describe this cause as that which works directly? The spirit is not helpless or needful of mediate organs. It has plentiful powers and direct effects. I am explained without explaining, I am felt without acting, and where I am not. Therefore all just persons are satisfied with their own praise. They refuse to explain themselves, and are content that new actions should do them that office. They believe that we communicate without speech, and above speech" (486).

Here Emerson explodes all talk of a "deeper" or "First Cause" as a thing in itself. All we know of "cause" is its manifestations in "that which works directly." The spirit's power is not to be reified and isolated, as is language's tendency, but is actually inseparable from its enactments and embodiments *in* life, in "new actions" that "refuse to explain themselves." With discursive explanation rendered irrelevant by "plentiful powers and direct effects," Emerson stops at the surface, keeping it clean of impediments derived from guilt or vanity, leaving no "crevice for a repentance or an approval" (478). In Wittgenstein's parlance, Emerson inhabits the domain of "showing."

As part of what "works and is," we move within the flow as we gradually acquire the modes of engagement (habits and routines) that minimize conscious intellectual control and enable our easy skating. Fluency occurs in the "tacit dimension" where "unbridled lucidity can destroy our understanding of complex matters," as Michael Polanyi observes (*Tacit* 18). In short, the ordinary "just shows up for us as what it is," Noë remarks of the "familiar world" (121). Emerson, employing tautology to make the point, notes that "direct effects" "work directly"—"I am explained without explaining." This world, where "new actions" are all the explanation one gets or requires, "baffles" "intellect" for it renders superfluous a search for essential causes and leaves "the noblest theory of life" "powerless and melancholy" (*Essays* 478).

Such noble theories help inspire essays such as "Experience" but in that same essay its author ambushes theory: "The intellectual tasting of life will not supersede muscular activity. If a man should consider the nicety of the passage of a piece of bread down his throat, he would starve" (478). Emerson turns once again against his own intellectual discourse, mocking his work as full of "fineries or pedantries": "What help from thought? Life is not dialectics. . . . Life is not intellectual or critical, but sturdy" (478). Nietzsche makes explicit what is implicit in Emerson and in late Wittgenstein: "We simply have no organ for *knowing*, for 'truth'" and consciousness is "basically superfluous." It is born of the pressure of the need to communicate, a necessity for a vulnerable species that must preserve and protect itself. If one were solitary and absorbed wholly in the business of living, one would have no need for consciousness: "We could think, feel, will, remember, and also 'act.' . . . All of life would be possible without, as it were, seeing itself in the mirror" (*Gay* sec. 354).

Gliding, clutching, slipping; by these mindless motions we arrange ourselves in a freedom of air. Contrary to a shared reputation as exponents of radical individualism, both Nietzsche and Emerson dismantle the self-determining subject, the former regarding it as an "ultimately Christian compensatory fantasy," in the words of Robert Pippin (73). Nietzsche dismisses motives, goals, and intentions, these venerable elements of free agency. Emerson does no less. In "Spiritual Laws" Emerson remarks the lightness of great men, their "self-annihilation," and ascribes the "extraordinary success" of a Caesar, a Napoleon not to their imperial will but to their serving as "an unobstructed channel; and the wonders of which they were the visible conductors seemed to the eye their deed. Did the wires generate the galvanism? It is even true that there was less in them on which they could reflect, than in another; as the virtue of a pipe is to be smooth and hollow" (*Essays* 306–307). Just as counter-intuitive is his depiction of the "great man" as the "impressionable man," possessed of the delicacy and susceptibility of a woman. "Women, as most susceptible, are the best index of the coming hour." Like them, the "great man" "feels the infinitesimal attractions . . . he yields to a current so feeble as can be felt only by a needle delicately poised" (965).

Such androgyny and lability are receptive to a world where "all that we reckoned settled shakes and rattles" and "every ultimate fact [is] . . . only the first of a new series," where "there is no outside, no inclosing wall, no circumference to us," and the "pulses" of the heart "tend outward with a vast force" (408, 404–405). In response to the fact that "life is a series of surprises, and would not be worth taking or keeping, if it were not," spontaneity, whim, and intuition flower (483). "Beyond the energy of his possessed and conscious intellect, he is capable of a new energy . . . by abandonment to the nature of things" (459). To our "involuntary perceptions a perfect faith is due" (269). Emerson is alert to the faint irony in this directive (enthroning the involuntary instills it with regularity); analogously Nietzsche urges not becoming "stuck"—to people, fatherland, pity, science, or "to one's own detachment" and "to our own virtues." In short, don't get stuck on not being stuck (*Beyond* sec. 41).

The universe glimpsed above—the incessant outward pulsations of nature and bodies—testifies to what Emerson calls the "preponderance of nature over will in all practical life." This leads him to say not only that "there is less intention in history than we ascribe to it" but also that "life might be much easier and simpler than we make it; that the world might be a happier place than it is; that there is no need of struggles, convulsions, despairs, of the wringing of the hand and the gnashing of the teeth; that we miscreate our own evils" (306–307). The blitheness of Emerson's vision in "Spiritual Laws" regarding the "optimism of nature" that man "interferes with," oblivious that "laws . . . execute themselves," is attuned to the liberating sense of anonymous "fatality" Nietzsche will come to celebrate. This is a remarkable rehearsal of Nietzschean innocence and lightnesss, and as well a summary in miniature of why *On the Genealogy of Morals* would be irrelevant or barely comprehensible to Emerson. For Emerson's very blitheness immunizes him from any interest in pursuing what initiated the *Genealogy*— "the origin of good and evil." Whereas this "problem of the origin," Nietzsche tells us in the preface, preoccupied him from the age of thirteen and ordained that he would come to burrow into its depths ("Preface" 3). Inevitably, such a topic, since it requires turning back to grope among the dry bones of the past, partakes of the *ressentiment* it seeks to diagnose. In contrast, Emerson bestows upon himself the title "a professor of the Joyous Science" (in an 1841 journal passage) precisely because he will not search out origins. He dismisses "Ah ye old ghosts. Ye builders of dungeons in the air!" (qtd. Kaufmann 8). This passage, with its wariness of being trapped in "dungeons" and "ghosts" of the past, helps make sense of Nietzsche's 1884 comment that if only Emerson, with his "great and glorious nature . . . might have gone through some *strict* discipline, a really *scientific education"* (7). The American's blithe dismissal of depth, his indifference to engaging with origin, accounted for his profoundly superficial gayness but also, for the German, his limitation.

When Emerson does seek depth—in that most venerable wellspring, grief—it turns out to be shallow. Disintegrating our most cherished pieties, "Experience" goes "antagonizing on," rudeness being the very rhythm of free thought, how the "mind" conducts itself (483). Emerson opens up the topic of grief by wondering what happens when we encounter compelling moments of arrest, the "sharp peaks and edges of truth," those intimations of epiphanic revelation that we expect will act as precious hooks to grasp as we negotiate "the most slippery sliding surfaces." These sharp edges seem so pregnant with meaning, with lessons, that they refuse to let us forget ourselves. Among these hooks, grief is widely regarded one of the sharpest peaks of truth. In "Experience," though, Emerson dismisses it: "The only thing grief has taught me, is to know how shallow it is. That, like all the rest, plays about the surface, and never introduces me into the reality, for contact with which, we would even pay the costly price of sons and lovers" (472–473). He knew the price, having suffered the loss of his young son. This is early in the essay when Emerson has yet fully to accept that slippery surface *is* reality; he still has metaphysical yearning for access to a deeper, firmer stratum, where he can take hold of meaning. "I grieve that grief can teach me nothing, nor carry me one step into real nature." He had expected that it would teach him, had assumed the experience of grief to be a repository of bitter wisdom. But all it does is "play about the surface." In *On Certainty*, Wittgenstein asks, "But how does experience *teach* us, then? *We* may derive it from experience, but experience does not direct us to derive anything from experience" (sec. 130). Emerson concurs. The experience of grief itself does not offer up any wisdom; we extract it and understand it through "these colored and distorting lenses which we are" (*Essays* 487).

■

"Experience" commences with "ourselves" newly awake, asking a question: "Where do we find ourselves? In a series of which we do not know the extremes, and believe it has none. We wake and find

ourselves on a stair," with stairs "above and below us" (471). Evidently
Nietzsche was so compelled by this opening that he recast it to begin
his preface to *On the Genealogy of Morals.* "We are unknown to ourselves, we men of knowledge—and with good reason. We have never sought ourselves—how could it happen that we should ever *find*
ourselves?" Cavell calls this last question "Nietzsche's answer to the
question that opens 'Experience'—'Where do we find ourselves?' How
could this circuit be proved, that Nietzsche had Emerson in mind?
It could at least be thought through—given a sense of the intimacy
of Nietzsche's reaction to, or transcription of, passages of Emerson's
prose early and late in life" (*This New* 25). The preface continues:

> Whatever else there is in life, so-called "experiences"—which of us
> has sufficient earnestness for them? Or sufficient time? Present ex-
> perience has, I am afraid, always found us "absent-minded": we can-
> not give our hearts to it—not even our ears! Rather, as one divinely
> preoccupied and immersed in himself into whose ear the bell has
> just boomed . . . the twelve beats at noon suddenly starts up and asks
> himself: "what really was that which just struck?" so we sometimes
> rub our ears *afterward* and ask, utterly surprised and disconcerted,
> "what really was that which we have just experienced?" and more-
> over: "who *are* we really." . . . So we are necessarily strangers to
> ourselves, we do not comprehend ourselves; we *have* to misunder-
> stand ourselves . . . we are not "men of knowledge" with respect to
> ourselves. (*Genealogy,* "Preface" 1)

If, for Emerson, "the individual is always mistaken," Nietzsche
insists we *must* mistake ourselves. For both, the booming bell of
noon—when daily life maximally bustles—finds them not on the beat,
not with it, but lethargic. Each mocks our proud identity as "men of
knowledge" and the correlative belief that, in Emerson's words, we
live "in the kingdom of known cause and effect" presided over by "perfect calculation" and confident that "manly resolution and adherence
to the multiplication-table through all weathers will insure success"
(*Essays* 483). Why not be confident given that "in the street and in the
newspapers life appears so plain a business." We reside in this comfort-
ably upholstered kingdom of smug certitude, which is, says Nietzsche,
one reason why we are unknown to ourselves: we are too busy piling

up "*our* treasure"—"bringing something home," we busy bees and "honey gatherers" (*Genealogy,* "Preface" 1). Our bustle encourages our self-ignorance. How, though, are we "*necessarily* strangers to ourselves"? How to find a way out of this problem? *Is* it a problem?

That questions dangle may be Nietzsche's intention. In *Ecce Homo* he boasts that each of the openings to the three essays that comprise *Genealogy of Morals* is intended to mislead, to keep one in suspense. It is tempting to apply his warning to the opening of his preface to the *Genealogy* quoted above because the emphasis on being unknown to ourselves and the hollowness of our pretensions to be "men of knowledge" seem to promise that what follows will bestow upon us the wisdom we lack. They will acquaint us with ourselves. But, as section two of the preface announces and the *Genealogy* fulfills, the book concerns "the *origin* of our moral prejudices"—"the question of where our good and evil really *originated*" and "under what conditions did man devise these value judgments good and evil?" (*Genealogy,* "Preface" 2, 3). Of course in a general way the book provides us with self-knowledge: we discover the destructiveness of our moral ideals, grounded, as they are, in the Judeo-Christian tradition of asceticism and guilt that we have introjected as conscience.

Unexplained however in the *Genealogy* is the *necessity* of remaining a stranger to oneself. This seems a dilemma left in need of remedy. In *Ecce Homo* that question is resolved with compelling insouciance. As I noted at the opening of this book, Nietzsche describes his own self-formation as a triumph over self-knowledge. "'Willing' something, 'striving' for something, envisaging a 'purpose,' a 'wish'—I know none of this from experience" (255). What was troubling in the *Genealogy* turns out to be a condition of optimum possibility. We learn "the good reason" that "we have never sought ourselves": it nurtured in Nietzsche the capacity for a "*revaluation of all values*" to grow inside him: instinct and intuition thrived (254). He acknowledges that being a stranger to oneself saves one from the anxious certitude that keeps us on track, piling up riches. *Ecce Homo* portrays the effortless coming to being of the lightest, most "innocent" of selves, that is, one so free of *ressentiment* that the smooth sea of his future is a surface without a "ripple of desire" (255).

This self-portrait reveals the Nietzschean will to power as, to borrow Deleuze's words, *"essentially creative and giving:* it does not aspire, it does not seek, it does not desire, above all it does not desire power."* (And neither does the *Übermensch,* as Heidegger will argue below.) What the will to power wills "is a particular relation of forces, a particular quality of forces." "Only qualities are ever willed: the heavy, the light. What a will wants is always its own quality" (*Nietzsche* 84–85, 78). "Mainly, the question is how light or heavy we are," declares Nietzsche late in *The Gay Science.* Lightness, the quality of will of those who seek to glimpse "beyond" their time, emerges out of the sway of instinctive force against the drive for knowledge (*Gay* sec. 380). The achieved self is only an *effect* of the instinctual drive having been victorious. In this context Nietzsche can be seen as deflating the fervent proclamations of his own incomparable genius that dot *Ecce Homo.* As one commentator notes: "Nietzsche wrote such wise and clever books for the same reason the tomato plant grows tomatoes: *because it must,* because it could not have done otherwise" (Leiter 85). The plant metaphor is courtesy of Nietzsche: "Our ideas, our values, our yeas and nays, our ifs and buts grow out of us with the necessity with which a tree bears fruit" (*Genealogy,* "Preface" 2). He had earlier noted: "As he stands before the plants," so must the man of knowledge "stand before the actions of men and before his own" (*Human* vol 1: 2:107). One can admire their beauty and fullness but to praise them for it is absurd since they are natural facts. They could not be otherwise.

In Nietzsche's case his will of (or to) lightness renounces the vigilant drive that self-mastery requires and abandons as well the anchorage of a stable home. The rootedness of "Heimat" holds little appeal. The iron aloofness of Heraclitus is, as we have seen, his model. As a young man, Nietzsche saluted (and would later adopt) the ancient's "great pride": "His activities never directed him toward any 'public,' toward any applause from the masses. . . . To walk along a lonely street is part of the philosopher's nature." The "feeling of solitude" suffusing Heraclitus is part of his "regal self-esteem," his inhuman indifference to mankind, and can only be intuited "when we are freezing on wild, desolate mountains of our own" (*Tragic Age* 65–67).

Nietzsche's youthful fantasy of Heraclitus's "self-sufficiency . . . built of diamonds" includes the philosopher directing his gaze to eternity: a "lack of consideration for what is here and now lies at the very core of the great philosophical nature" (66). Gazing "beyond one's time" always attracted Nietzsche and his love of untimeliness (*Gay* sec. 380). So it is not surprising that, for all his esteem for the "astonishment" of the ordinary, he is less invested than Emerson and Wittgenstein in pausing to ponder the nuances of relaxing into the present moment. We know he esteemed surface and living in the now and urged a Goethean density of looking; but his freely confessed grandiosity often tilts his gaze *beyond*, a vertical inclination distinct from the more horizontal stances of Emerson and Wittgenstein.

These latter two are concerned with the challenge of taking things as they come, which returns us to the embodied image of such poise, the roses outside Emerson's window. They gesture to Angelus Silesius's serenely indifferent rose "perfect in every moment of its existence. . . . Its nature is satisfied, and it satisfies nature, in all moments alike." The rose is a terrestrial version of Nietzsche's fantasy of Heraclitus's perfected autonomy, and looks forward to symbolist aesthetics. Foucault writes of Mallarmé: "His poems are "a manifestation of a language which has no other law than that of affirming . . . its own precipitous existence; and so there is nothing for it to do but to curve back in perpetual return upon itself, as if its discourse could have no other content than the expression of its own form" (299–300).

Foucault evokes Mallarméan silence—the word "upon the whiteness of a piece of paper, where it can possess neither sound nor interlocutor, where it has nothing to say but itself, nothing to do but shine in the brightness of its being" (300). Here the white page and the self-illumined word summon both the rose without why and the *Tractatus*'s domain of silent showing. By the time of his later work silence remains tempting, now expressed in Wittgenstein's intellectual and visceral need to resign himself to the fact that explanation and justification, Philosophy's appointed tasks, come to an end somewhere, and "sooner than we expected" (*Investigations* sec. 1; Klagge, *Exile*

128). Toppling capital P Philosophy requires, Wittgenstein says, "a resignation, but one of feeling, not of intellect. And maybe that is what makes it so difficult for many" (*Occasions* 161). If "giving grounds" comes to an end then Philosophy as we know it might itself come to an end: "The real discovery is the one that makes me capable of stopping doing philosophy when I want to. The one that gives philosophy peace, so that it is no longer tormented by questions which bring *itself* in question" (*Investigations* sec. 133).

This passage is notoriously controversial; resolute readers find the phrase "real discovery" nonsense, strictly "chimerical," uttered to show (and make us ponder) the fatal attractiveness of believing in the possibility of making "fundamental philosophic discoveries" (Read 367). For other readers it seems to constitute an anti-philosophical moment. It wants an end to tormenting questions, that is, those aroused by the endless doubt spawned by Cartesian skepticism, i.e. does the external world exist? Such epistemological conundrums encourage language to "go on holiday," that is, become smitten with abstractions relished only in philosophy classes. But, as Louis Sass argues, sec. 133 may also be an "anti-anti-philosophical" move that seeks to "dissolve" not traditional thought but "his own form of philosophizing" since "the questioning that most brings philosophy into question is, of course, that of Wittgenstein himself" (124). Even the subtlest readers of Wittgenstein, Sass claims, do not take seriously enough "the degree to which Wittgenstein did, at times, adopt a position that is truly against all philosophizing, including even anti-philosophy, a position verging on the anti-intellectual" (125). He accounts for this "blindspot" among professional readers as a way to deny (by ignoring) how "ultimately unassimilable to academic philosophy" is Wittgenstein's willingness to end an activity that so alienated him.

In the meantime, one can conduct philosophical investigations that avoid skepticism's "chimeras." One habit to acquire, he tells us, is to "suppress the question 'why?'" Rather than trying to "grasp the *essence* of the thing" when "philosophers use a word," we should instead always ask ourselves: "Is the word ever actually used in this way in the language-game which is its original home. What *we* do is to bring words back from their metaphysical to their everyday use" (*Investigations* sec. 471, sec. 116). In everyday use when we are asked a question about practices that are normally taken for granted as simply what we do—e.g. "'how am I able to obey a rule?'—if this is not a question about causes, then it is about justification for my following the rule in the way I do. If I have exhausted the justifications I have reached bedrock, and my spade is turned. Then I am inclined to say: 'This is simply what I do'" (sec. 217). In this much-discussed moment Wittgenstein shrugs off the skeptic's endless anxious quest for epistemological certainty, a quest for fundamental reasons that is simply irrelevant in ordinary circumstances: "Well, how do I know?—If that means 'Have I reasons?' the answer is: my reasons will soon give out. And then I shall act, without reasons" (sec. 211). In his last book, *On Certainty*, he declares that certainty is "beyond being justified or unjustified" (sec. 359). No need to seek its verification; indeed such an effort is not even possible since certainties are non-empirical (not based on evidence), non-epistemic (not objects of knowledge), not even articulated, so not open to question. He imagines an interlocutor asking: 'But, if you are *certain*, isn't it that you are shutting your eyes in face of doubt?'—They are shut" (*Investigations* 224).

The calm of Wittgenstein's minimalist stance, embodied in his turned spade, his shut eyes, his animal certainty, is the calm of the rose without why. As an exasperated Bertrand Russell remarked in 1919: "He has become a complete mystic. He reads people like Kierkegaard, and Angelus Silesius, and he seriously contemplates becoming a monk" (*Cambridge Letters*, 140). As Russell wrote after the *Tractatus* was published, "he has penetrated so deep into mystical ways of thought and feeling . . . I think (though he wouldn't agree) that what he likes best in mysticism is its power to make him stop thinking" (qtd. Monk 183). Russell was on to something, in effect anticipating how Wittgenstein, in his final work, regards our calm about certainty as that of a "primitive being to which one grants instinct but not ratiocination" (*Certainty* sec. 475).

Wittgenstein's mood comes close to embodying what Heidegger, quoted earlier, found crucial and unsaid in Silesius's couplet, "that humans . . . first truly are when in their own way they are like the

rose—without why" (38). Heidegger's concern is that this relaxed indifference to justification or reasons, part of what he calls *Gelassenheit,*
or being that lets go ("lassen") of active willing, is imperiled under
modernity. Appropriately, Heidegger found G*elassenheit,* which is so
alien a concept to Enlightenment rationality, in Meister Eckhart and
in Zen Buddhism. Worth noting here is that the philosopher in 1946
started a collaborative translation of the *Tao Te Ching.* (The timing
is interesting, given that the year before, after undergoing a denazifi-
cation hearing, Heidegger had an emotional collapse and spent three
weeks in a sanitorium. Is his taking up of mystical detachment not
only an escape from modernity but, a commentator asks, an "evasion," a "fleeing before guilt"?) (Pöggeler 270, 304).

Modern reason, says Heidegger, is "slavish" to Leibniz's Principle
of Reason, which "decrees what may count as an object of cognition,
or more generally, as a being." It not only legislates "the being of beings" but in its "demand to render sufficient reasons for all cognition,"
the principle of reason drives technology and its project of unleashing
atomic energy; nuclear physics "pushes toward the greatest possible
perfection . . . based on the thoroughgoing calculability of objects" (120,
121). Heidegger is pertinent here because he puts Silesius's rose into dialogue with Goethe to recover the possibility of "reflective thinking"—a
"will-not-to-will," in Hannah Arendt's gloss, a "letting be as . . . thinking that obeys the call of Being" (*Life,* "Willing" 172, 178). This instills
a capacity for listening that might hear "the appeal of the word of being
that speaks in the principle of reason." Yet the appeal has been rendered
"mute" by the "clamor" of the claim of the Principle of Reason as "the
fundamental principle for all cognition" (128). So there is an imperative
to undertake this "leap of thinking" (53).

Heidegger finds help in Goethe's lines: "But research strives and
rings, never tiring, / After the law, the reason *why* and *how.*" Goethe's
words are prescient of the contemporary fact that "the authority of the
powerful fundamental principle of reason is the element in which the
sciences move just as fish do in water and birds do in air" (123). Goethe
"had an inkling of how the tirelessness of research, if it pursues its advance blindly, exhausts humanity and earth." His diagnosis confirmed,
Heidegger discerns the "appeal" audible "in the demand of the principle of reason" when we "open ourselves to what really speaks" in the

standard paraphrase of the principle "nothing is without reason" (122). Listening, we hear a new "pitch," a "different ring," when we stress for the first time "is" and "reason" rather than "nothing" and "without." Stressing "is" "sets the pitch that tunes everything" differently, for "is" is the word of being and by sounding it we make the Principle now "speak as a word of being" rather than as a legislator of cognition (125). This new tonality reveals that being is without why: "Since it is itself ground/reason" it "remains without a ground/reason. Insofar as being . . . grounds, it allows beings to be beings" (125). That is, being does not *have* a ground/reason but rather embodies—*is*—ground/reason and hence immune to "why."

This immunity is intolerable to metaphysical thinking, which requires, says Heidegger, "a first reason for being." This is the demand of the Principle of Reason. And so a vertiginous circularity ensues in response to the question What does "being" mean? Heidegger replies it means "ground/reason," but what does ground/reason mean? "Now, the only answer to this is: 'ground/reason' means 'being.' . . . Here everything goes round in a circle. We become dizzy." (125–126). How to stop this? How to arrest the insatiable "why" insisted upon by cognition which "stalks this interrogative word from one reason to another" and "allows no rest, offers no stop, gives no support" (126).

Here Heidegger again turns to Goethe, for he had not only captured in verse science's tireless pursuit of the "*why* and *how*," but also offered a hint of an antidote in two other lines: "How? When? And Where?— The gods remain mute! / You stick to the *because* and ask not *why*" (qtd. 126). Goethe's "because" is a guardian "against investigating the 'why'" and foundations: for Heidegger, "because" balks at getting to the bottom of things. For informal confirmation, consider the familial language-game where the parent of thinning patience replies to the young child's seemingly endless questions: "Because. Because I said so." It says everything and nothing.

Although Heidegger here does not invoke Angelus Silesius by name, the rose which "blooms because it blooms" is in the air: its "because" functions precisely as Goethe's in Heidegger's description; and probably Goethe had it in mind as well when he urged it as an antidote to "why." The tautological emptiness of "because" is part of its power: The line "blooms because it blooms," remarks Heidegger, "really says nothing, for the 'because' is supposed to supply something else, something we can understand as the reason for whatever is to be founded." Yet it simultaneously "says everything" about what can be said about reason and the "why" (43). Indeed, Heidegger will show that "because" points to the essence of grounds and of being.

He does so by examining "because" through its German etymology and, in a move Wittgenstein would appreciate, seeing how the word works in ordinary language. "Because" is related to *weil*—which is "while" in English, as in "one must strike while the iron is hot." "While" here means not "because" per se but "as long as" or during. The act of whiling, or the infinitive "to while" means "to tarry," "to remain still," "to pause and keep to oneself"; Heidegger points out that tarrying and whiling and abiding are rooted in "the old sense of the word 'being'" (127). Goethe's original "hint" ("You stick to the *because* and ask not *why*") now reads "stick to" whiling, to remaining still and relaxed, "and ask not why." This doing nothing, this simple abiding, suggests what Heidegger meant when he said that Angelus Silesius's "because" says at once nothing and everything.

For Heidegger "everything" means that the while or whiling that "every 'why' guards against names the simple, plain presence that is without why—the presence upon which everything depends, upon which everything rests." In whiling, being and ground/reason are the same: "Both belong together" (127). In sum, the now fully audible "appeal" of the principle of reason in its non-cognitive "pitch" says: "'Nothing *is* without *reason*' both speaks as a word of being and names this as the ground/reason." This "appeal," however, is currently "mute," ever since "Greek thinking was converted to Roman cognition" and human beings came to be defined by "ratio" (account), a word from commercial discourse. "Accordingly human beings are the *animal rationale,* the creature that requires accounts and gives accounts" (129). However, the reduction of the human to *"ratio"* does not "exhaust the essence of humanity.". An alternative exists, and it is a venerable one: "During the uncommonly long incubation period of the principle of reason [the 2,300 years before Leibniz formulated his Principle], the word of being always already appealed to Western humanity as the word of ground/reason. Without this appeal there would be no thinking in the form of philosophy. But also, without philosophy, there would be no Western European science, no unleashing of atomic energy" (128).

In the present age the "clamor" championing the cognitive claim drowns out the "appeal" to being, so Heidegger suggests that we remain "patient and watchful, awake enough for the stillness of the appeal in the word of being to prevail over the clamor. . . . It depends on whether the force of the claim of the 'why' submits to the enabling appeal of the 'because'" (128). Until the impasse is resolved the question remains an open one: will the "recklessness of exclusively calculative thinking and its immense achievements" exhaust the essence of humanity (as the rational animal that requires accounts) or is "the essence of being what still remains, and even more disturbingly, worthy of thought?" (129). Thinking will be "capable of responding to what is worthy of thought" only if we cease to be "enchanted by calculative thinking."

In attuning us to the "appeal" of "because" Heidegger not only "names the simple, plain presence that is without why," but points to where this presence resides. This is a region immune to the pressure of time, antithetical to the "painful frenzy" and "haste" that Nietzsche regarded as the enemies of thinking, a place of abiding, whiling, waiting, tarrying. These stances are distant from the hungry why of explanation that fuels the "clamor" of "boundless purely quantitative nonstop progress" (Heidegger, *What* 69). Some have compared this domain of "without why" to Zen's *sunyata* or full emptiness, less a concept than that which transforms our relation to the world and prompts an existential conversion into "the personal spontaneity of 'sheer elemental doing'" (G. Martin 107–108). Such "innocence" is germane as well to Wittgenstein's domain of *showing* as disclosing "a pure and undivided *manifestation* of 'Being'" (as Louis Sass has glossed "showing") (137), and to Emerson's "I am explained without explaining." Circulating here too is Wittgenstein's "This is simply what we do," as well as Nietzsche's remark that "no trace of *struggle* can be demonstrated" in his life (*Ecce* 255). In this realm of stillness we are relieved of the itch to explain, we learn to see, which becomes a practice of "letting things come," to recall Nietzsche, who added that this stance redefines "strong will-power" as the ability "precisely *not* to 'will'." Such calm nurtures our original "schooling in spirituality." Having led us to this realm of renunciatory silence, philosophy effaces itself, as Heidegger admits in a remark quoted in concluding this part.

■

This aesthetic utopia sketched above honors the strength not to will and implicitly offers relief from what Zarathustra calls the "great folly" that "lives in our will": "in willing itself there is suffering, based on its inability to will backward" (*Zarathustra* 111). Because the nature of willing is always to will forward, "it was" is an "immovable stone" in its path, and hence disgusts the will, which internalizes its revulsion and sense of impotence. "The will suffers from itself" and remains captive to time's "it was," says Heidegger of *Thus Spoke Zarathustra*. (*What Is* 92–93). What results is revulsion against everything that passes and endures; this is the spirit of revenge or *ressentiment* that rules human beings, most especially those whom Nietzsche, in *Zarathustra*, dubs "last men."

The way "last men" form ideas, says Heidegger, is unremittingly hostile: the last man "opposes everything that is and as it is" so "sets upon everything it sets before itself, in order to depose and decompose it" (74, 84). Thus the blossoming tree reduced to "brain currents" by scientific explanation. In the last men we see that "the spirit of revenge is the fundamental characteristic of all thought so far. That is to say: revenge marks the manner in which man so far relates himself to what is," as Heidegger notes, paraphrasing Nietzsche (97). Nietzsche saddles the "last man"—"the most contemptible human," so smug that he is unable "to have contempt for himself"—with a tick: "'We have invented happiness', say the last human beings, men, and they blink" (*Zarathustra* 10). Heidegger seizes on the blink, which Nietzsche repeats three times, as containing the etymological clue—from Middle English *blenchen*, to *blenken*, to deceive and to glitter and gleam—to the last man's "particular manner of forming ideas"—which "blink at everything and can do nothing else" (*What Is* 74, 85). While the "wink" is a "superficial and incidental" cousin of the globally ambitious blink, both signal deceit and ease with lies; this makes them adept at helping to create a world order based on "the mutual setup, agreed upon as true and valid—with the mutual tacit understanding not to question the setup" of governmental bodies—congresses, committees, subcommittees—all the "blinking organizations of blinking arrangements of distrust and treachery" that comprise a "world order" (82, 74, 84).

In this context Wittgenstein's shut eyes are an emblem of immunity to blinking. Like Heidegger, he despised the rule of calculative thinking and scientism; "the typical western scientist will not understand the spirit in which I write" (*Culture* 7). It is a spirit apart from the ideology of "progress," which is "occupied with building an ever more complicated structure. And even clarity is sought as a means to this end, not as an end in itself. For me, on the contrary, clarity, perspicuity, are valuable in themselves" (7). Wittgenstein's "spirit" of thinking occurs outside a horizon of the instrumental, so requires withdrawal from the strictly purposive. Closed to the blinking, winking mendacity of bureaucratic modernity, Wittgenstein's shut eyes are also a symbol of deliverance from the climate of revenge bred by rage at time's ceaseless "passing" and the compensatory "will to will," in Heidegger's phrase, that drives man's relentless self-assertion. "For once," urges Heidegger, let the blossoming tree "stand where it stands. . . . Thought has never let the tree stand where it stands" (*What Is* 44).

Wittgenstein came to crave the peace of living in the present tense after serving at the Russian front in 1916–1917, where he saw heavy combat. The experience evacuated his sense of will: "I cannot bend the happenings of the world to my will: I am completely powerless," he wrote in a notebook at the time (qtd. Klagge *Exile* 9). He recovered some sense of will by deciding to be stoical in the grim present, without hope or fear, a decision he reached with the help of Tolstoy's *The Gospels in Brief*, which became one of his favorite books. Tolstoy has Jesus say: "And so, be not downcast, but always live in the present by the spirit. For the life of the spirit there is no time. . . . Life is only for this, to exalt the Son of Man, and the Son of Man exists always. He is not in time; and therefore, in serving him, one must live without time, in the present alone" (qtd. Klagge 11). In a notebook Wittgenstein writes: "For life in the present there is no death. . . . If by eternity is understood not infinite temporal duration but non-temporality, then it can be said that a man lives eternally if he lives in the present." As James Klagge notes, "this self-coaching in the midst of battle then becomes proposition 6.4311 in the *Tractatus*," which begins: "Death is not an event of life. Death is not lived through." One consequence of his having attained this perspective *sub species aeternitatis* was receiving a medal for valor (10–11).

Wittgenstein's battlefield spiritual epiphany of a timeless present leaves him free of feeling the impotent revenge against time that animates Nietzschean ressentiment. In effect, he has a taste of the cure that Zarathustra articulates: the will must "become its own redeemer" and "unlearn the spirit of revenge," so that willing becomes "not-willing." Until then it will suffer its "gnashing of teeth" (*Zarathustra* 112).

"The space for freedom from revenge," says Heidegger, "is where Nietzsche sees the superman's essential nature" (*What Is* 86, 88). That pacific quality is the opposite of the superman's caricature as a monster of aggression. Reversing his earlier estimate of the Übermensch, Heidegger in *What Is Called Thinking* (1954) enlists Nietzsche in making a kind of companion argument to his re-attunement of the Principle of Reason. Concerned to locate a space of composure for meditative thinking, Heidegger argues that the superman's power is precisely in his freedom *from* the imperious angry demands of the will: "Superman is qualitatively, not quantitatively, different from existing man. The thing that the superman discards is precisely our boundless purely quantitative nonstop progress. The superman is poorer, simpler . . . quieter and more self-sacrificing" (69).

Against the "tireless advance" of the "why," which "allows no rest, offers no stop," the roses (as rendered by Emerson) "exist with God today. There is no time to them." Whiling, pausing, remaining still—this stance of renunciation that is "both in and out of the game"—occupies an ambiguous zone, holding time in abeyance while allowing a life in the present. Granting this allowance comes close to the task of philosophy, whose role in effect is to let go of its own will to appropriate, as Heidegger told Reiner Schürmann in 1966. Philosophy is "to open the way by which an unutterable experience may be given, but such an experience would no longer be answerable to philosophy; it would be the prerogative of the one to whom it was granted" ("Report" 71).

Part 7

ALTHOUGH AS COMMITTED to negation as Gould or Wittgenstein, Paul Celan and George Oppen pitch their arts of renunciation in a less severe key. Whereas the pianist and the philosopher had a slightly menacing pertinacity, reflecting the hermetic apartness they cultivated in order to achieve an obsessive, near obliterative level of concentration, Oppen had a sustaining marriage of six decades to the writer Mary Oppen, and Celan, alongside many love affairs, was married to a devoted wife, a graphic artist. She stayed by him when, for much of the last decade of his life, Celan suffered increasingly intense manic depression with violent episodes—some directed at her. His torment (hers was a different matter) in part grew out of repercussions from public suspicion fed by a spurious 1953 charge of plagiarism by the disturbed widow of a Jewish poet whom Celan had befriended.

The Second World War psychically scarred Oppen and Celan: the disaster set the terms of art and life to a significant degree. "Obsessed, bewildered // By the shipwreck / Of the singular // We have chosen the meaning / Of being numerous" run Oppen's most famous lines, written in the late 1960s (*New Collected* 166). Yes, we have "chosen" solidarity, but we make the choice within the engulfing fact of "shipwreck" that has left the "singular" embattled, frail, and in need. "We seem caught / In reality together," he tells his daughter in "Of Being Numerous" (181). Celan too resists isolation; he writes: "I cannot see any basic difference between a handshake and a poem" (*Collected Prose* 26).

Yet union does not erase anxiety or solitude; indeed, these states become entwined in various permutations, as, for instance, obscurity sponsors encounter in Celan's aesthetic. For both writers, doubt endures, symptom of an emotional fragility that was one legacy of the catastrophe they shared. Always insisting on the historical divide that the war imposed, Celan speaks of "the poem *today*: not joyfully expressive and in no way loquaciously communicative," it instead has an "ascetic character." Indeed, to speak of Art and of the lyrical "contributes to the murder of the poem." Near that notebook entry, Celan adds, "the time of programmatic explanations is over—we are alone" (*The Meridian* 151, 153). In a 1966 notebook George Oppen asks himself: "Is it perhaps abominable / In a time of atrocity / To write poems" (*Prose* 184). "The only poem for our time is something that refuses poetry," writes Oppen's friend Rachel Blau DuPlessis of both writers, in a discussion that is one of the very few to bring them together, however briefly (214).

Celan, who insisted on writing in German though he was a brilliant translator of English, French, Romanian, Russian, and American poetry (Skakespeare's sonnets, Dickinson, Rimbaud, Valéry), would retrospectively remark that his loyalty to the language of "murderous speech" held steadfast during the war, "remained secure against loss. But it had to go through its own lack of answers" (*Collected Prose* 15, 34). Going through meant refusing transfiguration or transcendence ("the poem does not stand outside time") and instead abiding, staying "en route" to "find out where" he was and where he was "going" (34). Oppen's words too came through, his poems also disdaining metaphor whenever possible and surviving to bear witness to their own inadequate adequacy: "I don't know how to say it / needing a word with no sound // . . . say as much as I dare, as much as I can / sustain I don't know how to say it" (*New Collected* 261).

Pinned down in a foxhole for nearly ten hours with two other soldiers in Alsace in April 1945, "on the edge of the Battle of the Bulge," George Oppen was the only one to survive. In a late poem ("Semite") he speaks of "guilts / of the foxhole"; it appears in the *Myth of the Blaze*, the 1975 collection whose title poem is about "the destroyed (and guilty) Theatre / of the War," in which Oppen wonders "why had they not // killed me why did they fire that warning / wounding cannon only the one round" (194, 251–252, 247). In an intensely focused single-page prose piece of 1974, "Non-Resistance, etc. Or: Of the Guiltless," Oppen presents guilt as an uncontrollable flood. From the second paragraph: "If I fought, and fought to kill, I would suffer guilt, the guilt of guilt AND the guilt of fear, the desire to run, the guilt that I've told of, the guilt of that foxhole" (*Prose* 46).

In circumstances never definitively explained, in late June of 1942 in Czernowitz, Bukovina, a province of the Austro-Hungarian Empire until 1918, then incorporated into Romania until 1944, the Nazis seized the parents of Paul Celan when their twenty-two-year-old son was out of the house. He never saw them again, later learning his father had died of typhus and his mother had been shot. For nineteen months Celan was imprisoned in a Romanian forced-labor battalion. He avoided speaking in precise detail of the war years; more certain is their effect on him. A friend once remarked: "Paul said his heaviest guilt was a betrayal"; another spoke of a "severe psychic shock he never overcame" (qtd. Felstiner, *Paul Celan* 15, 26). Quoting in a notebook a line he had read—"survival is everything" —Celan comments, "no, it is not everything; no, to survive is indecent, as survivor one has to write for one's life even more so" (*The Meridian* 156).

The torments of these two survivors casts new light on the notorious rhetorical gauntlet that Adorno threw down in 1949—that "to write poetry after Auschwitz is barbaric"—and, especially his later amendment: "Perennial suffering has as much right to expression as a tortured man has to scream; hence it may have been wrong to say that after Auschwitz you could no longer write poems. But it is not wrong to raise the less cultural question whether after Auschwitz you can go on living—especially whether one who escaped by accident, one who by rights should have been killed, may go on living" (*Negative* 362–363). Adorno's own words here are not without some measure of guilt—he goes on to speak of the "coldness" that "mere survival requires" as the "drastic guilt of him who was spared" (363). In the thirties he had prudently edited his Jewish patronymic (reducing Wiesengrund to a middle initial "W") and taken his Catholic mother's name for his own. In commencing his literary career in 1947 Celan renamed himself, erasing his too-Jewish birth name, Antschel, by inverting syllables after deleting "S" and "H"—Stalin and Hitler, as legend has it.

Celan and Oppen faced and endured in painfully literal ways both challenges that Adorno raises—the "cultural" one—whether poetry should be written after the Nazi genocide—and the psychic one: whether one "who escaped by accident . . . may go on living." Their work is written against and through this double pressure. They rise to Adorno's challenge by defying it, by refusing the command to renounce. Yet they do not simply ignore it; instead they internalize renunciation, turning it into a compositional resource. From the guilt of survival they make a poetry written out of the silence that ensues after devastation. In the wake of a tornado, what remains? As Oppen writes,

I saw . . . the trampled
countries of the driveways to face
the silence of the pebbles the whirl wind must

have scattered under the sun the scattered

words that we can muster where once
were the grand stairways. (*New Collected* 309)

The "silence" is the sound of belatedness—"where once . . ."—and shapes what poetry can do: it can retrieve, "can muster" that which remains "scattered"—pebbles of words. Poetry survives but "exposed in an unsuspected, terrifying way," as Celan says in 1958 (*Collected Prose* 35).

Each an avid reader of Heidegger, Oppen and Celan both insist that the poem is an existential act of truthful encounter, anything but the product of the "fury of self-assertion which is resolutely self-reliant," as Heidegger describes the orientation of technology with its "unconditional" willing (*Poetry* 116). The encounter is a way of bearing witness to horrors endured and outlasted, and a way to fashion poetry into a precarious space of openness, a "gift to the attentive" (Celan) won from silence. Celan and Heidegger had a complicated friendship (sketched below); and the poet admired Adorno but a bid at friendship foundered on the latter's animus toward Heidegger and on Adorno's Auschwitz dictum. Regarding the latter, Celan scorned it as based on a sentimental view of poetry, one confined to a "Nightingale or song thrush perspective" (qtd. Dischner 43).

Once, when asked about the "craft" of writing, Celan dispensed with formal matters and answered that "craft means handiwork, a matter of hands. And these hands must belong to *one* person, i.e. a unique mortal soul searching for a way with its voice and its dumbness. Only truthful hands write true poems" (*Collected Prose* 26). In a draft of his enigmatic and moving address upon being awarded the Büchner Prize in 1960, "The Meridian," Celan reiterates this identity when he speaks of "writing as a way of being" (*The Meridian* 134). Readers of Heidegger will hear in these passages echoes of the philosopher's discussion in the opening pages of *What Is Called Thinking* of the "craft of the hand"—"the hand extends itself, and receives its own welcome in the hands of others"—and thinking as "handicraft" (published six years before Celan's own re-thinking of poetry) (16). Readers of American literature will hear an echo of Whitman in Celan's stress on how the intimacy of a live encounter between poem and reader renounces any distinction between art and life. In "So Long" Whitman

writes: "Camerado, this is no book, / Who touches this touches a man
. . . / It is I you hold and who holds you" (613). Celan quotes these very
lines and ruminates upon them in his notes for "The Meridian" speech
(*The Meridian* 132).

Looking at the careers of Oppen and Celan in concert affords an
intimate perspective on how, for the scarred poet, survival demands
not only "extreme formulations" but also "formulations in extremis"
(Celan) that shape poetry into new forms of mystery, austerity, and
intensity (74). Within such extremity the poem seeks to attain the
opacity of a thing; "the poem is born dark," says Celan; and Oppen
speaks of "the pure joy / Of the mineral fact // Tho it is impenetrable." Both chime with Heidegger's praise of the "earth" as what
"shatters" "every attempt to penetrate it . . . every merely calculating intrusion" and "shows itself only when it remains undisclosed
and unexplained" (Oppen, *New Collected* 164; Heidegger, "Origin"
25). Opacity, however, does not negate encounter. Simultaneously,
the poem is also to be "a word for living creatures" (Celan); it wants
communion with the reader, the "other"; "the poem is lonely. It is
lonely and *en route.*" The poem "intends another, needs this other,
needs an opposite. It goes toward it, bespeaks it." This encounter locates the poem, roots it in "the here and now of the poem," in what
Celan will call "its own '20th of January,'" an enigmatic refrain in
"The Meridian," to which we will return (*The Meridian* 84; *Collected
Prose* 47–50). Part of this sensitivity to time is the realization that
after the Holocaust we must not "take art for granted, for absolutely
given." Celan finds earlier evidence of art's being put in question in
certain self-reflexive moments in the work of the nineteenth-century
dramatist Georg Büchner (the ostensible subject of "The Meridian").
Büchner implied a radical interrogation of Art, a "challenge" to which
all contemporary literature "must return if it wants to question further" (Celan, *Collected Prose* 48, 43).

Oppen too stresses poetry's acute registration of the temporal.
Indeed, one could say that Celan's caution—that we must never "take
art for granted"—defines Oppen's perspective. The time must be right
for poetry. Oppen quotes and concurs with Brecht who "once wrote
that there are times when it can be almost a crime to write of trees"
("Because it implies silence about so many horrors," Brecht adds). Says

Oppen: "I happen to think the statement is valid. . . . There are situations which cannot honorably be met by art. . . . The question can only be whether one intends, at a given time, to write poetry or not" (*Prose* 36). He lived this question.

Oppen's quarter-century withdrawal from writing began with the Depression, "the catastrophe of human lives in the 'thirties which seemed to me to put poetry and the purposes of poetry in question" (*Selected Letters* 186). He was born to a wealthy family but felt burdened by its privileges—"the noise of wealth, // the clamor of wealth . . . it is the voice // Of Hell," he wrote in "Guest Room," his great poem about the illusory immunity of money, the "safe harbor" of wealth that "closes / Now like a fortress" against death: "It is the courage of the rich // Who are an *avant garde* // Near the limits of life" (*New Collected* 107–109). An inheritance allowed Oppen to live frugally and to avoid being tied to a profession for the freedom to explore the world. In a 1968 interview he said: "In a way I gave up poetry for the pressures of what for the moment I'll call conscience. But there were some things I had to live through, some things I had to think my way through, some things I had to try out—and it was more than politics really; it was the whole experience of working in factories, of having a child and so on" (*Speaking With* 20). He became a father, a union organizer, a tool and die maker, a metal worker in an aircraft factory, a furniture craftsman and, in 1942 at the age of thirty-four, enlisted in the army infantry.

A dozen years later Oppen called this commitment to finding out for himself a "poetic exploration at the same that it was an action of conscience. . . . And I thought most of the poets didn't know about the world as a life—so that I fairly easily gave up a great many poetic friends" (218). What made exploration "poetic" was that his experience as a maker, engaged with obdurate materials (*The Materials* is the title of his first book after resuming writing), bred respect for hands-on know-how. This, in turn, sharpened his engagement with poetic materials, faithful small words. He now found the "weakness of Imagism" (a style made famous by his mentor Pound) to be the very literariness that the movement had been devised to extirpate; "a man writes of the moon rising over a pier who knows nothing about piers" (*Prose* 82). Oppen not only regarded Pound as bookish but possessed of an "operatic quality" of aggressive masculinity that replaced reality with "a swirl of heroes and words" (qtd. Nicholls 40). His reaction to Pound held for high poetic modernism in general. Yeats, Eliot, and company were too full of ideas and arguments. Moreover, their goal was mastery—incarnated in authoritarian *Weltanschauungs* that explained everything. Pound "knew what he thought. The fact ruined much. . . . For me, the writing of a poem is the process of finding out what I mean, discovering what I mean" (qtd. Nicholls 38–39).

Oppen's critique of his former mentor Pound was at once a literary and a political rebuttal from the left to Pound's right-wing views, a critique also enacted in that quarter-century abandonment of writing. Oppen's rigorous silence enacted his separation of poetry from the pursuit of social justice and the demands of raising a daughter. His renunciation "hung over" the younger generation "like the extreme act of a saint," not least for being resolutely anti-heroic, not "glamorous," a word used by one observer of the poet who says the absence of this last characteristic discomfits those of Oppen's admirers who long for a hero (Weinberger xiv; Longenbach). Rather than taking refuge like Pound in literary and political myth making, Oppen could not insulate his relation to poetry from historical contingencies. Even after he returned to writing by 1960, his acute sense of art's fragility remained. In 1969, during the Vietnam War, Oppen found it "difficult again to believe in the importance of poetry. The army tightens up, some kids surely will be shot soon. Art becomes (again) more and more a struggle *against* the artworld, the art-attitudes . . . and against little else" (*Letters* 187). He drew the inevitable conclusion: "I perhaps cannot write poetry in wartime. I couldn't before and perhaps cannot now. I become ashamed, I become sick with shame" (qtd. Nicholls 85). When he was awarded the Pulitzer Prize that same year for *Of Being Numerous* he had a difficult time with sudden fame and canceled a number of scheduled readings.

In the remarkable single-page prose meditation of 1974, mentioned earlier, "Non-Resistance, etc. Or: Of the Guiltless," Oppen gives voice to the tormenting legacy of the Second World War: "If I fought, and fought to kill, I would suffer guilt, the guilt of guilt AND the guilt of fear, the desire to run, the guilt that I've told of, the guilt of that foxhole. . . . If I killed, I would suffer guilt. If I did not, I would suffer. . . . I don't even know a word, a name for what I would suffer" (*Prose* 46).

Because no single word or name is adequate, the poetic "necessity," for Oppen, is to evoke "the feeling of presence, not concept" (borrowing a line of Robert Duncan's) (47). Rather than naming his pain, folding it neatly into a concept, Oppen releases the spiraling anguish that commences within himself and spreads beyond him:

> —that I did not exist and never had, the terrible knowledge of a fake, a lie, that nothing had been as I said, pretended, that I had loved no one, that those that had loved me or anyone like me had deceived themselves, pitifully, tragically had deceived themselves, had drawn the simplest, delusory mere warmth from my presence, had been deceived, betrayed, demeaned, had given all they could give for nothing, to nothing, had been nothing—In the last moments they would know this. Die like me, or fight with nothing, without what they had thought was themselves, without a past, with nothing. Thrown away, unloved, shamed, degraded—stripped naked, herded into the gas ovens. *Think* Think also of children. The guards laughing (46)

The title, "Non-Resistance, etc. Or: Of the Guiltless," acquires an irony that undoes each term: "Non-Resistance" is redefined as the "presence" of pervasive impotence, which testifies to the fact that there is *no* resistance and *none* can remain guiltless when faced with "a force such as the force of Hitler." Oppen's torrential prose is analogous to that force, as the early repeated conditional "if" moves from pondering his guilt to envisioning "those that had loved me or anyone like me" being destroyed, stripped of every vestige of moral authenticity. By the end of the paragraph all will be sent to the ovens, the "I," the "those," all at one with the helpless children. All are swept up in the tidal wave of this eruptive contagion; or, if surviving, live to record the drowning. "We deceive ourselves" in thinking otherwise. In sum, the Nazi "force" devours distance, destroys any illusion that if "we release bombs from the air" or "aim a rifle at an unknown man and pull the trigger" we have established distance and won immunity (46). No strike is surgical. The war and survival taught him the utter folly of believing in one's powers of mastery. Hence Oppen resumes writing attended by humility, which will shape his poetry's form and subjects.

What might mitigate the poet's guilt and shame? Declaring in 1963 his "freedom from the art subject," from "histrionics," from "the trick of gracefulness" and the "cocoon of 'Beauty' . . . an art of the masseur and the perfumist," Oppen speaks of poetry's "test of truth." This is a seeking to "disclose"; "the image is encountered, not found; it is an account of the poet's perception, the act of perception; it is a test of sincerity, a test of conviction, the rare poetic quality of truthfulness." The "test" has no patience for "generalization" (*Prose* 30–32) because Oppen wants not concepts but

> Clarity
> In the sense of *transparence*,
> I don't mean that much can be explained.
>
> Clarity in the sense of silence. (*New Collected* 175)

Oppen brings this encountered clarity to poetic life in his best-known short poem, "Psalm" (1965):

> In the small beauty of the forest
> The wild deer bedding down—
> That they are there!
>   Their eyes
> Effortless, the soft lips
> Nuzzle and the alien small teeth
> Tear at the grass
> . . .
>   The small nouns
> Crying faith
> In this in which the wild deer
> Startle, and stare out. (99)

Such rapt attention to what is already "there!" possesses a spiritual intensity (encouraged by the title); indeed, to borrow a quotation from Malebranche that Celan will cite in "The Meridian," here "attention is the natural prayer of the soul." Attention is an act of witnessing, for "truth is empirical," says Oppen, "has to be encountered" unexpectedly, as a "disclosure." The exclamation "That they are there!" registers the poet's astonished sense of how profound the simple fact of the living moment of presence and of being is. "Being" here is less a noun than a verb, an emphasis that Oppen found affirmed in reading

Heidegger, who, as we know, decries the "forgetting of being." In a notebook Oppen writes: "Heidegger: Man creates not being but the *there* of being-there (Das Sein [sic])" (*Prose* 142–143, 146).

This silent watching of "wild deer" being there, preceding the poet, effaces any desire in the observing ego to exert authority. Rather, the poet exclaims in gratitude and by the end acknowledges "faith" in language: "The small nouns / Crying faith / In this in which the wild deer / Startle, and stare out." Oppen exposes artifice in the form of grammar but not in order to undermine the reach of reference: the speaker's sudden attention to his own medium in no way detracts from the poem's commitment to the presence of the "wild deer," who seem poised to flee, startled. By personifying "the small nouns"—they cry out—"Psalm" in a sense accords them creaturely life, as if the nouns are companions of the deer (they are the forest of words in which the deer bed), and Oppen affirms implicitly the power of words to bring us to the phenomenal. In an interview he called this affirmation a faith that "nouns do refer to something; that it's there, that it's true . . . that appearances represent reality, whether or not they misrepresent it" (*Speaking* 11). That the deer "stare out" in their otherness, at one with the "small nouns" that have summoned them to us, testifies to Oppen's trust in poetry to render singularity, what he often designates with the word "impenetrable"—not the unintelligible but the irreducibly different. "That" incites thought. To apprehend this quality involves what Oppen calls a "lyric reaction to the world" (12).

This last phrase recalls Oppen's "poetic exploration" of the world after quitting poetry. He had to spend decades earning his faith in small words. "Faith" meant reference, naming things of this world, but it did not mean making a fetish of small words. He did not share William Carlos Williams's love of American vernacular speech, the doctor's desire to record "the speech of Polish mothers." Instead he seeks to render the "life of the mind" and "the virtue of the mind / Is that emotion / Which causes / To see." As Oppen elaborates in an interview: "The mind is capable not only of thinking but has an emotional root that forces it to look, to think, to see," a unity of thinking and feeling that is found in William James's theory of emotion, to which Oppen alludes (*Speaking* 19, 201, 204). He seeks a "bounded whole," as "Psalm" presents (39).

Even when in interviews and letters Oppen declares his "peculiar faith in small words, a feeling that they are in immediate touch with reality, with unthought and directly perceived reality," he qualifies his claim of "immediate touch." He carefully avoids a William Jamesian frustration with concepts as obstacles to one's pursuit of the "real." Oppen avoids too "Hemingway's implication that the small words have a more intrinsic honesty" (Kenner 169). "The words distort," says Oppen, "but are our mode" (*Letters* 242). Oppen accepts, as he says in a major poem, "Route," that "Words cannot be wholly transparent. And that is the / 'heartlessness' of words" (*New Collected* 194). Dilating upon his anti-romantic acceptance, he notes: "But, except for the number of letters in the words and the age of the words, it ['there is a tree'] is precisely the same kind of statement as it is to say 'it is a monocotyledonous plant.' Even those simplest or at least commonest words—'tree', 'table' or 'chair'—so often appealed to as an escape from philosophic muddying of the waters are classificatory words, are in fact 'taxonomy' . . . things we invent for ourselves. Nevertheless, there are certain ones without which we really are unable to exist" (*Letters* 62).

Even if they inevitably regulate and pacify we must believe in some words as a matter of life and death. That caution and conviction informs the first poem he writes after twenty-five years, "Blood from the Stone" (1962). Surveying the interim by splicing together the bleakness of the thirties and the terror of wartime in the early forties, the poet ponders what is required morally and aesthetically to resume his craft. The poem commences with a woman in a doorframe, "carrying bundles," perched on the threshold of a new life: "Everything I am is / Us. Come home." Bridging the space (literalized in the line break) between "I" and "Us," individual and collective, domestic and political, will be one effort the poem will attempt. Its second section invokes "The Thirties. And / A spectre // In every street, / In all inexplicable crowds, what they did then / Is still their lives." And the poet interrogates his own aesthetic responsibility: "Belief? / What do we believe / To live with? Answer. / Not invent—just answer—all / That verse attempts. / That we can somehow add each to each other?" The next section moves to the next decade, to the war, and its "frightful danger" of ambush and exposure: "To a body anything can happen."

Oppen juxtaposes jarring memories of "joy" coming across a French farmyard and the "smell of wood-smoke" when suddenly Nazi troops appear: "In boots. Steel helmet. Monstrous. Standing / Shut by the silent walls," the poet barely avoids them as they march past. From "walls" and "cobbles," we move to "stone" in the final section.

The poem obeys its taboo against invention and the imperative of making "answer" by ending with an unyielding summary of the two decades: "Blood from a stone, life / From a stone dead dam. Mother / Nature! because we find the others / Deserted like ourselves and therefore brothers. Yet // So we lived / And chose to live // These were our times" (*New Collected* 52–54). Both mother (echoed in the pun on "dam") and nature have shriveled into barrenness, "stone dead," but they still yield a minimal "life" and "blood" for the "deserted like ourselves" to subsist on. The survivors form a brotherhood. Earlier, the poet had remarked: "Among the others," among the "pavements" and "streets," "we were lucky—strangest word." The indigence of the poem's last three lines, both verbal and tonal, still manages to affirm a stoic solidarity, even if minimally registered in "we" and "our." So concludes Oppen's first poem ending his renunciation.

Gratitude for luck and resolve to keep faith with this poverty permits Oppen to earn his postwar return to writing. "Answer. Not invent" is the demand, that is, to be *answerable* in the present to what he and others have suffered in the past. Then it is "Possible / To use / Words provided one treat them / As enemies. / Not enemies— Ghosts / Which have run mad / In the subways . . . / If one captures them / One by one proceeding // Carefully they will restore / I hope to meaning / And to sense" (*New Collected*, "A Language of New York" 116). The memory of the war has seeped into language; ghosts now inhabit words and must be tracked down, restored to sense. The poetic task of "purifying the words of the tribe," as Mallarmé had put it (in a line that T. S. Eliot borrowed) requires Oppen's permanent enlistment. "They await // War, and the news / Is war / As always," he writes a few lines later.

About ten years later, the ghostly enemy now is no longer words but "desks." "Two Romance Poems" begins: "something wrong with my desk / the desk / the destroyer, desk is the enemy." Oppressed by the act and scene of composition, Oppen expresses anxiety in a counterpoint of self-doubt as he imagines "adventure" on "sea," "islands," and "beach." He juxtaposes to the desk "bright light of shipwreck beautiful as the sea / and the islands I don't know how to say it / needing a word with no sound // but the pebbles shifting on the beach the sense / of the thing, everything, rises in the mind the / venture adventure // say as much as I dare, as much as I can / sustain I don't know how to say it // I say all that I can" (261). The poem seems to be simultaneously making and unmaking itself.

Oppen is not the first to narrate his own internal struggle and self-doubt in order to make a poem, but even this last word, he cautions, may be too ambitious—rather, "would be the poem // If one wrote it" (261). He keeps the poem's very existence conditional, setting himself against the medium—he is "Needing a word with no sound"—and against the means, the (literal) support—the desk. In a note he warns himself: "Not to make noise: to keep one's attention outward toward silence" even while knowing that "silence is impossible" (qtd. Nicholls 56). In other words, Oppen's return to poetry does not repudiate silence but is sustained by it as he creates poetry almost *malgré lui*, out of the tension between his "faith in small words" and "distrust of language" when it grows large and false with fluency and self-regard ("relevant thought begins" with this distrust). "I dislike most of all the theatrical ethic, the ethics of posture" (*Prose* 181, 190). Language is to be mined from silence—hence his late work's halting cadences achieved via caesuras and enjambment: "to read Oppen means reading more and more slowly" (Taggart). Poetry is to be won from the clutches of Art and Politics. Though a member of the Communist Party for decades, Oppen never wrote poetry in support of the Party. In the thirties, he recalled four decades later, he argued that "Henry James and not Hemingway was the useful model for 'proletarian' writers" (*Letters* 241). He kept his distance from the siren calls of those he named philistines and bohemians, respectively, partisans of poetry as political engagement ("left-wing 'cultural workers'") and advocates of the "onanism" of "pure" poetry, the latter also dismissed by Celan as purveyors of "lyrical potpourri" (*Letters* 241; *Prose* 30; *The Meridian* 138).

To be sure, Oppen's was always a poetry etched in spareness; the poems from his debut volume *Discrete Series* (1934) are all miniatures, one poem per page, chiseled, precise observation. "She lies, hip high, / On a flat bed / While the after- / Sun passes. //Plant, I breathe— / O Clearly, / Eyes legs arms hands fingers, / Simple legs in silk" (*New Collected* 20). Typical here is not the eroticism but the structurally static form—a detached observer (here imaged as a silent self-contained "plant" in the room) surveys, at times voyeuristically, an object. Oppen's severity of style was nurtured by his affiliation with the "Objectivist" school, which began at the start of the 1930s and derived from Pound's imagism with its "direct treatment of the 'thing.'" The goal of Objectivism, to quote Hugh Kenner, was "self-sufficient adequacy" and its aesthetic of "sincerity" (Louis Zukofsky's word) was, as Kenner says, "as puritan in its formulations as in its exemplars. . . . Implying as it did a perfect indifference to any reader's approval, tending as it did to thrust arrangements of speech into the perfect thinghood of a snail shell (shaped, achieved, at rest), it comported with a latent sense that the arts ought not exhilarate, save austerely, and that in a gray time (1931) they had best be gray" (Kenner 166–168).

After resuming his career Oppen's poems maintain his minimalist style (though there is critical debate about the degree and depth of continuity) but he abolishes the distance and spectatorship intrinsic to the subject/object dichotomy. Unbound by this constriction, Oppen's new poetry becomes in form and content a "process of finding out" what the world discloses. This effort blends a philosophical expansiveness— nurtured by Oppen's intuitive discovery of his affinities with the anti-subjectivist emphases of Heidegger and the neo-Thomist aesthetician Jacques Maritain—with a reliance on the elliptical, the gnomic, and on "transparence" that is vivid and opaque: "I don't mean that much can be explained" (*New Collected* 175). Hence the poet's fondness for Henry James. Maritain helped Oppen look beyond a strictly rational understanding of the intellect to discover its "preconceptual life," a "more profound—and more obscure life" that comprises "the hidden recesses of poetry" (Maritain 4).

Reaching the hidden refreshes one's engagement with the phenomenal, the "arduous path of appearance," in words of Heidegger that Oppen used as an epigraph to *This In Which* (1965). Aquinas's "Truth follows upon the existence of things" became another key motto ("*Veritas sequitur . . .*" is the epigraph of "Psalm,"), alongside Maritain's "We awake in the same moment to ourselves and to things." To allow the world to shine out from things is the poem's aim and this shimmering luster is the root of *claritas* for Aquinas. Inevitably the freshness of awakening to present discovery is shadowed by Oppen's past: the bruising intensity of his quarter century of living, the life of those unwritten years, now overflows in the absence of the impersonal camera-eye controlling the early poems, releasing a tenderness and sympathy that by accepting the "guilts / of the foxhole" mitigate the pain of survival: "even sorrow // or most terrible // wound prove us part / of the world not fallen" (*New Collected* 301). To be "part of the world" is to move about in it, not noisily but "unarmed / And unarmored," keeping "one's attention outward toward silence." In that attunement outward to the impenetrable, "the mind rises // Into happiness, rising // Into what is there. I know of no other happiness" (109, 155).

Oppen's "Psalm," though untypically accessible, is regarded as his signature poem, distilling his faith in reference and giving gratitude for what is "there"—"the fact of actualness" (*Speaking* 55). Celan also has a "Psalm," one of his best-known poems, and its opening stanzas (three of four) introduce us to his world.

In the translation by Felstiner it begins: "No one kneads us again out of earth and clay, / No one incants our dust. / no one. // Blessèd art thou, No One. / In thy sight would / we bloom. / In thy / spite. // A Nothing / we were, are now, and ever / shall be, blooming: / the Nothing-, the / No-One's-Rose" (Felstiner, *Paul Celan* 167). This is a psalm bereft of comfort, a psalm for the post-genocidal world Celan inhabits, a world in which the Hebrew God Yahweh's unpronounced name presides as "No one" and offers "Nothing." "We" maintain only a defiant vow to live ("bloom") amid the barrenness left in the wake of God's abandonment. The pun on "kneads" (in Felstiner's translation) draws out the cosmic indifference that engulfs us. Upon this world will be imposed "the rule of Nobody," as Max Weber defined bureaucracy, whose watchword is "without regard for persons." We stubbornly subsist in this blighted world nonetheless, almost out of "spite," and so does beauty, orphaned but enduring—the "No-One's-Rose," the "Niemandsrose," the title of Celan's volume. No wonder Celan will say in another text that those who are writing poetry now are "unsheltered even by the traditional tent of the sky, exposed in an unsuspected, terrifying way" as they "carry their existence into language" (*Collected Prose* 35).

In this exposed and forsaken time what is the place—is there a place—for poetry? Celan calls it a "letter in a bottle thrown out to sea," headed if it is lucky "toward something open . . . an approachable you" (35). In 1958 Celan sums up poetry's prospects and outlines the direction his work would take. His summary, quoted below, intersects broadly with Oppen's postwar aesthetic commitments. Striking as the parallels are, even more notable is how different are the bodies of work each man produced:

> No matter how alive [German poetry's] traditions, with most sinister events in its memory, most questionable developments around it, it can no longer speak the language which many willing ears seem to expect. Its language has become more sober, more factual. It distrusts "beauty." It tries to be truthful. . . . It is a "greyer" language, a language which wants to locate even its "musicality" in such a way that it has nothing in common with the "euphony" which more or less blithely continued to sound alongside the greatest horrors.
>
> This language . . . does not transfigure or render "poetical"; it names, it posits, it tries to measure the area of the given and the possible. True, this is never the working of language itself, language as such, but always of an "I" who speaks from the particular angle of reflection which is his existence. . . . Reality is not simply there, it must be searched and won. (*Collected Prose* 15–16)

As he implies above, Celan finds in renunciation the pulse of the poet's aesthetic responsibility to his historical moment. Yet Celan's career commences with a refusal to renounce the language of the Nazis. In an oft-quoted statement he speaks of his choice to write poems in the language through which he came to know death, the language that remained unlost though it "had to go through . . . terrifying silence. . . . It went through. It gave me no words for what was happening, but went through it. Went through and could resurface, 'enriched' by it all" (*Collected Prose* 34). As deliberately as he designs his pen name Celan, he turns his loyalty to the German tongue (not only his mother tongue, but his mother's, who taught him high German and its literature) into an endowment that entangles language, death, silence, and time. The poem "claims the infinite" but does so through time, "not above" it (34). This emphasis on remaining within time is perhaps what Celan meant by language emerging enriched by passing through the war's "terrifying silence." As one commentator has remarked: "Celan may well be suggesting that from language's very mode of remaining or surviving, of *going through* a kind of death, there comes a knowledge of time. . . . Language is 'enriched' by time, but not in the manner of a regeneration or through a dialectical sublation of the 'death' through which it has gone." Rather, "language now offers itself in its historicity and as the ground of a relation that is radically finite" (Fynsk 138–139). Taking up the bloody, mute language soaked in its deathly moment, Celan builds a poetics upon a double renunciation: of "Art, that is the artificial, the faked," which seeks to impose a factitious order and control upon experience, and of art's venerable mandate to be timeless.

Abandoning Art as transcendence, as triumph of order and control, Celan finds a new task for poetry: "The poem estranges. It estranges by its existence," as he writes in notes toward "The Meridian" (*The Meridian* 124, 107). In that address, he enacts this estrangement as subject and strategy by, we will see, repeatedly invoking a particular date—January 20th—until it acquires a haunted status. The bearer of estrangement is what Celan calls the *"Gegenwort,"* the counter-word; and a major translator of Celan, Pierre Joris, has suggested that in the face of Adorno's ban Celan offers his work as a counter-word that implies *"only* poetry is possible after Auschwitz" (qtd. Fynsk 141).

Within his poetics of "estrangement" and "obscurity" the poem takes precarious steps in search of "open, empty, free spaces—we have ventured far out"; indeed he is speaking not of an actual but "the absolute poem," one seen in a "u-topian light" (*Collected Prose* 50–51). In this venturing forth to the no place of utopia, the poems have a companion in silence, which Celan uses with "non-verbal rigor," as Blanchot characterizes it. Celan's silence creates "a void," but one that is "less a lack than a saturation, a void saturated with void" ("The Last" 228). Silence is somehow made visible, an expressive presence. Death—inscribed with his mother's murder—is often the face of silence become visible in language, at times all four—silence, death, language, mother—becoming one. So even in poems of stark brevity framed on a white page certain words ("you" below) are layered like a palimpsest:

> You were my death:
> you I could hold
> while everything slipped from me. (Felstiner, *Paul Celan* 233)

■

As early as 1945 Celan began writing the poem that after his first collection appeared in 1952 would win him international fame—Clement Greenberg translated it in *Commentary*—but whose popularity would torment him. First entitled "Tangoul Mortii" ("Death Tango") and originally published in Bucharest in Romanian, it was then translated by Celan into German and re-named "Todesfuge" ("Death Fugue"). The title referred to the music the SS ordered Jewish musicians to play in the camps to accompany grave digging, torture, and execution. The poem's musicality is built on repetition and, as translated by Felstiner, begins: "Black milk of daybreak we drink it at evening / we drink it at midday and morning we drink it at night / we drink and we drink / we shovel a grave in the air where you won't lie too cramped" (31). In postwar Germany it became a classroom set piece. Rather than evoking horror, some younger students heard it as a nursery rhyme: "A man lives in the house he plays with his vipers he writes / he writes when it grows dark to Deutschland your golden hair / Margareta / he writes it and steps out of doors and the stars are all sparkling / he whistles his hounds to stay close / he whistles his Jews into rows has them shovel a grave in the ground / he commands us play up for the dance" (31). Then: the opening tercet that begins "Black milk of daybreak we drink"—returns, the second of four repetitions. "Death is a master from Germany his eyes are blue," Celan writes. High school seniors, according to a 1957 account by a teacher in a journal of pedagogy, evidently were taught to ignore this fusion of the Aryan nation and destruction and concentrate on another German master. They read the poem as a Bach fugue: "theme . . . countertheme . . . motif . . . repetition . . . variation . . . modulation . . . coda," all worked through so pain would be "purified" into "'forgiveness and reconciliation.'" The journal's editor saw "Todesfuge" as assisting young Germans to "grasp, master, and surmount" the Nazi past (118). Students were not the only ones mesmerized. A critic praised the poem's "lyrical alchemy." Celan was lauded in a prestigious literary review for "mastering" unimaginable horrors "with a few simple paradoxes": for "singing" of atrocity "so that it escapes history's bloody chamber of horrors to rise into the ether of pure poetry." And then the predictable reference to Mallarmé (71, 79).

The cultural politics of this reading are imperative to sketch. In the wake of Nazism, Germany undertook a collective project known as "coming to terms with the past"—*Vergangenheitsbewältigung*—which was pledged to healing the German psyche as well as to facing the past to prevent collective forgetting. The above critic's rhetoric of mastery and transcendence was basic to the pacifying redemptive aspect of this project (79). Hence, against his intentions, Celan found his work enlisted to help ease the horror—a man unappeasably melancholy, hypersensitive to perceived slights, soon suicidally depressed, known to recite "Todesfuge" in a "cold heat," as a listener said of one of his much noted recordings of the poem. Felstiner asks us to "imagine Paul Celan at a newsstand in Paris, seeing 'the words he spoke so as to live' (Celan on Eluard now applied to himself) labeled 'finger exercises.' At least, he would never write another poem like 'Todesfuge.' At best, his credo spoke straight to himself: 'Whichever stone you lift— / you lay bare / those who need the protection of stones . . . / Whichever word you speak— / you owe / to destruction'" (71).

In other words, the jarring reception of "Todesfuge" revealed an unanticipated twist on Adorno's 1949 claim: after Auschwitz, *reception* of poetry can be "barbaric"—when a country desperate for moral renewal converts art into therapy and transfigures pain out of existence, or turns it into a sedative. The fact that Adorno admired "Todesfuge" and grasped its horror did not mitigate the poet's frustration. But the public reaction taught Celan a pivotal aesthetic lesson, contained in what Felstiner calls Celan's "credo"—"Whichever word you speak— / you owe / to destruction." To inscribe your words with the "destruction" wrought by the Nazis is achieved only via renunciation of the beautiful, the musical, the lyrical, even of metaphor, all elements of the "song thrush perspective." By the late fifties he forswore similitude: "No one person is 'like' another; only 'distanced' can my reader understand me" (qtd. 108). By 1960 Celan had found a word for all he renounced: "Art, that is the artificial, the faked, the synthetic, the manufactured." To Art, he counterposes the "human and creaturely" realm of poetry (*The Meridian* 124, 149).

What does "creaturely" poetry that renounces Art sound like? Celan gives us an answer in "Tübingen, January," which commemorates his 1961 visit to the tower by the Neckar river where the mad genius Hölderlin, a hero of Celan's, spent the last thirty-six years of his life, tended by the joiner Zimmer and his family. The poem opens in vertiginous motion, with eyes blinded by the Hölderlin towers that seem to be "floating, gull enswirled" and words refuse to hold fast.

> Visits of drowned joiners to
> these
> plunging words:
>
> Came, if there
> came a man,
> came a man to the world, today, with
> the patriarchs'
> light-beard: he could,
> if he spoke of this
> time, he
> could
> only babble and babble,
> ever- ever-
> moremore.
> ("Pallaksch. Pallaksch.") (qtd. Felstiner, *Paul Celan* 172)

Not only stalled in impotent repetition, words by the poem's end have become terminally opaque, as we conclude with the double dose of "Pallaksch. Pallaksch" confined between parentheses. We must discover for ourselves that these are the nonsense syllables Hölderlin invented, which meant both yes and no, depending on his mood. This final word—these final words—registering a poet's confinement in solitude, locks away speech in the privacy of madness, far from any possibility of translation into intelligibility. "Tübingen, January" neither translates nor transfigures, nor does it poeticize this damaged discourse. Instead, it simply inundates us with an outburst of distressed babbling. The poem neither represents nor refers but incarnates. It is not "about" anything but its own "plunging"—formally and thematically—that unmoors language's anchorage in reference, reducing it to the nonsense of pure sound. Poetry becomes not an art, not mimesis, but a creaturely act in itself, a step, a "turning."

"Tübingen, January" suggests that Hölderlin's unintelligible stammering is a legacy to some contemporary wise man, a bearded Jewish patriarch come to address us. Language, though, defeats this figure of authority: he seems to lack any control over words. In sum, poetry seems impossible "today"—or, more precisely, any poetry founded on eloquence and lyric flights that soar above the earth. The verticality with which the poem commences—gulls and towers—quickly plunges to earth (or into the Neckar) as if dragged down by the gravity of the horizontal, the dead weight of history that mocks any efforts to render history coherently. The poem thus concludes not with the enunciation of a bewildering yet life-generating sacred word triply repeated—say, "The Waste Land's" "Shantih"—but rather with doubly repeated nonsense syllables of a wrecked genius. Deprived of epiphany, and an orienting footnote (which Eliot had provided for the Hindu), Celan's reader dwells in poverty—refused reference, translation, stable meaning.

Celan emphatically denied that the Holocaust defined his literary identity. Instead of making the Nazi genocide their explicit subject, Celan's poems foreground its aftermath, specifically his linguistic and historical plight: the struggle of names and words to survive, to maintain the power of naming and reference. Here is an entire poem, in Celan's late (1967) minimalist mode, as translated by Michael Hamburger:

To stand in the shadow
of the scar up in the air.

To stand-for-no-one-and-nothing.
Unrecognized,
for you
alone.

With all there is room for in that,
even without
language. (Celan, *Poems* 233)

Here the referential struggle of language "to stand" in the "shadow" of pain (memorialized in "the scar")—to signify, bear witness, to maintain the power to communicate, to establish an intimacy between speaker and reader—"for you / alone"—seems to require the negation of reference—"To stand-for-no-one-and-nothing"—and, finally of language: "even without / language." Silence, what is "unrecognized," then, is what holds the possibility of recognition. One hesitates to call it intersubjective recognition, given the isolation of the "you," which is made even more emphatic by the next word. So concentrated is the address to "you / alone" that any context or historical markers are stripped away: the only witness is the "scar," which hangs "in the air" as if a star, part of mute nature. Yet what remains is not sterile anonymity but "room," space, for silent encounter between poet and "you," a hermetic austerity that somehow permits intimacy.

Adorno's 1970 summary description of the poet's extremity remains powerful. He notes that in Celan, "the experiential content of the hermetic is the opposite of what it used to be" (say, in Mallarmé's "totally purified art"). "His poetry is permeated by a sense of shame stemming from the fact that art is unable either to experience or sublimate suffering." (Recall the belatedness of "To stand in the shadow / of the scar up in the air.") Continues Adorno: "Celan's poems articulate unspeakable horror by being silent, thus turning their truth content into a negative quality. They emulate a language that lies below the helpless prattle of human beings—even below the level of organic life as such. It is the language of dead matter, of stones and stars. . . . The language of the lifeless is the only form of comfort in a world where death has lost all meaning" (*Aesthetic Theory* 444). In effect, this explains why Adorno would grant Celan exemption from his edict calling post-Auschwitz poetry barbaric.

Received wisdom tells us that in trying to represent the Holocaust, literature is pushed to the "limits of representation"—"inadequacy . . . assails us in the face of 'Auschwitz,'" notes the historian Saul Friedlander introducing a collection, *Probing the Limits of Representation* (1992) (5). Nazi barbarism not only perpetrated unspeakable horrors on an inconceivable number of innocent people but also eviscerated language, making it an accomplice in enforcing a debased, bureaucratic emptying out of meaning; to now use German for aesthetic ends turns poetry to ash. These familiar literary critical truisms are one thing. Celan's *living* them is another. In his lived experience, rather than being "assailed" by "inadequacy," Celan took it for granted, making it the condition of poetry. The inadequacy of any comprehension of the genocide and the inadequacy of the German language are givens. Note his response to work sent by his friend, the Jewish poet Nelly Sachs, in 1958. He thanks her for raising "all the unanswerable questions in these dark days. This ghastly mute Not-yet, this even ghastlier, muter No-longer and Yet-again, and in between, what cannot be overcome, even tomorrow, even today" (qtd. Felstiner, *Paul Celan* 112). "Unanswerable," "ghastly mute": this is the "'greyer' language"—edging toward "babble"—in which Celan surveys in the most abbreviated fashion the suspended redemption of Jewish suffering (hanging in the "Not-yet"), the Nazi past ("no-longer"), its revivals ("Yet-again"), all hovering against the backdrop of "what cannot be overcome"—because it is the very condition of surviving in this time and place. Sachs, like Celan, had to be hospitalized at times for emotional breakdown. Stressing the *un*-mastered past, "what cannot be overcome," and German's "ghastly" inadequacy, Celan has no room in his ethics or poetics for nationalist redemptive projects. They amount to a collective work of euphemism and Celan's oeuvre is a sustained attack on euphemism in all its oblivion-inducing smoothness (Guyer 338). He would have nodded with recognition at Claude Lanzmann's later claims that understanding the Holocaust is an "obscenity" and incarnation rather than representation describes his own ten-hour documentary *Shoah* (1985).

Immersing himself maximally in estrangement, Celan had moved to Paris in 1948 to commence a literary career in a place where he was unknown, writing in the language of—but refusing to live in—the lethal country where he was gaining a reputation. Gone was the city of his youth, Czernowitz, by 1950 made part of the Ukraine—a city where he had spoken Romanian in school and Yiddish with friends. "It was a region in which people and books were alive," he later remarked of the former Austro-Hungarian province, "which now suffers the fate of existing outside history" (qtd. Olschner 61). In Paris Celan would eventually earn a living at the École Normale Supérieure, where he taught German language and literature. In 1952 Celan married a gifted graphic artist from an aristocratic French Catholic family, Gisèle de

Lestrange. *Nomen est Omen*. His wife's mother, a widow, distressed at the marriage, entered a convent. In her estrangement, she would speak to her daughter and son-in-law only through the iron bars of the convent's grille, an experience that Celan turned into an organizing metaphor of an entire collection, *Sprachgitter* (1959) *(Speech Grille)*. An early poem in it opens: "There will be another eye, / a strange one, beside / our own: unspeaking / under its stony lid" *(Poems* 107).

Celan's biography is a dense web of historical, linguistic, geographical, and familial tumult. I am "one of the last who must live out to the end the destiny of the Jewish spirit in Europe," he said in a 1948 letter, because a poet cannot stop writing "even when he is a Jew and the language of his poems is German" (qtd. Felstiner, *Paul Celan* 57). Dedicated to remaining perpetually unsettled, he built his creative life upon a nomadic "destiny" as a homeless "Jewish spirit" who regards poetry as perpetually "en route." Celan's sense of being "one of the last" suggests he understood his life as an allegory of exile; as he told his friend Yves Bonnefoy: "You are at home in your language, your reference points," among the books, the works you love. "As for me, I am on the outside" (qtd. Bonnefoy, "Paul Celan" 11). To hear some envy or regret in this declared dissonance is apt as long as one makes room for Celan's pride in these words. Like the wanderer Rimbaud, whose "Le bateau ivre" he translated, Celan seemed to disdain most every form of stability and unity. Indeed, the notion of counter-statement, the precious counter-word—the *Gegenwort*—is the anti-definition he offers of poetry in "The Meridian."

Celan's poetry may be notorious for its hermetic obscurity. Like Joyce, he has kept the professors busy for generations, and with no sign of abatement. Unlike Joyce, however, this is not Celan's intention (Derrida 27). Rather, his obscurity, we will see, is in dialectical relation to a nearly opposite motive—an encounter between poem and reader. Multiply uprooted, Celan makes his poems partake of the chaos that constituted his life; hence he constructs them as palimpsests of linguistic echoes, puns, and allusions to a range of personal, biblical, and literary histories. Another layer of imagery has a source in philosophical interests that Celan shared with Heidegger, with whom he had an improbable, ambivalent friendship. Philippe Lacoue-Labarthe goes so far as to claim that "in its entirety" Celan's poetry "is a dialogue with

Heidegger's thought. And essentially with the part of this thought that was a dialogue with Hölderlin's poetry" (33).

Opting to write his poems in German but refusing confinement to its blood-stained legacy, Celan ransacks from a variety of sources—Middle High German as well as Northern and Southern dialectics from Austria—and draws his vocabulary from the natural sciences, botany, ornithology, geology, geography, mineralogy, and medicine. Felstiner, describes Celan's poetry as a "semantic explosion" that "practically crackles with polyglot, heterogeneous formations . . . odd compounds and fractures, disruptive syntax, repeated or truncated syllables, and his arcane, archaic, technical, playful, or neologized German" (*Paul Celan* 171). Critics have noted that Celan is often untranslatable into current ordinary German. At times, no less than eight languages circulate through his work, and at one point Felstiner, while explicating the poem entitled "Radix, Matrix" (root, womb), says: "no amount of ambidexterity can catch the puns that Celan generates" (177). Lacoue-Labarthe observes: "Especially in his late work, prosody and syntax do violence to language: they chop, dislocate, truncate or cut it" (12). Celan leaves upon German, says Derrida, a "scar, a mark, a wound. . . . Within the German language, he welcomed a different kind of German, or other languages, or other cultures, since there is in his writing quite an extraordinary crossing—almost in the genetic sense of the term—of cultures, references, literary memories, always in the mode of extreme condensation, caesura, ellipsis and interruption. . . . He was a migrant himself, and he marked in the thematics of his poetry the movement of crossing borders" (100).

All of this movement amounts to an assault on the purity of the German tongue, cutting against Heidegger's Nazi-inflected fetish of rootedness, the "*volkisch* bond to the homeland," that is the measure by which he judges the superiority of Germany (Bambach xx). Heidegger (disingenuously) professed not to know that Celan was a Jew, indeed a rootless cosmopolitan, to use the codeword for Jews in the discourse of anti-Semitic nationalism. Only after his 1967 meeting with Heidegger did Celan realize that the philosopher would fail to deliver on his private pledge to the poet to make himself publicly accountable regarding his Nazi past—"a hope, today, / for a thinker's / (un- / delayed coming) word"—as Celan had optimistically put it in the first version of

"Todtnauberg," his poem about their visit (Felstiner, *Paul Celan* 246).
Celan believed that such a disclosure might have helped discourage
rising neo-Nazism in Germany (Lyon 202, 178). The poet grew despair-
ing after the visit (as Lacoue-Labarthe was told by more than one friend
of Celan's) (94). In later versions of the poem he deleted "un / delayed,"
a gesture of (futile) patience that comports with the fact that, as James
Lyon points out, Celan did not break with Heidegger but instead met
him several more times, including a month before his suicide. Found
on Celan's desk after his death was the draft of an unsent letter to
Heidegger that read, in part, "that through your attitude, your posture,
you are weakening decisively what poetry is . . . and what thought is, in
their ardent urge, both of them, toward responsibility" (qtd.Felstiner,
"The One and Only Circle"). By not uttering the "coming word" (an
allusion to Hölderlin), instead taking refuge in silence, Heidegger refuses to be answerable. Such evasiveness casts incriminating light on
the philosopher's reverence for the silence of what is "without why."

The great energizing paradox of Celan's poetic enterprise is its entwinement of apparently opposite motives: it "demands the risk" of
hermeticism and obscurity not for the purpose of alienating the reader
but rather "for the sake of an encounter": indeed "this obscurity has
been bestowed on poetry" so that the encounter might occur and is
a "mark of attention—even respect—with regard to the encounter"
(*Collected Prose* 46; Lacoue-Labarthe 56–57). Celan always denied his
poetry was hermetic. Typically, though, he gave the word his own idiosyncratic meaning: in notes prepared for "The Meridian," he writes:
"hermeticism, today: to close oneself to the [conventional] [compro-
mised] 'beautiful,' in order to open up to something true. . . . I would
speak here of hope; the poem 'tests the wind' . . . like the hunted creature" (*The Meridian* 149). Thus the hermetic, for Celan, involves a
two-step move, closing down art for the sake of opening to poetry.

If one does not perceive the whole circuit, the hermetic can seem a
dead end or even an expression of a "pre-suicide, a not-wanting-to-be,
a flight from the world," as Primo Levi has described his response to
Celan's "obscurity." Levi grants that it reflects neither contempt for

the reader, inadequacy, nor laziness. Rather, Celan's obscurity, writes Levi, "truly is a reflection of the obscurity of his fate and his generation, and it grows ever denser around the reader, gripping him as in an ice-cold iron vise." Commencing with "the raw lucidity" of "Death Fugue" this "darkness grows from page to page [of Celan's oeuvre] until the last inarticulate babble consternates like the rattle of a dying man, and that is just what it is." Celan wrote as though he were alone, dying. But "as long as we live," says Levi, we are not alone and "we have a responsibility: we must answer for what we write . . . and make sure every word reaches its target" (173–174).

Likely, Celan would have agreed about "responsibility"—note his rebuke of Heidegger above—but would construe it in a way nearly opposite from Levi's. In a remark that might have pleased, if surprised the chemist, whose commitment to reference ("every word reaches its target") convicts Celan of babbling, the poet states that "poems are not first of all written records"; "poems are also gifts—gifts to the attentive" (*The Meridian* 76; *Collected Prose* 26). This is the second step—the opening of the hermetic. "The attentiveness of the reader: a turning-toward the poem" is affirmed in the fact that a poem pays attention "to all that it encounters . . . by a kind of concentration mindful of all our dates. 'Attention,' if you allow me a quote from Malebranche via Walter Benjamin's essay on Kafka, 'attention is the natural prayer of the soul'" (*Collected Prose* 50). Today, though, "instead of real responsibility" we have "cultural busy-ness rather than simple attentiveness" (*The Meridian* 169).

As "The Meridian" discloses, Celan does not simply honor but tests our capacity to be attentive; or rather he exposes its limits as the very basis of an encounter. His logic seems to be that if transparency reigned, "strangeness and distance" would be banished and with them the possibility of the poem's hopes "to speak on behalf of the *strange . . . on behalf of the other*, who knows, perhaps of an *altogether other*" (*Collected Prose* 48). He stresses *"the mystery of encounter"* (49). To enact this mystery the poem must be resistant; Celan will speak of its "darkness" and "thingness." Adorno imparts this logic in another context. Critiquing the esteem and demand for unconditional intimacy, he notes that "retention of strangeness is the only antidote to estrangement" (*Minima* 94).

■

Celan estranges attentiveness at the very moment he affirms it. Here is one audacious instance at the heart of "The Meridian." When he remarks that "attention" is achieved "by a kind of concentration mindful of all our dates," this phrase looks back to two earlier moments in the address. "Perhaps we can say that every poem is marked by its own '20th of January'? Perhaps the newness of poems written today is that they try most plainly to be mindful of this kind of date" (*Collected Prose* 47). In turn, this allusion to January 20th refers to a slightly earlier passage that quotes the opening of Georg Büchner's novella *Lenz* (based on Jakob Michael Reinhold Lenz (1751–1792), student of Kant's, obsessive emulator and "fan" of Goethe, chief dramatist of the *Sturm und Drang*, and sufferer of schizophrenia who eventually died insane). *Lenz* begins: "On the 20th of January" Lenz "was walking through the mountains" (46). It happens that "to be mindful of this kind of date" involves more than an allusion to *Lenz:* "20th of January" is also the date of the Wannsee Conference in 1942 when Nazi leadership convened to complete planning for the "final solution." But nowhere does "The Meridian" identify this reference. An editor noted it in preparing for publication some 314 pages of preliminary notes and drafts, typed and handwritten, from which Celan had distilled "The Meridian," a lecture of less than twenty pages. The archive was first published in 1999. What is Celan's point in using the *Lenz* "January 20th" as a placeholder, from which emanates a ghostly reference that by 1960 would be caught only by a handful of listeners?

The nearly invisible Nazi referent for "January 20" seems to possess a status even more fugitive than a claim Celan makes in a draft note for "The Meridian": "the poem is untranslatable." However, he cancels (places a line through) "untranslatable," graphically rendering its double status: here/not here (74). The Wannsee "January 20" doesn't even reach this level of flickering ambiguity. It remains "untranslatable," or, more precisely, deliberately so. Yet, especially as "The Meridian" draws to a close, Celan cannot stop hinting at its presence just out of reach. It hovers and beckons in the text of the address. Celan recalls another Büchner work, one he finds "full of words which seem to smile through invisible quotation marks," words that act like "rabbit's ears, that is, something that listens, not without fear, for something beyond itself, beyond words" (54). This image of alarmed animal alertness, attuned to possible danger "beyond words," comments obliquely on what is present obliquely—the mute presence of the Nazi reference. "Beyond words": but between the lines. Recall that, like the rabbit, the poem "'tests the wind' . . . like the hunted creature" (*The Meridian* 149).

Celan continues this indirection as he suddenly decides to conduct "a bit of topological research" on "the region from which hail" the pioneering editor of Büchner's complete works, as well as the historical Lenz. I have met both of them, he says, "on my way here and in Büchner's work. I am also, since I am again at my point of departure, searching for my own place of origin. I am looking for all this with my imprecise, because nervous, finger on a map—a child's map, I must admit. None of these places can be found. They do not exist. But I know where they ought to exist, especially now" (*Collected Prose* 54). His nervousness connects him to the uneasy rabbit scenting danger. Then Celan announces what he does find on the map: the "consoling" image of a meridian, what encircles the globe and—like poetry—binds and connects.

The appearance of the embracing meridian does not erase the image of the poet as anxious child, searching in vain for his "place of origin" on his painfully out-of-date child's map, a map made irrelevant by the history set in motion at a meeting on January 20, 1942, six months prior to his parents' seizure. This silent history bears on a cluster of interlocked claims made late in "The Meridian" about poetry's precariousness: that "the poem today . . . clearly shows a strong tendency towards silence," that the poem "stands fast at the edge of itself" (in Felstiner's version), enduring by constantly calling "itself back from an 'already-no-more' into a 'still here,'" and that the "poem is lonely. . . . Its author stays with it. Does this very fact not place the poem already here, at its inception, in the encounter, *in the mystery of an encounter?*" (*Collected Prose* 48–49). Creating part of that "mystery" is Celan's keeping the Wannsee Conference to himself, so to speak, as a private reference—present but off-stage.

Celan's insistence on "obscurity" in effect enacts his conviction that poetry is indifferent to art's established norms, conventions, or rules—for instance, making "sure every word reaches its target" (Levi). Rather than goal-directed, poetry is "language actualized, set free un- der the sign of a radical individuation which, however, remains as aware of the limits drawn by language as of the possibilities it opens" (*Collected Prose* 49). At once limit and possibility, the "final solution" hovers about the edges of "The Meridian." As do other unsaid possi- bilities. The exiled Jewish literary figures that Celan weaves unobtru- sively into his address—Benjamin, Kafka, Lev Shestov among them— constitute a gallery of guardian angels that form an implicit literary counter-history to the German canon circa 1960. In this inferential context the "20th of January" Wannsee reference takes its place as a silent pledge of fidelity to historical specificity—the doomed fate of the European Jews. From this "origin" the poems of Celan spring. Such a pledge at last makes sense of a Celan remark: "Perhaps the newness of poems written today is that they try most plainly to be mindful of this kind of date? But do we not all write from and toward some such date? What else could we claim as our origin?" (47).

The Wannsee silence begs comparison with "'Pallaksch. Pallaksch,'" the opaque piece of language that concludes "Tübingen, January." It is a word that mocks the possibility of stable reference. Hölderlin's arbitrary sign—his way of saying yes/no—functions as a kind of meta-obscurity, a laying bare of Celan's refusal to identify it, an exposure of his *not* making a connection that would dispel obscurity and permit "every word" to "reach its target." In sum, "'Pallaksch. Pallaksch'" is less a "lack" than "a void saturated with void," to re- call Blanchot. Whereas the Wannsee referent of "January 20th" is only a distant reverberation, heard by the rabbit's anxious ears and felt by the poet's shaking finger on his old map. The shadowy status of "January 20th"—the date commemorates a wounding, as if projecting "the shadow/ of the scar up in the air" bearing witness—is bereft of full or accessible presence . "There is no transparency," Celan once remarked. "Things, words have a thickness, a density, also a shadow" (qtd. Daive, *Under the Dome* 117). Hence, to respect the reality of this "shadow" world requires we respond with something akin to "free" or "ex-posed" understanding (in Hamacher's sense cited earlier), that is, a "turning toward" silence, for then "something is 'understood' . . . only because it is not 'understood'" (Hamacher 21, 10). As Celan wrote in an early poem: he "Speaks true who speaks shadow" (qtd. Felstiner *Paul Celan* 80).

The "unsaid" of "January 20th" insures the opacity and presence of the Other—which Celan deems crucial: from it emanates the "mystery" or secret at the heart of encounter. Yet why does encounter require mystery, beyond the salutary retention of strangeness and distance noted above? A response might begin with a remark of Celan's from 1960: "We live under dark skies and—there are few human beings. Hence, I assume, so few poems. The hopes I have left are small. I try to hold on to what remains" (*Collected Prose* 26). What remains is the precarious freedom "in the here and now of the poem—and the poem has only this one, unique, momentary present." The poem embodies an "'open' question 'without resolution,' a question which points towards open, empty, free spaces" (50). Yet this openness is not unconditional; it coexists with what is "most" the poem's "own: its time." Here "January 20th" becomes again pertinent but differently. While one understanding of the date's mystery and opacity relies on its *unsaid* qualities—what we have just seen—another, equally vital understanding relies on what was *said* on "January 20th" in Wannsee.

To grasp what poetry's fragile openness is up against, what shadows it, indeed what (de)forms it at and from birth, we must remember "its time" as measured by having survived "through the thousand darknesses of murderous speech." That linguistic darkness includes the deadly ambitions hiding in plain sight in that antiseptic phrase "the final solution." With this "murderous" euphemism, the destruction of millions is ordained, as Nazi plans are formalized at a brisk meeting in late January. Celan's "January 20th" was, analogously, hiding its own lethal meanings in plain sight (or hearing) of the audience of "The Meridian." This disturbing analogy is one way Celan in his 1960 address stages—exposes and defers—the "lack of answers," the "terrifying silence," the darkness of deadly speech that is "January 20th"— what is "most its own: its time."

Though he refused to live in Germany, Celan, as we know, became entangled against his will in its postwar project to face and overcome its past. This nationalist effort ignited the state's political and cultural ambitions for formal mastery and control, triggering zeal to arrest and classify meaning. Horror was heard as nursery rhyme. Celan, as noted earlier, regarded what happened to "Todesfuge" as a desecration of his mother's grave. It taught Celan to set poetry against final solutions in any form, including and especially bureaucracy's identity principle of the fungible. After "Todesfuge," his poetry will refuse the lethal euphemisms manufactured by the assimilative machinery of the state apparatus. Celan states it this way: "The poem estranges. It estranges by its existence, by the mode of its existence, it stands opposite and against one, voiceful and voiceless simultaneously" (*The Meridian* 107). What drives his poetry is its constitutive negativity, its non-identity: that to be itself is always to be other than it is. Poetry fulfills its estranging function by at once invoking and rendering ghostly the ghastly "January 20th" with its declaration of the deadly definitive.

The commitment to estrangement—of being against—is the imperative to be "a word against the grain," what Celan, as noted above, calls a *Gegenwort*. This describes the function of poetry (40, 52). Powerful poetry breaks the closed circuit of identity, is always exceeding the familiar rhetorical and formal trappings of art, and instead acts as a "counter-word," a "counterstatement" (*Collected Prose* 40). Poetry, for Celan, "preserves for itself the darkness of the 'illegitimate'; it presents itself without references, without indications" (*The Meridian* 85). Abiding in estrangement and seeking to estrange, it takes us by surprise and takes away our breath. Near the end of "The Meridian" Celan finds in Büchner's play *Danton's Death* a (necessarily) improbable appearance of poetry as *Gegenwort*. After flowery speeches rich in "artful, resonant words" at the base of the guillotine by Danton, an early architect of the French Revolution, and by Danton's fellow revolutionaries—who are being executed, victims of the reign of terror—amid this theatrical eloquence, "here Lucile, [wife of a fellow revolutionary] who is blind against art, Lucile for whom language is tangible and like a person, Lucile is suddenly there with her 'Long live the king!'" She is seized at once and led away. Lucile here appropriates a royalist slogan as a suicidal act. (Evidently this mode of self-destruction was not unheard of in its day.) "True, it sounds . . . at first like allegiance to the 'ancien regime.' But it is not," Celan assures us (*Collected Prose* 40). "This is not homage to any monarchy, to any yesterday worth preserving. It is homage to the majesty of the absurd, which bespeaks the presence of human beings. This, ladies and gentlemen, has no definitive name, but I believe that this is . . . poetry" (40). In sum: an artless person utters an inexplicable piece of language at a moment that insures her doom: in these maximally unpropitious circumstances—summed up as "the majesty of the absurd"—Celan discovers poetry.

"After all these" eloquent "words on the platform (the guillotine, mind you)—what a word!" From Lucile, the unfathomable erupts—an ungraspable "word against the grain" bursts forth, beholden to no authority, neither speaker nor poet, nor any other external source. Neither representation nor essence but an uncanny event, it eludes expectations and context, defies interpretive efforts to pin down its meaning. For who knows what motivates Lucile's "Long live the king!"—is it insight, insanity, solidarity? Unanchored to any clear intention, her phrase empties language of transparency. Its yes/no flickers as illegibly as "'Pallaksch. Pallaksch.'" Improbable, vulnerable, unknowable, abandoning logic and meaning, the words of Lucile are a performative possessed of suicidal force, therefore "an act of freedom. It is a step" (40). Hence, in its very absurdity, it is breathtaking. Poetry is a turn of breath, an "atemwende" (breath-turn) (47).

In evoking while estranging a familiar political phrase, Lucile the proto-poet can be said, borrowing Celan's terms, to "darken" her words, to make them a "thing," i.e. what is "not transfigured, not heightened, not dipped into a symbolic vagueness—but looked at" (The Meridian 148). As a phenomenal "thing" impervious to hermeneutic probing or to assimilation, it is not to be recoded, for instance, as counter-revolutionary political discourse. "Long live the king!" is an existential commitment that "bears witness to mankind's here and now," what Celan calls "the majesty of the absurd" (Jerry Glenn translation (175). Derrida points out that in German the "majesty of the present" is Gegenwart and that "this Gegenwort speaks in favor of the majesty of the Gegenwart" (116). He attends as well to Celan's use of "majesty" as subverting conventional notions of political rule or sovereignty; "there is something 'more majestic' than the majesty of the King," "more sovereign and otherwise sovereign, the majesty of poetry, or the majesty of the absurd insofar as it bears witness to human presence." To embrace the absurd is to embrace faith—"faith in poetry as faith in God, here in the majesty of the present" (117). The poet's faith is reflected in his careful qualification—that the meaning of Lucile's words escapes a "definitive name," but "I believe" they are "poetry." A poem asks of its reader to make a leap of faith: "the image has a phenomenal trait, intuitively recognizable—What separates you from it, you will not bridge; you have to make up your mind to jump" (*The Meridian* 74).

Two years after Celan's fatal jump into the Seine in 1970, Bonnefoy remarked: "I believe Paul Celan chose to die as he did so that once, at least . . . words and what is might join. In fact, we can say of Celan as of no other poet: 'his words did not recover his experience.'" ("Paul Celan" 9). Consider Celan's basic equations: "The darkness of the poem = the darkness of death. The humans = the mortals. Therefore the poem, remaining mindful of death, counts among the most human side of man" (*The Meridian* 89). True to the logic of his meridian image, death joins with life to complete "the human side of man." Celan's poems are equipment for living: in an unsent letter to René Char he says never forget that "poetry is something one breathes; that poetry breathes you in" (qtd. *Selections*, "Letter #3" 184). "Poems are *sketches for existence:* one has to live them, for the sake of their truth" (*The Meridian* 120). Recall Celan's quoting of Whitman's "this is no book, / Who touches this touches a man."

Part 8

AGNES MARTIN WOULD likely be receptive to Celan's and Whitman's imperative of intimacy—not merely to write but to live one's art while embracing the reader. "The life of the work depends upon the observer," she says (qtd. Glimcher 63). Yet dependency and intimacy are hardly words that one associates with this flinty isolata whose signature stance was "with my back to the world." The only outward drama and mystery in Martin's life involves an act of renunciation: in the summer of 1967, a week after Ad Reinhardt's death, in the midst of a flourishing career, she left New York without explanation; she gave away her art supplies and tools and traveled around Canada and the Far West for eighteen months. Martin would not resume painting for seven years, after settling on top of a mesa in New Mexico and becoming a desert recluse until her death at ninety-two in 2004. The last member of the Abstract Expressionist generation, born the same year as Jackson Pollock and a year before her mentor and friend, Reinhardt, Martin outlived both by many decades. Her career was slow in taking off, gaining momentum by the late fifties and early sixties. Until the move west her paintings had largely combined drawn grids on painted neutral monochrome fields; afterward she also filled canvases with bands and stripes of pale tonalities of pink and blue and green.

By 1993 she was dubbed "the most famous unknown artist in America." Two decades later this paradox has been retired, for now Martin has become—no surprise—a brand, an art world "truism verging on cliché": the beloved cranky visionary hermit, a self-sacrificing feminist heroine "renewed through the crucible of renunciation": this is the Agnes Martin constructed by the critics and by her own gnomic utterances (Eisler 70; Hudson 120). On an art tour of Santa Fe the literary critic Terry Castle invoked Martin in 2010 as a "private talisman, my anti-O'Keefe" and with all due respect dubbed her "the ultimate Connoisseur's Good Taste Vaccine" (135). For an artist committed to self-abnegation and an abhorrence of prestige, her new fame and iconic status are ironies that prove yet again the enduring public fascination with renunciation narratives.

Though in life Martin minimized dependency and kept her distance, believing solitude the way to clear the mind, she was as determined as Celan and Whitman to make aesthetic experience grip the beholder. Yet while the poets describe a tactile bond, Martin seeks "abstract response"—"infinite, dimensionless"—by which she means reproducing in the viewer something of the "mystery of beauty" and "sublimity of reality" that the painter first feels in her mind in the "retreat" of her studio as she "pursues the truth relentlessly" (*Writings* 93, 95). "Interruptions are disasters" because they spoil the freedom of "abstract response" by letting the "concrete environment" intrude with its hungers and "yearning." Martin was known to not eat (or would gobble food) while painting for hours on end, so intent was she to remain in the flow of "abstract response": "to hold on to the 'silver cord', that is the artistic discipline" (93). The "manipulation of materials in art work is a result of this state of mind" of unbroken intensity, which she calls "complete consciousness" (95). That state of heightened awareness of feeling is always "present to us" but we "reject it" in order to express our "ideas" and "prejudices," distractions that, like our unavoidable appetites, diminish "response." We grow "blissfully aware" when we are willing to "relinquish our ideas in favor of response" (*Writings* 95).

Martin affiliates with Whitman, apostle of openness, when she ends her best-known essay-poem "The Untroubled Mind" (1972) with a Whitmanesque dismissal of hierarchy: "The wiggle of a worm as important as the assassination of a / president" (44). Earlier she had invoked another pantheist, William Blake: "Blake's right about there's no difference / between the whole thing / and one thing" (alluding to his "To See a World in a Grain of Sand"). "When your eyes are open / you see beauty in anything" (40). Too often though eyes are closed to beauty, absorbed instead by pride and ambition. After all, "The ideal in America is the natural man / The conqueror, the one that can accumulate / The one who overcomes disadvantages, strength, courage" (37). To this cultural "ideal" she responds: "My painting is about impotence" (40). "Impotence" short-circuits this nationalist rhetoric of virile power and is her idiosyncratic way of putting what "these paintings are about"—"freedom from the cares of this world / from worldliness" (39). Freedom from the worldly involves acknowledgment that "we are ineffectual," that we routinely live with "failure" and "helplessness" (116), which, after they run their course, prove salutary as the discipline of defeat, a basis of ridding the ego of pride. Pride's anxious aggression might also ease if it stepped back to take a larger perspective than pursuit of self-interest. Then the prideful might see that while "We seem to be winning and losing, / but in reality there is no losing. . . . There is only the all of the all / everything is that / every infinitesimal thought and action is part and parcel of / a wonderful victory" (44).

It is tempting to dismiss her cosmic optimism, as some have, as "New Age effluvia of a Zen that eschewed the ego" and tacitly reliant on a brand of feminism built on binaries (Hudson 120). Martin was not, however, a proponent of a body of knowledge or doctrine—feminist or religious. Such advocacy would be at cross-purposes with the "un-learning" needed "so that one can be led by Tao / Be a child of Tao" (Chuang Tzu 133). A lifelong reader of Buddhism, mystic Christianity, and Taoism (particularly Lao-tzu and Chuang Tzu, whose line "free and easy wandering" she quotes), Martin attended Suzuki's Columbia seminar in the early fifties (*Writings* 71). She practiced daily medita-tion and her spiritual sensibility, nurtured from a variety of sources, dismissed concepts, categories, classifications, and deductions as "dis-tractions of mind that we wish to hold free for inspiration" (*Writings* 153). When Jill Johnston asked her if being a woman artist had made it hard to gain a reputation, Martin replied, "I'm not a woman and I don't care about reputations" (qtd. Crimp 71). This refusal of gender assignments and dismissal of ambition was more of what she meant by "freedom from the cares of this world." Like a fictional counterpart, Seymour Glass, she believed in reincarnation, another mode of de-tachment. So, from the perspective of eternity, gender was an illusion. Martin spent a lot of time doing what Wittgenstein called the "ter-ribly hard work" of dismantling "the edifice of your pride." She made millions of dollars but never owned any property because she found the pride of ownership intolerable. She told her dealer and friend Arne Glimcher not to *sell* her work but if someone wanted to buy, he should let them. She loathed what she called "reputation art" and the "pres-tige buyers" who acquired it (Glimcher 103). She refused awards or honorary degrees because she did not feel "responsible" for her paint-ing; she was simply a medium—the "locus" is her word—obeying the voices in her head. She called this obedience "inspiration." There is some justice in the remark that "John Cage talked a lot about silence, but Agnes Martin lived it" (Baas 214)

"That one can conjunct making a painting and making a life struck me as an achievement of Agnes Martin early on," remarked her friend, the artist Richard Tuttle, after her death (qtd. Zegher and Teicher 155). Both makings thrive on the fullness of emptiness. "Unattached," "un-subjective," "abstract": these values underwrite the continuity of her life and art. The hinge joining these realms is a clarified understanding of inspiration, which pivots on renunciation and detachment: "What you do is get rid of everything / freedom from ideas and responsibil-ity / If you live by inspiration then you do what comes to you / you

can't live the moral life, you have to obey destiny / you can't live the
inspired life and live the conventions / you can't make promises / The
future's a blank page" (*Writings* 38). Solitude is essential, as Kafka
knew, and is synonymous with a freedom that entails erasure of self
and others: "Others do not really exist in solitude, I do not exist / no
thinking of others even when they are there, no interruption / a mystic
and a solitary person are the same" (42). She is careful to insist that
there is "nothing religious"—she was not a believer in Christianity—
in her mode of being nor is it a source of privileged revelation; "being
detached and impersonal" is available to any of us (40, 38).

Above all, for Martin, to live the inspired life meant making her
life and art an intimate unity grounded in an ethic of humility, though
"ethic" is too regulatory, too much a deliberate project, given that,
as she said above, "you can't live the moral life." The *practice* of humility is more precise, though the practice is as "empty" as Eckhart
would envision. In a short poem she writes of "Humility, the beautiful daughter / She cannot do either right or wrong / She does not do
anything / All of her ways are empty / Infinitely light and delicate"
(qtd. Glimcher 48). Humility obviously personifies the Zen ideal
of an empty mind. Absence of ego and aggression creates a psychic
"lightness" which Martin often calls happiness, innocence, and beauty—the "sublimity of reality" (*Writings* 93). The artist "tries to live
in a way" that will make possible "greater awareness" of lightness
and happiness; her canvases achieve lightness by a commitment to
"formlessness, breaking down form" (7). On a visual level, the contrast to the darkness of Reinhardt's late work and its effect on viewers is stark. Where Reinhardt roiled spectators, his blackness read as
indifference to understanding, Martin's radiant serenity is closer to
her friend Newman's desire to affirm the beholder's sense of place in
the "now." On another, mystical level, one of which Reinhardt and
Martin might well have been aware, the polarity dissolves in the Black
Light or Luminous Night of the Sufis: a glaring white light blacks out
everything, as God's nearness renders all else invisible. Merton once
referred to "Ad Reinhardt the Sufi . . . the constant black white that is
like Reinhardt" (*When Prophecy* 261).

Martin's empty paintings, at once intricate and simple, are void of
figuration, curves, objects, and organic shapes of any kind. Yet there is

tension. Martin cultivates it by employing a square frame but only to soften what she finds is this shape's intrinsic harshness: "My formats are square, but the grids never are absolutely square; they are rectangles, a little bit off the square, making a sort of contradiction, a dissonance. . . . When I cover the square surface with rectangles, it lightens the weight of the square, destroys its power" (*Writings* 29). The grid introduces another tension. Although obviously "antinatural" (as Rosalind Krauss describes it), an icon of bureaucratic rationality, the grid first appeared to Martin as a "tree" (other times as blades of grass) bathed in "innocence." For one thing, it eliminates hierarchy and the fetish of difference. The oddity of her conjoining of grid and innocence is dispelled when one recalls other counter-intuitive uses of the grid; for Mondrian and Malevich, notes Krauss, "the grid is a staircase to the Universal," as it becomes for Reinhardt: recall his cruciform grids within the black paintings (Krauss, "Grids" 52).

By overlaying her hand-penciled grid of horizontal and vertical lines, making thousands of tiny rectangles (she used a ruler or string) on the canvas, Martin allows her colors to avoid the homogenous uniformity of the monochrome often achieved with a spray gun or roller. The result is that her pale grayish, bluish, whitish, reddish colors float rather than assert. From the middle distance her canvases can seem majestic graph paper and from afar the grids disappear into opacity. Close up we see the tactile materiality of her medium—often linen fabric canvas is the support; its uneven rough texture is more responsive to touch and to encouraging irregular graphite lines than is the slick flatness of paper or fiberboard. Tactility is her priority, attested to by her fingerprints left at the painting's edges (Rosenberger 104, 107). Occasionally she varies the thickness of paint, and sometimes she places a field of wash under the grid; this destabilizing of the surface achieves a depth of field that injects dynamism. The canvas seems to vibrate, its color in elusive motion, appearing differently when one is close up versus at a distance.

The result can be hypnotic. "Once you are caught in one of her paintings," said Kasha Linville in a landmark 1971 essay, "it is an almost painful effort to pull back from the private experience she triggers to examine the way the picture is made" (qtd. Crimp 67). Another critic (Peter Schjeldahl) accepts being "caught" as the point: "My analytic faculties, after trying to conclude that I am looking at one thing or another, give up, and my mind collapses into a momentary engulfing state that is either 'spiritual' or nameless" (qtd. Rosenberger 104). Anne Wagner puts it this way: "In some basic sense, a Martin painting can never really be seen in its entirety. There is no vantage point from which to take it in. . . . A painting by Martin will not—cannot—be seen as a unified presence, an impregnable whole. Instead, the work goes on undoing itself" ("The Cause" 234).

Martin acknowledges motion but less as elusiveness than as serene flow; she compares the subdued open expanses of her canvases to the ocean: "You wouldn't think of form by the ocean. You can go in if you don't encounter anything. A world without objects, without interruption, making a work without interruption or obstacle. It is to accept the necessity of the simple direct going into a field of vision" (*Writings* 7). Rather than a passive, detached gaze at a static object, looking at her work requires an entering into, a going, and she invites the viewer to join this process. Martin builds this sharing into her sense of perception: "*Perceiving* is the same as *receiving* and it is the same as *responding*. Perception means all of them. . . . Perception is a function. A function is part of a process. It does not identify. We are not identified by perception" (89). To identify is a defensive maneuver, an effort to fix and resolve, offering the mind a specious clarity by fastening a label on the perceived. Identifying is a mark of anxious thinking; "it compares everything" rather than receiving and responding (89). Imposing concepts, the work of thought is impatient with the unbidden happening of "inspiration"; hence reliance on the intellect "leads to pride, identification, confusion and fear" (90). Martin's train of thought here is distinctly Jamesian. James summarizes how from the "perceptual flux" of "this aboriginal sensible muchness, attention carves out objects, which conception then names and identifies forever" (*Writings* 2:1008). A likely mediator of James's thinking to Martin was Dewey's *Art as Experience,* which she encountered as a student at Columbia Teachers College in 1941 and a decade later when she returned for a graduate degree and also took Suzuki's class (Baas 214).

Martin is "interested in experience that is wordless and silent, and in the fact that this experience can be expressed for me in artwork which is also wordless and silent" (*Writings* 89). In other words, she would agree with Wittgenstein that ethics and aesthetics are what can be shown, enacted, but not talked about. Yet like Reinhardt with his garrulous pleas for the purity of "art as art," Martin surrounds her self-effacing art with commentary. Her statements are unabashedly prescriptive; immune to the modernist allergy to "meaning" or "about-ness," indifferent to establishing pristine autonomy, she tells you how to approach her art, what truth it attests to. Doesn't all this guidance violate Zen's esteem of the ineffable? One critic thinks her prose preachy, "vastly more Western, even dogmatic, than its Zen trimmings would suggest. . . . Zen holds fast to a notion that while insight may be learned it cannot be straightforwardly taught." But Martin's "oracular" "proclamations" ignore this; her "rhetoric of humility and egolessness" turns out to be merely that (Katz 179–180).

Yet this assessment is built on a misassumption that Martin means her statements as Zen teachings. She never mentions the word "Zen" and has no mandate to promulgate it. Her idiom and ideas are her own homegrown concoction of Eastern thought, Greek idealism, the Emersonian tradition, and Calvinism (her beloved grandfather's creed) that fed her obsession with the blindness inflicted by pride and the redemption found in obeying inspiration. After interviewing her, one critic called Martin an "austere and primitive" presence, elemental qualities that comport with her conviction in ancient ideas of fate and necessity, what she calls "destiny" (Gruen 77). Martin says destiny is "like a dignified journey with no trouble and no goal on and on" (Writings 43). This image and the words animating it summon the pre-determined form of the grid, the baseline upon which she conjured the sublime. Assent to necessity—which evacuates the ego's delusions of responsibility—explains her dislike of the centrality of chance in the work of her fellow Suzuki seminarian John Cage (Mansoor 160). Like Emerson at the end of "Fate," Martin "build[s] to the Beautiful Necessity . . . which rudely or softly educates" us "to the perception that there are no contingencies; that Law rules throughout existence . . . not personal nor impersonal,—it disdains words and passes under-standing; it dissolves persons; it vivifies nature; yet solicits the pure in heart to draw on all its omnipotence" (Essays 967–968).

Whatever one thinks of Martin's prose, it works as a kind of ver-bal hum that starkly sets off the austerity of the artifact. In other words, her statements set a context or atmosphere for reception and response without preempting the force of an encounter with her painting. That encounter asks that we surrender to the inwardness of feeling that her art communicates, as she suggests in her comment about a suite of thirty screenprints of gray-lined grids entitled *On a Clear Day*. She made them in 1974 as a return to art after her seven-year hiatus. Abstract art "holds meaning for us that is beyond expression in words. These prints express innocence of mind. If you can go with them and hold your mind as empty and tranquil as they are and recognize your feelings at the same time you will realize your full responses to this work" (qtd. Glimcher 60). "If you can go with them" enables the mimetic reciprocity that makes the viewer a participant: "When you have inspiration and represent inspiration / The observer makes the painting. . . . If there's life in the composition it stimulates your life movements" (*Writings* 36).

When we stay within the "abstract response," undistracted by the solicitations of the "concrete," we are "blissfully aware" (95). The awareness is bliss because it is free of the urge to identify. Hence Martin fiercely denied that her stripes and bands of pink and blue washes made any external reference, be it the wheat fields of her native Saskatchewan or the vast New Mexico sky and light. Her denial was loyal to Reinhardt's ban on reference. At other times, though, she granted that the vastness of western space had gotten into her paintings. Arne Glimcher made what he saw as an "irresistible" association visiting her studio when the sun was setting and beginning to turn pink: "the space and color in the paintings seems to have slipped down from the sky" (77). Certainly many of her titles, at least early in the sixties, invoked nature: *Night Sea, Flower in the Wind, The Beach*. Limitless meadows and water seem incarnated in these images of flowing, exultant tranquility: the "concealed landscapes of the 'abstract sublime'" (Krauss "Agnes Martin" 85). This smacks of romantic nostalgia—and at odds with her commitment to classicism (sketched below)—to some critics (Krauss and others) who reject it but at the price of making Martin's paintings purely self-referential semiological systems. James Elkins splits the difference: he finds the paintings peaceful but also "*about* the strain of moving away from landscape, toward abstraction, and back again." He calls his "wavering indecision about what" he is seeing "a failed sublime or truncated sublime" (*Six Stories* 40, 43).

Sublime or not, *Night Sea* is particularly compelling, a "shimmering golden grid that seemed to hover above a velvety blue ground," as Benita Eisler described it (71). Yet as an expert on Martin's technique points out, "the ground of the painting is not blue but white," comprising "titanium, lead and zinc pigments" to "provide a more reflective surface." Upon the white ground of *Night Sea*, Martin "painted a highly reflective coat of blue paint. She devised a grid of 2,976 rectangles on the blue paint, each individually colored with a flat, matte-sea-green paint. The artist then reinforced the grid lines with gold leaf." By using two different paints Martin "creates greater chromatic depth" and the "brightness of the white ground illuminates the painting from within, providing the luminosity—'the shimmer'—to which Eisler responded" (Rosenberger 107–108).

Martin never discussed technique, concerned perhaps that it might eclipse her emphasis on the spiritual, yet her technical virtuosity involved a casting off of the self of greed and pride, enabling absorbed manipulation of art materials. This state was at once impersonal, yet also, to be effective, required "awareness" of one's own state of mind. Once aware she can then invite us to enlarge our affective capacities via attunement with her art: "If we can see ourselves in the work . . . ourselves when viewing the work then the work is important. If we can *know our response*, see in our selves *what we have received* from a work, that is the way to the understanding of truth and all beauty" (*Writings* 89). In other words, as Anne Wagner has remarked, "her paintings are not windows but mirrors, and their repetitive surfaces are as profound or superficial as we make them" ("The Cause" 237).

When beholders respond they will "realize they make responses that are completely abstract and that their lives are broader than they think," Martin said in a filmed interview shortly before her death (Lance, *With My Back to the World*). This hope to inspire psychic openness recalls Kazimir Malevich's aim as a pioneer in monochrome abstraction circa 1915. Invoking a metaphorical space that Martin would later literalize, Malevich says he was drawn forth into the "'desert,' where nothing is real except feeling": no "practical values, no ideas, no 'promised land'" of "objective representation." In his Suprematist manifesto he writes: "In my desperate attempt to free art from the ballast of objectivity, I took refuge in the square form and exhibited a picture which consisted of nothing more than a black square on a white field." His black square was greeted with bewilderment: "The public sighed, 'Everything which we loved is lost. We are in a desert.'" Yes, Malevich famously replied, "a desert of pure feeling" ("Kazimir Malevich: Suprematism"). For Malevich this desert instilled "a white state of mind" where projects and plans, meanings and goals recede before the blinding light of immediacy (Harries 107, 67).

Martin links her belief in the liberating power of the abstract to the primacy of consciousness in Greek idealism ("Just follow what Plato had to say"). They "realized that the mind knows what the eye has not seen but / that what the mind knows is perfection" (*Writings* 117). There are no perfect lines or circles in nature, only in the mind. Hence the "classicism" she admires is a stringent idealism: it "is not about people / and this work [her painting] is not about the world . . . Classicists are people that look out with their backs to the world / It represents something that isn't possible in the world / More perfection than is possible in the world" (37). To live in the mind is to value feelings suffused in memory more than actuality; "experiences recalled are generally more satisfying and enlightening than the original experience." She refers to Wordsworth's daffodils: "They flash upon that inward eye / Which is the bliss of solitude" (94). The critic Briony Fer has linked this preference for recalling to Martin's preference for repetition in her painting: "Recollection is somehow more vivid, or put another way, original experience is a pale reflection of its repetitions. Repetition is understood as a means not of deadening but heightening experience . . . [it] creates maximum difference." It is (close to) interminable, like infinity: and "the thing about infinity is that it is not a thing. It exists only in the imagination" (191).

The interplay between repetition and difference is expressed on—as—the grid, which works doubly and dissonantly: at once a ready-made geometric template of paratactic repetition and a set of hand-penciled lines that in their varying degrees of manual pressure register repetition as infinitesimal difference. Thus in her deployment of the grid—"an emblem of modernity," as Krauss calls it—Martin opens the uniform and mechanical to particularity, turning a tool of impersonal management and affective neutrality into something handcrafted and frail, or "fugitive," to borrow Fer's word (Krauss, "Grids" 52). Of Martin's graphite notation, Fer says it is "fading even as it covers the uneven ground of the canvas," a white field of "light acrylic wash." "It is almost as if it is the ghostly trace of something marginal and ephemeral. Not so much obsolescence as the act of disappearing" (189).

The painterly "undoing" noted by Wagner and Fer resonates beyond Martin's canvases to point to a disquieting fact: that painting dedicated to "happiness" turned out to require its creator's own act of disappearing into ascetic isolation. This ratio suggests a cost in *unhap-piness*; "stand with your back to the turmoil," to cite a Martin remark that hints at why one might elect to turn one's "back to the world" (*Writings* 36). Arne Glimcher begins his 2012 book, *Agnes Martin: Paintings, Writings, Remembrances*, by disclosing the "turmoil" of Martin's lifelong suffering from schizophrenia that "from time to time required hospitalization. . . . Agnes would recover from an episode and start painting again and live a sedate life, her condition under control" (8). In a fittingly matter-of-fact tone he gives a name to what was known since a 1993 *New Yorker* profile where Benita Eisler wrote of Martin's "descents into uncontrollable panic" and of her "paranoia," as her friend Tuttle put it (78, 82). (Understandably, given the date, Eisler left open the other "open secret" of the artist's lesbianism.)

Eisler correctly notes that Martin herself had been candid, even vivid in writing about the psychic torment inflicted by prolonged solitude. "The solitary life is full of terrors," she wrote in a 1973 address, "On the Perfection Underlying Life." Her mental anguish seeps through the ostensible occasion—an address to "art students" who "feel inadequate and defeated" in the face of the frustrations inherent in making art. Before long Martin is dwelling on "the panic of complete helplessness" and the "fantastic extremes" it drives us to. She moves on to the "terrors" of solitude that are the artist's lot and soon is describing the "pervasive fear that is always with us" and what is "worse than the terror of fear"—the "self-destructiveness" she dubs "the Dragon" (*Writings* 70–72). This address is slightly out of control, driven by the intensity of her need to disclose her own psychic pain while also consoling anxious students. Martin ultimately prescribes a dose of stoic necessitarianism: not only will fear and dread eventually prove rewarding correctives to pride but our mistakes and errors are not what they seem—"it all has to be done. That which seems like a false step is just the next step" (73). And the strength is already within you; simply consult your memory and "recall" those moments when we learned "what it feels like to move freely, not held back by pride and fear. . . . The recall of these moments can be stimulated by freeing experiences including the viewings of works of art" (74).

Glimcher's memoir is based on thirty years of studio visits to New Mexico that grew into friendship on the condition of his heeding Martin's initial warning: "Remember Arne, we are not friends—I have no friends" (120). His book is a memorable portrait; it reveals not only Martin's orneriness (likeable and scary) but also how utterly her daily life was shaped by obedience to her "voices" that warned of pride and "distraction." "I don't have a dog because they demand love," she remarks, and tells Glimcher: "I am restricted from having music—not even one little note, and travel, because it would interrupt my state of mind" (77, 104). As her reputation grew in New York in the sixties, the "spectre of pride" increasingly haunted her, says Glimcher, "resulting in her decision to abandon painting" (9). Her voices had been telling her not to seek help, and she suffered some bad episodes. After years of effort, Glimcher finally convinced her to take medication. When she resumed painting and the Whitney Museum in 1980 wanted to arrange her first major retrospective, Martin refused because the show would include a catalogue of essays on her work. As "merely the locus where" the paintings "happened," Martin found a catalogue impertinent; "the idea of achievement must be given up," she wrote to the museum, if we are "to live truly and effectively" (qtd. Glimcher 120). By 1992 she relented. In later years, Glimcher notes, she grew more relaxed about the sin of pride and her colors flowed.

It might be tempting to seize on schizophrenia as the figure in the carpet and to regard Martin's mental illness as the "truth" of her creativity and the motive of her renunciation. The actuality is more complicated because the "voices" are not reducible simply to symptoms. While obviously at times destructive, the voices were also enabling when her psychic economy productively assimilated them; then the voices made pride the enemy and pride's defeat the (paradoxically non-egotistic) triumph of painting. Martin was able "to serve happiness," synonymous for her with life and beauty (135).

The presence of mental illness in Martin's renunciatory life of art does not isolate her from the other renunciants discussed, but rather reminds us that all of them worked in distinctive ways within the hazards of psychological extremity. Fear of going mad afflicted Kierkegaard, Kafka, and Wittgenstein; Nietzsche succumbed to derangement. Pollock courted and achieved violent self-destruction, as did Celan. They cluster at the far end of a continuum; but all along it the other renunciants are found. Each is an irreducibly unsettling figure, uneasy with the demands of civic or communal life (even if, like Wittgenstein, they show us how those forms of life work). Undoing their own authority, refusing exemplarity, they gain most of what they need—including joy and energy and certainty—not by explaining, not by knowing, nor even by thinking—but rather by finding freedom in logics of abdication. "There is no why, I simply don't. This is how I act," to recall Wittgenstein about why he doesn't make sure he has two feet when he rises from a chair. "Aiming but no aiming," as Salinger describes Seymour's marble shooting skill. Martin puts it this way: "To try to understand is to court misunderstanding. Not to know, but to go on" (qtd. Glimcher 41). She is at one with the Emerson who says, "Silence is a solvent that destroys personality, and gives us leave to be great and universal" (*Essays* 426).

■

Agnes Martin is my concluding figure and also a culminating one. She exemplifies the Eastern and Christian mystic imperative to live without why—when "you wake up and feel very happy about nothing, no cause, that's what I paint," she says at the start of the filmed interview *My Back to the World*. And she had the "courage to be an absolute nobody." The gauntlet Franny Glass throws down Martin seizes with joy, making her unique among her fifties cohort. Indeed, the reduction to "nobody" was the condition of her creativity: "When I paint . . . I have to be not there, not thinking at all, and only then can I paint the truth and bliss and divine" (qtd. Glimcher 118). Martin breaks free of the compulsive apophasis of her mentor Ad Reinhardt and his quixotic pursuit of the last painting even as she continues by other means his war against subjective expression and instrumentality. She continues by living a life of inspiration grounded in an overcoming of basic Western assumptions: that we are "supposed to be individuals" and are "conditioned by self-assertion" (qtd. Glimcher 118).

Compared to the monk Merton, Martin's renunciation has centripetal force, shaping a life gathering toward ever more disciplined (obsessive) concentration. Merton's renunciation is centrifugal; from his Kentucky monastery emanate across the globe spiritual, intellectual, and erotic energies and curiosity. Martin turned her hermitage into an "adventure in the dark," with the desert emptiness the perfect landscape to host the ongoing ferment of relinquishment: "Night, shelterless, wandering / I, like the deer looked / finding less and less . . . wandering away from everything / giving up everything, not me anymore, any of it / retired ego, wandering / on the mountain" (*Writings* 42). While Oppen's deer in "Psalm" bed down and stare out, Martin's are in movement. As is the painter: like Angelus Silesius and Eckhart in their own "wandering joy," Martin in her "wandering" steps with the lightness of a self dispossessed: releasement.

Remarkably given her reclusiveness, she wanted to share with the world, beyond the mute presence of her paintings, her art and life of renunciation: hence the lectures, essay-poems, and interviews. Was it a bid for publicity, exposure for the sake of burnishing the Agnes "icon"? Hardly. For, after all, she had nothing to show and nothing to hide. The rigor of her self-effacement had taken care of all that. "I spend my whole life thinking of perfection," she told Glimcher (104). And added that "if someone makes a film of me, they would have the opposite of what I am. My life is nothing—there is no incident—it's as though I never existed."

Acknowledgments

AT A VERY early stage in my writing of this book, Sharon Cameron insisted on more clarity and coherence and sparked crucial rethinking. I thank her for that. I first knew Branka Arsić as the author of an indispensable book on Emerson. Now she is also a wonderful colleague and interlocutor. Since I met him in Berlin in the late nineties, Heinz Ickstadt has been my ideal of the great generalist and I continue to be inspired by his intellectual curiosity and engagement. I am happy to say the same about two other friends closer to home, Paul Grimstad and James Livingston. Jack Barth has been a most instructive mentor about art and I appreciate our conversations with Rochelle Gurstein over many years. Richard Shiff took the time to offer helpful suggestions and information at several points. I also benefited from the computer savvy and Sinological rigor of Abigail Stuart. As well, I want to express my gratitude for various forms of valued input from David Bergman, Sara Blair, Casey Blake, Zoe High, David Kurnick, Tim Parrish, Marc Posnock, Nancy Ruttenburg, George Shulman, and Johannes Voelz. I much appreciate Kate McIntyre for her careful indexing.

Some themes explored in this book build upon discussions initiated in very different form in *Daedalus* and in *Raritan* and I thank the editors for the opportunity to develop my ideas in those earlier articles.

I am especially indebted and grateful to four people who have been engaged with this book and its ideas in ways vital and sustaining. From the start Gregg Crane has been a fount of advice, feedback, acuity, and encouragement. It is hard to imagine an intellectual life without him. Joan Richardson's reading of an early draft of the whole was richly attuned and incisive, complementing her own books and our many conversations, which always leave me inspired and full of new things to read. Not least of what I owe Joan is introducing me to Herwig Friedl.

In his scrupulous reading of a late draft of the book, Herwig gave generously of his immense erudition, of range and precision, concerning American and European intellectual history and Eastern thought. It is a great pleasure to thank him here for his help and above all for his embodiment of the life of the mind. With her witty, incisive literary and verbal sensibility, the delightful Jessica Burstein educated me in the subtleties of J.D. Salinger and decisively enlarged my understanding. She also made a number of important suggestions about other matters and graciously, patiently bestowed upon this book her editorial acumen and rigor.

Works Cited and Consulted

Adler, Renata. *Gone: The Last Days of* The New Yorker. New York: Simon and Schuster, 2011.

Adorno, Theodor. *Negative Dialectics*. Trans. E. B. Ashton. New York: Continuum, 1973.

———. "Commitment." In *Aesthetics and Politics*. Trans. Ronald Taylor. London: NLB, 1976.

———. "Letter to Benjamin." In *Aesthetics and Politics*. Trans. Ronald Taylor. London: NLB, 1976.

———. *Minima Moralia*. Trans. Edmund Jephcott. London: New Left, 1978.

———. *Prisms*. Trans. Samuel Weber and Shierry Weber. Cambridge, MA: MIT Press, 1981.

———. *Aesthetic Theory*. Trans. Christian Lenhardt. Boston: Routledge, 1985.

———. *Notes to Literature*. 2 vols. Ed. Rolf Tiedemann. Trans. Shierry Weber Nicholsen. New York: Columbia University Press, 1992.

Agamben, Giorgio. *The Highest Poverty: Monastic Rules and Form-of-Life*. Trans. Adam Kotsko. Stanford, CA: Stanford University Press, 2013.

Altieri, Charles. "Aesthetics after Aesthetic Ideology." In *Beyond Representation: Philosophy and Poetic Imagination*, ed. Richard Eldridge. Cambridge: Cambridge University Press, 2011.

Anderson, John. "A Mystery Woman's Eye on the World." *New York Times*, March 21, 2014, AR12.

Anderson, Mark. Afterword to *The Loser*, by Thomas Bernhard, 173–190. New York: Knopf, 1991.

Ankersmit, Frank. "Between Language and History: Rorty's Promised Land." *Common Knowledge* 6, no. 1 (Spring 1997): 44–78.

Antin, David. *Radical Coherency: Selected Essays on Art and Literature, 1966 to 2005*. Chicago: University of Chicago Press, 2012.

Arendt, Hannah. *The Life of the Mind*. New York: Harcourt Brace Jovanovich, 1981.

———. *The Human Condition*, 2nd ed. Chicago: University of Chicago Press, 1998. First published 1958.

Arsić, Branka. *On Leaving: A Reading in Emerson*. Cambridge, MA: Harvard University Press, 2010.

Artaud, Antonin. *Selected Writings*. New York: Farrar, Straus and Giroux, 1988.

Ashbery, John. "The Art of Poetry no. 33: Interview by Peter Stitt." *Paris Review*, no. 90 (Winter 1983). Available online at http://www.theparisreview.org/interviews/3014/the-art-of-poetry-no-33-john-ashbery

———. *Reported Sightings: Art Chronicles, 1957–1987*. New York: Knopf, 1989.

———. *Other Traditions*. Cambridge, MA: Harvard University Press, 2001.

Baas, Jacquelynn. *Smile of the Buddha: Eastern Philosophy and Western Art*. Berkeley: University of California Press, 2005.

Badiou, Alain. *Wittgenstein's Antiphilosophy*. Trans. Bruno Bosteels. New York: Verso, 2011.

Bambach, Charles. *Heidegger's Roots: Nietzsche, National Socialism, and the Greeks*. Ithaca, NY: Cornell University Press, 2005.

Barthes, Roland. "The Death of the Author." In *Image-Music-Text*, trans. Stephen Heath, 142–148. New York: Hill & Wang, 1977.

———. "Lecture in Inauguration of the Chair of Literary Semiology, Collège de France, January 7, 1977." Trans. Richard Howard. *October* 8 (Spring 1979): 3–16.

———. "The Reality Effect." In *The Rustle of Language*, trans. Richard Howard, 141–148. Berkeley: University of California Press, 1987.

———. *The Neutral: Lecture Course at the Collège de France (1977–1978)*. Trans. Rosalind Krauss and Denis Hollier. New York: Columbia University Press, 2005.

———. *The Preparation of the Novel: Lecture Courses and Seminars at the Collège de France, 1978–1979 and 1979–1980*. Trans. Kate Briggs. New York: Columbia University Press, 2011.

Bazzana, Kevin. *Wondrous Strange: The Life and Art of Glenn Gould*. Oxford: Oxford University Press, 2004.

Bearn, Gordon C. F. *Waking to Wonder: Wittgenstein's Existential Investigations*. Albany, NY: SUNY Press, 1997.

Bell, David. "The Art of Judgment." *Mind* 2, no. 96 (1987): 221–244.

Bellow, Saul. *Conversations with Saul Bellow*. Ed. Gloria Cronin and Ben Siegel. Jackson: University Press of Mississippi, 1994.

———. *Herzog*. New York: Penguin, 1996. Originally published 1964.

———. *Letters*. Ed. Benjamin Taylor. New York: Penguin, 2010.

———. *There Is Simply Too Much to Think About: Collected Nonfiction*. Ed. Benjamin Taylor. New York: Viking, 2015.

Belting, Hans. *Likeness and Presence: A History of the Image before the Era of Art*. Trans. Edmund Jephcott. Chicago: University of Chicago Press, 1994.

Belz, Corrina, dir. *Gerhard Richter Painting.* New York: Kino Lorber, 2012. DVD.

Benjamin, Walter. *Selected Writings,* vol. 2, pt. 1: *1931–1934.* Trans. Rodney Livingstone et al. Cambridge, MA: Harvard University Press, 2005.

Bernhard, Thomas. *The Loser.* Trans. Jack Dawson. New York: Knopf, 1991. Originally published 1983.

Bernstein, J. M., ed. *Classic and Romantic German Aesthetics.* Cambridge: Cambridge University Press, 2003.

———. *Against Voluptuous Bodies: Late Modernism and the Meaning of Painting.* Stanford, CA: Stanford University Press, 2006.

Bersani, Leo. *The Death of Stephane Mallarmé.* Cambridge: Cambridge University Press, 2009.

Bersani, Leo, and Ulysse Dutoit. *Arts of Impoverishment: Beckett, Rothko, Resnais.* Cambridge, MA: Harvard University Press, 1993.

Blanchot, Maurice. "The Last One to Speak." In *Translating Tradition: Paul Celan in France,* ed. Benjamin Hollander. 228–241. San Francisco: Acts, 1988.

———. *The Work of Fire.* Trans. Charlotte Mandell. Stanford, CA: Stanford University Press, 1995.

Blumenberg, Hans. *Shipwreck with Spectator.* Trans. Steven Rendall. Cambridge, MA: MIT Press, 1997.

———. *Care Crosses the River.* Trans. Paul Fleming. Stanford, CA: Stanford University Press, 2010.

Bois, Yves-Alain. "The Limit of Almost." In *Ad Reinhardt,* 11–33. New York: Rizzoli, 1991.

———. *Painting as Model.* Cambridge, MA: MIT Press, 1993.

Bonin, Vincent. Review of "Variations VII," concert performance by John Cage. Daniel Langlois Foundation, http://www.fondation-langlois.org/html/e/page.php?NumPage=611

Bonnefoy, Yves. *Rimbaud.* Trans. Paul Schmidt. New York: Harper, 1973.

———. "Image and Presence." Trans. John Naughton. *New Literary History* 15, no. 3 (Spring 1984): 433–451.

———. "Paul Celan." In *Translating Tradition: Paul Celan in France,* ed. Benjamin Hollander. 9–15. San Francisco: Acts, 1988.

———. *The Act and the Place of Poetry : Selected Essays.* Chicago: University of Chicago Press, 1989.

———. "Lifting Our Eyes from the Page." Trans. John Naughton. *Critical Inquiry* 16 no. 4 (Summer 1990): 794–806.

———. "The Art of Poetry no. 69: Interview by Susha Guppy." *Paris Review,* no. 131 (Summer 1994). Available online at http://www.theparisreview.org/interviews/1790/the-art-of-poetry-no-69-yves-bonnefoy

Braver, Lee. *Groundless Grounds: A Study of Wittgenstein and Heidegger.* Cambridge, MA: MIT Press, 2012.

Breslin, James E. B. *Mark Rothko: A Biography.* Chicago: University of Chicago Press, 1998.

Broch, Hermann. *The Death of Virgil.* Trans. Jean Starr Untermeyer. New York: Grosset and Dunlap, 1965.

———. *Hugo von Hofmannsthal and His Time: The European Imagination, 1860–1920.* Trans. Michael Steinberg. Chicago: University of Chicago Press, 1984.

Brooks, Cleanth. *The Well-Wrought Urn.* Garden City, NY: Mariner, 1956.

Brown, Peter. *The Body and Society: Men, Women, and Sexual Renunciation in Early Christianity.* New York: Columbia University Press, 1998.

Bryson, Norman. Review of *Devant l'image: Question posée aux fins de l'histoire de l'art,* by Georges Didi-Huberman. *The Art Bulletin* 75, no. 2 (1993): 336–337.

Cage, John. *Silence: Lectures and Writings.* Middletown, CT: Wesleyan, 1961.

Calasso, Roberto. *La Folie Baudelaire.* Trans. Alastair McEwen. New York: Farrar, Straus and Giroux, 2012.

Camille, Michael. Review of *Bild und Kult,* by Hans Belting. *The Art Bulletin* 74, no. 3 (1992): 514–517.

Candida-Smith, Richard. *Mallarmé's Children: Symbolism and the Renewal of Experience.* Berkeley: University of California Press, 2000.

Carson, Anne. *Economy of the Unlost (Reading Simonides of Keos with Paul Celan).* Princeton, NJ: Princeton University Press, 1999.

Castle, Terry. *The Professor and Other Writings.* New York: Harper, 2010.

Cavell, Stanley. *Themes out of School: Effects and Causes.* Chicago: University of Chicago Press, 1988.

———. *This New Yet Unapproachable America: Lectures after Emerson and Wittgenstein.* Albuquerque, NM: Living Batch Press, 1989.

———. *Must We Mean What We Say?* Cambridge: Cambridge University Press, 2002. Originally published 1969.

———. *Cities of Words: Pedagogical Letters on a Register of the Moral Life.* Cambridge, MA: Harvard University Press, 2005.

Celan, Paul. *Collected Prose.* Trans. Rosemarie Waldrop. Manchester: Carcanet, 1986.

———. *Poems of Paul Celan. A Bilingual German/English Edition.* Trans. Michael Hamburger. New York: Persea Books, 1995.

———. "The Meridian." Trans. Jerry Glenn. Appendix to *Sovereignties in Question,* by Jacques Derrida. New York: Fordham University Press, 2005.

———. *Selections.* Trans. with an introduction by Pierre Joris. Berkeley: University of California Press, 2005.

———. *Correspondence: Ingeborg Bachmann and Paul Celan.* Trans. Weiland Hoban. Chicago: Seagull, 2010.

———. *The Meridian: Final Version—Drafts—Materials.* Ed. Bernhard Boschenstein and Heino Schmull. Trans. Pierre Joris. Stanford, CA: Stanford University Press, 2011.

Chapman, John Jay. *Letters.* Ed. Mark De Wolfe. Boston: Houghton Mifflin, 1937.

Chuang Tzu. *The Way of Chuang Tzu.* Ed. with an introduction by Thomas Merton. New York: New Directions, 1965.

Clark, Elizabeth. "The Ascetic Impulse in Religious Life: A General Response." In *Asceticism,* ed. Vincent Wimbush and Richard Valantasis, 505–510. New York: Oxford University Press, 1995.

———. *Reading Renunciation.* Princeton, NJ: Princeton University Press, 1999.

Clark, T. J. *The Painting of Modern Life.* Princeton, NJ: Princeton University Press, 1982.

———. *Farewell to an Idea: Episodes from a History of Modernism.* New Haven, CT: Yale University Press, 1999.

———. *The Sight of Death.* New Haven, CT: Yale University Press, 2006.

Collins, Douglas. "1933, December: 'Terrorists Ask No Questions.'" In *A New History of French Literature,* ed. Denis Hollier, 914–919. Cambridge, MA: Harvard University Press, 1994.

Conant, James. "Throwing Away the Top of the Ladder." *Yale Review* 79, no. 3 (1991): 328–364.

———. "Putting Two and Two Together: Kierkegaard, Wittgenstein, and the Point of View for Their Works as Authors." In *The Grammar of Religious Belief,* ed. D. Z. Phillips, 248–331. New York: St Martins, 1996.

———. "On Going the Bloody Hard Way in Philosophy." In *The Possibilities of Sense,* ed. J. H. Whittaker, 85–130. New York: Palgrave, 2002.

Cooke, Lynne. " . . . in the classic tradition . . ." In *Agnes Martin,* ed. Lynne Cooke et al., 11–26. New York: Dia Art Foundation, 2011.

Cooke, Lynne, Karen J. Kelly, and Barbara Schröder. *Agnes Martin.* New York: Dia Art Foundation, 2011.

Coomaraswamy, Ananda Kentish. *The Transformation of Nature in Art.* New York: Dover, 1956.

Cooper, David D. *Thomas Merton's Art of Denial: The Evolution of a Radical Humanist.* Athens: University of Georgia Press, 2008.

Cooper, David E. "*Verstehen,* Holism, and Fascism." In *Verstehen and Humane Understanding,* ed. Anthony O'Hear, 95–107. Cambridge: Cambridge University Press, 1996.

Corris, Michael. "The Difficult Freedom of Ad Reinhardt." In *Art Has No History!: The Making and Unmaking of Modern Art,* ed. John Roberts, 63–110. New York: Verso, 1994.

Cotkin, George. *William James, Public Philosopher.* Baltimore: Johns Hopkins, 1990.

Cott, Jonathan. *Conversations with Glenn Gould.* Boston: Little, Brown, 1984.

Crimp, Douglas. "Back to the Turmoil." In *Agnes Martin,* ed. Lynne Cooke et al., 58–77. New York: Dia Art Foundation, 2011.

Cronan, Todd. *Against Affective Formalism.* Minneapolis: University of Minnesota Press, 2013.

Crow, Thomas. *The Rise of the Sixties.* New York: Abrams, 1996.

Daive, Jean. *Under the Dome: Walks with Paul Celan.* Trans. Rosemarie Waldrop. Providence, RI: Burning Deck Press, 2009.

Danto, Arthur. "Some Remarks on the Genealogy of Morals." In *Nietzsche, Genealogy, Morality,* ed. Richard Schacht, 35–48. Berkeley: University of California Press, 1994.

———. *After the End of Art.* Princeton, NJ: Princeton University Press, 1997.

———. *Philosophizing Art.* Berkeley: University of California Press, 2001.

Davenport, Guy. *7 Greeks.* New York: New Directions, 1995.

———. *The Hunter Gracchus and Other Essays.* Washington, DC: Counterpoint, 1996.

Dayan, Peter. *Art as Music, Music as Poetry, Poetry as Art, from Whistler to Stravinsky and Beyond.* Burlington, UK: Ashgate, 2011.

de Bolla, Peter. *Art Matters.* Cambridge, MA: Harvard University Press, 2003.

de Certeau, Michel. *The Mystic Fable.* Trans. Michael Smith. University of Chicago Press, 1992.

de Duve, Thierry. *Kant after Duchamp.* Cambridge, MA: MIT Press, 1996.

———. *Look: 100 Years of Contemporary Art.* Trans. Simon Pleasance and Fronza Woods. Brussels: Ludion, 2001.

———. *Clement Greenberg between the Lines.* Trans. Brian Holmes. Chicago: University of Chicago Press, 2010.

Deleuze, Gilles. *Nietzsche and Philosophy.* Trans. Hugh Tomlinson. New York: Columbia University Press, 1983.

———. *Francis Bacon: The Logic of Sensation.* Trans. Daniel Smith. Minneapolis: University of Minnesota Press, 2003.

de Man, Paul. *Blindness and Insight,* 2nd ed. Minneapolis: University of Minnesota Press, 1983.

Derrida, Jacques. *Sovereignties in Question: The Poetics of Paul Celan.* Ed. Thomas Dutoit and Outi Pasanen. New York: Fordham University Press, 2005.

Desmond, William. *Art, Origins, and Otherness.* Albany, NY: SUNY Press, 2003.

de Vries, Hent. *Philosophy and the Turn to Religion*. Baltimore: Johns Hopkins University Press, 1999.

Dewey, John. *Art as Experience*. New York: Perigee, 1980. Originally published 1934.

Diamond, Cora. "Throwing Away the Ladder." *Philosophy* 63, no. 243 (January 1988): 5–27.

Didi-Huberman, Georges. *Confronting Images: Questioning the Ends of a Certain History of Art*. Trans. John Goodman. University Park, PA: Penn State University Press, 2009.

Dilthey, Wilhelm. *Selected Writings*. Ed. H. P. Rickman. New York: Cambridge University Press, 1976.

Diogenes Laertius. *Lives of Eminent Philosophers*. Trans. R. D. Hicks. Cambridge, MA: Harvard University Press, 1925.

Dischner, Gisela. "'Flaschenpost' and 'Wurfholz': Reflections on Paul Celan's Poems and Poetics." In *German and European Poetics after the Holocaust*, ed. Gert Hoffmann, 35–52. Rochester, NY: Camden House.

Dreyfus, Hubert. "Overcoming the Myth of the Mental." *Topoi* 25 (2006): 48.

Du Bois, W. E. B. *Writings*. New York: Library of America, 1986.

DuPlessis, Rachel Blau. "'Uncannily in the Open': In Light of Oppen." In *Thinking Poetics: Essays on Oppen*, ed. Steve Shoemaker, 203–227. Tuscaloosa: University of Alabama Press, 2009.

Dworkin, Craig. *No Medium*. Cambridge, MA: MIT Press, 2013.

Dylan, Bob. *Chronicles*. New York: Simon & Schuster, 2005.

Eckhart, Meister. *Selected Writings*. Trans. Oliver Davies. London: Penguin UK, 1994.

Edwards, James C. *Ethics without Philosophy: Wittgenstein and the Moral Life*. Gainesville: University Press of Florida, 1985.

Eisler, Benita. "Life Lines." *The New Yorker*, January 25, 1993, 70–83.

Elderfield, John. "Transformations." In *Seeing Rothko*, ed. G. Phillips and T. Crow, 101–122. Los Angeles: Getty Research Institute, 2005.

Elie, Paul. *The Life You Save May be Your Own*. New York: Farrar, Straus, Giroux, 2003.

Eliot, T. S. "From Poe to Valéry." In *Literary Opinion in America*, vol. 2, ed. Morton D. Zabel, 626–638. New York: Harper, 1962.

Elkins, James. *On Pictures and the Words That Fail Them*. New York: Cambridge University Press, 1998.

———. *Six Stories from the End of Representation: Images in Painting, Photography, Astronomy, Microscopy, Particle Physics, and Quantum Mechanics, 1980–2000*. Stanford, CA: Stanford University Press, 2008.

Elkins, James, and David Morgan, eds. *Re-Enchantment*. New York: Routledge, 2008.

Ellison, Ralph, and Albert Murray. *Trading Twelves: The Selected Letters of Ralph Ellison and Albert Murray*. Ed. John Callahan and Albert Murray. New York: Modern Library, 2000.

Emden, Christian J. *Nietzsche on Language, Consciousness and the Body*. Urbana: University of Illinois Press, 2005.

———. *Friedrich Nietzsche and the Politics of History*. Cambridge: Cambridge University Press, 2011.

Emerson, Ralph Waldo. *Essays and Poems*. New York: Library of America, 1996.

———. *Later Lectures*, vol. 2. Ed. Ronald Bosco and Joel Myerson. Athens: University of Georgia Press, 2010.

———. *Selected Journals: 1820–1842*. New York: Library of America, 2010.

Engelmann, Paul. *Letters from Wittgenstein, with a Memoir*. New York: Horizon, 1974.

Esteve, Mary. "Shipwreck and Autonomy: Rawls, Riesman and Oppen in the 1960s." *Yale Journal of Criticism* 18, no. 2 (Fall 2005): 323–349.

Feinstein, Howard M. *Becoming William James*. Ithaca, NY: Cornell University Press, 1999.

Felstiner, John. "The One and Only Circle: Paul Celan's Letters to Gisèle." Stanford University, https://web.stanford.edu/group/mantis/cgi-bin/files/article_pdfs/Celan%20Felstiner.pdf

———. *Paul Celan: Poet, Survivor, Jew*. New Haven, CT: Yale University Press, 2001.

Fer, Briony. "Drawing Drawings: Agnes Martin's Infinity." In *3x an Abstraction: New Methods of Drawing*, ed. Catherine M. de Zegher and Hendel Teicher, 185–195. New Haven, CT: Yale University Press, 2005.

Fisher, Philip. *Making and Effacing Art: Modern American Art in a Culture of Museums*. Oxford: Oxford University Press, 1991.

Flaubert, Gustave. *Letters 1830–1857*. Ed. Frances Steegmuller. Cambridge, MA: Harvard University Press, 1980.

Forster, E. M. *Two Cheers for Democracy*. New York: Harcourt, 1951.

Fosburgh, Lacey. "J. D. Salinger Speaks about His Silence." *New York Times*, November 3, 1974, 1.

Foster, Hal. "The Expressive Fallacy." *Art in America* 71 (January 1983): 59–77.

Foucault, Michel. *The Order of Things*. New York: Vintage, 1973.

Francis, Richard, ed. *Negotiating Rapture: The Power of Art to Transform Lives*. Chicago: Museum of Contemporary Art, 1996.

Franke, William, ed. *On What Cannot Be Said: Apophatic Discourses in Philosophy, Religion, Literature, and the Arts*, vol. 1: *Classic Formulations*. South Bend, IN: University of Notre Dame Press, 2007.

———. *On What Cannot Be Said: Apophatic Discourses in Philosophy, Religion, Literature, and the Arts,* vol. 2: *Modern and Contemporary Transformations.* South Bend, IN: University of Notre Dame Press, 2007.

Freedberg, David. *The Power of Images.* Chicago: University of Chicago Press, 1989.

Fried, Michael. "Art and Objecthood." In *Aesthetics Today,* ed. M. Philipson and P. Gudel, 214–239. New York: New American Library, 1980. Originally published 1967.

Friedl, Herwig. "Fate, Power and History in Emerson and Nietzsche." *ESQ: A Journal of the American Renaissance* 43, nos. 1–4 (1997): 267–294.

———. "Global Aspects of American Pragmatist Thinking: William James and Kitaro Nishida on the Purity of Pure Experience." *AmerikaStudien/American Studies* 46, no. 2 (2001): 177–205.

Friedlander, Eli. *Signs of Sense: Reading Wittgenstein's* Tractatus. Cambridge, MA: Harvard University Press, 2001.

———. *Walter Benjamin.* Cambridge, MA: Harvard University Press, 2012.

Friedlander, Saul. Introduction to *Probing the Limits of Representation,* ed. Saul Friedlander. Cambridge, MA: Harvard University Press, 1992.

Fynsk, Christopher. *Language and Relation: That There Is Language.* Stanford, CA: Stanford University Press, 1996.

Gann, Kyle. *No Such Thing as Silence: John Cage's 4'33".* New Haven, CT: Yale University Press, 2011.

Gasché, Rodolphe. *The Honor of Thinking: Critique, Theory, Philosophy.* Stanford, CA: Stanford University Press, 2007.

Gass, William H. *Fiction and the Figures of Life.* New York: Knopf, 1970.

Gaukroger, Stephen. *Descartes: An Intellectual Biography.* Oxford: Oxford University Press, 1995.

Geuss, Raymond. *Public Goods, Private Goods.* Princeton, NJ: Princeton University Press, 2003.

Glatzer, Nahum. *Franz Rosenzweig: His Life and Thought,* 2nd ed. New York: Schocken, 1986.

Glimcher, Arne. *Agnes Martin: Paintings, Writings, Remembrances.* London: Phaidon, 2012.

Goehr, Lydia. "For the Birds/Against the Birds." In *Action, Art, and History,* ed. D. Herwitz and M. Kelly, 43-81. New York: Columbia University Press, 2007.

Goodman, Russell. *Wittgenstein and William James.* Cambridge: Cambridge University Press, 2002.

Gould, Glenn. *Concert Dropout: In Conversation with John McClure.* Columbia/CBS Masterworks, 1968, audio CD.

————. *The Glenn Gould Reader*. Ed. Tim Page. New York: Alfred Knopf, 1985.

————. *Glenn Gould's Solitude Trilogy: Three Sound Documentaries*. CBC Records, 1992, audio CD.

Greenberg, Clement. *The Collected Essays and Criticism*, vol. 1: *Perceptions and Judgments, 1939-1944*. Ed. John O'Brian. Chicago: University of Chicago Press, 1986.

————. *The Collected Essays and Criticism*, vol. 2: *Arrogant Purpose, 1945-1949*, ed. John O'Brian. Chicago: University of Chicago Press, 1986.

————. *The Collected Essays and Criticism*, vol. 3: *Affirmations and Refusals, 1950-1956*, ed. John O'Brian. Chicago: University of Chicago Press, 1993.

————. *The Collected Essays and Criticism*, vol. 4: *Modernism with a Vengeance, 1957-1969*, ed. John O'Brian. Chicago: University of Chicago Press, 1993.

Grosz, Elizabeth. *The Nick of Time: Politics, Evolution, and the Untimely*. Durham, NC: Duke University Press, 2004.

Gruen, John. *The Artist Observed: 28 Interviews with Artists*, 77–86. Chicago: A Capella Books, 1991.

Gumbrecht, Hans Ulrich. *Production of Presence: What Meaning Cannot Convey*. Stanford, CA: Stanford University Press, 2004.

Guyer, Sara. "Breath Today: Celan's Translation of Shakespeare's Sonnet 71." *Comparative Literature* 57, no. 4 (Autumn 2005): 328–351.

Hacker, P. M. S. *Wittgenstein: Connections and Controversies*. Oxford: Oxford University Press, 2001.

Hadot, Pierre. *Philosophy as a Way of Life: Spiritual Exercises from Socrates to Foucault*. Trans. Michael Chase. Malden, MA: Blackwell, 1995.

————. *What Is Ancient Philosophy?* Trans. Michael Chase. Cambridge, MA: Harvard University Press, 2004.

————. *The Veil of Isis: An Essay on the History of the Idea of Nature*. Trans. Michael Chase. Cambridge, MA: Harvard University Press, 2006.

————. *The Present Alone Is Our Happiness*, 2nd ed. Trans. Marc Djaballa and Michael Chase. Stanford, CA: Stanford University Press, 2011.

Halsall, Francis, Julia Jansen, and Tony O'Connor. *Rediscovering Aesthetics: Transdisciplinary Voices from Art History, Philosophy, and Art Practice*. Stanford, CA: Stanford University Press, 2009.

Hamacher, Werner. *Premises: Essays on Philosophy and Literature from Kant to Celan*. Stanford, CA: Stanford University Press, 1999.

Hannay, Alastair. *Kierkegaard: A Biography*. New York: Cambridge University Press, 2001.

Harries, Karsten. *The Meaning of Modern Art*. Evanston, IL: Northwestern University Press, 1968.

Hauser, Arnold. *The Sociology of Art.* Trans. Kenneth Northcott. Chicago: University of Chicago Press, 1985.

Haynes, Todd, dir. *I'm Not There.* Los Angeles: The Weinstein Company, 2007. DVD.

Heidegger, Martin. *Discourse on Thinking.* Trans. John Anderson and Hans Freund. New York: Harper Torchbooks, 1966.

———. *What Is Called Thinking.* Trans. J. Glenn Gray. New York: Harper, 1968.

———. *Poetry, Language, Thought.* Trans. Albert Hofstadter. New York: Harper, 1975.

———. *The Principle of Reason.* Trans. Reginald Lilley. Bloomington: Indiana University Press, 1991.

———. "The Origin of the Work of Art." In *Off the Beaten Track,* Trans. Julian Young and Kenneth Haynes. Cambridge: Cambridge University Press, 2002.

Herrigel, Eugen. *Zen in the Art of Archery.* Trans. R. F. C. Hull. New York: Vintage, 1999. Originally published 1953.

Hofmannsthal, Hugo von. *The Lord Chandos Letter.* Trans. Joel Rotenberg. New York: NYRB, 2005. Originally published 1902.

Hölderlin, Friedrich. "Oldest Programme for a System of German Idealism." In *Classic and Romantic German Aesthetics,* ed. J. M. Bernstein, 185–187. Cambridge: Cambridge University Press, 2003.

Hollywood, Amy. *The Soul as Virgin Wife.* South Bend, IN: University of Notre Dame Press, 1995.

———. Introduction to *Cambridge Companion to Christian Mysticism,* ed. Amy Hollywood and Patricia Beckman. Cambridge: Cambridge University Press, 2012.

Honegger, Gitta. *Thomas Bernhard: The Making of an Austrian.* New Haven, CT: Yale University Press, 2001.

Horkheimer, Max, and Theodor W. Adorno. *Dialectic of Enlightenment.* Trans. John Cummings. New York: Continuum, 1972. Originally published 1944.

Horwich, Paul. *Wittgenstein's Metaphilosophy.* Oxford: Oxford University Press, 2013.

Howard, Richard. *Alone with America,* enl. ed. New York: Atheneum, 1980.

Howe, Irving. "More Reflections in the Glass Mirror." *New York Times Book Review,* April 7, 1963, 4.

Howe, Susan. "The End of Art." In *The ABCs of Robert Lax,* ed. David Miller and Nicholas Zurbrugg, 81–91. Exeter, Devon, UK: Stride Editions, 1999.

Hudson, Suzanne. "Agnes Martin, On a Clear Day." In *Agnes Martin,* ed. Lynne Cooke et al., 118–131. New York: Dia Art Foundation, 2011.

Izenberg, Oren. *Being Numerous: Poetry and the Ground of Social Life.* Princeton, NJ: Princeton University Press, 2011.

James, Henry. *The American Scene*. London: Chapman and Hall, 1907.

———. *Views and Reviews*. Boston: Ball Publishing, 1908.

———. *The Ambassadors*, in *Novels: 1903–1911*. New York: Library of America, 2010.

———. *The Art of the Novel: Critical Prefaces*. Chicago: University of Chicago Press, 2011.

James, William. *The Letters of William James*, vol. 2. Boston: Atlantic Monthly Press, 1920.

———. "The Thing and Its Relations." In *Essays in Radical Empiricism*, 45–59. Cambridge, MA: Harvard University Press, 1976. Originally published 1905.

———. *Writings*, vol. 1: *1878–1899*. New York: Library of America, 1992.

———. *Writings*, vol. 2: *1902–1910*. New York: Library of America, 1992.

———. *The Correspondence of William James*, vol. 10. Ed. Ignas K. Skrupskelis and Elizabeth M. Berkeley. Charlottesville: University of Virginia Press, 2002.

Jameson, Fredric. *The Antinomies of Realism*. New York: Verso, 2013.

Jauss, Hans Robert. "Poiesis." Trans. Michael Shaw. *Critical Inquiry* 8 (Spring 1982): 591–608.

Jones, Caroline. "Finishing School: John Cage and the Abstract Expressionist Ego." *Critical Inquiry* 19 (Summer 1993): 628–665.

———. *Eyesight Alone: Clement Greenberg's Modernism and the Bureaucratization of the Senses*. Chicago: University of Chicago Press, 2006.

Joseph, Branden W. *Random Order: Robert Rauschenberg and the Neo-Avant-Garde*. Cambridge, MA: MIT Press, 2003.

Kafka, Franz. *Diaries, 1910–1923*. Ed. Max Brod. London: Penguin, 1972.

———. *Letters to Felice*. Trans. James Stern and Elisabeth Duckworth. New York: Schocken, 1988.

Kahler, Erich. *The Disintegration of Form in the Arts*. New York: George Braziller, 1968.

Kahneman, Daniel. *Thinking Fast and Slow*. New York: Farrar, Straus and Giroux, 2011.

Kant, Immanuel. *Critique of Judgement*. Trans. James Creed Meredith. Oxford: Oxford University Press, 1978. Originally published 1790.

Kaprow, Allan. *Essays on the Blurring of Art and Life*. Berkeley: University of California Press, 2003.

Karmel, Pepe. "Pollock at Work: The Films and Photographs of Hans Namuth." In *Jackson Pollock*, ed. Kirk Varnedoe, 87–137. New York: MoMA, 1998.

"Kazimir Malevich: Suprematism." Moodbook.com, http://www.moodbook.com/history/modernism/malevich-suprematism.html

Katz, Jonathan. "Agnes Martin and the Sexuality of Abstraction." In *Agnes Martin*, ed. Lynne Cooke et al., 170–197. New York: Dia Art Foundation, 2011.

Kaufmann, Walter. Translator's introduction to *The Gay Science*, by Friedrich Nietzsche. New York: Vintage, 2010.

Kenner, Hugh. *A Homemade World: American Modernist Writers*. New York: Knopf, 1975.

Kerouac, Jack. *The Dharma Bums*. New York: Penguin, 1991. Originally published 1958.

———. *On the Road*. New York: Penguin, 1999. Originally published 1957.

Kierkegaard, Søren. *The Journals*. Trans. Alexander Dru. New York: Harper, 1959.

———. "On the Difference between a Genius and an Apostle." In *The Present Age*, trans. Alexander Dru. New York: Harper, 1962. Originally published 1849.

———. *The Point of View for My Work as an Author*. Ed. Benjamin Nelson. Trans. Walter Lowrie. New York: Harper, 1962. Originally published 1859.

———. *Philosophical Fragments; or, A Fragment of Philosophy by Johannes Climacus*. Trans. David Swenson and Howard V. Hong. Princeton, NJ: Princeton University Press, 1967. Originally published 1844.

———. *Concluding Unscientific Postscript*. Trans. David Swenson & Walter Lowrie. Princeton, NJ: Princeton University Press, 1968. Originally published 1846.

———. *Attack on "Christendom."* Trans. Walter Lowrie. Princeton, NJ: Princeton University Press, 1972. Originally published 1855.

———. *Papers and Journals: A Selection*. Trans. A. Hannay. New York: Penguin, 1996.

———. *A Literary Review*. Trans. Alastair Hannay. New York: Penguin, 2001. Originally published 1846.

———. *Fear and Trembling*. Trans. Alastair Hannay. New York: Penguin, 2003. Originally published 1843.

———. *The Book on Adler*. Trans. Howard V. Hong and Edna H. Hong. Princeton, NJ: Princeton University Press, 2009. Originally published 1872.

Klagge, James C., ed. *Wittgenstein: Biography and Philosophy*. Cambridge: Cambridge University Press, 2001.

———. *Wittgenstein in Exile*. Cambridge, MA: MIT Press, 2014.

Kneller, Jane. *Kant and the Power of Imagination*. Cambridge: Cambridge University Press, 2007.

Krauss, Rosalind E. "Grids." *October* 9 (Summer 1979): 50–64.

———. "Agnes Martin: The /Cloud/." In *Bachelors*, 75–93. Cambridge, MA: MIT Press, 2000.

Lacoue-Labarthe, Philippe. *Poetry as Experience.* Trans. Andrea Tarnowski. Stanford, CA: Stanford University Press, 1999.

Lance, Mary, dir. *Agnes Martin: With My Back to the World.* Corrales, NM: New Deal Films, 2002. DVD.

Lao Tzu. *Tao Te Ching.* Trans. Victor Mair. New York: Bantam, 1990.

Largier, Niklaus. "Mysticism, Modernity, and the Invention of Aesthetic Experience." *Representations* 105 (Winter 2009): 37–60.

———. "'The Plasticity of the Soul': Mystical Darkness, Touch, and Aesthetic Experience." *MLN* 125, no. 3 (April 2010): 536–551.

Lasch, Christopher. *The Revolt of the Elites and the Betrayal of Democracy.* New York: Norton, 1996.

Leavis, F. R. *The Critic as Anti-Philosopher: Essays and Papers.* Chicago: Ivan Dee, 1982.

Leiter, Brian. *Nietzsche on Morality.* New York: Routledge, 2003.

Leonard, George. *Into the Light of Things: The Art of the Commonplace from Wordsworth to John Cage.* Chicago: University of Chicago Press, 1994.

Levi, Primo. *Other People's Trades.* Trans. Raymond Rosenthal. New York: Summit, 1989.

Lippard, Lucy. *Eva Hesse.* New York: NYU Press, 1976.

Lipsey, Roger. "Do I Want a Small Painting? The Correspondence of Thomas Merton and Ad Reinhardt: An Introduction and Commentary." *The Merton Annual* 18 (November 2005): 260–314.

Longenbach, James. "A Test of Poetry." *The Nation,* February 11, 2008, 29–31.

Lyon, James. *Paul Celan and Martin Heidegger: An Unresolved Conversation, 1951–1970.* Baltimore: Johns Hopkins University Press, 2006.

Lyotard, Jean-Francois. *The Inhuman.* Trans. G. Bennington and R. Bowlby. Stanford, CA: Stanford University Press, 1991.

Mailer, Norman. *Advertisements for Myself.* Cambridge, MA: Harvard University Press, 1992. Originally published 1959.

Malcolm, Janet. "The Silent Woman-I, II, III." *The New Yorker,* August 23, 1993, 84–159.

———. "Justice to J. D. Salinger." *New York Review of Books,* June 21, 2001, 16–22.

Mallarmé, Stéphane. *Divagations.* Trans. Barbara Johnson. Cambridge, MA: Belknap Press of Harvard University Press, 2007.

Mansoor, Jaleh. "Self-Effacement, Self-Inscription: Agnes Martin's Singular Quietude." In *Agnes Martin,* ed. Lynne Cooke et al., 154–169. New York: Dia Art Foundation, 2011.

Maritain, Jacques. *Creative Intuition in Poetry.* New York: Pantheon, 1953.

Marks, Laura U. *The Skin of the Film: Intercultural Cinema, Embodiment, and the Senses.* Durham, NC: Duke University Press, 2000.

Martin, Agnes. *Writings.* Ed. Dieter Schwarz. Winterthur, Switzerland: Kunstmuseum/Edition Cantz, 1992.

Martin, Glen. "Deconstruction and Breakthrough in Nietzsche and Nāgārjuna." In *Nietzsche and Asian Thought,* ed. Graham Parkes, 91–111. Chicago: University of Chicago Press, 1991.

Mason, Wyatt. Introduction to *I Promise to Be Good: The Letters of Arthur Rimbaud.* New York: Modern Library, 2003.

May, Todd. *Gilles Deleuze: An Introduction.* Cambridge: Cambridge University Press, 2005.

McCarthy, Mary. "J. D. Salinger's Closed Circuit." *Harper's Magazine,* October 1962. Available online at http://harpers.org/archive/1962/10/j-d-salingers-closed-circuit/

McConathy, Dale. "Ad Reinhardt 1913–1966: A Chronology." In *Ad Reinhardt: Last Paintings,* ed. Heinz Liesbrock, 130–157. Dusseldorf: Richter Verlag, 2011.

McDowell, John. "Wittgenstein on Following a Rule." In *Mind, Value, and Reality,* 221–262. Cambridge, MA: Harvard University Press, 1998.

———. "Wittgensteinian Quietism." *Common Knowledge* 15, no. 3 (Fall 2009): 365–372.

McEvilley, Thomas. *Art and Discontent: Theory at the Millennium.* Kingston, NY: McPherson & Company, 1991.

———. *The Exile's Return.* Cambridge: Cambridge University Press, 1993.

McGinn, Marie. "Saying and Showing and the Continuity of Wittgenstein's Thought." *Harvard Review of Philosophy* 9 (2001): 24–36.

McGrath, Charles. "J. D. Salinger, Literary Recluse, Dies at 91." *New York Times,* January 29, 2010, 1.

McGuinness, Brian. *Young Ludwig. Wittgenstein's Life 1889–1921.* Oxford: Oxford University Press, 2005. Originally published 1988.

McManus, Dennis. *The Enchantment of Words: Wittgenstein's* Tractatus Logico-Philosophicus. Oxford: Oxford University Press, 2006.

Meier, Heinrich. *Leo Strauss and the Theologico-Political Problem.* Cambridge: Cambridge University Press, 2006.

Mendelsohn, Daniel. "Rebel Rebel." *The New Yorker,* August 29, 2011, 8–22.

Merleau-Ponty, Maurice. *The Visible and the Invisible.* Trans. Alphonso Lingis. Evanston, IL: Northwestern University Press, 1968.

———. "Cézanne's Doubt." In *The Merleau-Ponty Aesthetics Reader,* ed. Galen Johnson, 59–75. Evanston, IL: Northwestern University Press, 1993.

———. "Eye & Mind." In *The Merleau-Ponty Aesthetics Reader,* ed. Galen Johnson, 121–149. Evanston, IL: Northwestern University Press, 1993.

———. *Phenomenology of Perception.* Trans. Colin Smith. New York: Routledge, 1995. Originally published 1962.

Merrill, Linda. *A Pot of Paint: Aesthetics on Trial in Whistler v. Ruskin.* Washington, DC: Smithsonian Institution, 1993.

Merton, Thomas. *Conjectures of a Guilty Bystander.* Garden City, NJ: Doubleday, 1966.

———. *Mystics and Zen Masters.* New York: Farrar, Straus, Giroux, 1967.

———. *Zen and the Birds of Appetite.* New York: New Directions, 1968.

———. *New Seeds of Contemplation.* New York: New Directions, 1972.

———. *The Asian Journal of Thomas Merton.* New York: New Directions, 1975.

———. *The Hidden Ground of Love: The Letters of Thomas Merton on Religious Experience and Social Concerns.* Ed. W. H. Shannon. New York: Harcourt, 1993.

———. *The Road to Joy: Letters to New and Old Friends.* Ed. R. Daggy. New York: Harcourt, 1993.

———. *Journals,* vol. 3: *A Search for Solitude: Pursuing the Monk's True Life: 1952–1960.* Ed. Lawrence S. Cunningham. New York: Harper, 1997.

———. *The Seven-Storey Mountain: An Autobiography of Faith.* New York: Harvest/Harcourt, 1999. Originally published 1948.

———. *When Prophecy Still Had a Voice: The Letters of Thomas Merton and Robert Lax.* Ed. Arthur Biddle. Lexington: University of Kentucky Press, 2000.

Meyer, Steven. *Irresistible Dictation: Gertrude Stein and the Correlations of Writing and Science.* Stanford, CA: Stanford University Press, 2003.

Miller, Henry. *The Time of the Assassins: A Study of Rimbaud.* New York: New Directions, 1962.

Mitchell, Stephen. *Dropping Ashes on the Buddha.* New York: Grove, 1994.

Monk, Ray. *Ludwig Wittgenstein: The Duty of Genius.* New York: The Free Press, 1990.

Moran, Dermot, "Meister Eckhart in 20th Century Philosophy." In *Companion to Meister Eckhart,* ed. J. M. Hackett, 669–698. Boston: Brill, 2013.

Moyn, Samuel. *Origins of the Other: Emmanuel Levinas between Revelation and Ethics.* Ithaca, NY: Cornell University Press, 2006.

Murdoch, Iris. *Metaphysics as a Guide to Morals.* New York: Penguin, 1992.

Nabokov, Vladimir. "On a Book Entitled *Lolita.*" In *Lolita.* New York: Vintage, 1997.

Newman, Barnett. *Selected Writings and Interviews.* New York: Alfred Knopf, 1990.

Nicholl, Charles. *Somebody Else: Arthur Rimbaud in Africa 1880–91.* Chicago: University of Chicago Press, 1999.

Nicholls, Peter. *George Oppen and the Fate of Modernism.* Oxford: Oxford University Press, 2007.

Nietzsche, Friedrich. *Philosophy in the Tragic Age of the Greeks*. Trans. Marianne Cowan. Washington, DC: Regnery, 1962.

———. *The Will to Power*. Trans. Walter Kauffmann and R. J. Hollingdale. New York: Vintage, 1968. Originally published 1901.

———. *Ecce Homo: How One Becomes What One Is*. Trans. Walter Kauffmann. New York: Vintage, 1969. Originally published 1908.

———. *On the Genealogy of Morals*. Trans. Walter Kaufmann. New York: Vintage, 1969. Originally published 1887.

———. *Beyond Good and Evil*. Trans. Walter Kaufmann. New York: Vintage, 1989. Originally published 1886.

———. *Human All Too Human*. Trans. R. J. Hollingdale. Cambridge: Cambridge University Press, 1996. Originally published 1878.

———. *Daybreak*. Trans. R. J. Hollingdale. Cambridge: Cambridge University Press, 1997. Originally published 1881.

———. *Twilight of the Idols*. Trans. Richard Polt. Indianapolis, IN: Hackett, 1997. Originally published 1889.

———. *Untimely Meditations*. Trans. R. J. Hollingdale. Cambridge: Cambridge University Press, 1997.

———. *The Birth of Tragedy*. Trans. Douglas Smith. Oxford: Oxford University Press, 2000. Originally published 1872.

———. *The Gay Science*. Trans. Josefine Nauckhoff. Cambridge: Cambridge University Press, 2001. Originally published 1882.

———. *Writings from the Late Notebooks*. Trans. Kate Sturge. Cambridge: Cambridge University Press, 2003.

———. "On Truth and Lies in a Non Moral Sense." In *The Nietzsche Reader*, ed. Keith Ansell Pearson and Duncan Large, 114–123. Boston: Wiley Blackwell, 2006.

———. *Thus Spoke Zarathustra*. Trans. Adrian Del Caro. Cambridge: Cambridge University Press, 2012. Originally published 1883.

Nixon, Mignon, and Cindy Nemser. *Eva Hesse*. Cambridge, MA: MIT Press, 2002.

Noë, Alva. *Out of Our Heads: Why You Are Not Your Brain, and Other Lessons from the Biology of Consciousness*. New York: Hill and Wang, 2009.

Northrop, F. S. C. *The Meeting of East and West: An Inquiry Concerning World Understanding*. Oxford: Oxbow Press, 1979.

Olschner, Leonard. "Anamnesis: Paul Celan's Translations of Poetry." In *Translating Tradition: Paul Celan in France*, ed. Benjamin Hollander, 54–89. San Francisco: Acts, 1988.

Olsen, Tillie. *Silences*. New York: Feminist Press at City University of New York, 2003. Originally published 1978.

Oppen, George. *The Selected Letters of George Oppen*. Ed. Rachel Blau DuPlessis. Durham, NC: Duke University Press, 1990.

———. *Selected Prose, Daybooks, and Papers*. Ed. Stephen Cope. Berkeley: University of California Press, 2007.

———. *New Collected Poems*. Ed. M. Davidson. New York: New Directions, 2008.

———. *Speaking with George Oppen: Interviews with the Poet and Mary Oppen, 1968–1987*. Ed. Richard Swigg. Jefferson, NC: McFarland, 2012.

Ostwald, Peter F. *Glenn Gould: The Ecstasy and Tragedy of Genius*. New York: Norton, 1997.

Owens, Craig. *Beyond Recognition: Representation, Power, and Culture*. Berkeley: University of California Press, 1994.

Oxenhandler, Neal. *Rimbaud: The Cost of Genius*. Columbus: Ohio State University Press, 2009.

Patterson, David. "Cage and Asia: History and Sources." In *John Cage*, ed. Julia Robinson, 49–72. Cambridge, MA: MIT Press, 2011.

Pawel, Ernst. *The Nightmare of Reason: A Life of Franz Kafka*. New York: Farrar, Straus and Giroux, 1992.

Pillow, Kirk. *Sublime Understanding: Aesthetic Reflection in Kant and Hegel*. Cambridge, MA: MIT Press, 2003.

Pippin, Robert B. *Nietzsche, Psychology, and First Philosophy*. Chicago: University of Chicago Press, 2010.

Plath, Sylvia. *Ariel*. New York: Harper, 1966.

Pöggeler, Otto. *The Paths of Heidegger's Life and Thought*. Trans. John Bailiff. Atlantic Highlands, NJ: Humanities Press, 1997.

Poirier, Richard. *Poetry and Pragmatism*. Cambridge, MA: Harvard University Press, 1992.

Polanyi, Michael. *Personal Knowledge: Towards a Post-Critical Philosophy*. Chicago: University of Chicago Press, 1962. Originally published 1958.

———. *The Tacit Dimension*. Chicago: University of Chicago Press, 2009. Originally published 1966.

Pollock, Jackson. "My Painting." In *Reading Abstract Expressionism: Context and Critique*, ed. Ellen Landau, 139–140. New Haven, CT: Yale University Press, 2005.

Porete, Marguerite. *The Mirror of Simple Souls*. Trans. Ellen Babinsky. New York: Paulist Press, 1993.

Posnock, Ross. "'Don't think, but look!': W. G. Sebald, Wittgenstein, and Cosmopolitan Poverty." *Representations* 112 (Fall 2010): 112–139.

———. "The Salinger Riddle." Public Books, November 1, 2014, http://www.publicbooks.org/fiction/the-salinger-riddle

Powers, Richard. *The Goldbug Variations*. New York: Harper, 1993.

Putnam, Hilary. *Jewish Philosophy as a Guide to Life: Rosenzweig, Buber, Levinas, and Wittgenstein*. Bloomington: Indiana University Press, 2008.

Ransom, John Crowe. "Criticism as Pure Speculation." In *Literary Opinion in America*, vol. 2, ed. Morton D. Zabel, 639–654. New York: Harper, 1962.

———. *The World's Body*. Rpt. Baton Rouge, LA: LSU Press, 1968. Originally published 1938.

Read, Rupert. "'The Real Philosophical Discovery': A Reply to Jolley." *Philosophical Investigations* 18, no. 4 (October 1995): 362–369.

Reinhardt, Ad. *Art-as-Art: The Selected Writings of Ad Reinhardt*. Ed. Barbara Rose. Berkeley: University of California Press, 1991.

———. "Oral History Interview with Ad Reinhardt, circa 1964." Archives of American Art, Smithsonian Institution, http://www.aaa.si.edu/collections/interviews/oral-history-interview-ad-reinhardt-12891

Reznikoff, Charles. *The Manner Music*. Santa Barbara, CA: Black Sparrow, 1977.

Richter, Gerhard. *The Daily Practice of Painting*. Trans. D. Britt. London: Thames & Hudson, 1998.

Rieff, Phillip. *Freud: The Mind of the Moralist*. New York: Anchor, 1961.

———. *The Triumph of the Therapeutic: Uses of Faith after Freud*. New York: Harper, 1966.

———. *Fellow Teachers: Of Culture and Its Second Death*. Rpt. Chicago: University of Chicago Press, 1985. Originally published 1973.

———. *Sacred Order/Social Order*, vol. 1: My *Life among the Death Works: Illustrations of the Aesthetics of Authority*. Charlottesville: University of Virginia Press, 2006.

———. *Charisma: The Gift of Grace, and How It Has Been Taken Away from Us*. New York: Pantheon, 2007.

———. *Sacred Order/Social Order*, vol. 2: *The Crisis of the Officer Class: The Decline of the Tragic Sensibility*. Charlottesville: University of Virginia Press, 2008.

———. *Sacred Order/Social Order*, vol. 3: *The Jew of Culture: Freud, Moses, and Modernity*. Charlottesville: University of Virginia Press, 2008.

Riley, Bridget. *The Eye's Mind: Collected Writings 1965–2009*. London: Thames & Hudson, 2009.

Rimbaud, Arthur. *Complete Works, Selected Letters*. Trans. Wallace Fowlie. Chicago: University of Chicago Press, 1966.

———. *I Promise to Be Good: The Letters*. Trans. Wyatt Mason. New York: Modern Library, 2007.

———. *Illuminations*. Trans. John Ashbery. New York: Norton, 2012.

Robb, Graham. *Rimbaud: A Biography*. New York: Norton, 2001.

Rorty, Richard. "The Pragmatist." *The New Republic*, May 9, 1983, 32–36.

———. "Some Inconsistencies in James's *Varieties*." In *William James and a Science of Religion*, ed. Wayne Proudfoot, 86–97. New York: Columbia University Press, 2004.

Rosen, Charles. *Freedom and the Arts: Essays on Music and Literature.* Cambridge, MA: Harvard University Press, 2012.

Rosen, Stanley. *The Elusiveness of the Ordinary: Studies in the Possibility of Philosophy.* New Haven, CT: Yale University Press, 2002.

Rosenberg, Harold. "American Action Painters." In *Reading Abstract Expressionism: Context and Critique,* ed. Ellen Landau, 189–198. New Haven, CT: Yale University Press, 2005.

Rosenberger, Christina Bryan. "A Sophisticated Economy of Means: Agnes Martin's Materiality." In *Agnes Martin,* ed. Lynne Cooke et al., 102–116. New York: Dia Art Foundation, 2011.

Rosenzweig, Franz. *The Star of Redemption.* Trans. William Hallo. South Bend, IN: University of Notre Dame Press, 1985.

———. *Understanding the Sick and the Healthy.* Trans. Nahum Glatzer. Cambridge, MA: Harvard University Press, 1999.

———. *Philosophical and Theological Writings.* Ed. Paul W. Franks and Michael L. Morgan. Indianapolis, IN: Hackett, 2000.

Ross, Alison. *The Aesthetic Paths of Philosophy: Presentation in Kant, Heidegger, Lacoue-Labarthe, and Nancy.* Stanford, CA: Stanford University Press, 2007.

Ross, Kristin. *The Emergence of Social Space: Rimbaud and the Paris Commune.* New York: Verso, 2008.

Roth, Philip. *The Human Stain.* New York: Vintage, 2002.

Royce, Josiah. *Studies of Good and Evil.* New York: D. Appleton, 1906.

Russell, Bertrand. *Selected Letters,* vol. 1. Ed. Nicholas Griffin. Boston: Houghton Mifflin, 1992.

Said, Edward. "The Music Itself: Glenn Gould's Contrapuntal Vision." In *Glenn Gould: Variations,* ed. John McGreevy, 45–56. New York: Quill, 1983.

———. "The Virtuoso as Intellectual." In *On Late Style: Music and Literature against the Grain,* 115–133. New York: Vintage, 2006.

Salinger, J. D. *Franny and Zooey.* New York: Bantam, 1964. Originally published 1961.

———. "Hapworth 16, 1924." *The New Yorker,* June 19, 1965, 32–113. Available online at http://www.goingwimax.com/wp-content/uploads/1.pdf

———. *Nine Stories.* Boston: Little Brown, 1991. Originally published 1953.

———. *Raise High the Roof Beam, Carpenters* and *Seymour: An Introduction.* Boston: Little Brown, 2001. Originally published 1963.

Salinger, Margaret. *Dream Catcher: A Memoir.* New York: Washington Square Press, 2001.

Santayana, George. *Persons and Places: Fragments of Autobiography.* Cambridge, MA: MIT Press, 1986.

———. *The Genteel Tradition in American Philosophy* and *Character and Opinion in the United States*. Ed. James Seaton. New Haven, CT: Yale University Press, 2009.

Sass, Louis. "Deep Disquietudes: Reflections on Wittgenstein as Anti-Philosopher." In *Wittgenstein: Biography and Philosophy*, ed. James C. Klagge, 98–155. Cambridge: Cambridge University Press, 2001.

Schaeffer, Jean-Marie. *Art of the Modern Age: Philosophy of Art from Kant to Heidegger*. Trans. Steven Rendall. Princeton, NJ: Princeton University Press, 2000. Originally published 1992.

Schelling, F. W. J. *The Grounding of Positive Philosophy: The Berlin Lectures*. Trans. Bruce Matthews. Albany, NY: SUNY Press, 2012.

Schiller, Friedrich. "Kallias or Concerning Beauty." In *Classic and Romantic German Aesthetics*, ed. J. M. Bernstein, 145–183. Cambridge: Cambridge University Press, 2003.

———. "On Naïve and Sentimental Poetry." The Schiller Institute, http://www.schillerinstitute.org/transl/schiller_essays/naive_sentimental-1.html

Schonbaumsfeld, Genia. *A Confusion of the Spheres: Kierkegaard and Wittgenstein on Philosophy and Religion*. Oxford: Oxford University Press, 2010.

Schopenhauer, Arthur. *The World as Will and Representation*, vol. 1. Trans. E. F. J. Payne. New York: Dover, 1966. Originally published 1818.

Schulte-Sasse, Jochen. "1735: Aesthetic Orientation in a Disordered World." In *A New History of German Literature*, ed. David Wellbery and Judith Ryan, 350–356. Cambridge, MA: Harvard University Press, 2004.

Schürmann, Reiner. "Reiner Schürmann's Report of his Visit to Martin Heidegger." *Graduate Faculty Philosophy Journal*. 19:2/20:1, 1997: 67–72.

———. *Wandering Joy: Meister Eckhart's Mystical Philosophy*. Trans. Reiner Schürmann. Great Barrington, MA: Lindisfarne, 2001.

Schwartz, Sanford. *Artists and Writers*. New York: Yarrow Press, 1990.

Sells, Michael A. *Mystical Languages of Unsaying*. Chicago: University of Chicago Press, 1994.

Serra, Richard. "'Thou Shall Not.'" *Brooklyn Rail*, December 2013/January 2014, 2.

Sextus Empiricus. *Outlines of Pyrrhonism*. Trans. R. G. Bury. Cambridge, MA: Harvard University Press, 1939.

Sharf, Robert. "The Zen of Japanese Nationalism." *History of Religions* 33, no. 1 (August 1993): 1–43.

Sheed, Wilfrid. "The Exile." *New York Review of Books*, October 27, 1988.

Shiff, Richard. "An Interview with Katy Siegel," *The Brooklyn Rail*, April 2008.

———. "Sensation in the Wild." In *Rediscovering Aesthetics*, ed. Francis Halsall et al., 75–86. Stanford, CA: Stanford University Press, 2009.

————. "On 'Between Sense and de Kooning.'" *Montreal Review* (online magazine), September 2011, http://www.themontrealreview.com/2009/Between-sense-and-de-Kooning-by-Richard-Shiff.php

————. *Doubt*. New York: Routledge, 2012.

————. "Watch Out for Thinking (Even Fuzzy Thinking): Concept and Percept in Modern Art." *Common Knowledge* 19, no. 1 (2013): 65–87.

Siewert, Charles. "Intellectualism, Experience and Motor Understanding." In *Mind, Reason, and Being-in-the-World: The McDowell-Dreyfus Debate*, ed. Joseph Schear, 194–226. New York: Routledge, 2013.

Simonds, Charles. "Ad's Quest and a Flat Black Shining Moment." *Brooklyn Rail*, December 2013/January 2014, 19.

Sluga, Hans. Introduction to *Cambridge Companion to Wittgenstein*, ed. Hans Sluga and David Stern. Cambridge: Cambridge University Press, 1996.

Smith, Steven B. *Reading Leo Strauss: Politics, Philosophy, Judaism*. Chicago: University of Chicago Press, 2007.

Sontag, Frederick. *Wittgenstein and the Mystical: Philosophy as an Ascetic Practice*. Atlanta, GA: Scholars Press, 1995.

Sontag, Susan. Introduction to *Artaud: Selected Writings*, by Antonin Artaud. Berkeley: University of California Press, 1976.

————. "Thirty Years Later." In *Against Interpretation*. New York: Picador, 1996.

————. *Reborn: Journals and Notebooks, 1947–1963*. New York: Farrar, Straus and Giroux, 2008.

————. *Essays of the 1960s and 70s*. New York: Library of America, 2013.

Stach, Reiner. *Kafka: The Decisive Years*. Trans. Shelley Frisch. Princeton, NJ: Princeton University Press, 2013.

————. *The Years of Insight*. Trans. Shelley Frisch. Princeton, NJ: Princeton University Press, 2013.

Starkie, Enid. *Arthur Rimbaud*. New York: New Directions, 1962.

Starobinski, Jean. *Montaigne in Motion*. Trans. Arthur Goldhammer. Chicago: University of the essay Chicago Press, 1985.

Stein, Gertrude. *Writings 1932–1946*. New York: Library of America, 1998.

Steiner, George. *Real Presences*. Chicago: University of Chicago Press, 1991.

Stone, Martin. "Wittgenstein on Deconstruction." In *The New Wittgenstein*, ed. A. Crary and R. Read, 83–117. New York: Routledge, 2000.

————. "On the Old Saw 'Every Reading of a Text is an Interpretation': Some Remarks." In *The Literary Wittgenstein*, ed. John Gibson and Wolfgang Huemer, 186–209. New York: Routledge, 2004.

Storr, Robert. "Diogenes of the Funny Pages." In *How to Look: Ad Reinhardt Art Comics*, 5–19. New York: David Zwirner.

Strauss, Leo. *Jewish Philosophy and the Crisis of Modernity*. Ed. Kenneth Hart Green. Albany, NY: SUNY Press, 1997.

Stroll, Avrum. *Wittgenstein*. Oxford: Oneworld, 2002.

Suzuki, Daisetz. *Zen Buddhism: Selected Writings of D. T. Suzuki*. Ed. William Barrett. New York: Doubleday Image, 1996. Originally published 1956.

Swami Nikhilananda, *Vivekananda: A Biography*. New York: Ramakrishna-Vivekananda Center, 1989. Originally published 1953.

Sylvester, David. *The Brutality of Fact: Interviews with Francis Bacon*. London: Thames and Hudson, 1988.

Symons, Arthur. *The Symbolist Movement in Literature*. New York: Dutton, 1958.

Taggart, John. "Walk-Out: Rereading George Oppen." *Chicago Review* 44, no. 2 (Spring 1998): 29–93.

Taylor, Charles, "Retrieving Realism." In *Mind, Reason, and Being-in-the-World: The McDowell-Dreyfus Debate*, ed. Joseph Schear, 61–90. New York: Routledge, 2013.

Taylor, Mark. *Disfiguring: Art, Architecture, Religion*. Chicago: University of Chicago Press, 1992.

Thoreau, Henry D. *Walden, Civil Disobedience, and Other Writings*. Ed. William Rossi. New York: W. W. Norton & Company, 2008.

Toews, John Edward. *Becoming Historical: Cultural Reformation and Public Memory in Early Nineteenth-Century Berlin*. Cambridge: Cambridge University Press, 2004.

Valéry, Paul. *The Collected Works*, vol. 7: *The Art of Poetry* (Bollingen Series). Trans. Denise Folliot. New York: Pantheon, 1958.

———. *The Collected Works*, vol. 12: *Degas, Manet, Morisot* (Bollingen Series). Trans. David Paul. New York: Pantheon, 1960.

———. *The Collected Works*, vol. 5: *Idée Fixe* (Bollingen Series). Trans. David Paul. New York: Pantheon, 1965.

———. *The Collected Works*, vol. 8: *Leonardo, Poe, Mallarmé* (Bollingen Series). Trans. Malcolm Cowley and James Lawler. Princeton, NJ: Princeton University Press, 1970.

———. *The Collected Works*, vol. 9: *Masters and Friends*. (Bollingen Series). Trans. Martin Turnell. Princeton, NJ: Princeton University Press, 1968.

———. *The Collected Works*, vol. 14: *Analects* (Bollingen Series). Trans. Stuart Gilbert. Princeton, NJ: Princeton University Press, 1972.

Vila-Matas, Enrique. *Bartleby & Co*. Trans. Jonathan Dunne. New York: New Directions, 2004.

Wagner, Anne Middleton. *Three Artists (Three Women): Modernism and the Art of Hesse, Krasner, and O'Keeffe*. Berkeley: University of California Press, 1996.

———. "The Cause of the Response." In *Agnes Martin,* ed. Lynne Cooke et al., 228–239. New York: Dia Art Foundation, 2011.

Waismann, Friedrich. "Notes on Talks with Wittgenstein." *Philosophical Review* 74 (January 1965): 12–16.

Walsh, David. *The Modern Philosophical Revolution: The Luminosity of Existence.* Cambridge: Cambridge University Press, 2008.

Weinberger, Eliot. Preface to *New Collected Poems,* by George Oppen. New York: New Directions, 2008.

Weschler, Lawrence, and Robert Irwin. *Seeing Is Forgetting the Name of the Thing One Sees: A Life of Contemporary Artist Robert Irwin.* Berkeley: University of California Press, 2008.

Whistler, J. M. *Whistler on Art: Selected Letters and Writings.* Washington, DC: Smithsonian Institution Press, 1994.

Whitman, Walt. *Poetry and Prose.* New York: Library of America, 1982.

Wilde, Oscar. *The Artist as Critic.* New York: Vintage, 1970.

Wilkinson, John. "The Glass Enclosure: Transparency and Glitter in the Poetry of George Oppen." *Critical Inquiry* 36 (Winter 2010): 218–238.

Williams, J. P. *Denying Divinity: Apophasis in the Patristic Christian and Soto Zen Buddhist Traditions.* Oxford: Oxford University Press, 2000.

Williams, R. John. "*Technê*-Zen and the Spiritual Quality of Global Capitalism." *Critical Inquiry* 37 (Autumn 2011): 17–70.

Willis, Ellen. *Beginning to See the Light: Pieces of a Decade.* New York: Knopf, 1981.

Wilson, Edmund. *Axel's Castle: A Study in the Imaginative Literature of 1870–1930.* Rpt. London: Fontana, 1982. Originally published 1931.

Wisdom, David. "Kierkegaard and Euthyphro." *Philosophy* 62 (1987): 221–226.

Wittgenstein, Ludwig. *Philosophical Investigations,* 3rd ed. Trans. G. E. M. Anscombe. New York: Macmillan, 1968. Originally published 1953.

———. *Zettel.* Trans. G. E. M. Anscombe. Berkeley: University of California Press, 1970.

———. *On Certainty.* Trans. Denis Paul and G. E. M. Anscombe. New York: Harper, 1972.

———. *Culture and Value.* Trans. Peter Winch. Chicago: University of Chicago Press, 1984.

———. *Notebooks 1914–1916.* Ed. Elizabeth Anscombe. Chicago: University of Chicago Press, 1984.

———. *Wittgenstein's Lectures: Cambridge: 1930–1932.* From the Notes of John King and Desmond Lee. Chicago: University of Chicago Press, 1989.

———. *Philosophical Occasions.* Ed. James Klagge and Albert Nordmann. Indianapolis, IN: Hackett, 1993.

———. *Tractatus Logico-Philosophicus.* Trans. C. K. Ogden. New York: Dover, 1999. Originally published 1922.

———. *Wittgenstein in Cambridge.* Ed. Brian McGuinness. Malden, MA: Wiley-Blackwell, 2012.

Wordsworth, William. *Poetry and Prose.* Ed. Nicholas Halmi. New York: Norton, 2013.

Yard, Sally. *Willem De Kooning: Works, Writings, Interviews.* New York: Distributed Art Pub Incorporated, 2007.

Yusa, Michiko. *Zen and Philosophy: An Intellectual Biography of Nishida Kitaro.* Honolulu: University of Hawaii Press, 2002.

Zegher, M. Catherine de, and Hendel Teicher, eds. *3x an Abstraction: New Methods of Drawing by Hilma af Klint, Emma Kunz, and Agnes Martin.* New Haven, CT: Yale University Press, 2005.

Zerilli, Linda M. G. "Doing without Knowing: Feminism's Politics of the Ordinary." *Political Theory* 26, no. 4 (1998): 435–458.

Zinoman, Jason. "A Comic Quits Quitting." *New York Times,* August 18, 2013, AR1.

Index

abandonment, 7, 15, 23, 28–29, 44, 60, 85, 100, 198, 252, 277, 316; "without why," 2, 11, 41, 183, 285, 296; of writing, 22, 26–27, 54, 84, 91, 337; and silence, 26–27, 35, 41, 48, 54, 296, 337, 345. *See also under* Emerson; renunciation
abstract expressionism, 30, 98, 105, 126, 128
Adler, Renata, 171
Adorno, Theodor, 8, 41, 44, 47, 120–121, 123, 140; and Celan 38, 42, 120, 333–334, 337, 349, 352, 357; and understanding, 119. *See also under* Heidegger; nuance
aesthetic autonomy, 13, 15, 97, 113, 125, 140, 146, 149, 151, 154; and silence 35, 38, 321. *See also* Kant: blind intuition; Valéry
aesthetic education, 15, 124, 164
aesthetic idea (Kant), 35–38, 68, 98, 113, 119, 122, 152, 168–169, 257; anti–concept 35–36; non–discursive 36, 152, 167
aesthetic living, 20, 63, 65–66, 139, 140, 158–159, 164, 172
Angelico, Fra, 57–58, 65
Angelus Silesius (Johannes Scheffler), 3, 10–11, 306, 321, 323–326, 378. *See also under* Heidegger; "without why"
Anscombe, Elizabeth, 238–240
Antin, David, 203–204
anti–philosophy, 107, 322
apophasis, 19, 187, 377. *See also* negative theology
apotaktikoi, 33
Aquinas, Thomas, 344–345
Arendt, Hannah, 1, 16, 51–52, 62, 263–264, 324
Arnold, Matthew, 65, 154–155, 232

Artaud, Antonin, 72, 74–75
asceticism, 19, 21, 26, 27, 34, 134, 201, 319
Ashbery, John, 117, 256; and understanding, 118
Ashton, Dore, 197

Bach, Johann Sebastian, 241, 248, 257, 259, 261, 348
Bacon, Francis, 102–103, 109–110, 122, 127
Badiou, Alain, 284
Banville, Théodore de, 86
Barnes, Djuna, 22
Barthes, Roland, 17, 23, 31, 73, 133, 140, 179, 199; *The Neutral* 138–139, 141, 147, 149. *See also under* nuance
Baudelaire, Charles, 75, 83, 86, 255
Bauer, Felice. *See under* Kafka
Baumgarten, Alexander, 5, 156, 198
Bearn, Gordon C. F., 282
Beckett, Samuel, 42, 47, 113, 182, 206
Beethoven, Ludwig van, 245
Bellow, Saul, 46–47, 136, 181
Belting, Hans, 111, 208–209
Benjamin, Walter, 1, 8, 31, 238, 254–255, 357, 360
Bergson, Henri, 52, 68, 70, 79, 97
Bernhard, Thomas 1, 12, 29, 35, 238–241, 255, 257–262, 268. *See also under* Gould; Wittgenstein
Bersani, Leo, 92, 94, 113
betrayal, 225, 333; writing as 57, 147, 153, 211, 213, 228–229, 264
Bhagavad Gita, 33, 55, 184
Bierce, Ambrose, 54
Blake, William, 160, 188, 366
Blanchot, Maurice, 79–80, 93; on Rimbaud 18, 53, 66, 90; on Celan 347, 360

Blood, Benjamin Paul, 72
Blumenberg, Hans, 64
Bochner, Mel, 268
Bois, Yves–Alain, 75, 197, 203
Bonnefoy, Yves, 40, 66, 78, 89, 108, 284,
    354, 364
Brecht, Bertolt, 335
Breton, André, 116
Broch, Hermann, 41, 115
Brod, Max. See under Kafka.
Brooks, Cleanth, 127
Brown, Norman O., 135, 219, 221
Brown, Peter, 43
Bryson, Norman, 58
Buchloch, Benjamin, 103–104
Büchner, Georg, 334–335, 358–359, 362
Buddhism, 141, 146, 190, 309, 324, 367;
    Gautama, 160; sunyata, 33, 327. See
    also Zen
Burnett, Whit, 142

Cage, John, 75, 77–78, 121, 199, 204,
    244; and Zen 13, 30, 33, 48, 76, 97,
    152, 164–165, 190, 197, 371; 4'33"
    30, 48, 97; and silence 30, 60, 176,
    205–206, 367. See also under listening
Calasso, Roberto, 111
Calvin, John, 71
Calvinism, 371
Carnap, Rudolph, 265, 268, 274, 276, 279
Cartesianism. See under Descartes
Castle, Terry, 365
Cavell, Stanley, 1, 158, 284–285, 287,
    293, 318
Celan, Paul, 13, 54, 86, 345–365, 377;
    and Oppen 12, 42–43, 330–335,
    339, 343, 345–346; on "exposed
    understanding," 38, 120; and Nazis
    42, 332–333, 346, 349, 351–353,
    355–356, 358–359, 361; "Todesfuge"
    42, 348–349, 362; "The Meridian"
    334–335, 339, 347, 354, 356–362; and
    Büchner 335, 358–359, 362; and the
    "20th of January" 335, 347, 358–362;
    Gegenwort 347, 354, 362, 363; and
    Hölderlin 350–351, 355–356, 360.
    See also under Adorno; Blanchot;
    Heidegger; Oppen
Cézanne, Paul, 111; in Merleau–Ponty
    101–103, 110, 130; in Deleuze
    102–103, 110

Chapman, John Jay, 70, 78
Chappelle, Dave, 15–16, 18, 21
Chuang Tzu, 367
Clark, T. J., 100, 104, 127
Columbia University, 24, 132, 142, 195;
    Suzuki's seminar at 32, 164, 367, 370
Conant, James, 276–277
Coomaraswamy, Ananda Kentish,
    197–198
Courbet, Gustave, 96

Dada, 30, 116, 120, 165, 197
Danto, Arthur, 46, 164, 170, 303
Darwin, Charles, 273
Davenport, Guy, 193
de Certeau, Michel, 10
de Duve, Thierry, 4, 23, 63, 65, 98, 112,
    167. See also under looking
Degas, Edgar, 111–112. See also under
    explanation
de Kooning, Elaine, 200
de Kooning, Willem, 97, 179, 233
Deleuze, Gilles, 102, 108–110, 122, 320.
    See also under Cézanne
de Man, Paul, 78, 105
Derrida, Jacques, 105–106, 108, 355,
    363
Descartes, René, 6, 8, 27, 40, 64, 75, 157,
    226, 303; Cartesianism 165, 305
Desmond, William, 152
detachment. See under Eckhart,
    Heidegger, Salinger. See also:
    Heidegger: Gelassenheit, Eckhart:
    releasement.
Dewey, John, 52, 105–106, 155, 157–158,
    302; and aesthetics 5, 97, 167; Art as
    Experience 5, 97, 370. See also under
    Martin, Agnes
Diamond, Cora, 276–277
Dickinson, Emily, 21, 27, 117, 332
Dilthey, Wilhelm, 52; on understanding,
    157–158
Diogenes the Cynic, 28–29, 32–34, 60,
    107–108, 204, 290
disappointment 16–17, 80, 136
disenchantment thesis (Weber), 224,
    255, 308
Dreyfus, Hubert, 174
Du Bois, W. E. B., 10, 124–125
Duchamp, Marcel, 23, 75, 99, 102, 135
DuPlessis, Rachel Blau, 331

Dylan, Bob, 10, 12, 14–15, 20, 114–115, 117, 151, 193, 249. *See also under* explanation; Rimbaud

Eckhart, Meister, 52, 55, 61, 70, 135, 182–188, 201–202, 263, 368; and *Gelassenheit* (detachment) 11, 13, 184–187, 193, 197, 309, 324; releasement, 11, 13, 20, 25, 153, 185, 194–196, 198, 378; and Merton, 13, 184, 188, 190–191, 193–197, 368, 378; and Reinhardt, 13, 182, 194–198, 201–202, 260; and Salinger 13, 135, 153, 188, 190, 195, 197. *See also* Heidegger: *Gelassenheit*; "without why": and Eckhart
Edwards, Jonathan, 123, 166
Eisler, Benita, 373, 375
Eliot, T. S., 25, 29, 75, 116, 125, 127, 231, 271, 337, 342, 351
Elkins, James, 110, 372
Ellison, Ralph, 21, 117, 181
Emerson, Ralph Waldo, 4, 6, 8, 18, 32–33, 49–50, 57, 63–64, 70, 102, 117, 123, 128–129, 131, 155, 187, 212, 216, 262, 282–297, 300–302, 304–306, 308, 312–318, 327, 330, 371; and abandonment, 2, 7, 11, 27, 41, 48, 285, 296, 316; "Circles," 2, 286, 289, 308; "Self-Reliance," 11, 293–294, 296, 310, 313; and silence, 12, 24, 27, 41, 45, 47–48, 67, 188, 211, 291–292, 294–296, 321, 377; "Experience," 45, 311, 313–314, 317–318; "Nominalist and Realist," 294–296. *See also under* ethics; explanation; looking; Martin; Nietzsche; Rimbaud; surface; "without why"; Wittgenstein
Epicurus, 264
epistemology, 6, 73, 106, 271
ethics, 293, 343, 353; in Emerson, 291–294, 297, 371; in Wittgenstein 62, 267, 272, 274, 279, 291–292, 294, 371
explanation, in Emerson, 8, 50, 155, 296, 301–302, 305, 311, 314, 321, 327; in Dylan, 12, 15, 30, 114–117; in Rimbaud, 12, 30, 53, 114, 116, 118; refusal of, 29, 38, 51, 54, 104, 111, 157, 296; in Faulkner, 30, 117; in William James, 36, 56, 104, 155, 157, 302; in Kant, 36, 38, 119, 157; critique of, 46,

51, 155, 157; in Nietzsche, 50, 54, 157, 296, 298–299, 301–302, 305, 311, 321, 327–328; in Wittgenstein, 50–51, 158, 272–273, 305, 307, 311, 314, 321, 327; in Richter, 104, 113, 118; in Degas, 111; in Henry James, 157–160

faith: in art, 4, 65–66, 111, 193, 195, 197, 202–203, 230, 244; in images, 4, 126, 202–203; in words, 4, 57, 74, 95, 126, 187, 211, 224, 336, 340–343, 364; in attunement, 8, 66, 357; in Kierkegaard, 207, 211, 213, 217, 225–230, 233, 272; as revelation, 213, 216, 224
Farber, Manny, 134
Faulkner, William, 10, 30, 52, 117, 125, 208, 211. *See also under* explanation
Fechner, Gustav, 157
Felstiner, John, 345, 348–349, 355, 359
Fer, Briony, 374–375
Fish, Stanley, 105
Fisher, Philip, 111
Flaubert, Gustave, 26, 138
Forster, E. M., 24
Foster, Hal, 105
Foucault, Michel, 321
Franklin, Benjamin, 31, 117
Freedberg, David, 209
Freud, Sigmund, 41, 218–219, 221–222, 225–226, 231. *See also under* Rieff, Phillip
Fried, Michael, 166
Friedl, Herwig, 72
Friedlander, Saul, 352
Frost, Robert, 71
Fuller, Buckminster, 76
Futurism, 75, 116

Garbo, Greta, 21, 136
Gass, William H., 269
Gautama. *See under* Buddhism
Gelassenheit. See under Eckhart; Heidegger.
Ginsberg, Allen, 27, 181
Glass, Philip, 133
Glimcher, Arne, 367, 372, 375–376, 78
Goethe, Johann Wolfgang von, 215, 231, 304–306, 321, 324–326, 358. *See also under* Heidegger
Goodman, Russell, 269

Gould, Glenn, 14–15, 18, 22, 25, 30–31, 34, 41, 60, 66, 114, 242–266, 330; and Thomas Bernhard 12, 29, 35, 238–241, 255, 257–262; "the idea of north" 25, 253, 256; and Richard Powers 29, 256–257; and contrapuntal radio 248–250. *See also under* listening; negation; Rimbaud

Greenberg, Clement, 13–14, 46, 95, 111, 114, 132, 134, 163–164, 171, 175, 348; and the "grunt" 15, 170, 179; and Kant 35, 98, 166–167, 169; on Pollock 96–97, 99, 132; versus Harold Rosenberg 97, 99, 128; versus thinking, 97–98, 169. *See also under* looking; modernism; revelation

Grosz, Elizabeth, 106

Gumbrecht, Hans Ulrich, 105

Guston, Philip, 1–2, 164

Hacker, P. M. S., 155

Hadot, Pierre, 20, 107, 118, 264, 268, 288

Hamacher, Werner: on understanding as "ex-posed," 119–120, 360

Hannay, Alastair, 228

haptic, 82–83, 101, 163

Hauser, Arnold, 172

Hawthorne, Nathaniel, 27–28, 185

Haynes, Todd, 115

Hegel, Georg Wilhelm Friedrich, 25, 36, 68, 79, 209, 212–213, 215–216, 226, 250, 306, 308

Heidegger, Martin, 73, 122, 153, 264, 340, 344; and Nietzsche 52, 285, 304, 308–309, 320, 327–328, 330; and Wittgenstein 52, 107, 285, 304, 306–309, 323, 326–327, 329–330; and Adorno 121, 334, 357; *Gelassenheit* 304, 309, 324; on Goethe 304, 306, 324–326; on Angelus Silesius 306, 323–326; and detachment 309, 324; and Celan 330, 334–335, 354–357. *See also under* "without why"

Hemingway, Ernest, 81, 117, 142, 341, 343

Heraclitus, 118, 299–300, 313, 320–321

Herrigel, Eugen, 149

Hess, Thomas, 130

Hesse, Eva, 13, 182–183, 200

Hindu. *See* Vedantism

Hofmannsthal, Hugo von, 12, 23, 80–83, 103

Hölderlin, Friedrich, 36, 350–351, 355–356, 360. *See also under* Celan

Hopkins, Gerard Manley, 26

Horkheimer, Max, 41–42, 44

Howard, Richard, 31

Howe, Irving, 136

Hume, David, 52, 71, 165

Huysmans, Joris–Karl, 84, 253

immanence, 45, 77, 179, 270, 311, 313

impersonality, 3, 86, 125, 132, 199

Impressionism, 75, 82, 96, 110

Irwin, Robert, 13, 40, 78–19, 103

Jackson, Laura Riding. *See* Laura Riding

James, Henry, 1, 10, 26, 116, 118, 142, 242, 343–344; and quest for "no-knowledge," 158–159; *The Ambassadors*, 159. *See also under* explanation

James, William, 1, 5, 11, 28, 31, 44, 52, 56–57, 63–64, 72–74, 77–79, 106–108, 124, 155, 157, 160, 172–173, 189, 211–212, 216–217, 271, 285, 288–289, 340; and critique of concepts, 6, 14, 32, 36, 45, 67–71, 78, 80, 165, 260–270, 302, 370; *The Varieties of Religious Experience*, 7, 10, 69, 108, 162, 216, 269; and painting, 12, 70–71, 78, 95, 97, 100, 104, 128, 130, 158, 163, 206, 370; radical empiricism, 36, 165; *A Pluralistic Universe*, 67, 106; *The Principles of Psychology*, 71, 270. *See also under* explanation; Martin; poverty; revelation; Wittgenstein

Jameson, Fredric, 73

Jefferson, Thomas, 31

Jesus, 33, 58, 168, 206, 311, 329

Johnston, Jill, 367

Jones, Caroline, 171

Joris, Pierre, 347

Joyce, James, 25–26, 103, 116, 354

Kafka, Franz, 13, 21, 23, 26, 147, 153–154, 217, 233–238, 357, 360, 368, 377; and Bauer, 12, 24, 234–237; and Brod, 237

Kahneman, Daniel, 174

Kant, Immanuel, 35, 37, 65, 98, 117, 130, 151–153, 166, 169, 172, 213, 250, 289, 303, 308, 358; reception by

German romantics, 36, 152, 167; on
understanding, 36, 38, 119, 122, 157,
167–168, 198; on aesthetics 68, 152,
156, 167, 198, 250; and "blind" intuition, 164, 168–170. *See also* aesthetic
idea; explanation: in Kant; Greenberg:
and Kant; sublime: in Kant
Kaprow, Allan, 13, 176; on Pollock 97,
101, 132, 146, 151
Kees, Weldon, 54
Kenner, Hugh, 22, 344
Kerouac, Jack, 14, 27, 165, 181
Keynes, John Maynard, 266, 268
Kierkegaard, Søren, 21, 134, 147,
153–154, 208–213, 230, 233, 249;
and Wittgenstein, 13, 158, 217, 265,
271–272, 284–285, 323, 377; on
profundity, 206, 265; on Christianity,
207, 209–210, 225–227; on the
"unrecognizables" 227; engagement,
228–229, 234. *See also under* faith;
revelation; Rieff
Klein, Yves, 199
Kleist, Heinrich von, 134
koan. *See under* Zen
Krauss, Rosalind, 369, 374
Kuhn, Thomas, 172

Lacan, Jacques, 108
Laclos, Pierre Cholderlos de, 232
Lacoue-Labarthe, Philippe, 354–356
Laing, R. D., 219
Lange, Carl, 157
Lanzmann, Claude, 353
Lao-tzu, 56–58, 143, 160, 367; and *Wu-
wei* 55, 61
Larsen, Nella, 54
Lasch, Christopher, 220
Laughlin, James, 189, 193
Lawrence, D. H., 102–103
Leary, Timothy, 27
Leavis, F. R., 34
Lebensphilosophie (life-philosophy), 52,
157
Leibniz, Gottfried Wilhelm, 306, 308,
324, 326. *See also under* "without
why"
Lenz, Jakob Michael Reinhold, 358–359
Levi, Primo, 356–357
Lincoln, Abraham, 160
Linville, Kasha, 369

listening, 38, 161, 324–325; in Cage, 13,
48, 77, 244; in Gould, 14, 66, 243–250,
254, 257, 261
looking, 127, 130, 139, 140, 151, 160,
204, 224, 260, 335, 359, 370; in de
Duve, 4, 63, 167; in Emerson, 4,
49, 63, 70, 262, 305, 308, 321; in
Nietzsche, 4, 49, 63, 70, 262, 304–305,
308, 321; in Greenberg, 15, 167, 170;
in Stein, 15, 170; as "hermit vision,"
51; versus "looking through," 51, 125,
305; in Wittgenstein, 51, 282, 305,
308, 321; in Whistler, 114, 125.
Lyon, James, 356
Lyotard, Jean-Francois, 108–109, 130

MacLeish, Archibald, 181
Maier, Vivian, 114
Mailer, Norman, 135–136, 139, 232
Malcolm, Janet, 54, 136
Malevich, Kazimir, 75, 369, 373–374
Mallarmé, Stéphane, 14, 53, 84, 91–96,
114, 116–117, 125, 195, 342, 349; and
silence, 12, 26, 30, 149, 181, 321, 352.
See also under Rimbaud
Malraux, André, 53
Mapplethorpe, Robert, 233
Marion, Jean-Luc, 280
Maritain, Jacques, 344
Martin, Agnes, 11, 61, 127, 164,
364–378; and Reinhardt 13, 199,
364–365, 368–369, 371–372, 377; on
"impotence" 366; on gender 367; and
Dewey, 370; and William James, 370;
and Emerson, 371, 377.
Mason, Wyatt, 91
mastery, 15, 58, 91, 96, 159, 309,
312, 320, 338, 349, 361; and the
Enlightenment, 5, 41, 44; in Zen 138,
143, 149–152
McCarthy, Mary, 136
McEvilley, Thomas, 133, 202
McGuinness, Brian, 273, 282
McLuhan, Marshall, 249
McManus, Dennis, 277–278
Melville, Herman, 26–28, 30, 99; *Billy
Budd*, 24; "Bartleby the Scrivener," 28,
147, 175–176; *Benito Cereno*, 28, 177
Merleau-Ponty, Maurice, 14, 63, 73,
101–104, 107, 110, 130, 307. *See also
under* Cézanne

Merton, Thomas 151, 188–197; and
   Reinhardt, 12–13, 24, 75, 194–197,
   203–204, 368, 378; and Zen, 13, 151,
   164–165, 190, 196–197, 368; and
   Salinger, 190. See also under Eckhart
Michaels, Walter Benn, 105
Mies van der Rohe, Ludwig, 16
Mill, John Stuart, 3
Miller, Henry, 27, 100, 189, 192
mimesis, 42, 95, 229, 351
minimalism, 16, 175, 192
modernism, 9, 25–26, 30, 47, 71, 74–78,
   120, 141, 147, 153, 189, 337; in
   Greenberg, 13–14, 46, 95, 132, 171; in
   Sontag, 14, 74–75, 119, 132, 181, 221,
   229–230
Monet, Claude, 71, 102
Montaigne, Michel, 27, 45, 58–59,
   283–284, 313
Motherwell, Robert, 100, 200
Mozart, Wolfgang Amadeus, 232, 259
Murdoch, Iris, 274
mysticism, 20, 75, 128, 163, 186, 206,
   323; Christian, 18, 61, 162, 190

Nabokov, Vladimir, 5, 14–15, 164, 172
negation, 19, 83, 187, 352; in Gould,
   25, 250–252, 330; in Reinhardt, 196,
   199–200, 205, 365
negative theology, 11, 57, 135, 141, 290,
   203. See also apophasis
New Criticism, 38, 125–126; affective
   fallacy, 39
Newman, Barnett, 108, 112, 127–131,
   368
Nietzsche, Friedrich 11, 14, 22, 44, 52,
   61–62, 80–81, 88, 108, 134, 157, 215,
   217, 244, 262, 298–304, 309, 319–320,
   330; and Emerson, 2, 4, 6–7, 12, 41,
   45, 47–50, 63, 70, 102, 187, 282–290,
   295–297, 300–302, 305, 308, 310–312,
   315–316, 318, 321, 327, 330, 377;
   on "becoming what one is," 3, 310;
   and silence, 12, 28, 41, 45, 47–48, 54,
   66, 134, 295–296, 321, 328, 377; and
   "letting the hermit speak," 48; and
   skepticism, 48–50, 60. See also under
   explanation; Heidegger; looking; surface; "without why"; Wittgenstein
Nirvana, 62, 165, 177
Nishida, Kitaro, 32–33, 72–73

Noë, Alva, 173–174, 314
Northrop, F. S. C., 165
Norton, Charles Eliot, 124
Novalis, 122–123
nuance, 159, 193, 256, 321; in Adorno,
   38, 140; in Salinger, 38, 138–141, 149;
   in Barthes, 138–141, 149

Objectivism, 344
O'Hara, Frank, 31
O'Keefe, Georgia, 365
Olsen, Regine. See under Kierkegaard
Olsen, Tillie, 26
opacity, 37, 104, 115, 239, 268, 335; and
   presence, 4, 29, 40, 110, 208, 361; of
   the medium, 98–99, 175, 369
Oppen, George, 22, 31, 47, 61, 64,
   336–338, 340–344, 378; and Celan, 12,
   42–43, 330–335, 339, 343, 345–346;
   and war, 12, 42, 331–332, 337–338,
   341–342
Oppen, Mary, 331
optical, 41, 58, 82–83, 101, 121, 167, 171

Paolozzi, Eduardo, 268
Pascal, Blaise, 284, 312
Pasolini, Pier Paolo, 23
Picasso, Pablo, 15, 23
Pillow, Kirk, 169
Pippin, Robert, 315
Pirsig, Robert, 76
Plath, Sylvia, 41, 53–54
Plato, 7, 49–50, 107, 156, 374; Euthyphro
   272
Poe, Edgar Allan, 37, 96, 122–123
Poirier, Richard, 292
Polanyi, Michael, 172–173, 314
Pollock, Jackson, 41, 96, 99, 121, 146,
   151; the drip paintings, 12, 30, 97,
   101; and Reinhardt, 12, 60, 75,
   132, 200, 365, 377. See also under
   Greenberg; Kaprow; Salinger
Pop Art, 75
Porete, Marguerite, 18–19, 185
Porter, Fairfield, 118
positivism, 7–8, 65, 80, 274
postmodernism, 4–7, 50, 105, 108, 110,
   130, 171, 307–308
Pound, Ezra, 189, 231, 236, 336–337, 344
poverty, 49, 85, 133, 342, 351; in
   William James, 7, 26, 69–72, 108, 269;

in Wittgenstein, 7, 51, 108, 269; in Eckhart, 70, 185–186, 190, 263

Powers, Richard, 29, 256–257. *See also under* Gould

pragmatism, 5, 69–70, 106–108, 211

privacy, 171, 180, 205, 243, 246 250

Proust, Marcel, 16, 25, 179

Puritan, 17–18, 35, 123, 133, 344

Putnam, Hilary, 217

Pynchon, Thomas, 114

quietism, 17, 62, 273

Ransom, John Crowe, 14, 126

Rauschenberg, Robert, 176, 233

Reed, Lou, 232

refusal, 24, 27, 54, 59, 113–114, 117, 137, 157, 231, 246, 257, 296, 346, 360; of meaning, 28, 30, 37–38, 40, 79, 104, 115, 128, 133, 141, 207, 303; in Reinhardt, 29, 207, 303; in Valéry, 30, 37–38, 40, 133; in Wittgenstein, 37, 44, 51, 367. *See also under* explanation; renunciation

Reinhardt, Ad, 1, 12–14, 60, 65, 75, 111, 132, 182, 194, 198, 206–207, 303, 364, 371–372, 377; black paintings, 17, 24, 29, 195–197, 199–205, 368–369. *See also under* Eckhart; Martin; Merton; Pollock; negation; refusal

releasement. *See under* Eckhart

renunciation: as abandonment, 7, 11, 15, 22–23, 26, 29, 35, 41, 44, 48, 54, 60, 84–85, 91, 100, 198, 252, 296; as freedom, 9, 43–44, 67, 80, 84–85, 185, 192–193, 198, 219, 264, 284, 330, 367; and refusal, 24, 28–29, 40, 44, 51, 54, 59, 79, 104, 113, 137, 141, 207, 246, 296, 346, 367; generative, 41, 48, 54–55, 58, 61, 66, 100, 175, 284; terminal, 41, 53–55, 80; and anti-Cartesianism, 51–52. *See also* abandonment; disappointment

revelation, 7, 25, 37, 129, 215, 224, 231, 235, 317, 368; in William James 45, 63, 128, 130, 212, 216; in Greenberg, 128, 134, 164, 166; in Kierkegaard 134, 208–210, 212–213, 265; in Rosenzweig, 213, 215–216. *See also under* faith

Reznikoff, Charles, 46–47

Richards, I. A., 156

Richter, Gerhard, 103–104, 112–113, 118. *See also under* explanation.

Riding, Laura, 21

Rieff, Phillip, 12, 22, 24, 31, 217–222, 224–233; identification with Kierkegaard 13, 24, 217, 225–230, 233; on Freud 218–219, 221–223, 225–226, 231; and "deathworks" 229, 231. *See also under* Sontag

Riley, Bridget, 78, 110

Rimbaud, Arthur, 27, 64, 78, 85–89, 118, 122, 135, 189, 332, 354; and Dylan, 12, 30, 114–115, 249; and Gould, 12, 18, 22, 25, 30–31, 34, 41, 66, 114, 241, 249, 256; and Mallarmé, 12, 26, 30, 53, 84, 91, 96, 114, 116; and the Paris Commune of 1871, 31, 74, 86; in Africa, 73, 90–91. *See also under* Blanchot; explanation

Rimbaud, Frederic, 91

Rorty, Richard, 5, 105–106

Rosen, Stanley, 267

Rosenberg, Harold, 97, 99, 128, 195. *See also under* Greenberg

Rosenzweig, Franz, 1, 213–217, 281. *See also under* revelation

Roth, Henry, 21

Roth, Philip, 1–2, 44, 127

Rothko, Mark, 112–113, 127, 132, 200, 207

Royce, Josiah, 70

Ruskin, John, 113, 124–125, 131

Russell, Bertrand, 106, 239–240, 266–269, 277, 323

Sachs, Nelly, 353

Said, Edward, 242–243, 248, 250

Salinger, J. D., 10, 14–19, 21, 31–32, 38, 114, 122, 135–155, 171–172, 195, 197, 217, 266; and "the courage to be an absolute nobody," 12, 188, 377; Franny Glass, 13, 138, 142–143, 162, 181–184, 190, 294; "Hapworth 16, 1924," 136, 144, 178–179; *The Catcher in the Rye*, 18, 135, 190; *Seymour: An Introduction*, 43, 137, 143, 145, 147, 149, 160; Seymour Glass, 43, 136–141, 143, 146–147, 149, 151, 153–155, 162–164, 175–180, 377; Buddy Glass, 136, 138–142,

Salinger, J. D. (*continued*): 146–147, 149, 153–155, 163, 179–180; *Franny and Zooey*, 142; and detachment, 143, 184; and Pollock, 146. *See also under* Eckhart; Merton; nuance; Whitman

Santayana, George, 1, 22, 59–60, 70, 124

Sass, Louis, 322, 327

satori, 43, 179. *See also* Zen

Saussure, Ferdinand de, 141

Schaeffer, Jean–Marie, 123

Schelling, F. W. J., 210, 212–214

Schiller, Friedrich, 36, 47, 309; and reenchantment, 308

Schlegel, Friedrich, 122–123

Schopenhauer, Arthur, 62, 166, 190, 215, 247, 288–289, 308

Schumpeter, Joseph, 76

Schürmann, Reiner, 20, 184, 186, 188, 194, 196, 330

Schwartz, Sanford, 248

scientism, 7, 80, 141, 155, 157, 273–274, 279, 329

Sebald, W. G., 108, 268, 398

Serra, Richard, 200

Serrano, Andres, 232

Sextus Empiricus, 50

Shakespeare, William, 67, 160, 297

Shawn, William, 171

Sheed, Wilfrid, 180

Shestov, Lev, 360

Shiff, Richard, 5–6, 98

silence, *See under* abandonment; Cage; Emerson; Mallarmé; Nietzsche; Sontag; withdrawal; Wittgenstein; Zen

Simmel Georg, 253

skepticism, 1, 19, 38, 48, 50–51, 60, 110, 176, 322

Socrates, 106–107, 207, 263–264, 268–269, 303. *See also under* Wittgenstein

Sontag, Susan, 15, 38–39, 123, 131–134, 154, 164, 175, 181, 202, 241, 256; and Philip Rieff, 12, 24, 217–222, 229–230; on modernism, 14, 74–75, 119, 132, 181, 221, 229–230; aesthetics of silence, 132, 135, 149, 218

Spinoza, Baruch, 215, 303

spirituality, 9, 132, 183, 195, 206, 224, 304–305, 327; and letting go, 20

Starobinski, Jean, 45

Stein, Gertrude, 15, 25, 70–71 *See also under* looking

Steiner, George, 208, 280

Stevens, Wallace, 7, 53, 71, 117

Strauss, Leo, 206, 213–216

sublime, 51, 57, 64, 68, 108, 129–131, 298, 371–373; in Kant, 35, 130, 152, 168–169, 250

sunyata. See under Buddhism

surface, 15, 83, 98, 124, 126, 175, 206, 222, 235, 258, 369, 373; and Nietzsche, 3, 45, 134, 298, 301–302, 304, 310, 319, 321; and Emerson, 45, 102, 129, 292, 301–302, 304, 310, 313–314, 317, 321; and Wittgenstein, 51, 279, 314, 317, 321

surrealism 54, 100, 193

Suzuki, Daisetz, 367, 370; and Zen 32–33, 164–165, 179, 190, 371. *See also under* Columbia University

Symons, Arthur, 29

Tagore, Rabindrath, 279

tao, 55–57, 135, 137, 139–141, 165, 184, 195, 202, 311, 324, 367

Tarkovsky, Andrei, 22

Taylor, Charles, 6, 106–107, 173

Thoreau, Henry, 22, 27–28, 33, 117, 123, 131, 253; *Walden*, 44, 128

Toomer, Jean, 21

Traven, B., 54

Trilling, Lionel, 134, 155

Tudor, David, 148

understanding. *See under* Adorno; Ashbery; Dilthey; Hamacher; Kant; Valéry

Valéry, Paul, 1, 22, 37, 45, 84, 89, 92, 94, 112, 180, 265, 269, 332; and aesthetic autonomy, 13, 38, 125; on presence 14, 39–40, 83, 109, 122, 133; and symbolism, 25, 83; on understanding, 30, 38–40, 66, 118, 285. *See also under* refusal, Wittgenstein

Van Gogh, Vincent, 96

Vedantism, 33, 62, 153, 177, 351

Velazquez, Diego, 109

Verlaine, Paul, 85, 87–89, 93–94

via negativa, 18, 190

Vidal, Gore, 31
Vila–Matas, Enrique, 28
Vivekananda, Swami, 32, 153
Vorticism, 116

Wagner, Anne Middleton, 370, 373, 375
Wagner, Richard, 80, 243
Walsh, David, 77, 210
Wannsee Conference, 358–359
Weber, Max, 77, 80, 218, 220, 224–225,
    230, 231, 247, 308, 345
Weil, Simone, 134, 217
Whistler, J. M., 113–114, 118–119, 125
Whitman, Walt, 17, 27–28, 52, 99, 123,
    128, 159, 160–161, 287, 365–366; in
    Salinger, 139, 153; and Rimbaud, 88,
    241; and Celan, 334–335, 364
Wilde, Oscar, 119, 133
Williams, Tennessee, 189
Williams, William Carlos, 340
Willis, Ellen, 117
Wilson, Edmund, 25–26
Wilson, Robert, 133
"without why," 31, 109, 147; and
    Angelus Silesius, 3, 10–11, 306, 321,
    324–326; and Nietzsche, 3–4, 11, 41,
    52, 287, 304, 321, 327; and Emerson,
    4, 41, 188, 287, 304, 306, 321, 321;
    and Heidegger, 4, 52, 188, 304, 306–
    307, 324–327, 356; and Wittgenstein
    10, 52, 268, 287, 304, 306–307, 321,
    326–327; and Eckhart 11, 52, 183–184,
    186, 188, 324; and Leibniz 306, 324,
    326. See also under abandonment
Wittgenstein, Ludwig, 13, 51, 158, 272,
    307, 323, 326, 329; and Bernhard 1,
    12, 29, 238–240, 268; and William

James, 1, 6–7, 10, 12, 32, 44, 52,
    64, 67–68, 97, 106–108, 158, 217,
    269–271, 285; and Emerson 6–7, 12,
    20, 32, 50, 64, 67, 282–294, 304–306,
    308, 311, 314–315, 317, 321, 327,
    330, 371, 377; and Nietzsche, 6–7, 12,
    44, 50, 52, 60, 62, 108, 217, 282–290,
    303–305, 308–309, 311, 315, 321, 327,
    330, 377; and silence, 12, 30, 37, 55,
    67, 135, 165, 267, 271, 274, 280–281,
    291–292, 294, 321, 367, 377; and
    quietism, 17, 62, 273; Tractatus, 20,
    37, 55, 68, 265–267, 271, 273–278,
    280; and Valéry, 37; "don't think, but
    look" 51, 97, 108, 151; and Socrates
    106–107, 268–269, 303; and Carnap,
    265, 268, 274, 276, 279; Philosophical
    Investigations, 270, 277, 281, 285;
    and certainty, 280, 285, 304, 308,
    314, 323, 377. See also under ethics;
    explanation; Heidegger; Kierkegaard;
    looking; poverty; refusal; surface;
    "without why"
Wordsworth, William, 47–48, 254, 374
Wu–wei. See under Lao–tzu

Zen, 13, 17–18, 32–33, 73, 97, 135, 141,
    143–144, 146–147, 150–153, 164–165,
    179–180, 183–184, 186, 190, 196–197,
    324, 327, 371; empty mind, 11, 48,
    368, 372; and openness, 11, 43, 48,
    76, 140, 366; koan, 19, 20, 29, 43, 72,
    275; and silence, 19, 27, 30, 36, 43, 48,
    135, 149, 181. See also under Cage;
    mastery; Merton; Suzuki; See also
    Buddhism
Zukofsky, Louis, 192, 344

CPSIA information can be obtained
at www.ICGtesting.com
Printed in the USA
BVHW040017120522
636361BV00007B/131/J